# SAL MINEO

CROWN
ARCHETYPE
NEW YORK

# SAL MINEO

A BIOGRAPHY

MICHAEL GREGG MICHAUD

All rights reserved.
Published in the United States by Crown Archetype,
an imprint of the Crown Publishing Group,
a division of Random House, Inc., New York.
www.crownpublishing.com

Crown Archetype with colophon is a trademark of Random House, Inc.

All photographs are from the collection of the author unless otherwise credited.

Back jacket photo captions: *top row (left to right):* With James Dean in *Rebel Without a Cause,* 1955; with Jill Haworth in Cyprus, 1959; with friends, the Bronx, July 1956; *bottom row (left to right):* at the Gotham Health Club, New York, 1956; with Courtney Burr III, Norfolk, England, 1971; with Gigi Perreau at the Chinese Theatre, Hollywood, 1956.

Library of Congress Cataloging-in-Publication Data is available upon request.

ISBN 978-0-307-71868-6

Printed in the United States of America

DESIGN BY BARBARA STURMAN

10 9 8 7 6 5 4 3 2 1

First Edition

Sal Mineo, 1955

THIS BOOK IS DEDICATED TO

JILL HAWORTH AND COURTNEY BURR—

two very different people who loved the same complicated man.
Without their loving recollections and willingness to
bravely and graciously share their stories with me,
this book would not have been possible.
In writing this story, I have learned why Sal loved them both.

# CONTENTS

# FOREWORD

In 1957, a magazine editor asked eighteen-year-old Sal Mineo to write an autobiographical feature article for an upcoming issue. The young star was riding high, having earned nominations for an Academy Award and an Emmy Award for his acting abilities.

"It's hard to write about yourself," Sal said at the time. "I just wanted to do a story about a boy who gets into show business. I wanted to do it in the third person, and then at the end say, 'And, by the way, his name happened to be Sal Mineo.' But the editor said that wasn't being fair with the readers. That it was a freshman-theme device. So I had to do it over. And I really labored. How can you tell all about yourself in four thousand words? If you leave something out, then it isn't true."

# PART ONE

# THE BOY FROM
# THE BRONX

Sal, the Bronx, 1950

# 1.

"Should I spend all of my time dancing to become like Fred Astaire or all of my time with a bat and ball and be Phil Rizzuto?"

The winter was mild with little snow in New York City in 1939. Just east of town, in a marshy wasteland in Flushing Meadows, construction proceeded on exhibition halls and pavilions for the 1939 New York World's Fair. In spite of the dark war clouds hovering over Europe, the fair's theme was one of international cooperation. The exciting lure of the World's Fair went unnoticed by most immigrant families trying to survive in an unsteady economy and struggling to pay fourteen cents for a quart of milk and nine cents for a loaf of white bread.

On Tuesday, January 10, a child was born to a Sicilian immigrant and his American-born Italian wife in an apartment in Harlem. As is the old Sicilian custom, this third son would be named after his father. Salvatore Mineo Jr. was a healthy baby.

"The original pronunciation of our family name was 'Min-ayo,'" Sal explained, "but we use the Americanized 'Min-ee-o,' with the accent on the first syllable."

Josephine, a short, well-proportioned woman, was adamant that only English be spoken in her home. Quiet by nature, Mr. Mineo was always self-conscious about his accent, though he was fluent in English. With the exception of a few words and phrases, Sal never learned to speak Italian.

Two days after Salvatore Jr. was born, a gangster was murdered just outside the Mineo apartment, and his parents decided to move their family immediately. They took a small, three-room, cold-water flat on the fourth floor of a brick building in an Italian section of the Bronx. The monthly rent was $20. The bathtub in the middle of the room doubled as a dining table. "The move," said Sal, "was a step up."

"My father was born in Sicily," Sal explained. "He came here when he was sixteen, and for two years he could only get odd jobs, doing all kinds of dirty work." Salvatore Mineo Sr. was tall, lanky, and darkly handsome. He fled Sicily in 1929 with nothing more than a sense of adventure and a wooden mandolin strapped to his back. In the daytime he sawed wood for carpenters, laid bricks, and carved little animals in ivory and wood that he sold on the street. In the evening, he courted a young, American-born Italian girl named Josephine Alvisi.

"My mother was born in New York City of Neapolitan parentage," Sal recounted. "My dad tried to date her, but she wouldn't go out with him—not unless he could speak English. When he finally took her out, she was amazed at how quickly he had learned the language. Here's a guy with ambition, she felt."

Salvatore married Josephine in 1931 when they were both eighteen years old. He was working as a cabinetmaker and finish carpenter when their first child, a son named Victor, was born in 1935. A second son, named Michael, was born two years later.

When Salvatore Jr. was born in 1939, his father had begun working for the Bronx Casket Company. In the beginning, Salvatore hand-finished the coffins. "My father was so good," Sal said, "they made him a foreman. He worked like a dog—even nights. It was my mother though who really made him. Here you are, she told him, working like a dog for others. You should be working for yourself, and for your children."

The family struggled for several years. The three boys slept in one bed in a small room off the kitchen. Sal wore hand-me-down clothes. Their baby sister, Sarina, born three years after Sal, slept in a nearby crib. "We always had plenty of food," Sal recalled, "but we did eat lots of spaghetti."

"Pop and Mama came to realize that they couldn't make a go of it on the money he was earning," Sal explained. "And so Pop decided to borrow money and start a business of his own. He knew something about coffin making and chose that as the business he'd sink or swim with. My father didn't have a dime, but friends insisted on putting up the money to back him. So, in 1946, he went into business with my uncle, and they opened up Universal Casket Company."

To begin, the Mineos rented the basement of the building they were living in for the coffin business. A small room was used to show two casket models for prospective clients. Salvatore worked slowly and meticulously, crafting one or two caskets each week.

Josephine decided her husband needed a secretary. She scraped together a staggering $160 and took a business course by correspondence. At first, she did her husband's accounting at night. But Josephine was ambitious. She told her husband that in addition to doing all the bookkeeping, she would solicit orders on his behalf so he could concentrate on making coffins.

Her husband worried about their four young children. Josephine had this problem figured out as well. "Some days," she said, "so they don't forget who are their parents, they come to the shop and they stay with us.

"Of course," Josephine explained, "I had to take them to the shop more than I thought I'd have to. Because they were only children and they couldn't seem to stay home all day without me and not get into some kind of mischief."

The boys loved to play jacks and marbles in the gutter and swing like monkeys on the fire escapes, climbing up one and down the other. They played stickball with broom bats in the street, and Sal and Mike regularly got into trouble for dropping piss bombs (urine-filled balloons) on unsuspecting, and sometimes targeted, passersby beneath the roof of their building.

Kathy Schiano, a childhood friend, recalled Sal fondly. "Sal was just so little, and always trying to keep up with his older brothers. He just threw himself in the mix. Victor stuck close to his younger brothers, but Sal and Mike were thick as thieves."

"The first five years were the toughest," Sal recalled. He never forgot what it was like for his father in those early days. "I never saw a man age so fast. He and my uncle used to do all the work themselves—hauling lumber, making the caskets, painting them, even delivering them. My mother used to go down every day. And as soon as they were old enough, my two older brothers worked at the company. And as soon as we were old enough to handle tools, Pop taught us how to pitch in and help with the repair work. Soon all of us boys could use a paintbrush, splice a wire, and solder a pipe."

Sal's main job was staying at home and babysitting his sister. "I guess that's why I'm so close to her," he said. "I took care of her—everything from feeding to good-night stories when my parents were working late. Sure, I wanted to be out playing with the other kids, but we all had to help out."

Every penny Mr. Mineo earned went back into the business, and still they struggled. But Mr. and Mrs. Mineo somehow managed to ensure that none of their children ever wanted for anything. "Even if they had to deprive themselves," Sal added. All three sons got the same treatment, too. If one boy wanted a bike, then all three boys got bikes.

The kids in the neighborhood challenged Sal all the time about his father's business. "A guy would come up to me and ask, 'What does your father do?' knowing exactly what he did," Sal said. And Sal would defiantly clench his fists and answer, "He makes caskets. What are you going to do about it?"

Josephine instilled a healthy fear of God in her children. Sal was six when he received his first communion at the Holy Family Church on Castle Hill Avenue in the Bronx. A devout, churchgoing Catholic, she enrolled her children in parochial school. He was confirmed at the age of seven.

Sal was introduced to acting at the age of eight, when he attended St. Mary's Parochial School in the Bronx. "The sisters asked me to play the Savior as a boy. I was like a kid dumbstruck. I had seen the movies and knew there was such a thing as acting. But to have these women ask me to portray Jesus as a youth—well, that was something beyond my understanding," Sal said.

"I was scared at first; I was afraid that it would be wrong. That afternoon I took home the script and studied it as though my life depended on it. A few days later in a religious book I was studying I saw a picture of Christ as a boy. In it he was carrying a staff. I decided I wanted one. The sisters told me it wasn't necessary to have one in the play, but I had become a stickler for realism. I had to have a staff. Someone suggested a sawed-off broomstick. I wouldn't hear of it. By the afternoon of the play I still didn't have a staff. We dressed in one of the classrooms. When I was ready, I walked down the corridor to the rear of the stage entrance. I felt awful without the staff.

"And then I saw it. It was hanging on the wall. A fire hook over a sign: 'For Emergency Only.' For me, this was a genuine emergency! I took the hook down, and I tied a blue ribbon from my costume on the top. Can you picture me walking onto that stage, so happy, with that fire hook? Anyway, I couldn't stop thinking of the stage."

Sal's days at St. Mary's School were numbered. He was sensitive about his size, being slight for his age, and was often picked on by other boys. Sal always met their challenge, though, and he was quick with his little fists. He was expelled from the fourth grade for slugging a rival boy.

Josephine appealed to a priest who helped enroll Sal in another parochial school called Holy Family. In fact, she wouldn't leave the priest's office until he accepted Sal. The discipline-minded nuns found him too much to handle, though, and again he was expelled for fighting in the school yard, and for being incorrigible.

"Sal's our baby brother," recalled Victor Mineo, "but he's the toughest guy in the family. If Mike or I got into fights with the boys around the neighborhood, Sal would always come running, fists flying."

In a couple of years, the Mineos managed to repay some of their debt to friends and family, and the coffin business began to turn a small profit. In an effort to get their family away from bad "city" influences, they found a dilapidated, three-story, wood-shingle house in the Throgs Neck section of the Bronx at 2485 Wenner Place near East 217th Street and the Bronx-Whitestone Bridge. The Mineos moved into the top two floors and rented out the first floor to help pay the mortgage. Josephine was relieved that her children could safely play in open fields instead of the streets. There was a nearby creek where the kids went fishing, and a swimming hole. On one side of the house a lane led down to the sound.

Sal Sr. converted an extra kitchen tucked into an eave on the third floor into a makeshift bedroom for Sal. The sink and kitchen cabinets remained, and it was painted pale blue—Sal's favorite color. Sal loved his room, which was the smallest in the house, and enjoyed having privacy for the first time. Each child had a room of his or her own. Josephine converted the back porch into a home office where she could work.

To keep off the streets, Sal and his brothers spent Saturday mornings running errands for their father's business. Josephine would prepare a picnic lunch of sandwiches and hard-boiled eggs, which they'd share. Afterward, the boys played hide-and-seek among the unfinished caskets in the woodworking shop.

Once, Sal hid in a casket and the lid snapped shut, trapping him inside. Mike found him an hour later and asked him if he had been frightened. "No," Sal said. "I knew someone would come and find me pretty soon." Sal knew his brothers were always watching out for him.

"They didn't fight with me; they didn't tease me," he said. "They protected me."

Sal's experiences at his next school were no better than before. On his first day at PS 72 in the Bronx, the guys ganged up on him in the boys' room. Sal tried to fight them off one at a time but was quickly overtaken.

Soon, Sal established himself with his schoolmates, however. A bully pulled a switchblade on him in a school yard fight. Sal knocked the knife out of his assailant's hand with the buckle of his garrison belt. Then they had a bloody, vicious fight, until a teacher pulled them apart.

"If anybody won, I guess I did," Sal recalled. "But the important thing was that, for the first time, I felt the other kids were rooting for me. Y'know?"

Sal couldn't recall a time in his childhood when he wasn't running with a gang or getting into street fights. Still, he loved going to the movies, and it was his mother who introduced him to movie musicals. His love of Fred Astaire movies caused the kids in his neighborhood to call him a sissy. He quickly responded by beating them up. "I could have gone on the wrong track," Sal confided to columnist Sidney Skolsky years later. "I didn't get my nose busted acting in movies," he laughed.

Sal may have been perceived as a tough character in the neighborhood, but to his sister, he was the "most soft-hearted person" she knew. He walked home with Sarina after school and stayed with her until their mother came home from the shop.

Sarina said, "It was Sal who cheered me, cracking jokes and teaching me to play checkers and Monopoly whenever I was sick. To understand Sal, you have to realize he is strong and sensitive at the same time. He seems to know what you're thinking and feeling before you quite know it yourself. And then he's able to comfort and guide you, no matter what the trouble is."

ON A sweltering day in the summer of 1948, Sal was playing with his sister and some neighborhood boys on the sidewalk in front of their home. A man approached the children. Sal took Sarina's hand and looked at the stranger suspiciously.

"How would you kids like to be on TV?" the man asked. "Dancing and singing?"

The kids laughed, but Sal stood up to the man and said, "What we gotta do?"

"Take lessons," the man said. "After you take some lessons, I'll put you on TV."

Sal looked at his friends, who were snickering at the stranger. "I think you're fulla baloney," Sal snarled. Then he jumped on the curb and started to sing and dance to mock the man and amuse his friends.

"Son," the man said, "you have talent. Take me to your mother."

Moments later, the man was explaining his proposal to Josephine, who was skeptical. The man told her that Sal had potential and he was so appealing and good-looking. He assured her that he could get Sal on television, and he had connections to a dancing school in Manhattan that might have room for one more student. He promised to get Sal an audition for a popular local television program called *The Children's Hour.* Josephine was unconvinced.

Sal begged to attend the school. "Ma, send me, Ma. Give me lessons, Ma . . . huh?" He nagged his mother until she accepted the stranger's card. Josephine said she would talk it over with her husband and call him.

That night the Mineo family had a meeting. Josephine felt that something had to be done to keep Sal out of trouble, so she decided that Sal could get his dancing lessons, and Mike and Victor would get music lessons. They wanted to learn to play the saxophone and clarinet.

Josephine took Sal to the dancing school, but her skepticism was soon confirmed. The school wanted to charge the Mineos for photographing their son and requested a hefty enrollment fee. In addition, the stranger had no real connection to the school or any apparent connections to television. In spite of this, Josephine enrolled Sal.

"Since I was too small to be left home alone," Sarina said, "it was decided that I'd take singing and dancing lessons too, and while Mom took Sal and me to the school, the other two boys had a music lesson at home. In this way, we were all kept busy at the same time and no one got into trouble."

"We didn't have very much money," Josephine recalled. "To pay for the kids' music and dancing lessons, I used to do typing and bookkeeping at the school. It was worth it because Sal was in seventh heaven. I couldn't stop the boy from dancing."

The boys helped to pay for their lessons by maintaining paper routes. Sal went into the newspaper business at the age of nine. "I sold papers in the Bronx," Sal remembered. "My spot was near a subway kiosk and my brother Victor warned me never to get on the trains without him. But one afternoon I wanted to get on one and go. And all of a sudden I was on Broadway. A million miles of colored neon, earsplitting whistles, and those head-piercing police sirens. I thought the world had gone mad. And I was alone. I was so small, people fell over me.

"Then I saw a theater marquee. You know what I did? I counted the letters to see if my name would fit. 'Salvatore' was too long, so I changed it right then and there to 'Sal.'"

Sal and Sarina quickly outgrew the dancing school and Josephine found another, the Marie Moser Dance Academy. Her two youngest children were soon dancing again with renewed enthusiasm.

One evening Josephine was worried about Sal's disinterest in anything but his dancing lessons. "Salvatore," she said to her husband, "I can't get it out of my mind. Sal is such a nice little boy. He should be running and playing, not thinking all the time about work, and dancing and being an acrobat. Who knows what he'll think of next? It seems he doesn't want a childhood."

Sal thought about his mother's comments that night. He sat up in bed and wondered, "Should I spend all of my time dancing to become like Fred Astaire or all of my time with a bat and ball and be Phil Rizzuto?" Sal loved baseball. He collected baseball cards and he and Mike snuck into Yankee Stadium to watch games.

The next morning over breakfast he told his mother, "I really want to go to dance school. I've decided because if I become a ballplayer, I can't start working till I'm eighteen, but as an actor I can start tomorrow."

For two years, he would go twice a week for three hours straight of lessons.

"It was almost frightening the way Sal applied himself to his work," Josephine recalled. "Hour after hour, he'd practice in his own room. I'd have to make him go out and play."

Because of their financial limitations, Josephine couldn't afford dancing lessons *and* two sets of shoes for Sal, one for dancing and one for school. There was only one solution. Sal had to wear his tap shoes to school. "I'd walk in the dirt instead of the pavement so the kids wouldn't hear the big taps on my shoes," Sal said. But his dancing lessons still earned him many black eyes from his schoolmates. One particular brawl broke Sal's ten-year-old nose, making him more determined than ever.

"The dancing school had a Saturday afternoon program on TV," Victor recalled, "and Sal and Sarina were scheduled to dance. Then came the big day! Sal was so excited; you could hardly get him to talk about anything else." With Sal's carefully combed hair and natty suit, and Sarina's curls and crinoline dress, Josephine's youngest children smiled broadly beneath a sign that read MARIE MOSER'S STARLETS as the recital was broadcast locally in New York City. Their many weeks of rehearsals paid off. Shortly afterward, Sal and Sarina, and several other star pupils from the school, appeared on *The Ted Steele Show*, a variety program broadcast live from New York City.

Sal's appearance on this very popular show caused him problems with his schoolmates and friends, though. "The day after I danced on *The Ted Steele Show*, I was out of the gang again," Sal recalled. "I got the 'sissy' routine from them and I wound up in a long and bloody fight with the gang president. We got taken to the principal's office, and he wanted to know why I'd started the battle. So I told him. And I had to dance eight bars to prove it!"

School continued to be a problem for Sal, especially since he became interested in dancing and performing. He had aptitude but was easily distracted from his studies. "Sal is a bright boy," a schoolteacher wrote on his report card, "with great potential. Too often, though, his energy is channeled in the wrong directions." Sal was called into the principal's office weekly for brawling. He was even brought into the police station a few times to answer questions about his local gang's antics.

"We were just kids," Sal recalled, "and we were always getting into trouble. It wasn't anything really terrible—mostly things like breaking windows, stealing small things just for the hell of it. I was a hood. The school would call home, or the cops would, and my family couldn't stop me. Finally I got brought into court."

Sal's gang had decided to steal sports equipment from the school's locker rooms. Sal was the smallest kid, so he slipped into a basement window and handed the equipment up to his friends. They hid their stolen goods in an empty coffin in Mr. Mineo's shop.

The judge admonished Josephine and assigned a social worker to the case. "This boy will be sent to a correctional institution unless an alternative can be found," he said. Sal's teachers and the social worker felt he was causing trouble because he was bored rather than emotionally disturbed. They searched for a way to channel his energy into something more productive.

"They told my mother that she should send me to a school in Manhattan where I could study acting," Sal said. "They thought it would keep me too busy to raise hell—and they were right."

## 2.

> "It wasn't really acting. We just ran across the stage
> laughing and chasing the goat. But during that
> year, I began to want to be an actor."

Sal's court-recommended school in Manhattan accepted kids at very early ages and occupied them for four or five hours a day with singing and dancing lessons for a small enrollment fee.

Many years later, Sal recalled, "I thought it was a gag. And I told the buddies back home how I got out of going to a boys' school having a ball, singing and dancing and all that. Actually, most of the time I was playing cards in the washroom while everyone else was singing and dancing."

One day in early December 1950, Sal had accompanied Sarina to her dance class and was standing along the wall in the studio waiting for her lesson to conclude. Earlier in the year, their dancing had earned them a second appearance on *The Ted Steele Show* and an uncredited soft-shoe routine on *The Milton Berle Show,* the highest-rated show on television.

A casting agent, looking for children for a new Broadway play, had gone to the Bronx looking for "an Italian-looking" boy. He spotted Sal, wrote an address on his business card, and told him to be there the next afternoon.

A suspicious Josephine took Sal to a cavernous theater on Broadway the next day. Sal joined fifteen other boys onstage and confidently recited the line "The goat is in the yard." Daniel Mann, a director from the Actors Studio, and veteran producer Cheryl Crawford, picked Sal to play the part of Salvatore in *The Rose Tattoo,* a new play by Pulitzer Prize–winning author Tennessee Williams. Sal was instructed to come back to the theater in two days to begin rehearsing with the principal actors, Maureen Stapleton and Eli Wallach.

"Who's your agent?" Crawford asked Sal.

"What's an agent?" Sal answered, looking at his mother.

Crawford sent Mrs. Mineo and her son to a veteran theatrical agent named Alec Alexander at 70 East Fifty-sixth Street. With Sal's black curly hair, big brown eyes, and olive-colored skin, Alexander thought the boy looked "a little too ethnic." Still, knowing he had a sure bet since the kid had just been offered a role in a Broadway show, the savvy agent agreed to represent him.

Josephine sat in stunned silence all the way back to the Bronx. Clutched in her hand was an open-ended contract for her son to act in his first Broadway play for $75 per week. Eleven-year-old Sal would now be earning more money than his father.

The story, one of playwright Williams's most poignant, was set among Sicilian immigrant fishermen in a small village along the Gulf Coast of the United States. *The Rose Tattoo* told the story of Serafina Delle Rose, a restless widow, and the man she chose as her lover. Sal had a small part as a village boy. When the curtain rose, he chased a live goat across the stage and cried out, "The goat is in the yard!"

"After taking dramatic and dancing lessons for three years, I finally auditioned for a real big show," Sal recalled. "I was eleven at the time, and I had to show them I could read a script well, so I figured when they signed me that it was for a pretty good part. I can clearly remember how hurt I was when I showed up for the first rehearsal. My big fat part consisted of chasing a goat onstage. Worse still, that damn goat stole the scene every time. But it was Broadway!"

Sal went to the theater every day to rehearse his one line and running entrance. When he wasn't on the stage, he sat for hours carefully watching director Daniel Mann work with Stapleton and Wallach. Sal explained, "Daniel Mann taught me a great deal. I learned by watching him direct others, and I think this is an important part of any performer's career. He made me really want to act, and it gave me confidence."

Williams insisted his new play preview in Chicago. Sal's father was not pleased by the prospect of Sal's working and was especially concerned about putting his youngest son alone on a train bound for Chicago. Once again, five-foot-two-inch Josephine imposed her will, assuring her husband that Sal would be fine.

Sal's family and aunts, uncles, and cousins gathered at Grand Central Station to watch him board the train. "I cried when I left," Sal remembered. "This was the first time I had been separated from the family. But we all knew that this might be the beginning of a career."

*The Rose Tattoo* premiered on December 29 at the Erlanger Theatre.

The days in Chicago were exhausting and endless for the cast. Williams fussed with the script daily, adding or deleting lines and challenging the director's choices.

Sal had an indulgent and devoted family, he told columnist Hedda Hopper years later, but what he learned about life, he learned from theater people. "It was Eli Wallach who told me about the birds and the bees when we were in Chicago," Sal explained. "He once studied medicine and he gave me my first instruction in the facts of life. I had very little to do in the play so I helped Eli put on his makeup. One day, using all the correct terms, he told me about sex. When he got through I said, 'I know all that, only we used different words.' He nearly fell off the stool. Then when I told my family it was their turn to laugh."

*THE ROSE TATTOO* opened at the Martin Beck Theatre in New York on February 3, 1951, to glowing reviews. "I knew what I wanted to do," Sal recalled. "When I saw people performing on the stage and then saw the audience burst into applause for them, acting became my big dream. Everyone said, 'So you want to become a big star!' There's no harm in dreaming."

Sal's trying days of school and formal education ended once and for all when he was cast in Williams's play. He continued his dancing and drama lessons, but his irregular acting schedule, and now occasional trips to casting agents' offices, made it necessary for his mother to hire a private tutor.

Sal had always been curious and wanted to learn, and the tutor seemed to suit him very well. The older people Sal was now spending most of his time with encouraged him to study. He enjoyed reading classic plays. He became interested in writing, which would eventually become an ambition. Sal also liked to draw and paint.

Josephine and Mike shared the task of taking the daily bus and subway trips with Sal from the Bronx to Manhattan, which sometimes took an hour. Mike would usually take Sal in the early evening. They had to leave by 6:30 P.M. so Sal could make his 8:30 P.M. curtain. Mike would sometimes spend the day with him during matinee Saturdays and Wednesdays. Josephine would be waiting in the evening backstage when the show was finished to ride back to Wenner Place with Sal, who often fell asleep with his head in her lap as she read.

―――――

"I CAME home one day, full of 'Mineo the future star' plans as usual, to find the house empty," Sal recalled. "That seemed kind of funny, and I prowled around, wondering where all the family was. Then I found the note. It said for me to go to the hospital right away. I ran the whole distance, about half a mile, with my heart in my mouth and my whole body in a cold sweat."

Sarina had been admitted to the hospital and diagnosed with polio. The infection affected her throat, and she was soon breathing with the aid of forced oxygen. The doctors felt she might not recover.

Josephine was stoic and confident Sarina would recover. She sent her husband back to work and told the boys not to worry. "We tried, but it was hard to seem cheerful as we sat in Sarina's hospital room," Sal said. "All we could hear was the sound of my sister's labored breathing under the oxygen tent. But Mother insisted that we believe, and tell Sarina we believed, everything would be all right."

That evening, Josephine accompanied Sal on the long ride to the theater. They didn't talk about his sister's illness, though he knew from his mother's expression that Sarina's condition was at a critical point.

"Before I found out that Sarina was so sick," Sal said, "I used to spend all my spare time writing her crazy joke cards with drawings and pictures I used to take. Then, when I found out how serious her condition was, I somehow didn't feel like making the joke cards anymore or taking the crazy pictures. Instead, I began to sit down and write her letters as a much more mature person. I began to understand people a lot more and got a different outlook on life. Maybe this is how I began to become an actor."

Weeks passed, and Sarina gradually regained enough strength to be released from the hospital. Josephine set her up on the sofa in the front room so she could be a part of family activities. Sal stood by the sofa and began to cry. Sarina asked Sal why he was crying. "Because you're home," he said. "We're a family again."

After Sarina had recovered, Sal helped her regain strength by coaching her with some dancing and swimming lessons. "You can always count on Sal," Sarina said.

―――――

ON SUNDAY evening, March 25, 1951, the Mineo family listened to the Tony Awards presentation broadcast live over New York radio station WOR from the Waldorf Astoria Grand Ballroom. *The Rose Tattoo* won four Tony Awards, including Best Play. The next morning, Josephine sent eight-by-ten-inch portrait photographs of Sal, which he personally autographed, with a letter proudly stating that Sal was appearing in the best play on Broadway, to his many aunts, uncles, cousins, and family friends.

Sal enjoyed his role in *The Rose Tattoo*, but he had higher ambitions and made the rounds of casting agents' offices regularly, always accompanied by his brother Mike. "Call it ambition, call it drive, call it what you like," Sal said. "One weekend I remember there was an elevator strike. So I climbed up and down flights of stairs to ask producers, casting directors, and secretaries to place my photo in their files."

Josephine had ambitions of her own for her youngest son, and she set the tone for Sal's interviews and auditions. Since he was now appearing in the most popular and critically acclaimed show on Broadway, she was determined the attention should not go to his head. Keeping the family tightly together was her only defense. "If Sal was with his brothers," she explained, "he couldn't help but realize he was no better than the rest of them. When problems came up, we'd all sit down around the dining room table and thresh them out, no holds barred! Sometimes we'd sit up until two o'clock in the morning after Sal got home from the theater, just talking."

Sal worked well with his tutor, but he was anxious to prove himself as an actor. "I want to be a real professional," he told Josephine. "I want to be accepted in show business."

But Sal was still a scrapper and wasn't easily intimidated. He got into a backstage fistfight with one of his young costars in *The Rose Tattoo* and told his mother proudly, "Even if I am in show business, Ma, I don't ever want to become conceited."

Josephine's accounting chores now included managing Sal's acting income. Some portion of his earnings was diverted into his father's casket company, but the added paycheck proved to be a headache rather than a windfall for the family. His private tutor cost $500 each semester, his union dues were $115, his agent took 10 percent, and publicity photographs cost $150. Additional costs included buses, subways, and taxicab rides to and from the theater in Manhattan. His wardrobe, makeup, dramatic lessons and coaching, and daily meal and tip costs quickly added up. In fact, when the addition and subtraction was completed, Josephine was running in the red.

"But I didn't mind," she said. "I was investing in Sal's future. I believed in him, and I wanted him to have good clothes, good meals, and an education." Still, something had to give.

AFTER MONTHS of trudging the New York streets handing out photographs to agents, Sal was called to audition for the part of Candido in a Theatre Guild production of *The Little Screwball* at the Westport Country Playhouse in Connecticut. Film veteran Walter Abel was to star in the limited-run production. With Abel's approval, Sal won the role.

This new job offer provided two opportunities to Josephine. It gave Sal the chance to assume a larger role in a new Broadway-bound play for the prestigious Theatre Guild. Mike had been understudying the boys' roles in *The Rose Tattoo* for about a month. Sal stepped off the stage at the Martin Beck Theatre, and Mike assumed his little brother's part.

*The Little Screwball,* a heartwarming comedy written by Walt Anderson, opened in July of 1951 at the Westport Country Playhouse, not far from New York City. Later renamed *Me, Candido!* the play told the heartwarming story of a homeless eleven-year-old shoe-shine boy named Candido (played by Sal) who lives on the streets of New York. He is unofficially adopted by Papa Gomez, a poor immigrant Puerto Rican family man; a gruff restaurant owner named Mr. Ramirez; and an alcoholic but philosophical ex-longshoreman named Mike McGinty. The adoptive fathers save Candido from the streets and try to legally adopt him and keep him from being placed in an institution.

The play was successful and ran for several weeks. Sarina was also cast in a small role in the comedy. When Sal wasn't entertaining his sister, he was playing cards with the stagehands. Josephine now had three children gainfully employed. She took Sal and Sarina by train to Westport every day. Mike, now appearing in *The Rose Tattoo* on Broadway, had to fend for himself.

AFTER *THE LITTLE SCREWBALL* closed, Sal returned to New York and began visiting casting agents again. In September Sal read for the part of another shoeshine boy, in a new play called *Dinosaur Wharf.* He won the role and anxiously began two months of arduous rehearsals.

Sal's picture appeared in the *New York Times* on November 4, 1951, to promote *Dinosaur Wharf.* His mother and her friends bought many copies of the newspaper that day. Josephine began to compile a large scrapbook about her youngest son's burgeoning career and pinned a copy of the newspaper picture on the wall in her kitchen.

*Dinosaur Wharf* opened at the National Theatre on November 8, 1951, and closed on November 10, 1951. "Rehearsals passed quickly," Sal recalled. "My excitement was great that first night when I received telegrams from my family and friends. But the play was not a success, and when it closed after four performances, I learned another very important part of show business: disappointment."

# 3.

"I was pretty bad. I was playing the part of a prince
but onstage I walked and talked like a Bronx boy."

A gain I began visiting agents," Sal said. "There were no jobs and
this time I became depressed. In fact, I began to look upon myself as a failure. A failure at twelve and a half!"

"My other children slowed down and dropped out," Josephine
said. "Not Sal. Acting, dancing, show business, all of it was always running hard in his blood."

By the fall of 1951, Victor was busy in high school. Sarina had
completely recovered from the polio. Though she loved spending
time with Sal onstage in *The Little Screwball,* she decided she wasn't
interested in show business, but instead wanted to become her father's
secretary.

Sal's brother Mike was marginally interested in show business.
Sleepy-eyed and self-conscious, his acting abilities were limited. He
especially liked the girls backstage life attracted, though, and he enjoyed the attention paid to his little brother. Kathy Schiano recalled,
"After Sal got on a roll, Mike started slinking around after him instead
of the other way around. For him, it was an easy living. And the girls
were easy marks."

Josephine placed Mike's photo in an actors directory and handled
any calls or appointments for auditions until she convinced Sal's agent
to represent him as well.

RODGERS AND HAMMERSTEIN'S latest musical, *The King and I,*
had opened to much fanfare at the St. James Theatre in New York
on March 29, 1951. Based on the novel *Anna and the King of Siam,*
the story concerned the adventures of English schoolteacher Anna
Leonowens, who was hired to teach the many children of the king of
Siam. Directed by John Van Druten, the smash-hit show was choreographed by Jerome Robbins.

A casting agent working for Rodgers and Hammerstein had seen Sal
in the Theatre Guild production of *The Little Screwball* in Connecticut

and invited him to audition with a dozen other boys for the role of Crown Prince Chulalongkorn.

"I had to summon up all my nerve and keep the butterflies under control," Sal remembered. "The worst part of the audition was that I would have to sing. I hadn't known that, so I had prepared no song. All the other kids were smart. They all did 'Young Lovers' from the play, but not me. I ran out to a music store and grabbed the sheets on a thing called 'Down Yonder,' a real jumping hillbilly number. And I sang it. Man, it was a blast. Everybody was in hysterics, and I knew that was it. I was very much off-key. I had goofed. So then a guy ran up and said, 'You got it!' It was crazy."

Though Oscar Hammerstein had said about Sal, "Too short," he was hired as understudy for the role of the Crown Prince. Sal had to be at the theater one hour before curtain for each show. If the boy he was understudying was ill, or unable to perform, he had to step in as the replacement. Sal was fascinated with the theater, and always stayed each evening, observing the other actors and watching their techniques and carefully choreographed exits and entrances.

Sal was especially entranced by the broad theatrical gestures of Yul Brynner, the commanding actor who portrayed the King, and the graceful confidence of his leading lady, Gertrude Lawrence. He then decided he wanted to be a full-time actor rather than a dancer. "This was a brand-new challenge," Sal said, "and I simply had to lick it."

He began to think he would never get to play the role of the Crown Prince, but he memorized and imitated all the actors. Before long, he knew each part and could easily sing every song and dance every step. "I never got tired of standing backstage," he added, "because I kept learning something new every night."

Working again on Broadway qualified Sal to enroll at the Lodge Professional Children's School in Manhattan. Mike enrolled as well since Josephine was still concerned about her youngest son traveling alone in the city. For the boys, it was a daily one-hour bus ride to the school. In addition, the school was used by casting agents and producers to find new, young talent. Job opportunities were posted daily, and the flexible class schedule allowed the children to leave for auditions throughout the day.

Sal excelled at the Lodge School. The relaxed discipline was appealing. Besides routine acting classes, the children studied "cold-reading" techniques (reading aloud from a script without any rehearsal) and physical movement. To be surrounded by other children pursuing careers in show business was exciting and stimulating to Sal. He began to overhear other child actors his own age boast about appearing on television programs being shot in New York. Still just an understudy, Sal was a little frustrated at being unable to actually perform onstage and he asked his mother to let him audition for television plays.

"You gotta let me do TV," Sal pleaded.

"I don't gotta do nothing," Josephine said, "except see that you're raised a normal, decent boy."

In March of 1952, Josephine received a call from Sal's agent, Alec Alexander, with an offer for Sal to audition for an episode of the new and critically acclaimed television anthology called *Hallmark Hall of Fame*. The one-hour television special presentations, broadcast live from NBC Studios in Brooklyn, New York, were sponsored by the Hallmark greeting card company. Sal was determined to try his hand at television. Feeling that a full class schedule and a job at the theater were enough for Sal to handle, Josephine was opposed.

"I'd rather have a healthy son than a famous one," she said.

In an unusual show of will, Sal's father spoke on his behalf at a family dinner-table meeting. "Look, Jo," he said, "if he wants to take it, well, let's let him. We don't want the boy to be unhappy." The other children, excited at the prospect of seeing Sal in a dramatic role on television, sided with their father.

"The Vision of Father Flanagan" aired on March 30, 1952. The Mineo family gathered around their television set to watch Sal play the part of an orphan boy named Les who moves to a residential farm where other orphans, juvenile delinquents, and abandoned young boys found a loving home. Actress Sarah Churchill narrated the heartfelt story of the Catholic priest who founded Boys Town in Omaha, Nebraska.

That same evening, the sixth annual Tony Awards banquet was held at the Grand Ballroom of the Waldorf Astoria Hotel. *The King and I* was awarded five Tony Awards, including Best Musical Play. Within one year, thirteen-year-old Sal had appeared in the 1951 Best Play winner and the 1952 Best Musical winner.

IN THE spring, several of the child actors in *The King and I* contracted the measles. At last, Sal had his chance to actually appear on the stage. "One night I had to take the part of one of the king's young sons," Sal explained. "The original boy who played the role was sick and he was smaller than I was. But I got into his costume. It was so tight I could scarcely breathe. At one point in the play I had to bend over. As I did, my belt broke clean and fell to the floor and the velvet pants split right down the rear. And at that very moment I was forced to dance ring-around-the-rosy with the other children. We had to walk around the stage holding each other's hands. I was right in midstage when the pants dropped down to my ankles. The audience was hysterical at the craziest colored pair of shorts a prince ever wore. I was red as a beet and everyone laughed. Gertrude Lawrence got me out of my misery. She ad-libbed, patted me gently, and shooed me off the stage."

Sal made his second television appearance in a *Hallmark Hall of Fame* production called "A Woman for the Ages," on May 11, playing the son of President John Adams. Finally, Ronnie Lee, who had played the part of Crown Prince Chulalongkorn in *The King and I* for fifteen months, outgrew the role. Josephine and Sarina anxiously held hands when Sal made his first appearance as the Crown Prince on the stage of the St. James Theatre in October 1952.

"I was scared," Sal recalled. "I would be playing with Yul Brynner. There was something about the man that terrified me. I had watched Yul from the wings for a year. He was so very stern as the king with his unrestrained gestures, and very loud voice, that I thought he must be that way offstage too. I had heard he had a good sense of humor but I couldn't believe it. But there was nothing frightening in his offstage manner at all. When he came into the wings, he'd wave and nod to me just as he did to everyone else, but he'd never speak."

To play the prince, Sal had to wear "oriental" makeup. He asked Brynner's makeup man, Don Lawson, for help. Lawson told Sal to talk directly with Brynner.

Sal summoned the courage and went to Brynner's dressing room. "My knees literally shook," he remembered. "I waited for a long time before I knocked at his door."

Brynner surprised Sal by knowing his name. "Why, hiya, Sal. Come in, feller. I hear you are going on tonight."

Brynner got up from his seat in front of the dressing table. "Sit down," he said. "I'll tell you how to put the makeup on but I won't do it for you. You must learn to do it yourself."

Sal recalled, "He put a strong hand on my shoulder and added teasingly, 'Frankly, I don't see how makeup can help you.' He laughed and I laughed, too."

Brynner showed Sal how to apply the body makeup and how to fix his eyes with an eyeliner pencil. He then sent him on his way with a list of things he needed to buy. "From now on," Sal said, "I was informed, I was to apply the makeup myself."

The next time Sal saw Yul Brynner was onstage that night. "He whispered, Relax kid," Sal recalled. "All I remember of that performance was that his voice was so loud, so clear, and carried so far, that it made my own voice seem very small. After the show, he was the first to shake my hand. 'Nice job,' he said. That was all."

The cast became a second family to Sal. He sometimes saw more of them than his own family. Brynner became a second father to him. Sal didn't get home after the show until nearly one o'clock in the morning. By then, the rest of the house was sound asleep. Sal rarely saw his father during his run in *The King and I*. When Sal arose for school and another trip into New York City, his father had already left for work at the casket company.

As Sal stepped into the role of the prince, the cast had just accepted English-born Constance Carpenter in the role of Anna. Gertrude Lawrence, suffering from liver cancer, had left the show in mid-August 1952 and died three weeks later.

Cast member Helena Scott recalled, "We were more in love with Sal than we were with Yul Brynner, and we were plenty in love with Yul! You just couldn't help treating Sal like a prince."

Sal and Brynner's friendship grew and deepened, and the strong-willed veteran actor took the young boy under his wing. "Every night," Sal recalled, "we would meet in the wings before we went on, and he would talk to me as an equal. We discussed acting for one thing. Once, he presented me with a couple of books on acting. We talked a lot about water-skiing, one of his favorite pastimes. When he asked me if I liked it, I told him I liked the water and knew how to swim, but I didn't know a thing about water-skiing.

"One night Mr. Brynner called me into his dressing room to show me some skis he had made himself. When I admired them, he said, 'They're yours.' I couldn't find words to thank him. 'Oh, beat it,' he snapped good-naturedly, waving his arms."

Brynner was serious about his craft, but he was playful with the children, assuming the father role on and off the stage. He had clever ways of keeping the children at ease on the stage and teaching them acting lessons at the same time.

"There's a scene at the very end where the king is dying and is giving final instructions to his son," Sal remembered. "The king lies on a divan and the two keep on whispering to each other, while other stage business is going on. To make it appear that he really was giving me final instructions before his death, the king began telling jokes one night. Though at first I was completely thrown by his sense of humor, I had to use every acting trick at my command. Soon I realized there was method to his madness. This was Yul's rather unconventional way of teaching poise and balance. It was tough to take but I learned to laugh at it, since it proved invaluable experience."

In spite of Brynner's acting pointers, Sal admitted, "I was pretty bad. I was playing the part of a prince but onstage I walked and talked like a Bronx boy. Another thing, I never used to listen to anyone else speak their lines. Luckily, a private acting coach got hold of me and really taught me a thing or two."

Sal began acting lessons with the accomplished teacher Claudia Franck, who remembered Sal as fiercely earnest. She said, "It is not my rule to accept youngsters as pupils, but there was an unusual quality about this boy which came through to me, a fierce earnestness which was noticeable because it was combined with, and almost covered over by, a hesitant and appealing shyness. Even at that tender age, he had a strong desire to be helped toward a better understanding of the theater as well as acting, and I could see, even then, a very promising future for Sal."

With Miss Franck's encouragement, Sal began to observe the

"real people" whom he encountered and who were around him in the Bronx. She instructed Sal to absorb their mannerisms and idiosyncrasies so he could use them in his future acting assignments.

Sal became aware of his slight frame and began to exercise and use the weightlifting equipment that had been installed backstage for Yul Brynner's use. Brynner helped Sal create an exercise routine, showing him barbell exercises designed to add muscle to his young body, and deep breathing exercises to increase his stamina and projection onstage.

WHEN SAL was appearing in *The Rose Tattoo,* he was more interested in playing ball with his brothers and shooting dice with the other boy actors backstage than thinking about the little girls he worked with in the show. "Only sissies pay attention to actresses," he had told his mother.

In December of 1952, Josephine went shopping for Christmas gifts for Sal's fourteen stage "brothers and sisters." Brynner had planned a large holiday party for the cast. One of Sal's stage sisters, six months his senior, surprised him the night of the party.

"It happened backstage," Sal said, "and before I knew it, she leaned over my chair and kissed me. I figured maybe it was because I was a little kid, but she didn't kiss me like I was a little kid. And believe me, there's a difference."

Sal began to look for the girl whenever he arrived at the theater. They would sometimes sit beside each other in the balcony and talk until shortly before the audience trickled in to take their seats. They exchanged little gifts, and Sal soon found himself entangled in his first "puppy love" affair. At the time, he didn't tell his parents.

He had already begun to live two lives. His little world of the theater, which provided him with a window to escape from everyday life, was something he didn't particularly share with his family. And his family life, which he also loved, was something he didn't take to work.

"After a while," Sal admitted, "I got sort of tired of the girl in the show. It was around that time, I guess, that I got interested in girls in school. I got two passes to the show each week and had two girls out front. Before the performance they used to come to my dressing room and watch me put on my makeup."

Sarina's girlfriends from school would come to the Mineo house for any reason hoping to catch a glimpse of her "Broadway star" brother. They loved to go swimming with him and Sarina and watch him work in the yard bare chested. Sal playfully suggested his little sister should charge admission.

Sal was definitely beginning to feel his oats and realize the power provided to him by his good looks. His delicate features and pouty lips attracted the girls but also made him a target for bullies in his neighborhood and in Manhattan. He soon learned to hide his makeup kit in a paper sack after being chased down streets. Occasionally, he arrived at the theater with a bloody nose, scraped knuckles, and disheveled clothes.

Sometimes a theater usher who lived near Sal in the Bronx would accompany him home after the show. Usually, though, Sal traveled alone, which he never told his mother. He encountered young midtown thugs in the subways often, and he switched trains many times, dashing up and down stairs, in an effort to shake off assailants. Several times he was accosted by switchblade-wielding gangs.

Years later, Sal remembered those late nights. "By the time I got back to the Bronx, it was one in the morning. In the years I was working on Broadway, there wasn't one day in my life on those subways around Forty-second Street going toward the theater when I was not approached by a homosexual, and I mean by every form of homosexual, whether he was a cop, a priest, or a guy on the street."

Sal bought a little starter pistol and carried it with him when he traveled alone. One night he found himself alone on a subway car with an older man who tried to pick him up. The guy persisted, and Sal pulled out the gun and told the man to back away and get on his knees. When his stop came up and the train slowed down, Sal was unable to repress his anger any longer, and he pulled the trigger. "Jesus, the sound was so loud it scared the shit out of the guy. He thought he was dead. There was nothing wrong with him, but he started yelling. The doors opened and I ran like hell. I ran all the way home."

DURING THE day in Manhattan, between matinee and evening performances, Sal killed time window-shopping, exploring the tonier parts of the city, catching a John Garfield movie, or playing pool. Sometimes he'd skip over to the nearby Paramount Theatre and watch Gene

Krupa play the drums, eventually coaxing the drummer to give him a few lessons. Mike often left him alone, attending to his own auditions or chasing girls. Sal never told his mother, fearing she might yank him out of the show. The pool hall nearest the theater was frequented by show business people. He liked to listen to their stories about Broadway greats, and away from his mother's watchful eye, he could smoke and play poker.

He was also reluctant to talk about his newfound interest in girls with his mother. "When I was in junior high I didn't have too many dates. I was far more interested in baseball. Girls just didn't enter into it. But then I can remember a change at the Lodge School. I started dating about every two weeks at first. Then more often. I even went steady, I remember, for something like two weeks at a time. I decided baseball wasn't for me. Since then, I've been more romantic minded than sports minded. I was really swinging by fifteen."

Sal, though just a young teenager, was fast becoming savvy and worldly-wise. He lost his virginity early in the run of *The King and I* when an older girl who worked as a wardrobe mistress seduced him in his dressing room backstage and introduced him to fellatio.

IN THE spring of 1953, Sal began to experience a nagging pain in his right eye. He tried to ignore it, but before long, the pain became too sharp to neglect. "Whenever I walked out into the hot sun, it was as if my eye was on fire, and I felt feverish and dizzy," Sal remembered. "Finally I told my mom. She was fit to be tied. She couldn't understand why I hadn't said something about my eye before."

Josephine made an appointment with a recommended eye doctor in Manhattan. Sal was ordered to wear a patch over his eye for a few weeks so the eye could recover from the strain and irritation. "I was on Broadway," Sal explained, "and I couldn't wear a big black patch on my eye." Though Sal wore the patch for the short time he was at home, as soon as he left each day for school and the theater, he removed the patch. Several weeks later, his condition worsened and a small ulcer developed in the corner of his right eye.

Sal was accompanied by his mother to the Manhattan Eye and Ear Hospital the following morning for minor surgery. The doctor told Josephine he could not use any anesthetic because he needed to see how responsive Sal's eye would be to the procedure. Sal remembered the pain was horrible, though the entire operation lasted only a few minutes. He did wear a patch for a few weeks during the recovery whenever he could, but not onstage.

ONE DAY in June, Yul Brynner invited Sal to spend a weekend with him and his family at their Connecticut estate. "You've got the skis," he said to Sal. "I'll teach you how to water-ski."

The following Saturday evening after the show, Sal climbed into Brynner's car with the water skis Yul had given him, a suitcase his mother had packed, and a big block of lasagna wrapped in aluminum foil she had prepared as a gift for the Brynners. He had never seen such a luxurious home before and recalled being embarrassed when he handed Josephine's lasagna to Brynner's formally dressed chef.

"Though he loves to water-ski and spends hours at it," Sal said, "he took time out to teach me. He showed me the basic principles on the pier. He stayed with me, patiently coaching until he felt I caught on. He was so afraid that I might get hurt that he kept the motorboat going at a very slow pace. I remember yelling to him, 'Faster, faster.' "

"We went back to New York on Monday afternoon," Sal recalled, "just in time to make the show." When Sal got home from his weekend getaway, he excitedly told his mother about his newly acquired water-skiing skill. "Look, Ma," he boasted, "now we have to get a boat!"

SAL DID eight shows a week and he didn't seem to think it was enough," Josephine said. "He was going to school, too, and you would imagine he would crawl home exhausted each night. But he'd still go out in the afternoons and make the rounds of casting agencies. Sometimes he would land a job, but when the agency would phone me, I would say no."

Sal's mother was afraid his eye infection would return if he worked too hard and didn't get enough rest. She reminded him of the doctor's orders. But twice during the run of The King and I, Josephine relented.

Sal was cast as Paco, a little Spanish boy who desperately wants to be a toreador, in a drama called "The Capital of the World" for the Emmy Award–winning series, Omnibus.

"When I heard that Yul Brynner had been assigned to direct the television script in which I was to appear as a Mexican bullfighter, I was delighted," Sal remembered. "Yul, as a director, gives the actor a feeling of security. You just know you're going to be good if he's guiding you."

Brynner actually inspired Sal to become interested in directing. "Here he was," Sal said, "the star of the biggest musical on Broadway, and he was directing television shows on the side. And he directed me in my first lead on television."

Yul Brynner said, "He's the best kid I ever worked with, so respectful, so eager to please. Some kids, onstage, get to be brats. Not Sal. He treated me like a father. And to me he was like one of my kids. I think he had complete confidence in me. He confided his problems."

"The Capital of the World" was broadcast live on Sunday night, December 6, 1953. "Thanks to Yul's direction," Sal said, "I received many compliments on my performance."

In early 1954, shortly before *The King and I* closed, Sal appeared in one more television show, *Janet Dean, Registered Nurse.* Sal was awakened by his mother at six A.M. after only four hours of sleep so he could be at the television studio in Manhattan to begin work by eight A.M. on the day of filming. When he came home early the next morning after his performance in *The King and I* and a full day of filming the television show, he was exhausted. Josephine was waiting up for him. He told her he fell asleep on the TV set between shots.

"But," Sal told her, "I didn't fall asleep until after I had finished my scenes."

"The Garcia Case," Sal's episode of *Janet Dean, Registered Nurse,* was broadcast in March. Sal played Jose Garcia, a Mexican boy who wants to play baseball. Sal turned in an excellent performance as the little boy with a big ambition. He was appropriately belligerent, endearing, and coyly flirtatious.

*The King and I* closed on March 24, 1954, and a new company of actors was cast and prepared to tour the country. Though Josephine refused the producers' offer for Sal to continue his role in the road tour, Rodgers and Hammerstein reported, "Sal's the finest young actor we know."

A few weeks later, Sal landed his most unusual role to date when he was cast as the Page in the Richard Strauss operatic adaptation of

Oscar Wilde's drama *Salome* for *NBC Television Opera Theatre*. Sal's appearance in a "highbrow" show made his mother especially proud but gave his neighborhood chums something else to tease him about, as he was clad in only a white silk toga. The program, broadcast live on May 8, was very well received and earned Sal his first critical mention in the *New York Times* when critic Howard Taubman wrote, "Young Sal Mineo was the agreeable actor who played the page."

In early June, Philip Benjamin, a veteran agent with the Universal International Pictures casting department in Hollywood, arrived in New York City to cast the few remaining roles for a new motion picture called *Six Bridges to Cross*. The screenplay was a thinly disguised retelling of the famous 1950 Brinks armored car robbery in Boston.

Mike Mineo was called to read for the part of the lead character, Jerry Florea, as a boy. Jeff Chandler had been cast in the adult role of Florea. Benjamin felt he resembled Chandler as a young man. The tables were turned, and Sal accompanied Mike to the audition. While they were there, Benjamin asked Sal to read as well, "though, of course," he said, "you don't look anything like Chandler. But read."

The brothers left the audition uncertain, but Mike was buoyed when the casting director said he would call very soon with the results of the audition. Soon Josephine received the news that Mike had indeed been chosen for the role. One week later, Jeff Chandler dropped out of the movie. He was replaced by Tony Curtis.

"When Tony Curtis replaced Jeff Chandler in the lead role," Sal recalled, "I replaced Mike since I looked more like Tony. It was just my luck to have curly hair like Tony's. This began my motion picture career." Sal was very excited. Mike was disappointed but was expected to celebrate Sal's good fortune. Victor recalled his little brother's big break. "We knew Sal was in when he started that first picture, and, believe me, we were the happiest family in the world!"

In mid-June, Sal traveled to Boston with a guardian hired by his mother. All of his scenes would be shot on location, and he was paid $350 a week for the duration of filming. In spite of this large salary, Josephine still had a difficult time managing the money. To the existing expenses were added food and lodging in Boston, a private tutor, and $100 a week for his location guardian; Josephine was again spending more money than Sal was earning.

Sal had the time of his life in Boston. He was happy to meet Tony Curtis, one of his sister's movie idols. Curtis remembered Sal as "a gifted actor." They developed a friendship that lasted through the years. "Sal and I ended up being good friends," Curtis said. "He was a good guy, and you could see he loved working in movies."

Sal learned a valuable acting lesson from his first film's director, Joseph Pevney. Sal said, "He showed me the difference between stage and film techniques. I learned to control my actions, which were fine on the stage, but terribly exaggerated before the camera."

Mineo and Alvisi cousins from around the country sent Josephine different newspaper clippings about the making of *Six Bridges to Cross,* including a photo of Sal that appeared in the *New York Times* and was then picked up by the wire services. Her "kitchen wall of fame" was beginning to take shape. She also began a quaint, and wily, letter-writing campaign as Sal's career grew. She wrote thank-you letters to reviewers and reporters who wrote about her son. She kept a list of their names and addresses and sent them Sal's latest publicity photographs, and she sent Christmas cards signed by Sal.

Once filming on *Six Bridges to Cross* concluded, there was no work for Sal in the summer of 1954. He visited casting agents and auditioned for jobs, but his mother was becoming more selective with her choices. The family missed the much needed extra income, but Josephine was more conscious of building up a career for her young son rather than accepting any offer for work.

Victor, now nineteen years old and a college student, had a steady girlfriend and worked with his father at Universal Casket Company, located at 259 East 134th Street. He received a car for his eighteenth birthday, purchased with "family funds," so he was usually away from home until the appointed dinner hour.

Sal, Mike, and Sarina spent a conventional summer playing with friends, having barbecues, and going swimming. Sal was spending more time with girls and entertaining double dates with Mike. In fact, Josephine's youngest boy was single-minded when it came to pretty girls. Romance was a means to an end for Sal. Even at that young age, he recognized the power of charm and friendly persuasion.

Sal began to correspond with his first "girlfriend," the young actress he worked with in *The King and I.* Some of his friends teased him, and finally his family became aware of his early infatuation. Josephine didn't open Sal's mail, but she stood nearby while he read his first love letters with a weary smile frozen on her face and her hands firmly on her hips.

Sal missed the regularity of working. The only offers he got were little more than bit parts. In a bold move, Josephine turned down another offer from *Hallmark Hall of Fame*, believing the part was too slight. Earlier, she had refused a contract offer from the same producers for Sal to appear in several *Hallmark Hall of Fame* presentations.

Just as she had advised her husband years before to hold out for the right opportunity and turn down insignificant offers, she gambled with Sal's career. "If you don't get good parts," she told Sal, "I'd rather see you home."

# 4.

"I used to look at people and think, 'They're from Hollywood!'"

Hollywood's calling," Josephine yelled out the door at her youngest son. Sal was playing ball with his brother Mike and several neighborhood boys. Since completion of his first movie role in *Six Bridges to Cross* several months earlier, Sal had spent a quiet summer with his family in the Bronx. He and Mike had traveled often to Manhattan for casting calls and auditions, but no substantive offers had been made. Though Sal missed acting, he relished the time he was able to spend with his family, especially his father.

Since Sal's scenes in his first film were shot on location on the noisy streets of Boston, there were many problems with the sound. He would have to go to Hollywood to "loop" his lines and shoot a few pickup shots at Universal International Studios. Looping requires the actor to rerecord his lines in a recording studio. The newly recorded dialogue is then laid over the film, replacing the track that had been recorded on location.

The studio paid for Sal and a guardian to fly to Los Angeles in November 1954. Sal's aunt Millie, one of Josephine's younger sisters, was chosen to accompany him. Sal was thrilled, and again frightened to be so far from his family. Josephine dismissed her neighbors' concerns about her little boy being alone in what they called "good-time" Hollywood. "Nobody's going to turn Sal's head," she said with confidence. "Emotionally, he's been grown-up for years."

SAL AND his aunt Millie were overwhelmed by the sprawling, laid-back city of Los Angeles. A uniformed chauffeur in a studio limousine picked them up at the airport, and they were driven to a motel in North Hollywood near Universal International Studios. Sal called Josephine as soon as they checked into their room and anxiously told her about the palm trees, the beautiful people wearing bathing suits on the street, and the steamy heat.

"The first time I went to Hollywood," Sal said, "there I was, a green, scared kid from the Bronx. Hollywood is a very different world than any I had imagined. At first glance, it's strange and new and, well, it was awfully frightening. The thing is everyone is so terribly sophisticated. My parents brought me up with hopes of making a gentleman of me. But believe me, when I first saw those really big stars I couldn't help but feel like a nothing. It sounds so trivial. I mean, being nervous and shy around more sophisticated people. But it wasn't at all trivial to me. It was very, very important."

Determined to see for herself what her young nephew was about to undertake, Aunt Millie accompanied Sal to the studio on the first day. Alec Alexander, Sal's theatrical agent from New York, who had traveled to Hollywood the previous day, was waiting for him.

"My first morning at Universal, I started getting butterflies," Sal recalled. "The first familiar star I saw was José Ferrer. I started yelling, 'There's José Ferrer!' My agent had to hold me down and keep telling me to take it easy. I was just a little kid."

California state law required that child actors had to put in three dedicated hours of school on the set each day. Between takes, they had twenty-minute study periods. Sal found this discipline particularly difficult. "I didn't know whether to study geometry or rehearse my lines for the next scene," he complained. Gladys Hoene had been the resident teacher at Universal International for fifteen years. Her kindness, patience, and skills as a teacher were widely known in the industry. She was charmed by Sal's disarming personality and quickly became fond of her new student.

Looping took a little longer than originally anticipated, and the few additional days of shooting delayed Sal's return to New York. Sal and his aunt stayed in a motel for a little more than a week before she had to return to her own family. Mrs. Hoene explained, "The idea struck his aunt: Sal could live with us. She had been to our house, and she knew I had the room. I didn't even think it over once she'd said it. It seemed like a natural thing to do. Of course, Sal called home to get permission. I heard him saying on the phone, 'Yes, Mom, the school-teacher . . . Mrs. Hoene.' "

Sal's second home became a comfortable, rambling California ranch-style, four-bedroom house on a tree-lined dead-end street not far from Universal International in North Hollywood. The house, located at 4918 Rhodes Avenue, had a large backyard surrounded by hedges, fruit trees, and rosebushes. Sal had his own room and private bath.

It was agreed that Sal would pay Mrs. Hoene $100 a month for room and board. Josephine provided Sal with a twenty-dollar weekly allowance for his lunches and dates. Gladys Hoene became Sal's second mother, and she and her husband, Bernard, actually became Sal's legal guardians in California.

"He was part of the family right from the start," Mrs. Hoene said.

In late November, Sal overheard other young actors in the studio classroom talking about a new movie being cast on the lot. He read for a role and was cast as Cadet Sylvester Dusik in *The Private War of Major Benson*. He excitedly called his mother and told her about his good luck. He remained in California for another week for fittings and wardrobe test shots before flying home to the Bronx for a Christmas holiday.

"When Sal took his first trip to Hollywood," Sarina recalled, "we missed him terribly. When he came home, he brought each one a present. My gift was a beautiful bracelet and necklace set."

*SIX BRIDGES TO CROSS* previewed at the Hollywood Paramount Theatre on January 4, 1955. The film went into limited release the next day, and Sal received the first movie reviews of his life. On January 14, *Variety* wrote, "Sal Mineo does a credible job of playing Tony Curtis as a youth." That same day, the *Hollywood Reporter* offered, "A new actor, Sal Mineo, is a standout as the young hoodlum." Veteran Hollywood reporter Dorothy Manners wrote in the *Los Angeles Examiner,* "Jay C. Flippen and Sal Mineo are standouts in the supporting cast." Philip K. Scheuer reported in the *Los Angeles Times,* "Sal Mineo deserves special mention as the boy Jerry." And back home in the Bronx, the *New York Times* said, "As young Jerry, the budding delinquent, Sal Mineo contributes an effective bit in the best scene with George Nader."

Sal had returned to Los Angeles on January 2. Principal photography on *The Private War of Major Benson* began at Universal International the following day. His first day on the set was overwhelming and exhilarating, but he felt a little out of his element. Standing in a cavernous soundstage amid a swirl of actors and technicians, he felt alone.

He was ushered into the makeup department before his first shot. "On TV," he said, "and in the theater we always put on our own makeup, so when I began my first movie in Hollywood I really flipped when I discovered the studio had people to do this for you."

*The Private War of Major Benson* was shot in Technicolor on soundstages at Universal International Studios and on location at St. Catherine's Military School in Anaheim, forty miles south of Los Angeles. The imposing school buildings constructed in the late 1880s and stark campus grounds provided scenery for the film, and all of the students at the school were employed as extras.

The film was standard family fare. Starring Charlton Heston in the title role, the story concerned Major Benson, considered a hothead with a big mouth, who is given a choice to either leave the army or assume command of the ROTC program at Sheridan Academy and shape up the three hundred unruly preteen cadets before the school fails its next inspection.

Despite working with a studio dialogue coach, Sal's Bronx accent was apparent in the film. His distinctive ethnic looks further set Sal apart from the other experienced young actors. All but ostracized by his fellow boy costars during the ten weeks of shooting, Sal gravitated to the *real* boys who attended St. Catherine's. He regaled them with his tales of roughing it on the streets of New York City. During breaks in shooting, he joined them on the school's baseball diamond and sneaked contraband cigarettes to his new "cadet" friends.

Sal found Heston accommodating but brittle and self-possessed. He did not interact with the children off camera. The director, Jerry Hopper, provided little guidance. Shooting ended on February 26. The humorous though predictable film was slow moving and overlong.

"While he was making *Private War*," Mrs. Hoene said, "some of the agents here became interested in him, and he was given the script of a film about juvenile delinquents to read, called *Rebel Without a Cause*. I think from that moment he was really, seriously an actor."

## 5.

"If he put his arm around me, that was fabulous, because then I knew he meant it. I always felt he was just testing people, testing to see how far he could push."

In the early 1950s, teen crime soared in the United States. Teenage boys and girls, encouraged by new feelings of independence and empowerment, were becoming more aggressive in pursuing their own interests and dismissive of parental authority. The days of children being seen and not heard were about to end. Director Nicholas Ray, who had touched upon juvenile delinquency in two of his films, was intrigued by two feature articles in September 1954: "Our Vicious Young Hoodlums: Is There Any Hope?" in *Newsweek*, and "Why Teen-Agers Go Wrong" in *U.S. News and World Report*, which featured an in-depth interview with juvenile crime expert Richard Clendenen.

Juvenile crime had become the focus of the U.S. Congress in 1953 with the formation of the United States Senate Subcommittee to Investigate Juvenile Delinquency and the appointment of Richard Clendenen as the executive director. Originally formed to study the effectiveness of current laws, the subcommittee soon turned its attention to what many people felt was the real cause of the moral decline of America's youth—teenage popular culture. The emerging teen culture of rock and roll music, fashion, "hip" slang, fast food, automobiles, and open attitudes toward sex was viewed as a threat to the traditional family and the values that defined American living.

In addition, the number of teenage children doubled in the wake of the postwar baby boom. By the mid-1950s the United States was home to more than sixteen million teenagers. More young Americans were employed, and spending, like never before. Manufacturers recognized this new market, and products were created exclusively to appeal to this new consumer force. Accordingly, their newfound financial freedom emboldened young Americans to be more independent and curious.

Sal's arrival in Hollywood coincided with a shift in the consumer demographic. He represented the kind of product most appealing to a teenage consumer public, and for a young audience hungry for someone they could easily identify with on-screen, Sal fit the bill perfectly. His tough yet sensitive image appealed to both girls and boys.

AT THE age of forty-three, Nicholas Ray had established himself as a respected director beginning with his first film, *They Live by Night,* in 1948. In spite of his bohemian approach to directing, he had worked within the studio system with many of Hollywood's most established actors, and his credits included *In a Lonely Place, The Lusty Men,* and *Johnny Guitar.*

In the fall of 1954, Warner Bros. was looking for a product to appeal to the new teen market. Ray wanted to do a film about *average* kids, unlike those portrayed in his earlier films. The studio expressed an interest in working with him and suggested he adapt a book they had earlier purchased written by Dr. Robert Lindner called *Rebel Without a Cause: The Story of a Criminal Psychopath.* Ray was not interested, however, after reading the book.

Ray met with Steve Trilling, head of production at Warner Bros., and explained an idea of his own. Ray then wrote a seventeen-page treatment called *The Blind Run* that featured the exploits of three teenage companions: a heroic young man, a discontented young woman, and a lonely boy looking for love.

The studio bought the property immediately but insisted Ray use the title *Rebel Without a Cause,* even though he refused to use one word from the book. Upon reading Ray's treatment, though, it was dismissed as unfilmable and the director was asked to search the studio for a screenwriter.

Creating a screenplay from Ray's treatment would not be easy. Though he had a theme and intense character relationships, the story lacked plot. Ray proposed veteran writer Clifford Odets. Odets, a successful playwright, had written several classic plays about youth, including *Awake and Sing!, Waiting for Lefty,* and *Golden Boy.* Odets was Ray's neighbor at the Chateau Marmont Hotel in Los Angeles, and a longtime friend. Unfortunately, the studio balked at the idea of hiring an infamous, blacklisted writer. Still, during the tedious writing process and ultimate filming of *Rebel,* Ray would continue to consult with

Odets, who provided him with useful advice in terms of characterizing Jim Stark in the film. And it was Odets who provided one of the most momentous lines in the film, wailed by James Dean in the heartbreaking finale: "I got the bullets!"

Over the next few weeks, Ray worked with two studio-assigned writers, Leon Uris and Irving Shulman, and quickly rejected them both. But in December of 1954, Ray met Stewart Stern, a young writer, at a star-studded Christmas party hosted by Gene Kelly. Stern seemed to understand what Ray was looking for. They began an intensive working relationship that would be fruitful and contentious. And their efforts would ultimately lead to the final screenplay of *Rebel Without a Cause*.

The story centers around Jim Stark, who tries to deal with a henpecked father, a domineering mother, and life at another new school. Jim is arrested for being drunk in public. While awaiting his parents at the police station he notices two other youngsters. Judy was picked up for walking around alone at night, and Plato was arrested for shooting a litter of puppies with his mother's gun. The next morning, Jim sees Judy on the way to his new high school. The class goes to the planetarium for a field trip, where Jim becomes friendly with Plato, who explains that Judy is the girlfriend of Buzz, the leader of a dangerous school gang. In the parking lot, Jim and Buzz get in an argument and have a knife fight. They agree to meet later that evening to test each other's bravery by racing cars toward a cliff in a "chickie run." While all the kids watch, Jim jumps to safety, but Buzz plummets over the cliff to his death. Jim, Plato, and Judy flee before the police arrive. Jim and Judy, now allied in tragedy, go to a deserted mansion near the planetarium that Plato had pointed out during the school field trip. Plato arrives at the mansion, armed with a .45-caliber pistol, to warn Jim that Buzz's gang is looking for him. The three friends spend some peaceful time in the dark house. When Plato falls asleep, Jim and Judy wander off to explore. While they are away, three gang members arrive and attack Plato, who in his fear shoots one of his assailants. Plato runs to the planetarium to hide, followed by Jim and Judy. In a confrontation with the police, Plato is shot on the planetarium steps.

The entire story of *Rebel Without a Cause* takes place within a twenty-four-hour period of time. "The purpose of the film," Stern explained, "was to tell the story of a generation growing up . . . in one night."

IN EARLY March 1955, with a preliminary script in hand, Sal arrived at his appointed audition on the Warner Bros. lot for the part of one of the gang members. Several young actors had already been cast, including James Dean in the leading role of Jim Stark. Ray was able to persuade him to accept the role on January 4 before a script had even been completed. Sal looked oddly out of place in his preppy-boy clothes.

"I saw this kid in the back who looked like my son except he was prettier," director Nick Ray recalled. While working on the script of *Rebel Without a Cause,* Ray had actually modeled Plato after his own son.

Ray spotted Sal, who looked even smaller for his age as he stood in line with other sixteen- and seventeen-year-old actors, all of whom towered over him. Sal looked more like a choirboy than a thug. Ray called him over and asked him to read with Corey Allen, the young actor cast in the role of Buzz. After watching Sal, Ray thought he would be perfect as Plato.

Sal waited for hours until the other young actors had auditioned. Ray asked him to come to the Chateau Marmont, a castle-like hotel on Sunset Boulevard, on the following Sunday to read with James Dean. Ray maintained a small poolside bungalow at the industry-populated hotel. Sal hurried home to tell Mrs. Hoene.

"He was so excited," she recalled. "He couldn't stop talking about it, and none of us knew who James Dean was."

"I was almost sick, I wanted the part so bad," Sal said. "I thought I was dressed pretty sharp for those days, pegged pants, skinny tie, and jacket, until Jimmy walked in with his T-shirt and blue jeans."

Part of Ray's unconventional approach to directing was an effort to keep his actors on their toes, keep them wondering about what was expected. Newly turned sixteen, Sal's inexperience and naïveté served him well during his first intimate reading for the role. Not knowing what this process would entail, the young actor was excited and a bit anxious.

Without telling Sal what role he was to play, Ray explained a scene he wanted Sal and Jimmy to read and asked him what role was he interested in.

"Definitely you want a Plato," Sal stated.

Ray asked why Sal was interested in Plato.

"Well," Sal explained, "I just think it's a better role."

Ray briefly explained the setup preceding the scene, and Jimmy and Sal began to read. Ray watched and listened intently. Jimmy was well prepared, having worked with the director for several weeks, but Ray was very impressed with Sal's cold-reading skills and his lack of self-consciousness. After a few moments, Ray told the young actors to put aside the script and improvise.

Sal said, "I had no idea what he was talking about, but I wanted the role very badly. I picked it up from Jimmy, realized that he was doing the scene but making up his own dialogue, and that that's what improvisations are. So we 'improvised' the sequence.

"We went through a scene and nothing happened between us. Nick finally walked over and suggested we sit and talk for a while. When Jimmy found out I was from the Bronx, we started gabbing about New York and then progressed to cars, and before we knew it we were buddies. Then we went back to the script, and this time it went off like clockwork. When we reached a part where we were supposed to laugh hysterically, Jimmy gave out with that special giggle of his, and I couldn't help but follow along. Pretty soon we just couldn't stop laughing."

During that first reading, Ray stopped the actors and stepped in. "Sal," he said, "stop trying to be Plato, and be yourself. Now, think, is there anything in the world you want as much as Plato wanted a friend?"

Sal thought for a moment, then his eyes lit up. "My driver's license," he gushed.

"Fine," Ray responded. "Now look at Jimmy as if he is your driver's license."

Sal was instantly impressed by Jimmy's ease and lack of inhibition. Jimmy's brotherly attention and sense of teasing fun made Sal feel comfortable and safe. "I liked being near him. I liked talking with him more than anybody else," Sal recalled. "From the moment I met Jimmy my whole life took on a completely different meaning. I was in incredible awe of him in many ways, watching him do the things he did. He was really overwhelming."

The reading continued for another hour and then Jimmy took Ray aside with a peculiar idea. He said, "Tell Sal to look at me the way Natalie looks at me." Actress Natalie Wood had just been cast as the second teenage lead, Judy, Dean's love interest in the film.

It quickly became clear to Ray that Sal was attracted to Dean. He knew that Dean was bisexual and he persuaded him to encourage Sal's attentions. Ray was impressed by the repartee between Sal and Jimmy. Dean took notice as well, and following the reading, he and Ray decided they had found an actor who would give them what they had been looking for.

Ray decided to screen-test Sal in a scene with Wood and Dean. Wood began her film career in 1943 at the age of five. With numerous television roles, and more than twenty motion pictures to her credit, including *The Ghost and Mrs. Muir* and *Miracle on 34th Street,* Wood was the most experienced actor among the three young leads. Several months shy of her seventeenth birthday, she was desperate to make the transition from child star to leading lady.

Sal was acquainted with Wood. "One afternoon," Wood recalled, "a curly-haired boy walked into the classroom of the Universal International school and looked at me with an appraising smile. Although I never before laid eyes on him, he waved to me, came over, and jauntily said, 'Hi, doll!' I thought he was a fresh little thing." In spite of Sal's bold approach, they discovered they had a similar sense of humor and a definite pursuit of mischief. "He had a dazzling smile," she added, "that seemed to start at his toes and work all the way to his hairline." They quickly became friends, and Sal was happy to commiserate with someone so close to his age.

Ray chose the mansion sequence, a pivotal and romantic scene in the script, as Sal's ultimate test. On March 16, 1955, less than two weeks before filming was scheduled to begin, Sal was called to the set of *A Streetcar Named Desire* at Warner Bros. Studio. The abandoned set was used as the deserted mansion. Sal's test went very well. By the end of the day, he was signed to play the part of Plato, though the final casting news was not revealed in the trade papers until April 1. Sal's weekly salary was $600. He called Josephine that evening, awakening her from sleep. She dragged everyone out of bed to tell them the wonderful news.

The following day, Sal joined Dean and Wood at Ray's bunga-low for more rehearsals. The director soon departed from any working script and instructed his actors to improvise. He recorded their efforts on audiotape. At the end of the session, they would listen to playbacks and critique. Ray thought it was important for him to know as much about his actors' personal lives as possible. Accordingly, he could use his knowledge of their joys or sorrows to elicit the emotion he needed in the scene. Sal also learned an important acting lesson from James Dean, who told him to relax before an emotional scene. Though it sounded contradictory, Sal discovered it worked.

Ray filmed the final rehearsal of the mansion scene at the studio in black and white on March 23, 1955. Production of the film was set to begin the following week and last for only thirty-six days. Ray was also pressed for time since, on March 17, James Dean had signed to play the part of Jett Rink in the Warner production of Edna Ferber's novel *Giant*. The epic production, to be directed by George Stevens, was set to begin filming on May 23.

The sequence, beginning with Sal manically laughing and flirting with Dean, and ending with Sal, Dean, and Wood lying entwined on the floor, is one of the most intense, revealing, and erotically charged scenes ever filmed at that time. This test, which survives on film, first captured the naked emotion of the three young actors and the sublimi-nal sexual complexity of the story that explains the emotional power of the film.

The filmed rehearsal was important to Ray for several reasons. It provided him with an opportunity to explore the erotic tension he wanted to represent in the film, and it set the tone for the challenging and intriguing direction he intended for the character of Plato. Sal didn't realize what was being asked of him. "I couldn't understand," he said later, "couldn't comprehend what was happening. Something was happening to me. I had no idea or any understanding of affection between men. And for the first time I felt something strong."

Though Stern would later say there was never any gay element in his script, and, in fact, bristled at the idea, Ray was determined to mine the attraction and affection that the character of a lonely, father-less Plato would demonstrate as his friendship with Jim Stark blos-somed. The conservative moral climate of the 1950s would impose itself on issues concerning anything perceived as abnormal sexual behavior. Gayness was a subject hardly represented in popular fiction and certainly repressed in any motion picture representation. But Sal was a courageous and inquisitive actor. Without fully understanding the subtext Ray pursued, Sal willingly surrendered to his director's commands. "Sal is rich," Ray would later say. "That sounds ambitious. What I mean is that Sal is rich with the things that are important, rich with talent and imagination, with sincerity and family love."

Stern submitted his final script on March 25, the same day Ray began filming. At the same time, another movie about juvenile delinquency opened, which demonstrated the decided shift toward the youth market. *Blackboard Jungle,* produced by MGM Studios, opened with a blast, literally. The opening credits played over Bill Haley and the Comets' rock and roll hit "Rock Around the Clock." Riots were reported in theaters coast to coast as teenagers jumped on their seats and danced in the aisles. *Blackboard Jungle* portrayed adolescent rebellion as a social problem told from the point of view of the adults. It managed to capture some of the surprising violence and rebellion of teens but didn't consider the cause.

To promote his film project, and to address the attention *Blackboard Jungle* was generating, Ray was interviewed by Philip K. Scheuer for the *Los Angeles Times* on April 3, 1955. Ray explained, "This is no slum study like *Blackboard Jungle.* We have put what happens in the home, the middle-class home, ahead of that, ahead of the slum condition. These things are taking place on all social, economic, and cultural levels, wherever young people feel they are 'out of attention.' It is there and then that they are vulnerable to participating in and creating delinquent acts which will bring them back into attention, only this time it's negative."

Ray named home, school, economy, environment, the behavior pattern of parents, even a child's muscular development as contributing factors to the problem. But the home, he felt, was the principal area of interest. "What is done there," he explained, "can be constructive— or destructive. But there is no one answer. Take identical families—and you find one kid a leader of his school and another out on probation!"

GRIFFITH OBSERVATORY, an imposing concrete and granite structure, clings to the hillside of Griffith Park facing south, overlooking
the city of Los Angeles. The first day of principal shooting took place
in a parking lot next to the observatory. Sal reported to work on March
30, along with Wood and Dean, and a dozen young actors portraying
gang members. *East of Eden*, starring Dean, had just opened to wide acclaim, and reviews proclaimed a new Hollywood star was born. Consequently, Dean dominated the set of *Rebel*, and his fellow actors treated
him with deference and a small amount of cynicism.

For Dean's costars, though, his dominance had been established
weeks before in the comfort of Ray's bungalow. Sal and Natalie were
both seduced by Dean's charisma, mystery, and sexual ambiguity. They
also soon recognized his style, choices, and approach to acting represented the future of their profession. Ray had described the characters
of Plato and Judy as Jim Stark's two new worshippers in his original
film treatment. With seemingly little effort, James Dean managed to
earn the same loving devotion offscreen.

"We all tended to idolize him," Sal explained. "If he didn't say
good morning to me I'd be a wreck the whole day. If he put his arm
around me that was fabulous, because I knew he meant it. I always felt
he was just testing people, testing to see how far he could go."

Sal found Wood to be schoolgirlishly obsessive about Dean. "He
was all she could talk about," he said. "Every night for weeks in a row,
she went to see *East of Eden*. She must have seen it over fifty times. She
even taught me to play the theme song from the picture on the piano."

After several days on location at Griffith Observatory, Jack Warner
decided to halt production and reshoot the film in color. Without a
pause, filming continued, including reshooting three days at the observatory and then moving to Santa Monica High School, renamed
"Dawson High" for the film.

Despite his promise to Stern, Ray frequently made changes to the
script without consulting him. New script pages appeared every day.
His numerous changes meant the picture would fall behind schedule
and always be over budget.

FRIENDSHIPS, ROMANCES, and obsessions began to take hold of
the principal players as shooting entered its second week. Being the

youngest and closest in age, Sal and Natalie developed a friendship quickly. By law they were required to spend three hours each day with a tutor in school. Tom Hennesy, a six-foot-five-inch former policeman, was their on-set guardian. The imposing Hennesy was determined to protect his young charges. He was a watchdog on the set and tried to control any on-set profanity and shield them from any bad influences of adult cast members and the crew.

Keeping Natalie Wood in line was a daunting and full-time job since the years she had already spent in the business made her more advanced for her age. Unlike Sal, Wood was a good, attentive student but she balked at authority. At every opportunity, she would run off to Hollywood for an off-the-set lunch with actors Nick Adams and Dennis Hopper. When Hennesy complained to Ray and the film's producer, David Weisbart, they laughed at him. Natalie smoked cigarettes and swore more than most of the boys on the set. Sal smoked, too, but restricted his smoking to after working hours.

The guardian was not aware of anything that happened off the studio lot, which was one of the reasons Ray conducted rehearsals at his bungalow at the hotel. Sal may have thought he had seen it all, but he was a wide-eyed innocent in comparison to his new friends. Natalie was having an affair with Nick Ray and sleeping with Dennis Hopper as well. Dean was often with a young man named Jack Simmons, who most people believed was his lover. Both Natalie and Sal smoked dope with Ray and Dean regularly. Odets joined the group nightly and drank with Ray until the director became incoherent and the youngsters let themselves out. It didn't take Sal long, though, to join in the fun. Henry Vilardo, Sal's makeup man, said that one morning while Sal was in the makeup room, Sal looked in the mirror and opened his mouth. "Do you ever get syphilis of the mouth?" he asked.

Still, Sal was a novice in Hollywood, and he had trouble on the set fitting in with the rest of the young actors. "He tried to hang out with the kids on set but was left on the wayside," said Hennesy. Some of the other young actors who played gang members harassed him, and some actually called him queer behind his back. When he approached them on set, they would turn and walk away. Oddly, they treated him like their characters treated Plato in the film. As Ray focused the film on the three principal players, the other smaller roles were reduced and some were simply written out. This became a bone of contention for the young actors who watched their parts disappear. Natalie was too delicate and Dean too impressive to blame for the director's shift of focus, so the actors' ire was directed at Sal.

Hennesy recalled, "Sal was withdrawn and did not socialize much because of that. He was very sensitive. If you made a joke about something that he felt was connected to him, he brooded over it for days."

The more the other kids ostracized Sal, the more attentive and affectionate James Dean became to him. Gary Nelson, who was second assistant director on *Rebel*, said, "If anyone was a bit closer to Dean it was Sal Mineo. If he talked to anyone, it was Sal."

Dennis Hopper said, "Sal was under Jimmy's wing all the time. Those were the parts they were playing in the film. Jimmy was trying to help Sal; it just made things worse because everyone thought Sal was Jimmy's 'boy.' "

Natalie often brought her friends to the studio, but no one recalled Sal ever bringing a guest or being with anyone. If Sal had a life off the set, he didn't share it with his coworkers.

THE J. PAUL GETTY ESTATE, at the intersection of Wilshire and Crenshaw boulevards in the Hancock Park area of Los Angeles, had been used as the dilapidated mansion owned by Norma Desmond in Billy Wilder's classic film *Sunset Boulevard*. Location scouts for *Rebel* found the house, and Ray decided it was the perfect location for the all-important mansion scene in the film. Three gang members would confront Plato in the empty pool behind the massive house. The pool was not original to the property and had actually been constructed by studio carpenters for the production of *Sunset Boulevard*. The agreed-upon shooting dates were April 16, 18, 20, and 21.

The studio was pressuring Ray to film more quickly, especially on expensive locations. Although the time booked at the Getty estate was limited, Ray was still unwilling to sacrifice his ambitious vision. The first shot scheduled on the morning of April 16 was a grand master shot of the fight scene with Sal. A fifty-foot crane was late in arriving at the location. Ray had time for one quick rehearsal of the intended boom shot. The kids choreographed the complicated moves themselves. Ray had time to finish the boom shot and a few close shots of Sal before his camera time expired. Since he was a minor, Sal could not work past eleven o'clock in the evening. After a full day of tiresome rehearsals and delays, Sal collapsed in the middle of Ray's boom shot. In a memo to the studio, Ray wrote, "Mineo folded on me. I had to keep rolling while he revived in order to save the time absorbed by resetting and all the other mish-mash that goes on after a cut." When Sal regained his composure, Ray had just ten minutes to complete the shot.

Natalie Wood and James Dean joined Sal at the mansion on the morning of Monday, April 18. Wood was characteristically nervous about the love scene to be shot with Dean, who had just returned after a four-day break for a car race. The shot was delayed, so the cast and crew would shoot more of the gang's attack on Sal in the bottom of the empty pool.

In spite of Ray trying to maintain an amiable set, the pressure of time constraints was felt by everyone. A strange discomfort had developed between Wood and Ray, and it intensified as shooting progressed. Sal observed that Dean could be cruel and even contemptuous of Wood in front of others.

Ann Doran, who played Dean's mother in the film, said that Sal was advising Natalie how to deal with Jimmy. "Honey, it's his way of doing things," he would tell Wood. "Just get with him."

Sal was more comfortable with James Dean's constant improvisations and challenges. Unlike Wood, Sal found it easy to respond with creative reactions of his own. In a short time, Sal's bond with both his costars deepened. "Sal and I really became great pals on that picture," Natalie said.

"While we were working on *Rebel*," she remembered, "I got a new black toy poodle, and I mentioned that I had been unable to think up a name for him. 'I've got it!' Sal said, snapping his fingers. 'Why not call him Rebel in honor of being in the picture?' So I named him Rebel, and a strange thing happened. Soon after I named him, he was killed by a car."

THE PIVOTAL garden and gazebo scenes at the mansion delicately explored and ultimately revealed the intimate dependence the three lead characters had developed for one another. Considering the tensions, real and imagined, on set, it was Sal's fondness for Natalie and admiration of Jimmy that provided the palpable link on-screen. They all complemented and completed one another.

Illustrating Ray's eye for visual effects, the mansion is introduced on film in a classic horror-movie master shot on a dark, cloudy night. The startling sound of shattering glass cuts through the scene as Jim and Judy break into the house. Plato quickly arrives on his scooter. In a doleful moment, Plato, excluded again but anxious to warn Jim that Buzz's gang is looking for him, knocks on the imposing door.

When Jim lets him in, he finds Judy sitting on a sweeping staircase that the carpenters had imbedded with microphones to pick up Dean's mumblings. Playing out a fantasy, Plato pretends to be a real estate salesman who is showing the young couple the house. Sal said this was one of his favorite parts of the movie. Capturing Stern's imagined "night journey," the scene was full of mysterious darkness and shadows. Clutching a candelabrum, Plato leads the couple through the mansion. The candelabrum was actually connected to a gas line that went through Sal's arm and down his pant leg. The wire can actually be seen on-screen.

As they walk through the garden, screenwriter Stern provided touching dialogue revealing their naïve and wounded view of their parents. As affecting as the garden scene was, one of the most moving and controversial scenes, shot on Wednesday, April 20, followed it. After making their way through the shadowy garden, the trio walks across the bottom of the empty swimming pool. Ray captured the moment in a superb overhead crane shot.

When they finally reach the gazebo, Dean reclines in Wood's lap, and Sal sits on the floor at their feet. Plato talks introspectively about his absent parents, and the playful mood suddenly becomes painfully raw and tender. The universe seems to revolve around the three characters entwined on the floor.

The strength of this scene can be attributed to Ray's distinct visual style and the unself-conscious skill of the actors. The emotional core, though, is in the words of Stewart Stern. This respite the actors find in the privacy of the gazebo is a world imagined by Jim. He is the father, Judy the mother, and Plato their son. Jim is the benevolent protector, the kind of father he wishes his own was for him.

But more than familial relations are portrayed in these moments on film. An undercurrent of desire boils beneath the surface between all three characters that is startling and as groundbreaking as Ray had imagined. This scene, rehearsed just weeks before, had secured the role of Plato for Sal. In the filmed rehearsal, Sal and Dean maintain a lengthy and shockingly physical contact, with a fearless Sal literally running his hands up and down Dean's body. In the film, Ray restrained their contact, though Plato's position on the floor and the longing look in his eyes make a strong subversive statement. Dean seems to be as attentive to Sal as he is to Natalie, almost flirtatious when he smiles at him. Suddenly, Sal lays his head on Dean's arm, and the scene jumps from the screen. Ray not only pushed the envelope, but he crossed a boundary in the depiction of overt affection between two men in the chaste mid-1950s.

Stewart Stern believed this particular scene, so carefully written and filmed, was the beginning of a new freedom in popular American culture. "The whole movement toward getting in touch with your feelings, that whole flower child movement, it all happened in the wake of *Rebel,*" he stated.

As the gazebo scene in the film winds down, Plato actually falls asleep on the ground as Judy hums a lullaby and strokes his hair. Jim and Judy cover him with his coat, and just as they are about to leave him sleeping to explore the deserted house, they notice that Plato is wearing mismatched socks.

This curious detail of one red and one blue sock did not appear in the script, though. In a sleepy rush to get dressed, Sal had put on the wrong socks. Moss Mabry, the costume designer, hadn't noticed the mistake before the take began. Nicholas Ray, ever mindful of the power of image and the subtlety of human nature, shot a close-up of the mismatched socks for insertion in the final film many weeks later on May 14.

Ray was encouraging of his actors but rarely gave outright compliments. He felt this scene in the film, however, was one of the finest he had ever directed. "After an 'involuntary performance' the actor is kind of stunned and bewildered," the director explained. "He doesn't know what just happened to him. He is in shock at having caught sight of his own evasions, tricks, and clichés. At such moments the director knows he has found something, released something which nobody in the world could have told the actor was there." Everyone expected *Rebel* to catapult James Dean into superstardom, but Ray praised the sympathetically effective performance of Sal, saying it was Mineo who delivered an unfettered "involuntary performance" throughout *Rebel Without a Cause.*

DESPITE WARNER'S objections to the costs and inherent delays involved with location shooting, Ray moved his cast and crew to a suburban location in Baldwin Hills for the delicate scene between Plato and Jim in an alley. Though the call time was seven A.M., a thick fog caused a six-hour delay and shooting could not begin until later that afternoon. The scene was masterfully scripted by Stern and given intriguing nuance by Sal and Dean. The real drama, though, had happened behind the scenes, unbeknownst to the actors.

The subject of homosexuality was all but forbidden in the 1950s. Whatever Ray's intentions were in characterizing Plato and Jim, Stewart Stern's script did not suggest anything subversive in the developing relationship between the two characters. Ray may have had other ideas and flatly stated, "Warners didn't know what the hell I was doing." But Geoffrey Shurlock, a studio censor, wrote a curious memo to Warner, dated March 22, 1955: "It is of course vital that there be no inference of a questionable or homosexual relationship between Plato and Jim."

In a rambling, four-page memo of criticisms, executive Steve Trilling wrote in underscored longhand across the top of one page, "Jim kisses Plato?" There was nothing of the sort written in Stern's screenplay, though Ray, who constantly changed the scripted word, may have suggested it in the alley scene between Plato and Jim. Jim has taken a distraught Plato home after they witnessed Buzz drive off a cliff to his death. In the same memo, Trilling suggested a more acceptable alternative to a kiss. Jim Stark, he wrote, could "stroke" Plato's head.

What Stern had actually written was an awkward fit of laughter from Plato and Jim as they try to come to terms with the tragedy they had witnessed. As the boys laugh, Stern's written directions called for the boys to fall onto each other for a moment until Jim pulls away in tears. At this point in the script, Plato says, "Come home with me."

"This was an important scene from many points of view," Stern said. "It showed a reaction to tragedy which is not only bare and honest, but a reaction which, though probably the truest, has not been on the screen before, at least to my knowledge."

Strangely, the laughing fit would be cut from the film, but Plato's heartbreaking lines remain. "Why don't you come home with me?" he asks of Jim Stark. "I mean, nobody's home at my house, and I'm not tired, are you? I don't have many . . . people I can talk to." And then Plato says a line that was crafted by Ray *and* Sal. "Gee . . . if you could only have been my father."

When news of the cuts and Ray's improvised line reached Stern, he was mortified. He was angered by what was being done to his script, and this particular tampering prompted him to write to Steve Trilling. "I think that under no credible circumstances would he, even in hysteria, refer to Jim as his father here. It seems totally out of key and character and achieves with its boldness nothing that is not inherent in the story as it stands." Stern felt his screenplay was being destroyed by the studio's interference and by Ray's determination to explore his own psychological hang-ups. Stern continued. "The thing I feared most and expected least seems to be happening now, with a harrowing and bewildering thoroughness, a bit-by-bit emasculation of an original treatment in an effort to make it conform."

This lover-father blurring of attraction between Plato and Jim was deliberately invented and mined by Ray. Much has been speculated about the scene at the beginning of the film in the high school when Plato gazes at Jim Stark in his locker mirror. He actually angles the mirror for a better view. Attached to Plato's locker door beneath the mirror is a glossy photograph of handsome actor Alan Ladd.

Stern's intention was to suggest a sort of hero worship Plato may have had for Ladd. Signs of any deviant desire by Plato were the product of Ray's direction and simply not in Stern's script. Mineo's portrayal of Plato drops suggestive clues throughout the movie, including the way he rests his head on Jim Stark's arm in the gazebo, the way he softly touches Jim's shoulder in the planetarium and gazes at his face, and the way he physically surges toward Jim when he arrives at the fateful "chickie run."

"I heard Jimmy explaining things to Sal," Ray recalled. " 'You know how I am with Nat,' he said. 'Well, why don't you pretend I'm her and you're me? Pretend you want to touch my hair, but you're shy.' Then he said, 'I'm not shy like you. I love you. I'll touch your hair.' I took one look at the kid's face . . . he was transcendent, the feeling coming out of him."

Stern admitted, "Plato was the one who would've been tagged as the faggot character." He intended, and wrote, the relationship between the two boys to be less specific and more naïvely ambiguous. "The gay community just wanted to own that movie," he would later grumble.

Stewart's intentions aside, and despite his denials, the character of Plato—interpreted by Sal and Ray—represented a teenage boy that homosexual teenagers could recognize and empathize with. Sal's searing and sympathetic portrayal of Plato burned a hole in the movie screen and in the hearts of millions of teenage girls *and* boys. And whether the screenwriter liked it or not, the character of Plato eventually became known as the first gay teenager in the movies.

DESPITE THE sociological machinations in front of and behind the cameras, the cast managed to eke out some fun and horseplay in the little time they had off. Sal spent most of his time with Natalie, either working on the set or in school. But Sal and James Dean snuck off to smoke and play practical jokes on each other or unsuspecting people on the Warner Bros. lot.

John Gilmore, a would-be actor friend of Dean, remembers one day he joined Jimmy for lunch at the studio commissary. Sal was walking ahead of them, surrounded by various crew members. "Jimmy sneaked up behind him," said Gilmore, "and pinched him on the right cheek of his ass. Sal jumped, startled, his big brown eyes wide as cake plates. His face flushed red when he saw it was Jimmy, and then he giggled, which started Jimmy laughing. Sal's face beamed with admiration and awe."

Actress Carroll Baker had become acquainted with James Dean. She recalled the first time she met Sal. She had recently been cast in *Giant* and was called in one day for costume fittings. When she drove up to the Warner Bros. gate, she noticed the guard was slumped over his seat, his face covered by his uniform cap. She waited for a few seconds and then stepped out of her car and walked over to him.

Dean, and Sal dressed as the guard, were playing a practical joke on her. Dean had acted the part of the gate guard before and refused to let Baker onto the lot. She grabbed the cap off the fellow's head, thinking she would find James Dean again.

"But that round cherub face and those enormous brown eyes with long, thick lashes did not belong to Jimmy," Baker recalled. " 'Oh, I'm sorry. I thought you were someone else.' The beautiful cherub face broke into a radiant smile."

Then she heard Dean's laugh and he stepped from around the corner.

"Jimmy said, 'My buddy, Sal, here, and me . . . woo-eee . . . have we had a good laugh! You know my buddy Sal Mineo?"

Baker recalled, "I thought to myself, 'This Sal Mineo is an adorable little boy. I wonder if his mother knows he's playing with the big boys.' "

Dean wanted to take Baker for a ride but her car was still blocking the studio gate entrance. He told Sal to move her car, which he did. "I couldn't believe Sal was old enough to have a driver's license," Baker stated.

Despite studio pressure, Ray decided to shoot the finale his way. On May 16, the crew returned to Griffith Observatory and spent five days shooting *Rebel*'s original ending with Plato dramatically dying on the roof of the planetarium. Many shots were filmed during those days, including Plato falling from the dome, with Sal working tirelessly.

With just three shooting days left, Ray and the film's editor, William Ziegler, watched the finale footage Ray had shot on May 23. Reluctantly, Ray realized he could not shoot the finale as he had conceived it. With Stern's help, the director accepted the fact that Plato would have to be shot and die on the steps of the observatory. On the evening of May 24, the cast and crew returned to Griffith Observatory for the final scenes. Since the release of *East of Eden*, James Dean had become a star. Barricades were set up and the police were called to keep back hundreds of fans who had shown up that night. Between shots Dean signed autographs for the fans, while Sal and Natalie huddled in the back of a police car to stay warm.

After Plato is shot by the police, Jim screams, "I got the bullets!" Not knowing that he had removed the bullets from Plato's gun, the police killed the boy needlessly. Dean had trouble with the line, perhaps conscious of an audience of fans, or perhaps realizing the end had literally come. Dean required many takes, trying the line a number of ways.

"The day I got killed in the film was a very important day for me," Sal remembered. "The scene was that I ran out of the planetarium and got shot, and Jimmy discovers me dead and hovers over me, and expresses what he feels at the moment. So he had a number of choices to make."

Dean demonstrated his superior acting skills and ability to reach into his deepest emotions in the scene over Plato's body, stretched out on the cold cement. Dean crawls around him like a wounded animal in horror. When he gently straightens out Plato's leg, he notices the red and blue socks. At first, Dean laughs manically, and then he collapses in tears.

"And I wanted to do that scene over and over again," Sal said, "and each time we did it, he'd position me in the kind of repose that would work best for him to get the emotion going. It was very moving for me, because *he* was very moved. When you see the finished scene you can see how he broke up at the moment that was used in the film."

Dean was so consumed by the scene, so immersed in the moment; it seemed to become a part of his reality. He acted as if Sal himself had been shot. "Immediately after the scene," Sal said, "I noticed there was a change in the relationship. He was very protective, and for the whole time he'd never let me out of his sight. He was always there.

"In Plato's death scene I understood what being loved meant," Sal added. "Now here was the chance for me to feel what it would be like for someone close, someone that I idolized, to be grieving for me. It was an opportunity to experience what kind of grief that would be, what would he be like, what he would sound like, what would he be thinking.

"Jim had the hots for Natalie *and* me in the film. In those days, it could only end in one way. Ergo, I *had* to be bumped off, out of the way," Sal said later, believing the feelings of love Jim had for Plato condemned him to death.

The arc lights from the all-night shoot were so intense that residents called the police all night, fearing Griffith Park had caught fire. What would be the last scene in the movie was shot at 6:55 A.M. on May 25. Nicholas Ray, dressed in an overcoat, played a stranger who climbs the steps of the observatory unaware of the tragedy that has befallen as Jim Stark and his parents are driven away in a police car.

Partial sets had been reconstructed on stages 5 and 7 at Warner Bros. for completing many remaining connecting shots. The cast ran from setup to setup for the two final days of shooting. *Rebel Without a Cause* wrapped at 2:45 A.M. on May 27, 1955, eleven days over schedule.

Post-production work began immediately on *Rebel*. The studio wanted a quick release to cash in on Dean's fast-developing popularity. Due to extensive location shooting, an unusually large amount of looping had to be done. Sal, Natalie, and Jimmy returned to the studio to dub dialogue for a couple of days. Sal had to redo his dialogue to eliminate his strong Bronx accent ("You mean a head shrinkah?").

"Working on *Rebel* was like being part of a close-knit family," Sal said years later. "I've never experienced it in any other film. Everybody became very tight, and Jimmy was the focus of it. We all grew around him, and as a result we all tended to idolize him. At first, I was afraid of him, I was terrified of him. I really didn't know him at all, but I worshipped the way he dealt with people in a higher position. He'd never take anything from anybody, never take any nonsense from them no matter what the situation was."

JUNE 9, 1955, was mild and slightly overcast in the Bronx. Josephine had been working in the kitchen for two days preparing lasagna, manicotti, and meatballs. She had planned a raucous party for Sal, who had recently flown home from Hollywood. While Sal's aunts helped in the kitchen, his uncles huddled around a picnic table drinking beer and playing cards. A large banner proclaiming WELCOME HOME SAL fluttered over the back door in the afternoon breeze. Mineo and Alvisi cousins, along with dozens of Sal's neighborhood friends, spilled out of the kitchen and into the large backyard. They were ready for a cookout and dressed for the nearby beach. When Sal stepped out the back door to cheers, though, he was not the same little boy from the Bronx who had gone to Hollywood a mere six months before. He was dressed in a baby-blue tailored suit, white shirt and tie, and black leather shoes. He smiled broadly, clutched his sister, Sarina, and posed for pictures for reporters and photographers his mother had invited from the *New York Times* and *Photoplay* magazine.

# 6.

"If individualists are considered moody people,
then Jimmy was probably moody."

While Sal relaxed with his family in New York, post-production
work on *Rebel* was put on the fast track in Hollywood. Jack
Warner, anxious to see a rough cut of the film, pressured Ray
to edit his many hours of footage. In June 1955, Warner was scheduled
to testify in front of the Senate subcommittee investigating juvenile
delinquency. The cochair, Senator Estes Kefauver, traveled to the West
Coast to conduct hearings on what he characterized as the excessive
depiction of violence, brutality, and sex in motion pictures and its
negative impact on teenagers. The investigation, entering its second
year, had explored music and literature and was now focusing its attention on Hollywood. *Rebel Without a Cause* had already been placed
on the committee's "black list" of films featuring excessive violence,
and Warner was justifiably concerned about its effect on the box office
receipts. The studio boss was happy, though, after viewing Ray's edit
of the film.

Sal did not work during the summer of 1955. He was tired and
enjoyed being with his family. Soon after arriving home, Sal bought a
speedboat. In honor of his beloved pet boxer Bimbo, he christened his
new boat *El Bimbo II*. He casually dated a few local girls, double-dating
with his brother Mike, and spent hours water-skiing and swimming.
Mostly, he was content to spend time with Sarina and hang at coffee
shops with his buddies after being away for so long.

That summer, a much larger purchase was made with Sal's money
that he was entirely unaware of. The family celebrated Mike's eighteenth birthday on June 28. In keeping with Josephine's desire to treat
each son the same, his gift was a brand-new coupe automobile purchased with his little brother's earnings from *Rebel*.

Sal traveled to Manhattan for his twice-weekly acting lessons with
Claudia Franck, who joined him and his family August 2 for the open-
ing of *The Private War of Major Benson* at the Plaza Theatre in New
York City. Sal was the only star from the movie on hand that evening.

*Variety* reviewed *Private War*, writing that Sal was "very good," and the movie was a modest success.

JOSEPHINE NAÏVELY courted the press, and invited reporters into her home to interview and photograph her son and family. Sal's mother enlisted the aid of a neighbor and attended to the trickle of fan mail that came directly to the house or was forwarded by Universal International in Hollywood. She was careful to answer every letter, often coercing Sal to write responses in longhand and send little autographed picture cards to those who asked.

More important, Josephine made some critical decisions regarding her son's career. On January 11, 1955, Hedda Hopper had mistakenly reported to the *Los Angeles Times* that Sal had signed a long-term contract with Universal International Pictures. A seven-year contract had indeed been offered to Sal at the beginning of the year. Josephine, being uncomfortable with the expectations she associated with such an offer, and realizing her own influence would be diminished, if not eliminated altogether, instructed Sal's agent to pass on the offer.

With Josephine's blessing, Alec Alexander continued to negotiate contracts in California on behalf of the Mineo family. On October 1, 1955, Alexander and his wife, Helen, would actually close their New York office and move to Los Angeles to better represent Sal, their primary client. The agent's lack of Hollywood experience and connections would prove to be a hindrance in the long run, but Josephine's loyalty took precedence over any practicality or business acumen. This, too, would prove to be a professional mistake.

SAL RETURNED to California, and the home of Gladys Hoene, in early August. He was scheduled to begin work August 12 on his next film, *Giant*, based on the bestselling novel about a Texas family, written by Edna Ferber.

Sal had overheard James Dean talk about the picture when they were working on *Rebel*. Sal got a copy of the script and pursued the role of Angel Obregón II, the son of poor Mexican immigrants. James Dean told the director, George Stevens, that Sal "had the look of the angels," but the imposing Stevens did not have to be convinced. After a quick audition one morning between shots for *Rebel*, Sal had been signed for the part of Angel.

Touted by the press as the most prestigious motion picture of the year, *Giant* covered approximately thirty years in the lives of its characters, from 1923 to 1955. The serious-minded Stevens was loath to explain the underlying theme of his film, but press releases issued by his office promised a grand epic about the fortunes and misfortunes of an American family.

A George Stevens picture featured his obsessive attention to detail and a thorough exploration of every visual possibility of a scene. He shot take after take, from many different camera angles, and later spent weeks and sometimes months in the editing room.

By far, Stevens was the most experienced and decorated director Sal had worked with. He began his career in 1923, and his work as a cinematographer led him into writing, directing, and eventually producing motion pictures, including such classics as *Woman of the Year, A Place in the Sun,* and *Shane.* His four Academy Award nominations included one win as Best Director in 1952 for *A Place in the Sun.*

However, in spite of Stevens's impressive credits and awards, after the stimulating and challenging work environment Nicholas Ray had created on the *Rebel* set, Sal felt the slow, rigid work schedule of *Giant* was positively boring. There was no creative collaboration between the actor and the director on a George Stevens set.

Though the company had shot on location in Marfa, Texas, from the first of June until mid-July, all of Sal's scenes were shot on a soundstage at Warner Bros. For generations, his character's Mexican immigrant family had worked as farmhands for the wealthy Benedict family at their ranch, Reata. Dressed in a military uniform, Angel arrives at Reata to say good-bye as he's about to enter the army in World War II. Though his scenes were effective, Sal did not appear on-screen until halfway through the three-hour epic.

Sal's character had one of the most effective and dramatic moments in the sprawling film. Cutting away from Angel's good-byes at the ranch, the film reveals the Obregón family standing expectantly on a railroad platform, seemingly waiting for his return home from duty. When the train pulls away from the station, though, it reveals Angel's flag-draped coffin on a caisson.

Sal tried to convince the studio to use one of his father's caskets. " 'Please use one of Dad's coffins,' " he recalled saying. " 'After all, it's me who's going to lie in it.' But they wouldn't bite."

Sal had no scenes with James Dean and only ran into him on the lot or in the studio commissary a few times. He worked primarily with Rock Hudson and Elizabeth Taylor. Although Sal enjoyed Taylor's bawdy sense of humor and the chocolate martinis she created, he couldn't connect with Hudson, whose acting style was the complete antithesis of what he had experienced on *Rebel*. Sal missed the close interaction he had enjoyed with Ray but later admitted, "Stevens was a good director but a tough old buzzard. The best directors are usually tough nuts to crack, but the result's usually worth it." Still, Sal was proud of his role in the film. "I was only sixteen when I made the picture," he said, "but they had me playing an eighteen-year-old. I'm a Mexican. I go off to war a soldier and then come back a hero. In a casket."

MUCH TO Mrs. Hoene's consternation, Sal had passed his driving test and got his California license a few weeks before *Rebel* wrapped. He bought a 1949 Mercury like the car James Dean had driven in *Rebel*. "He practically rebuilt the Mercury from the motor out," Mrs. Hoene recalled.

Sal drove himself to the first preview of *Rebel Without a Cause* on September 1, 1955, at a theater in Huntington Park, California, a small working-class suburb of Los Angeles. The screening was very well received. Steve Trilling reported to his bosses at Warner Bros., "Story, performances, entire picture received excellently."

In spite of the audience's positive reaction, Jack Warner, who also attended the screening, thought the movie was a little slow. Thirteen cuts were made at the directive of the film editor's notes dated September 18, including a couple of scenes featuring Sal.

Sal returned to New York in mid-September when he was finished with *Giant*. Near the end of the month, Natalie Wood, accompanied by Nick Adams, flew to New York to join Sal for a publicity junket for *Rebel*. Nicholas Ray had missed the preview screening in California and was still in London working with the Warner Bros. publicity department about the upcoming British release of the film. James Dean had just finished his work in *Giant* and missed going to New York with Natalie and Nick Adams so he could enter his new Porsche Spyder in a race in Salinas, California. He was supposed to join them after the race.

On the evening of September 30, 1955, Sal, Natalie, and Nick Adams went to see Arthur Miller's new play, *A View from the Bridge*, starring Richard Davalos, who had played Dean's brother in *East of Eden*. After the performance, they all had a late-night dinner at a Chinese restaurant in Chinatown. Inevitably, they all began to share their experiences with Dean and agreed that Dean had a great future in Hollywood.

Unbeknownst to his young friends, James Dean had been pronounced dead several hours earlier, at 6:20 P.M. Pacific time, at Paso Robles War Memorial Hospital. Dean had died instantly when his Porsche struck another car in a remote intersection near Cholame, California.

Sal and Adams walked Natalie back to the Warwick Hotel, where they were all staying. Natalie went straight to bed since she had an early call the next morning for a live television "all-star" musical broadcast of *Heidi*. A studio chaperone intercepted Sal and Adams in the hotel lobby and took them aside to break the news of Dean's death. The young men were instructed not to disturb Natalie that night. Sal was so distraught, he didn't fall asleep until daybreak.

The next morning, Natalie's limo driver unwittingly broke the terrible news when he asked her if she'd heard about James Dean's death. When the live telecast was over, Natalie returned to the Warwick and sat in stunned silence in her room.

Shortly after, Sal called her. And in an odd reversal of the roles they played in *Rebel,* when Judy and Jim mourned the death of Plato, Natalie and Sal mourned the death of Dean together, commiserating late into the night.

EVERYONE ASKS me about Jimmy," Sal would say nearly a year later. "What is there to say? If there was one thing that bugged Jimmy it was hypocrites. I think that the most important reason we got along so well together was that we were always honest with each other and never pulled punches. He hated people who put up fronts.

"Jimmy was shy. He was so shy that he was hard to communicate with. Often you couldn't get to him and if you were lucky enough to talk to him, most often both of you were at a loss for words. But if by chance you could get through to him, and Jimmy liked you, then he would come out of his shyness and talk freely and honestly with you.

"Jimmy also wasn't moody, as everyone makes him out to be. Sure, he had his off-again, on-again times, as everyone has. He was an individualist. Maybe because he didn't do what everyone else did, wear what everyone else wore, and think like everyone else, people thought he was moody. Instead of insulting or laughing at him the people who knew him respected him for his individuality. If individualists are considered moody people, then Jimmy was probably moody.

"But the picture I remember of Jimmy is that of a wonderful, brilliant and young guy whom I admired like no one I have admired before."

Sal and James Dean, *Rebel Without a Cause,* 1955

# 7.

"I just want to be Sal Mineo."

Josephine was perplexed by the sudden change in her normally cheerful son. Sal glumly took to his room, preferring to be alone. He had never experienced the death of a contemporary, someone so close to his age, and the shocking, violent nature of Dean's accident made it even more difficult. He spent days alone, drawing and reading. He covered a wall in his room with movie magazine pictures of James Dean and displayed a handsome, brooding portrait of the actor on one of his artist easels.

His mother turned down all requests from the press wanting to know Sal's thoughts about the accident. It wasn't until many months later that he could expound on his feelings of loss. But the uncharacteristic depression that seemed to consume her son disturbed Josephine. Though Sal had often spoken of Natalie Wood, he had rarely talked about Jimmy Dean to his mother. The depth of his sorrow mystified her.

After a heart-to-heart talk with their local priest failed, Josephine enlisted the aid of Sal's old friend and mentor Yul Brynner, who invited Sal to stay at his Connecticut home. Yul's son, Rocky, recalled, "Sal, who was still like a son to Yul and a brother to me, came to stay with us briefly when it was feared he might become suicidal at the death of his friend."

Yul did not believe in surrendering to adversity. The time in Connecticut was healing and Sal was comfortable talking with Brynner about things he didn't necessarily share with others.

Ultimately, it was work that lured Sal out of his funk. His agent, who had just hung his shingle in Hollywood, had several attractive television offers for the Mineo family to consider. The days of Sal having to audition for a role were coming to an end.

ONCE AGAIN, Sal was cast in a special broadcast of *Omnibus*. Sal had been busy making four feature films in one year, so this was his first television role in nearly eighteen months. "A Few Scenes out of the

California Boyhood of William Saroyan: The Bad Men" was broadcast live from New York on CBS-TV on October 16, 1955. Sal played the part of Señor Cortez. A New York critic wrote of his performance, "He has the emotional grasp of actors two and three times his age."

Mike Mineo's lackadaisical interest in college concerned his mother. She continued to encourage him to pursue acting, constantly holding his little brother up to him as an example. Though Sal had his California driver's license, he could not drive in New York, and Josephine felt he should no longer be taking trains and subways, so Mike drove him into and out of the city.

ON OCTOBER 26, *Rebel Without a Cause* opened to mixed but generally supportive reviews. Sal attended the New York premiere at the Astor Theatre in Times Square with his mother, brothers, and sister. It was an exhilarating and melancholy time for Sal, who said his tuxedo and the black limousine made him feel like he was going to a funeral rather than a movie opening.

*Variety* reported the film was a "fairly exciting, suspenseful and provocative, if also occasionally far-fetched, melodrama." The *New York Times* critic Bosley Crowther complained that the film had "a pictorial slickness about the whole thing in color and Cinemascope that battles at times with the realism in the direction of Nicholas Ray. It is a violent, brutal and disturbing picture of modern teenagers . . . it is a picture to make the hair stand on end."

The *Hollywood Reporter* wrote, "Exceptionally fine is Mineo's sensitive study of lonely youth." And *Variety* praised Sal, saying, "Young Mineo stands out on performance and is an important value in the film."

Philip K. Scheuer of the *Los Angeles Times* wrote, "As melodrama, *Rebel Without a Cause* is smooth movie-making." He praised the performance of James Dean and added, "Miss Wood and Mineo are also uncommonly appealing."

Youthful audiences responded to the film enthusiastically, driving *Rebel* to number one at the box office almost instantly. The film made sympathetic and heroic teenage film icons of the three principal young stars that would define the era. And in its first week, it outgrossed Dean's first motion picture, *East of Eden.*

*Rebel Without a Cause* went into wide release nationally on November 9. In just a few days it became a solid success at the box office and stayed in the top ten for weeks. Literally overnight, Sal had developed an impressive fan base.

WORK BECKONED Sal back to the West Coast. He was cast as a juvenile delinquent in an episode of *Big Town*. The thirty-minute melodrama was the first television show Sal recorded on film. His episode, called "Juvenile Gangs," aired on November 1, 1955, on NBC-TV.

The success of *Blackboard Jungle* and *Rebel Without a Cause* ushered in an avalanche of juvenile-delinquency-themed motion pictures. Many were produced at independent companies like Allied Artists and Republic Pictures. This type of film was suited for independent production for a few reasons, including its low budgetary requirements and topical subject matter.

Acclaimed television dramatist Reginald Rose won an Emmy Award for his teleplay "Twelve Angry Men" in 1954. He had written a number of searing dramas for CBS-TV's hit anthology series *Studio One*. On March 8, 1955, his one-hour drama "Crime in the Streets" had been broadcast on *The Elgin Hour*. Rose adapted this work for the big screen. His screenplay was purchased by Allied Artists, an independent production company.

Although the official casting news was not printed until November 20, Sal began work on *Crime in the Streets* at Goldwyn Studios in Hollywood on November 5 in the supporting role of Baby Gioia.

*Crime in the Streets* tells the story of Frankie Dane, the leader of a neighborhood teenage gang, who lives in the New York slums with his single mother and little brother. Juvenile delinquency is depicted as a serious social problem caused by an unstable home life and bad parenting. Ultimately, though, *Crime in the Streets* portrays the boy's relationship with his father as the root cause. The results of a father's absence, neglect, or abuse could only be remedied by the sensitive and patient intervention of a kindly surrogate.

Don Siegel was hired to direct the picture. Siegel, a young maverick director, was responsible for the classic 1949 film noir classic *The Big Steal*. With a meager budget and a shooting schedule of only eighteen days, Siegel had his work cut out for him. Despite first-rate writing, tight direction, and compelling acting, the film suffered because of its low budget. Siegel was forced to shoot the entire film on soundstages or on the studio lot. Coupled with dark, moody lighting, the finished black-and-white film has a very staged, claustrophobic feel.

Though Sal had a supporting role, he again managed to make the most of his time on-screen, proving himself to be a determined and fearless actor. The confrontational scenes with his father, played by Will Kuluva, were not only compelling but heart wrenching. He connected well with fellow actors John Cassavetes and Mark Rydell, both from New York, and appreciated their introspective, brooding style of acting.

Principal photography for *Crime in the Streets* was completed on November 23, and the film was rushed into post-production. Sal had completed his work a few days earlier and quickly flew home to New York to join his family for Thanksgiving.

Sal picked up his required lessons at the Lodge School in New York and managed to squeeze in acting lessons with Claudia Franck during the ten days of rehearsals preceding his next television appearance, in an episode of *Goodyear Playhouse* called "The Trees." "Sal is a perfectionist," Franck said, "and after each role is completed, he tells himself, his director, and me, 'Next time I'll do better.' " Sal played another juvenile delinquent in the contemporary drama telecast on December 4.

The last month of 1955 would prove to be a busy one for Sal. "It's mainly the family," he said, regarding his source of advice. "Sure, I need their signature on contracts. But that's not the important thing. I wouldn't do a picture, I wouldn't do an interview unless they knew about it. I'm looking for one thing. That's to have a good career and a good name. Now, I may do things that I may feel are very good for me to do, but they look at it as a whole. They can see things that I don't see. So they'll advise me whether or not it's good. So far, anything they've suggested is good."

Josephine signed a contract for Sal to star as the title character in Reginald Rose's new dramatic teleplay called "Dino" for the television series *Studio One*. The one-hour drama anthology became a staple on CBS television beginning in 1948 and consistently drew high praise. With little time to waste before the January 2 live broadcast, Sal began rehearsals immediately in Manhattan. Mike Mineo secured a nonspeaking role as a young hoodlum and would also work as his little brother's stand-in.

Sal's salary for *Studio One* was $1,000, a staggering sum considering that President Eisenhower had increased the hourly minimum wage to $1.00 the previous August. In 1955, the average price of gasoline was twenty-five cents a gallon, and a new-model 1956 automobile cost $1,910.

Fan mail had begun to pour into the Mineo house. Josephine set up a makeshift office on the sun porch to handle Sal's correspondence. All the family was enlisted to open and read the mail and deal with fan requests. Even though savvy young fans found the Mineo household telephone number and called the house at all hours, Sal's mother refused Alec Alexander's advice to cancel the public listing and privatize the number. "If they want to talk to Sal, and he's here, what's wrong?" she wondered.

Sal managed to make time for his friends and run out to see a movie or hang out at a local diner. His friends didn't treat him with kid gloves or with any reverence, either, in spite of his fast-approaching stardom. In fact, Sal said most of his friends knew little of his show business career.

"They never developed a different attitude toward me. It was the same old crowd. We went to the same places together; we did the same things, until finally *Rebel* was released. Once that was released everybody was amazed. And there were about two weeks when they just couldn't believe it. They wondered why I'd kept it a secret."

Sal's popularity was on the rise, but because of his compelling television and screen roles, he was fast becoming a poster boy for juvenile delinquency. Perhaps concerned with the way this characterization affected the way her son was depicted in the press, or by the tone of some of his fan mail, Josephine declared, "My Sal is a good boy. He's no delinquent." With her priest's prodding, she accepted a role for Sal as a troubled boy on a popular Sunday-morning half-hour, religious-themed drama called *Frontiers of Faith*. Sponsored by the National Council of Churches, the stories highlighted everyday problems and their solutions as a result of divine intervention rather than the secular social workers her son's characters were more accustomed to.

"The Man on the 6:02" was shown on NBC on Christmas Day 1955. Josephine donated his salary to their local church.

IN THE fall of 1955, MGM Studios contracted Robert Wise, a veteran of Warner Bros. B movies, to direct *Somebody Up There Likes Me,* based on the bestselling autobiography of champion boxer Rocky Graziano. Wise's 1949 film, *The Set Up,* was considered to be one of the finest films about the boxing profession and won an award at the Cannes Film Festival. Ernest Lehman would write the screenplay based on Graziano's book. Lehman's screenwriting credits included *Executive Suite, Sabrina,* and *The King and I.*

*Somebody Up There Likes Me* told the rags-to-riches story of the boxer. While still a young man, Graziano is arrested for various crimes. In jail, and undisciplined, he constantly finds himself in trouble with other inmates and the authorities. Eventually he discovers boxing as an honest and quick way to earn money. Soon his estimable talents as a pugilist make him a boxing champion and public favorite.

After months of speculation, on December 30, it was announced that Sal would appear in *Somebody Up There Likes Me.* His salary was set at $1,000 a week, with a ten-week guarantee. Sal was cast to play Rocky Graziano's best friend, Romolo, who cannot escape the bad environment as Rocky does. Paul Newman, fourteen years Sal's senior, was cast as Graziano. Originally, Warner Bros. had agreed to lend MGM James Dean, who would play the part of Graziano. Upon Dean's death, the film project was put on hold temporarily. Eventually, Dean was replaced by Paul Newman, who had earlier starred on Broadway in *Picnic* and appeared in guest roles on numerous television programs. His one other feature film, *The Silver Chalice,* released in 1954, had been a critical and box office flop.

JOSEPHINE HOSTED a New Year's Eve party at the Mineo house to keep a watchful eye on her children, especially her youngest son, who was about to embark on the busiest year of his life. On the evening of Monday, January 2, 1956, *Studio One* broadcast "Dino" live from New York. Sal was directed by a young man named Paul Nickell, who had previously directed several episodes of *Studio One.*

Dino Manetti has just been released from reform school after serving time for his involvement in a murder. He reluctantly returns home to an abusive father and a time-ravaged mother. Dino is sullen and uncooperative and tries to deal with his deep-rooted anger and feelings of loneliness with the help of a sympathetic guidance counselor played by Ralph Meeker. Dino knows, despite the temptations, that if he returns to his life of crime, his adoring kid brother will follow him into that spiral of darkness and despair.

Sal's performance, which was corralled rather than dictated by Nickell, was riveting. Many years later, when she was about to work with him herself, actress Elaine Stritch recalled watching "Dino" on television with her friend Maureen Stapleton and described Sal's performance as one of those rare acting moments a person can never forget. "We all saw this kid," Stritch said. "We absolutely flipped out. It was rare to see that kind of reality in an actor that age. It scared me a little, it was so good. There was an element of danger in it and 'What's he going to do next?' You didn't know which direction this kid was going to take."

While preparing for his work on *Somebody*, Sal fulfilled another professional commitment to satisfy his mother. *Look Up and Live* was broadcast live Sunday mornings on CBS-TV from New York. The thirty-minute program featured teleplays designed to show the cause and effect of juvenile crime and present a means of eliminating the scourge of juvenile delinquency. The material was provocative but presented in ways to attract youthful viewers.

With a sulky-looking Mike Mineo finally cast in a small credited role, Sal starred in the episode of *Look Up and Live* called "Nothing to Do," which aired on January 15.

AFTER FIVE weeks at MGM Studios, the film company moved to New York for ten days of location filming, beginning on March 2. To save money, the film was shot in black and white and filmed on the studio back lot, designed to look like New York's Lower East Side tenements. Wise was dissatisfied with the way the sets looked in daylight and convinced the studio to shoot night exteriors and interiors on the lot but shoot daytime scenes on location in New York City.

In all, twenty-eight scenes were filmed at various sites, including the Brooklyn Bridge; Graziano's former home in Brooklyn, Stillman's

Gym; Astor Place; and Foley Square. The filmmakers and the Holly-wood stars stopped traffic for two days with final shooting on Henry, Houston, and Pitt streets, former haunts of the middleweight champion.

New York City police who were hired to patrol the film location on Pitt Street in the Lower East Side had a scare when a group of young neighborhood thugs broke through the security line and inter-rupted filming. They rushed a nervous Sal, who was sitting behind the cameras waiting for his call. Before the situation got out of control, though, the boys identified themselves as fans who only wanted the young star's autograph.

Hearing the news that a movie was being filmed in the city, and that the star was Sal Mineo, youngsters had begun to follow the crew from one location to the next to catch a glimpse of Sal. On the final few days of shooting, police on horseback were called upon to control hundreds of boys and girls who wanted to meet him. Many of the young girls, clutching autograph books and glossy photographs of Sal they had gotten at the movie theater, even brought him gifts. Sal loved the attention. He stood by the barricades and signed autographs when-ever he wasn't in front of the camera. He took the stuffed animals and other presents home to Sarina.

Sal flew to Los Angeles on March 12 to finish work on *Somebody Up There Likes Me*. He would be busy with his role until April 4. Sal was careful to observe the Actors Studio–trained Newman. He was especially interested in Newman's subtle use of his eyes and facial expressions to convey emotion, playing down rather than exploding physically. The younger actor said, "Paul was not only manly but kind and understanding. We used to talk about Jimmy Dean a lot. He felt Jimmy would have grown and developed had he lived, that his death was a real loss."

Newman's style represented the new breed of acting, and he played it close to the vest in his delivery, but Sal brought everything he could to the part of the boxer's best friend, sometimes appearing emotion-ally raw and making what convincingly seemed to be improvisatory moves. This set him apart from the tone of the film, and he played that to his advantage. Though he admired Robert Wise, Sal found his direction too restrained.

Sometimes appearing restless on-screen, Sal seemed to rail against the simplicity of Wise's vision. He managed to inject an ambiguous level of hero worship between his character and Graziano that some critics later compared to that between Plato and Jim Stark.

Beginning a pattern that would last for the rest of his life, questions from the press invariably turned to *Rebel* and James Dean. "I think my greatest lesson came from Nicholas Ray," Sal said. "I'll never forget his patient, understanding approach and advice. He spoke to me on my own level. He got a performance out of me I never would have delivered on my own.

"You know," he added, "*Rebel* was the first time I worked with a director. Up till then, I had done my own interpretations. If you're a good actor you should be able to do each part at least four or five different ways. I would like to redo my part in *Rebel*. It's not perfect yet. I liked only one scene. The last one, when Jimmy comes into the observatory and I give him my gun for his jacket."

In what would be his first nationally published interview, Sal spoke with a reporter in early 1956 for *New York TV and Radio Magazine* during the production of *Somebody*. The reporter inferred that most young actors were patterning their techniques after current stars and the "new breed" of movie idol. But not young Mr. Mineo.

"I just want to be Sal Mineo," he stated. "If some people liken my style to Marlon Brando, I can't help it, but I don't try to imitate other actors. I just act the way I feel."

BEING ACCUSTOMED to a houseful of immediate and extended family members, Sal did not like being alone. The Hoenes provided him with a good, loving "adopted" family but he still needed people around. He spent a lot of time with young actors he met in the studio schools, like Natalie Wood and another young starlet named Gigi Perreau. Perreau, two years Sal's junior, was the precocious young star of more than twenty-five films, including *Madame Curie* and *Green Dolphin Street*. Like Sal's father, Gigi's father was a European immigrant. Gigi had three siblings, including a brother with show business ambitions. Sal and Gigi went on a number of studio-arranged dates and posed for publicity photographs for movie magazines. A trip to Disneyland was covered by a phalanx of studio photographers. The kids passed time at some Hollywood diners, including one of their favorite spots, Googie's on Sunset Boulevard.

Perry Lopez, a handsome actor several years older than Sal, recalled meeting him at the school at MGM Studios during the making of *Somebody Up There Likes Me*. Sal and Perry became chums. "We had a lot of lunches together in the commissary," Lopez remembered. "He was a terrific kid. A great guy. He loved his family. We all hung out with Natalie Wood and Nick Adams at Patsy D'Amore's Italian restaurant Villa Capri in Hollywood."

Lopez added, "He was just a kid, not much younger than us. He was youthful and energetic and naïve but still had some real street smarts. He was disarming. You couldn't help but like him. Some others talked about him behind his back, made fun of him, but they were just jealous. He was delicate but just so damn good-looking. I had been good friends with Jimmy Dean. And Sal was close to Jimmy. Jimmy really liked him. Sal was the new kid in town and was sort of an underdog, and Jimmy gravitated to that type of person."

Sal had become more and more aware of his appearance, especially his physique. Standing at just over five feet six inches and weighing 118 pounds, he pushed himself to build up his muscles. Lopez was a well-conditioned athlete and helped Sal in the gym at the studio with weight lifting, gymnastics, and shadowboxing. "He was strong," Lopez said, "and he worked hard. Appearances were everything in Hollywood. I helped him, but he smoked too much. His teeth were yellow and I told him."

When Sal wasn't working on set, he set up a drawing board in his dressing room and sketched his coworkers. His teacher at MGM, Mary Lowe, reported he wasn't very interested in his required studies. "Sal wants to study playwriting and directing," she said. "He's the most ambitious young man I've ever met."

With his weekly allowance, Sal managed to start an impressive record collection, and Mrs. Hoene allowed him to host a group of friends at the house for sock hops on Saturday nights and Sunday cookouts in the backyard. Sal's girl-chum of choice was still Natalie Wood, though.

"Sal Mineo is the only boy I know who blushes," Natalie said. "He's like a happy, tail-wagging puppy who loves everyone and who has no doubt that everyone loves him. He's utterly convinced that the world is his romping place, and I think it's entirely possible that he may go through life without anyone having the heart to disillusion him.

"He has an irrepressible gift of gab. He's never at a loss for words, no matter what the occasion. I've never known anyone who was any faster or more disarming with the compliments than him.

"The nicest thing about Sal is that he doesn't change," Natalie added. "He wouldn't know how. He doesn't fall into the Hollywood mold. He just lacks the phoniness that surrounds many of the Hollywood pretty boys, and he has the talent that many of them lack.

"All I can say is that I'd hate to be taxed a nickel for every heart he's going to break."

# PART TWO

# MINEO MANIA

Sal, the Bronx, 1957

# 8.

### "I want to win the Academy Award."

On February 18, 1956, the Academy of Motion Picture Arts and Sciences announced the nominations for Academy Awards during a half-hour television program broadcast live from Hollywood. There was at least one person genuinely surprised to hear of the nominations that evening. Sal was at home in the Bronx preparing for a date when he heard his name as one of the nominees for Best Performance by an Actor in a Supporting Role for his work in *Rebel*. The other nominees were Jack Lemmon for *Mister Roberts,* Joe Mantell for *Marty,* Arthur O'Connell for *Picnic,* and Arthur Kennedy for *Trial*. Sal watched in shock as the camera panned across the audience on the program searching for him. "I'm here," he yelled at the set, "I'm here!

"I wasn't even invited to the affair," Sal later told Bob Thomas for an Associated Press interview. After a few minutes of adjusting to the news, Sal finished his dinner and got dressed for his date. Still, Sal stayed up all night trying to get used to the idea of an Oscar on the mantel.

Sal had been in New York for several weeks waiting for his scheduled work on *Somebody* to begin. His family had been perusing television and motion picture scripts, and Sal had busied himself with movie magazine interviews and pictorials, and his required curriculum at the Lodge School. He had no idea he was in the running for an Academy Award. Neither did Warner Bros. Studios.

The advertising campaign mounted by Warner Bros. for *Rebel Without a Cause* concentrated on promoting the stardom of James Dean. Natalie Wood was represented in the studio-crafted campaign, but Sal was virtually ignored. He was not pictured on any posters or even newspaper- and magazine-formatted advertisements. The studio intended to lobby for Oscar nominations for Dean and Wood for obvious reasons. Dean's tragic death was still the talk of the town, and Natalie was a Hollywood veteran even at her young age. Though highly regarded by studio executives and the critics, Sal's performance in the film was not considered viable for Academy Award attention.

The studio thought his very young age (Sal turned seventeen on January 10) and his lack of any real motion picture experience would be too problematic for Academy members.

Despite the death of Dean, Warner Bros. was determined to capitalize on his meteoric stardom and popularity. An Oscar nomination, and more important, a win, would add significant revenue at the box office. The Warner Bros. publicity department courted Academy members, placed extensive ads in industry publications, and scheduled carefully placed interviews with their actors and Hollywood's most famous columnists. The advertising blitz that preceded the nominations had been successful. *Rebel Without a Cause* earned three nominations, including Supporting Actor nods for both Natalie Wood and, surprisingly, Sal. But it was *East of Eden* that earned a Best Actor nod for James Dean.

It was not an oversight that Sal was not invited to the televised Academy Award nomination ceremony. The studio simply had no expectation that he could earn a nomination, so he was not included on the short list of attendees invited by Warner Bros. Studios. The young actor was not under contract to Warner; accordingly, the studio was not especially interested in promoting him. Neither did they offer to fly Sal from his home in the Bronx to Hollywood at their expense. And in spite of critical acclaim and the public's embracing of young Sal, no studio money would be appropriated to change or reinvent a costly advertising campaign to accommodate an independent actor's road to stardom.

"Any time you're with Sal," recalled Natalie Wood, "he's good for a surprise. For instance, when he was the only contender not invited to the Academy Award nominations on television, I was sure his feelings would be hurt. I phoned him the next day to offer my congratulations on his nomination and my sympathy at his having been slighted.

" 'Left out?' he laughed. 'Are you kidding, Nat? I was home having dinner and watching TV when I found out I was nominated. It's a good thing I wasn't there. I would have fainted. It was such a shock.' "

Sal's surprise was shared by his family, though Josephine later said she would have been surprised if her son *hadn't* garnered a prestigious nod from the Academy. "One of my biggest thrills so far is being nominated for the Academy Awards," he told a reporter. But he later said he never thought he would win the coveted award. In fact, he thought it was a fluke that he had been recognized at all. He became troubled when people around him, including his agent and his family, took the nomination seriously and became boastful of his accomplishment. So he wouldn't raise his hopes too high, Sal called Nicholas Ray to ask him what he thought were his chances of a win.

"No, he told me," Sal said. "Nick said, 'You won't get the award. But you don't need it. Someday you'll get it. But not now.'

"I was relieved," Sal recalled. "I felt definitely that I wouldn't get it."

In an interview with Bob Thomas, Sal said his greatest ambition was to win the Oscar, but he felt he would lose to Arthur Kennedy in *Trial*. "It's enough of an honor to be considered along with great actors like Kennedy, Joe Mantell, Arthur O'Connell, and Jack Lemmon," he added.

One immediate benefit of the nomination was an avalanche of movie offers. Only one film, which offered him the part of a young Cuban boy, especially interested Sal. The character was about as far away from a juvenile delinquent as he could get. Leland Hayward and Warner Bros. were set to produce *The Old Man and the Sea*, based on the novel by Ernest Hemingway. On the strength of his nomination, Sal was considered for the costarring role of the Boy. Alec Alexander quickly planted the news item in the industry trade papers. On February 29, 1956, the *Los Angeles Times* reported in their drama column, "Sal Mineo is the young lad most strongly mentioned for the boy role in *The Old Man and the Sea* in which Spencer Tracy is to star."

ON THE night of March 21, the motion picture industry focused its attention on the Pantages Theatre on Hollywood Boulevard for the twenty-eighth annual Academy Awards ceremony. Sal was not only a nominee, he was a presenter responsible for handing out an Oscar for Best Sound. Thousands of people were gathered on the world-famous street, straining to catch a glimpse of their favorite stars. Passes to the actual Academy Awards presentation are allotted to members of the Academy and the nominees only, but Sal's agent managed to secure a ticket for Sal's mother and brother Mike. On March 18, Josephine and Mike traveled to Hollywood for the first time. Gladys Hoene secured a hotel room for them near Universal International Studios.

Sal was his own chauffeur that evening. "I took my mother to the awards," he explained. "People kept asking, 'Who's your date?' And when I told them, 'My mother,' they all thought this was the most wonderful thing. Mother was so excited.

"When they announced, 'Mr. Mineo's car,' everyone expected a big new shiny Cadillac to draw up, and here I was in my old Mercury." Josephine and Mike watched as Sal was interviewed by reporters on the red carpet leading into the ornate theater. "The girls screamed so loud," Sal recalled, "that I screamed, too, and was scared and jumped back!"

Natalie Wood said, "It was the first time I'd ever seen him in a tuxedo and he was the picture of teenage dignity. We were at opposite ends of the crowded lobby when he spotted me. He suddenly forgot how solemn the occasion was supposed to be and how dignified an Academy Award nominee was supposed to act.

" 'Hey, Natalie!' he shouted. 'Hey, Natalie!'

"He kept pushing people aside until he got to me. Then he gave me his customary greeting, 'Hi, doll!'

"I told him he looked very dashing and handsome. He stood back to give me a once-over and, making like a connoisseur, he said, 'You look very European, yourself, very chic, baby doll.' "

The two teenage Oscar-nominated costars were quickly swarmed by reporters and studio publicists. Mike was asked to step aside as photographers snapped pictures of a beaming Sal and his mother, and a radiant Natalie Wood and her date, Tab Hunter.

Sal said, "I thought that she was counting on my getting it. Whereas she thought that I was counting on getting it. So we sat there and every once in a while I'd say, 'You know, Ma, there's a very slight chance of getting it.' Five minutes would go by and she'd say, 'You know, Sal, you shouldn't put your heart on this.' When Eva Marie Saint finally said, 'Now the winner of the Best Supporting Actor of the year,' I took a deep breath because that meant I was scared that I *would* get it! Then it hit me. It happened in such a split second. If I would get that award, when *Crime in the Streets* is released, people would expect so much of me. When they'd see *Giant* they'd expect even more. And I can't give it to them. So I was tense hoping that I wouldn't get it. And when she said, 'Jack Lemmon,' I smiled. I was so relieved. People came over and said, 'Don't worry.' But I was so happy about it. So relieved. My mother, too. Because my mother knew that if I would have gotten that award I wouldn't work as much as I am now. When you're an Oscar winner, you do only certain TV plays and you do certain pictures." Not only did Sal go home empty-handed, neither Dean nor Natalie won that evening.

After the ceremony, Mike was sent ahead to retrieve their car as Sal and his mother slowly made their way through the theater lobby. "Each of us thought the other needed comforting," Sal recalled. "But then people started coming up and congratulating us. They said it was an honor just being nominated. 'Look forward to the next movie,' they told me. 'That's the important thing.' "

Mike was long delayed with their car, so Sal and his mother took a taxi to the official after-party at Romanoff's restaurant in Beverly Hills, where they were treated to an elegant, formal dinner the likes of which Josephine had never experienced. They were carefully scrutinized by smiling but treacherous Hollywood columnists who were both charmed and bemused by their naïve ways. Josephine was speechless as some of the top stars of the day stopped at their table to congratulate her youngest son and pose for photographs. On the way back to their hotel, they stopped at the Villa Capri in Hollywood for a party in honor of James Dean.

The following day, Josephine and Mike returned to New York, and Sal went to Burbank Studios to film a segment that would be shown at the end of an upcoming broadcast of *Lux Video Theatre* to promote his next film, *Crime in the Streets*. Several compelling film clips were shown and Sal answered a few scripted questions put to him by the host, Gordon MacRae. The program, which normally garnered mediocre ratings, enjoyed an enormous viewership when the episode including Sal's appearance was later aired.

Near the end of March, Sal returned to New York, where he guest-starred on *Monitor*, a respected radio program on WRCA, broadcast on the evening of March 31. He spoke about his brush with Oscar, his upcoming film *Crime in the Streets*, and his personal life.

"I'm not for going steady, which a lot of fellows and girls today think the thing," he said. "Why go steady? There's too much to see and do to get tied down. No, I've never been in love. And I don't want to get married for a long, long time."

———

THE MORNING of April 7 was cloudy and cold in the Bronx. Intermittent showers had snarled traffic and delayed the delivery of Sal's newly fitted white suit from Manhattan. When the suit finally arrived from the tailor's, the trousers didn't fit, so Josephine washed and pressed Sal's black tuxedo pants to wear with the white jacket. The Mineo house was in a frenzy as the family scrambled to make themselves presentable for Sal's big night. While directing household chores, Josephine handled constant phone calls from family members and other well-wishers and friends, many of whom asked her for tickets to the New York premiere of *Crime in the Streets,* scheduled for later that day in Manhattan at the Victoria Theatre on Broadway.

Sal was blissfully unaware of the tumult downstairs. When he awoke that morning, he expressed concern to his sister that the bad weather might dampen the party that evening. This was his first personal appearance to promote a movie, and he was afraid no one would be at the theater to meet him.

Shortly before noon, Sal and Mike took a taxi to the theater. The studio had arranged a series of radio, newspaper, and magazine interviews inside the theater before festivities were to begin. Josephine, Sarina, and Victor would join them later, after picking up Sal's teacher Claudia Franck. Mr. Mineo would arrive at the theater at the end of his workday.

It was advertised that Sal would sign autographs in the theater before the movie screened. Sal said, "When I first got there, the streets were empty. Well, it was a cold, rainy day and I figured that maybe only a few kids would show up. At eight, I looked out and almost fainted. There was no longer a street, just a mass of people waiting. For me! There must have been ten thousand out in the street and a couple thousand more in the theater. And I was in the lobby, right in the middle."

Sal sat in the lobby and handed out autographed pictures. Mike and Victor stood on either side of him and collected flowers and gifts fans had brought for him. Unprepared for the number of people, Sal soon ran out of photographs to give away and the boisterous throng became unruly. Sal recalled, "The crowds broke through the police and began to swarm over me. It looked like it was going to turn into a riot."

When Sal and his family tried to leave to go to dinner, squealing teenagers who jammed the entrance to the theater and flooded into the street became a howling mob. They held up traffic for nearly half an hour until police on horseback drove them back from Sal's taxi.

The *New York Times*, coining the phrase "Mineo Mania," reported that "hysterical teenagers, banked ten deep," broke through the police barricades and surged toward Sal's waiting car. The police offered to lift him up onto the theater marquee. That way, they told him, he could wave to the crowd without running the risk of being trampled to death. But Sal didn't care for the idea. "I just couldn't stand on top of a Broadway theater marquee," he said. "I'm not that important."

"So they put me on a chair," Sal remembered. "I was crying and I couldn't control my emotions. I started mumbling something about my gratitude, and then the police lines broke." The officers grabbed Sal and pulled him back into the theater, where he and his family made a hasty retreat into the manager's office, but not before Josephine was knocked to the ground in the frenzy. "My clothes were ripped and after it was all over you couldn't recognize me," Sal recalled. "It was just wonderful!"

After dinner at Leone's Restaurant, Sal's taxi drove back up Broadway and passed the Victoria Theatre. It had begun to rain again. The crowds had finally dispersed, but at midnight the theater management, having recognized Sal's tremendous drawing power, had reconfigured the theater marquee. As flashbulbs popped and fans screamed, they changed the order of the names. Now, in bold letters, Sal's name had been moved above the title of the film. Sal's cab stopped, and he hopped out to be photographed in front of the theater. The photograph appeared the next morning in the newspaper.

When *Crime in the Streets* opened, no one was prepared for the public's reaction, which was nothing short of sensational. The studio's promotional campaign was designed to make Sal a bona fide movie star. Seemingly overnight, Hollywood's star-making machine focused on a new potential young idol. The carefully crafted newspaper advertisements, clever enough to take advantage of Sal's breakthrough performance in *Rebel*, appealed to a newfound movie audience of teenage boys and girls.

About *Crime in the Streets* and Sal's portrayal of Baby Gioia, the headlines screamed, *REBELS WITH CAUSE?*, COOL CATS, BUT THEY'RE ON FIRE INSIDE . . . AND THIS PICTURE TELLS WHY! THE STORY OF THE

WHOLE ROCK 'N ROLL GENERATION . . . SEETHING IN EVERY CITY, HUNTING THE TWISTED PLEASURES THEY CALL "KICKS"!, SAL MINEO, SENSATIONAL IN *REBEL WITHOUT A CAUSE*, RAGES TO FURIOUS STARDOM!; SOMEBODY'S GOT TO LOVE HIM . . . OR HE'LL EXPLODE!; SAL MINEO . . . THE SENSA-TION OF *REBEL WITHOUT A CAUSE* PLAYS THE FURIOUS ROLE THAT MAKES HIM A STAR!

Bosley Crowther of the *New York Times* was not so enthusiastic, though. Comparing the delinquents in *Crime* to the Bowery Boys of film fame a decade before, Crowther called *Crime in the Streets* "a meager drama of juvenile delinquents . . . and the picture itself looks exactly like some of those B-grade agonies of yore. John Cassavetes and Sal Mineo are the more credible of the boys. The production, which Donald Siegel has directed from the screenplay of the original author, Reginald Rose, is cramped and flimsy. It matches the rest of the show."

Los Angeles critics were kinder. The *Los Angeles Examiner* wrote, "MINEO TAKES OVER . . . young Mr. Mineo takes over and never lets you tear your fascinated attention away from him." The *Hollywood Reporter* gave Sal a glowing review: "There are some good things in the picture, the best being the performance of Sal Mineo, who delivers a pathetic picture of a good boy being pushed toward crime by a bad environment. He looks believably young and, in an incredible short time, he has so mastered screen technique that he is able to build a bridge of sympathy between himself and the audience."

SAL RETURNED to Los Angeles to attend the West Coast premiere of *Crime in the Streets*. The overwhelming fan response and critical praise provided him with a measure of consolation for losing the coveted role in *The Old Man and the Sea*. His agent had heartily campaigned on Sal's behalf, but the producer, Leland Hayward, had other ideas. It is likely that Hayward decided Sal's teenage appeal and strong association with juvenile delinquent roles would overshadow such a "serious work" as Hemingway's *Old Man and the Sea*, set to star one of America's most respected leading men, Spencer Tracy. Sal's agent discovered that "Mineo Mania" might be problematic. Instead of being cast in a role because he was Sal Mineo, for the first time he was *rejected* for a role because he was Sal Mineo. Leland Hayward cast Felipe Pazos, five years Sal's junior. This would be Felipe Pazos's first and only film.

Though he felt let down, Sal told a reporter, "I just usually laugh off disappointments. I wanted the part more than anything, more than the Academy Award. When they gave it to a discovery in Cuba, I just laughed it off."

On the heels of attending the Hollywood premiere of *Crime in the Streets,* Sal appeared at another spectacular event on April 12 at Grauman's Chinese Theatre. A large canvas tent covered the courtyard of the famed theater to protect the many stars attending the world premiere of the 20th Century Fox film *The Man in the Gray Flannel Suit.* Hundreds of fans on Hollywood Boulevard were not deterred by the heavy rain as they watched their favorite movie personalities scurrying down a soggy red carpet. The film's stars Gregory Peck and Fredric March attended the celebration.

Gigi Perreau, who played the teenage daughter of March in the film, arrived with Sal on her arm. But Sal proved to be the real star of the evening. Screaming teens greeted him, making it nearly impossible for the actual stars of the movie to be heard as they were interviewed by the attending press. Ushers held umbrellas over Sal's head as he stopped to greet fans. As dozens of teenage girls rushed him, Perreau was literally pushed aside. The photograph that appeared in papers the next day showed a beaming Sal, surrounded by girls, signing autographs while Perreau watched from a distance. She never appeared with him in public again.

IN SEPTEMBER, *Variety* reported that *Crime in the Streets,* with a negative cost (the actual production cost of the completed film) of $280,000, had earned a gross of $1.5 million, with the average movie ticket costing seventy-five cents at the time. With the movie studio switchboard and mailroom overwhelmed by young fans swept away by Mineo Mania, Sal had quickly established himself as a bona fide movie star.

# 9.

"No villains, marijuana, or juvenile delinquency,
just rock and roll and — girl happy!"

Standing in for Sal Sr., who could not attend his daughter's commencement, Sal was Sarina's chaperone at her graduation from the eighth grade at PS 72. The ceremony was interrupted by hundreds of young female fans who poured into the auditorium searching for the young star.

"The girls nearly tore him apart," Sarina said, "but he took it good-naturedly."

Later that evening, the entire Mineo family dined at a local restaurant and danced to a live band Sal had arranged for. Sal gave Sarina a painting he had done of her favorite film star, Tony Curtis. Sarina loved the attention, and Sal joked that his own graduation from the Lodge School several days before went virtually unnoticed compared to the fanfare accorded his sister.

Since returning home, Sal had little time for relaxation. With Mike at the wheel, he had been commuting to Manhattan for nearly a week to rehearse for his next television role as a musician in "The Magic Horn" on *The Alcoa Hour,* scheduled for broadcast on June 10, 1956. In addition, countless interviews and pictorials were scheduled. He was peppered with questions about his dating habits, marriage, juvenile delinquency, future film roles, and college ambitions. Sal invited some neighborhood buddies to watch him rehearse at the NBC studio, and have lunch in the commissary with him and Mike, just so he could do some small amount of socializing.

Josephine, having decided that the juvenile delinquent roles played by her youngest son were beginning to wear thin, continued to urge Sal to find more upbeat roles. Disappointed by his awkward appearance in a nineteenth-century Russian period piece for *Screen Director's Playhouse* a month earlier, Mrs. Mineo thought it was time to introduce music into the mix. After reviewing many scripts for films and television programs, the family had decided "The Magic Horn" would be another welcome departure. While they considered his next feature film project, the television broadcast would keep him fresh in the public's mind. But the reviews were lukewarm at best. Val Adams of the *New York Times* wrote, "Sal Mineo, as the boy, played his role competently but darkly in accordance with the script," but described the drama as "a rather weak fantasy."

About "The Magic Horn," Sal laughed with a reporter and pinched his nose in disgust. He said he just couldn't see the story or his portrayal of the role.

ON JULY 5, *Somebody Up There Likes Me* was released in New York City. The film opened with a bang and quickly went into a wide, national release.

Sal received wonderful notices. *Box Office Digest* wrote on August 10, 1956, "Sal Mineo is tops in the uniformly excellent support"; *New York World Telegram,* July 6: "The most vivid of Rocky's slumhood pals is Sal Mineo in viciously cunning mood"; *Variety,* July 3: "Sal Mineo is excellent"; *New York Morning Telegraph,* July 6: "Sal Mineo as a young street hoodlum contributes handsomely whenever called upon"; *Motion Picture Daily,* July 3: "Sal Mineo supplies a strikingly clear-cut supporting performance"; and finally, on July 3, the *Hollywood Reporter*: "Sal Mineo has the difficult job of protecting the symbol of what Graziano might have become. He is the slum child who doesn't escape and whose tragedy is the greater because he doesn't even realize that his fate might have been different. Young Mineo does a beautiful job!"

Several months before, two young screenwriters presented a script to Universal International Studios for consideration. Herbert H. Margolis and William Raynor had collaborated on the script starring Francis the Talking Mule called *Francis in the Haunted House.* Their new project, originally titled *Crazy Love,* was about a group of youngsters interested in forming their own rock and roll band and tales about their dating misadventures.

The script made its way to Sal and his mother. Rather than another downbeat juvenile delinquent story, *Crazy Love* was a lightweight "romance with music about the Coke-and-cheeseburger set" (per the studio press release). Josephine Mineo was anxious for her son to make it his next feature film, especially when she read a story in a trade paper that her son had "become the screen's foremost exponent of the teen-age candidate for the psycho ward."

The young actor's freelance contract with Universal International provided compensation of $3,000 per week with a five-week guarantee. More important, it provided Sal with his first star billing in a feature film. At Josephine's insistence, the contract further provided Sal with first-class transportation (railroad fares and Pullman) from New York City to Los Angeles and similar transportation back to New York upon completion of the film.

Directed by a young man named Richard H. Bartlett, *Crazy Love* was a low-budget black-and-white film, shot on the back lot of Universal International Studios. Though Sal was given star billing for the first time in his career, Sal's character, Nino Barrato, was not the star of the picture. The story concerned the adventures of Jimmy Daley and his high school orchestra. Sal played a flirtatious, womanizing drummer.

Five weeks of shooting *Crazy Love*, which was renamed *The Living End*, began in early July. The days were long, but Sal had a good time with the other young actors. He enjoyed playing a character with no problems except how to date every pretty girl in school. Talking with John L. Scott from the *Los Angeles Times*, Sal said, "No villains, marijuana, or juvenile delinquency, just rock and roll and—girl happy!"

Insisting on actually playing the drums himself in the film, Sal had two intensive weeks of lessons. Emulating his favorite drummer, Gene Krupa, he seriously sprained a thumb, which sidelined him for a couple of days. And he broke his nose when he fell flat on his face filming a picnic sequence in the sand on the beach in Santa Monica. Sal joked with the press, "There's nothing I won't do for art."

*The Living End*, retitled again with the more teen-friendly *Rock, Pretty Baby*, completed principal photography the first week of August. Before returning to New York, Sal made his first guest-starring appearance on a television game show. *Juke Box Jury*, hosted by a popular Hollywood disc jockey named Peter Potter, was broadcast from Los Angeles. Sal was reunited with his costar and friend Natalie Wood.

DESPITE SAL'S desire to move away from being pigeonholed as film-dom's reigning juvenile delinquent, his convincing portrayals and his willingness to expound upon teenage issues in the press made him somewhat of a young expert on the subject. And his mountainous fan mail proved the point. Teenagers looking for advice from someone they could identify with flooded the Mineo house with thousands of fan letters almost daily.

"Because I've played so many juvenile delinquent parts and because I'm a teenager myself, many think I'm an expert on the subject and write me about their own personal problems," Sal explained.

Though much of Sal's fan mail was from kids asking advice, many letters were from girls looking for a date. Often, they'd enclose their picture and even their telephone number. Sal joked that he had a date waiting in every city he had ever visited. He coyly confessed that he'd never gone on more than three dates with the same girl.

"I get all those letters," Sal said, continuing, "and some of those girls really do seem to have it bad. But it's hard to figure. Maybe it's because I don't get serious with girls. I'm always having a ball. Sometimes when I tell them they're beautiful, they laugh. They think I'm kidding. Usually, I am."

The Mineo house had become a star-making factory with Josephine at the helm. "At home," Sarina said, "he's just a boy full of fun. He does his chores around the house and we all pitch in to do what we can as a family to further his career."

Since he was not of an age to properly handle his own business affairs, Sal was not clear on how his finances were managed. "My money that I earn?" he said. "It goes into the bank for my education. I never see it. I get twenty dollars a week allowance and buy my lunches and my gasoline, and have my dates on that. It's plenty. In fact, lots of guys I pal around with don't have that much. People make too much fuss about money. It's enjoying life and doing things that's good.

"I'd be lost without my mother," Sal admitted. "There are a lot of things I can't handle. My schedule, for one thing. Mother keeps it for me, handing me a list each day. 'This is what you're doing tomorrow,' she says."

Since the Mineo telephone number was not only printed along with their address on Sal's stationery but also listed in the telephone directory (Talmadge 8-4583), Josephine found herself fielding phone calls constantly. Coupled with the mountains of mail flooding the house, it had become necessary to hire two full-time secretaries. Mrs. Mineo relished the limelight, inviting reporters and photographers into the house and even serving them lunch. As the "mother of the star," she all-too-willingly shared family stories and personal photographs with the press.

Josephine's willingness to accommodate every journalist's and photographer's request proved to be an embarrassing problem when an unscrupulous photographer was allowed to follow Sal to New York City's Gotham Health Club late in the summer. Sal was photographed in a pair of black boxer shorts working out with a trainer, lifting weights, riding a stationary bicycle, jumping rope, playing handball, and sparring with a punching bag. The photographs appeared in a feature article entitled "Boy, What a Man!" in the November 1956 issue of *Screen Stars* magazine. The "problem photograph" was a full-page picture of seventeen-year-old Sal soaping his naked body in the gym shower.

Sal's teenage girl followers may have swooned, but Josephine was none too happy to handle a rash of telephone and letter complaints. Within a couple of months, the photo had been reprinted in dozens of magazines around the world. Although proud of his body, Sal was embarrassed by the revealing nature of the photograph.

"I used to be completely open," Sal said. "I had no reason to hide anything. I'm not that free and easy anymore."

After months of negotiations, Alec Alexander delivered a movie contract for Mrs. Mineo's perusal. The contract with Philip A. Waxman Pictures Inc. guaranteed two feature films to star her son, with an option for a third picture. Under the contract, Sal would be paid $3,000 a week for his first film. His next film called for a flat payment of $25,000 plus 2.5 percent of the net profits. The agreement gave Waxman an option for a third film, which provided a flat payment of $35,000 and the same 2.5 percent. This was a nonexclusive contract that allowed Sal to pursue other work in films, television, and theater. The generous compensation was remarkable at that time for a seventeen-year-old actor. Sal and his mother and father signed the primary contract on September 28, 1956.

It was surprising that Josephine agreed to the Waxman contract after turning down numerous contract offers over the past couple of years, including a coveted seven-year contract from Universal

International. Of the various producers and production companies to lobby for her son's services, Waxman seemed the least likely to deliver the best film projects for her consideration.

Philip Waxman began his career in show business with a Broadway flop in 1945. His production of *Star-Spangled Family* closed after four performances. Waxman's career in the film business was spotty at best. His company, Philip A. Waxman Pictures Inc., had previously produced only one film, the forgettable 1951 film noir *The Big Night* starring John Drew Barrymore.

IN 1956, *The Perry Como Show* was one of the top ten programs on television. The season premiere, broadcast live and in color (still a rarity at the time) on September 15, was presented from the new NBC studio in the famed Ziegfeld Theatre in New York City. Josephine, a devoted Perry Como fan, insisted her son accept the invitation to appear on his first variety program. Como wanted Sal to play the drums on the show. Sal agreed but didn't tell Como that he had just learned to play for his recent film role. After the show, Como gave a customized drum set to Sal as a remembrance of his stellar performance.

The day after the telecast, the *New York Times* reported that the *Motion Picture Herald*'s annual poll of theater operators forecast Sal as one of ten actors most likely to be "stars of tomorrow."

SAL, ACCOMPANIED by his brother Mike, flew to California in mid-September to film an episode of *Climax!* for CBS-TV. He played a character named Miguel in a dramatic one-hour episode called "Island in the City."

On October 2, the *New York Times* reported that Sal had been cast in a costarring role in *The Cunning and the Haunted*, to be produced by Philip A. Waxman for a Columbia Pictures release. Written by Richard Jessup, *The Cunning and the Haunted* was a contemporary pulp novel popular with young readers. Waxman bought the rights to the book and hired Jessup to adapt his book for the screen. This would be Sal's first picture under his contract with Waxman, providing him with a weekly salary of $3,000.

The addendum to Sal's original contract with Waxman, also dated September 28, 1956, not only provided for Sal's round-trip, first-class transportation from New York City to the film's location in Savannah, Georgia, lodging accommodations, and meals, but Mike Mineo's travel and accommodation as well. The producer agreed to pay Mike the standard Screen Extras Guild daily rate for his services as Sal's stand-in. Sal also agreed to three consecutive weeks of personal appearances in connection with the release and promotion of the motion picture. For this service, Sal would receive an additional 2.5 percent of the net proceeds derived from the film.

Sal and Mike flew to Georgia in early October. Waxman managed to secure the historic Bethesda Home for Boys near Savannah for the movie locale. Founded in 1740, the imposing brick school with its five-hundred-acre grounds was located outside Savannah. Location scouts spent nearly two months in the area and finally decided upon fourteen different sites for filming, eight of them deep in the pine forest and swamp area. Twenty-five acres of land were sprayed to control insects, and production assistants were constantly on the lookout for dangerous water moccasins and rattlesnakes native to the area.

The story of *The Cunning and the Haunted,* soon to be retitled a more dramatic *The Young Don't Cry,* concerns a seventeen-year-old orphan named Leslie, played by Sal, who is forced to choose between a millionaire who made his money through unscrupulous business dealings and a chain-gang convict, played by James Whitmore, who believes in the honest way of life. Sal was reunited with Whitmore, with whom he had worked in *Crime in the Streets.*

"Sal was self-assured," Whitmore recalled. "He didn't have the trappings of a formally trained actor, but his instincts were great. He was a kid with a youthful energy about him, a little innocence and a little wickedness. He had already developed a keen sense of the power over people that celebrity handed him. He could be suave and gentlemanly with the girls, and he could smoke and curse and be a little tough guy around the fellas. I could sense a reckless streak in him. I believe he had gotten by on his wits from an early age."

Alfred L. Werker directed the film, which would be his last. Having begun his motion picture career with silent movies, Werker had a long list of impressive credits, including *The Adventures of Sherlock Holmes* and the classic *He Walked by Night.* Often overcome by the oppressive heat and humidity, the frail Werker spent most of his time in an air-cooled trailer. The actors would meet with him there for direction. Sal was diplomatic when he spoke to the press about the director, who had virtually left the young actor alone to his own theatrical devices. "His quiet urging and sound advice were something I'll never forget," he said.

News of the young star's presence quickly swept through sleepy Savannah. Hundreds of girls overran the Hotel DeSoto, where Sal was staying. The stately, antebellum-style hotel and the properly mannered citizens had never experienced such Hollywood-type attention. Local police had a difficult time controlling the youngsters who stole into the legendary hotel at all hours of the night, blocked staircases and fire escapes, and disturbed the other hapless guests.

*The Young Don't Cry* provided Sal with his most physically demanding role to date. The film called for him to wade in murky swamp waters teeming with snakes, run through the woods in merciless late-season humidity, and engage in fistfights with other young actors and adults. "It was a rough shoot," Whitmore said. "Very physical, but Sal never complained once. What a mess with the bugs, the snakes, the swamp, and the girls hiding behind trees to catch a glimpse of him."

SAL RETURNED to Los Angeles in mid-November to promote the back-to-back openings of his latest films. *Rock, Pretty Baby* opened on November 20, 1956, to lukewarm reviews. The *Hollywood Reporter*'s praise was measured: "It is a clever screenplay and the younger members of the cast all come off well. Mineo is allowed to play a normal youth for a change, and he is appealing without losing his special qualities." The *Los Angeles Examiner* was more kind: "Mineo as the love-happy drummer has too little to do for an actor of his established ability, but registers well, as usual."

After many months of post-production, *Giant* went into wide release on November 24. The immense public interest in seeing James Dean in his final performance made the Hollywood premiere the most anticipated event of the season.

Josephine decided this was the perfect time to properly celebrate the stardom of her son. With Victor and Sarina by her side, she flew to Hollywood with other family members to attend the world premiere. Sal's earnings paid for the flights and everyone's accommodations.

Mrs. Hoene arranged a special tour of Universal International Studios for the Mineo family and hosted a special luncheon in the studio commissary.

Despite the extravagance and first-class treatment, Mrs. Mineo was unimpressed. She embarrassed Sal when she complained about the studio food, worrying that her baby boy was not being "properly fed" by studio chefs.

Josephine also expressed her disappointment in Sal's less than minor role in the completed film. Taking advantage of his popularity, Warner Bros. prominently featured Sal's name and likeness in the publicity campaign surrounding their big-budget gamble, even though he was virtually cut from the final print. "*Giant* was filmed a long time ago," Sal said reasonably. "I made it while I was still green in the business. When we finished it, the film was five and a half hours long and somebody had to be cut out. I was one of the somebodies."

With a negative cost of $14 million, *Giant* would earn $35 million in domestic theatrical rentals, making it number three in the top ten movies of the year for box office receipts. This film's gross, combined with the box office revenues of Sal's other 1956 films, put him at number 80 in the top 100 box office stars of the 1950s at that time.

In November, readers of *Movie Stars Parade* magazine named Sal the "Most Exciting Bachelor of the Year." In a story accompanied by a shirtless Sal reclining in bed and another picture of the seventeen-year-old flexing his muscles as he lifted weights, Sal said, "When I have troubles, I go to my dog. He never answers me back."

With Mike acting as his little brother's traveling companion and bodyguard, Sal traveled by train through the Midwest to make a few personal-appearance stops to promote *Rock, Pretty Baby*. Thousands of teenage fans and local chapters of the Sal Mineo Fan Club swamped him at train stops and theaters along the way.

SEVERAL MONTHS earlier, in the summer of 1956, Allied Artists purchased the feature film rights to "Dino," which Sal had previously starred in for a *Studio One* telecast. Reginald Rose was hired to adapt his original teleplay to the big screen. Sal's name was associated with the project from the start, though publicly he had been trying to distance himself from this type of role. When the producers agreed to his salary demands, Sal committed himself to re-creating the role of Dino for the big screen. The official announcement was not made until the day before Christmas.

Originally, Sal was reluctant to accept another "downbeat" part. The initial plan to film *Dino* in New York City near his home was appealing, but more important, such a good role could not be denied. But, he told reporters, this would be his last juvenile delinquent role. "Besides," he added, "I'll be eighteen in January and it's about time I played a part where I get the girl."

Sal did admit, though, "I like doing juvenile delinquent roles because they're meaty roles with a lot for an actor to do. But people are beginning to think that maybe I can't do anything else and I want to prove I can."

Usually open to any media intrusion in the home, Josephine had resisted the blandishments of Edward R. Murrow, who wanted to pay a visit with the crowd-pleasing television program *Person to Person*. Murrow hosted the show from the comfort of a television studio and used a satellite hookup live from his subjects' homes. "Because our rooms are so small I don't think they could get the cameras in," Josephine had said. "If they can, we would be honored to have Murrow visit us, even though our house is ordinary, plain furniture and the garbage can in front of the house."

On December 14, the neighbors at Wenner Place watched as truckloads of technicians ran cables down the street and through the Mineo house. More and more fans gathered until the police were finally called to clear the street. Sal and his family in the Bronx, along with millionaire financier Cyrus Eaton and his family at their two-hundred-acre estate in Ohio, were the guests on CBS-TV's *Person to Person* that evening.

The opening shot revealed an unobtrusive brown-shingled house. "Though not quite eighteen," Murrow told his television audience, "he is already a star of television and motion pictures and an idol of the teenagers. Sal Mineo was born in the Bronx, grew up in the Bronx, and was discovered six years ago by a talent scout while attending dancing school. Since then, Sal has appeared in three Broadway plays, twenty television shows, and seven movies . . ." The camera panned across the living room of the Mineo house as Murrow concluded his introduction. The entire family surrounded Sal on a sofa.

The televised interview included the whole family—with Josephine often speaking over her son—and lasted for about twelve minutes of broadcast time. Sal was the youngest person ever to be profiled by the veteran journalist. This particular episode of *Person to Person* was the highest-rated of the television season.

Sal on *The Perry Como Show*, 1956.

## 10.

"Tell the people I'm not really a juvenile delinquent."

On January 10, 1957, Sal turned eighteen years old. As had his two older brothers, Sal got a car for his eighteenth birthday, but it was purchased with his own money. "When I knew Sal was coming home," Josephine said, "I called up an automobile agency and ordered a Thunderbird in Sal's favorite color—blue. I told the salesman, 'Put on all the trimmings! Heater, radio—even an electric shaver! I want my boy to have the finest birthday present in his life!' "

The day Sal picked up his iridescent blue hardtop convertible with custom New York license plates (SM-95) he drove to his father's casket shop to show off the extravagant gift. And then, as he had promised, his first passenger was Sarina, whom he picked up at her high school after class.

Such a high-profile car for a young movie star proved to be a problem, though. Many mornings Sal awakened to find lipstick scribblings of girls' names and telephone numbers, marriage proposals, and love pronouncements covering his convertible. "I need a bodyguard for my car," Sal joked, "or a full-time car washer!"

Sal had little time to enjoy his new toy. He and Mike flew to Los Angeles a couple of days after his birthday to begin work on *Dino*. Sal reported to the set at Allied Artists Studio in the San Fernando Valley on January 14. Thomas Carr had been hired to direct the film. Susan Kohner, a beautiful, petite brunette, was signed to portray Sal's screen sweetheart. The twenty-year-old daughter of Hollywood agent Paul Kohner and Mexican leading lady Lupita Tovar had appeared on Broadway with Tyrone Power and in several feature films.

Written by Reginald Rose, the story of *Dino* closely followed the original story broadcast a year earlier on *Studio One*. The black-and-white film was shot mostly on the studio lot. Earlier, Sal had purchased a drum set so he could continue to practice while staying with Gladys Hoene in California. To ease the intensity of the film's subject matter, he brought his drums to the set and constantly entertained his coworkers during breaks in the production.

"We got pretty loud a few times and almost drove the director crazy," Sal said, "but you would be surprised how a little rhythm can set an entire company on its toes."

Sal's first screen kiss was with his costar Susan Kohner. Reported to be the "longest teenage screen kiss ever filmed" at four minutes and sixteen seconds, it was anything but romantic. More than twenty technicians, including cameramen, costumers, makeup artists, and hairstylists, surrounded the young actors for a total of nine takes of the carefully choreographed kiss and embrace. "It's like being home," Sal laughed. "Everybody's watching!"

On January 22, Sal took time out of his busy filming schedule to register for the draft at the Hollywood Draft Board at 5507 Santa Monica Boulevard. With reporters and photographers in tow, Sal said, "I dig brass buttons. Maybe it's corny but I think two years of service is little enough for a guy to give in exchange for the privilege of living in this country."

Though Sal enjoyed working, he still felt the pressure of success. "I don't have ten spare minutes a day for myself, as things work out now." Sal preferred to spend time with his friends on weekends when he could. He joked about often being dateless and having nothing to do but table-hop at Googie's in Hollywood with other "Lonesome Joes." He missed his Thunderbird and arranged to have the car shipped to California by train.

Proud of his new car, Sal planned to enter a few road races, but Allied Artists had another idea. The studio halted Sal's plan to race in Palm Springs. Reluctantly, Sal canceled his run. "I have a lot of catching up ahead of me," he complained. "While other kids were playing baseball or football I was working. I had to attend professional school—no football team and no class parties. Education, yes, high school fun, no. I missed all those things that fill a teenager's life."

*TV Guide* interviewed Sal during the making of *Dino*. The reporter asked Sal why American teenagers became hysterical over certain entertainers. "I think they idolize actors who are on their side, who are all for them. Kids get pushed around a lot—by parents, teachers, rules—and when they find somebody who they think understands their problems, they make him a hero."

Despite the critical praise for his acting skills, Sal expressed a strong interest in directing. "An actor," he said, "creates a character, sure; but a director is far more creative. He's the one who brings a story to life.

"Listen, do me a favor, will ya?" Sal added. "Tell the people I'm not really a juvenile delinquent."

Principal photography on *Dino* was completed near the end of February. This would be the last time Sal played the part of a juvenile delinquent in a motion picture.

ON FEBRUARY 28, a *Los Angeles Times* headline was an unpleasant and embarrassing end to a few uncomfortable days in superior court for the young movie star. SAL MINEO PROMISES TO SAVE, GETS CONTRACT OK. JUDGE BALKS AT APPROVAL WHEN ACTOR'S PAY SEEMS TO BE LESS THAN HIS EXPENSES.

Sal had been called to court for approval of his contract with Philip A. Waxman Pictures Inc. Uncommon at that time, multipicture contracts between independent producers and minors were routinely reviewed. Los Angeles Superior Court Judge Clyde C. Triplett was bothered by the agreement, signed in September of 1956, because it appeared to provide Sal with less income than the detailed accounting of his yearly expenses that had been ordered as evidence by the court.

"This leaves nothing for him to save," Judge Triplett said, "and this court does not approve contracts for minors unless there is a savings plan." The accounting records presented to the judge for review revealed that Sal had earned a total of $85,000 in 1956. The detailed analysis also revealed his expenses for that same year exceeded his earnings. The financial reports and accounting prepared by a court-appointed accountant clearly indicated that the meteoric increase in Sal's popularity had caused an overwhelming increase in the financial demands against the young man.

"First," Sal explained, "my manager [Josephine Mineo] gets fifteen percent of my income. My agent gets ten percent. Federal and state taxes eat up at least twenty percent. And fifteen percent is laid aside by California law in U.S. Savings Bonds, which I can't touch until I'm twenty-one. That's sixty percent whacked out of my earnings right there."

Sixty percent of $85,000 amounted to $51,000, which left Sal with $34,000. When Sal revealed that he received a weekly allowance of $20 for pocket money and minor expenses, the judge wondered what happened to the rest of his money.

"I spend it—and more," Sal stated. "Thanks to interest from my bonds, I just about break even. My expenditures total more than thirty-four thousand dollars annually. Everything is necessary. And everything is in black and white for Uncle Sam and everyone to see."

According to Josephine, who did not appear in court with her son, Sal's single biggest expense was the handling of his fan mail. Until recently, fan mail had been handled from the sun porch of the Mineo house in the Bronx. Beginning in the later part of 1956, nearly five thousand letters a week were delivered to Sal's home. Josephine, with the help of her other children and a couple of additional assistants, could no longer process the mail. Josephine had recently rented an office in New York City and hired a full-time secretary and two office aides, which cost Sal $1,140 monthly.

In addition to the office rent and salaries, Sal spent $1,200 for printed stationery, fan club pin-back buttons, and photographs annually, and more than $1,200 in postage. His fan mail expense came to over $16,000 a year. His mother paid an outside accountant $20 a month to keep a check on the fan mail division and tabulate the appropriate taxes for the government. And she retained a lawyer for $100 a month to review his movie and television contracts.

Since Sal split his time between both coasts, telegraph and long-distance telephone bills were exorbitant. Though he lived at home in the Bronx, Sal had to pay his monthly rent in Los Angeles year-round. He had monthly automobile expenses of about $150. The costs of eating out and traveling on personal-appearance tours averaged around $5,200 annually.

And professional wardrobe expenses for a movie star making numerous publicized appearances each week were daunting. Sal's clothes needed to be in perfect condition. Josephine said that her son never made a personal appearance without losing buttons or even having sleeves ripped out of the armholes. The annual wardrobe, cleaning, and tailor bills totaled more than $1,800 a year.

Sal maintained his private acting lessons in New York with Claudia

Franck. Life and disability insurance premiums exceeded $480 annually. He also paid for automobile insurance and liability insurance at his New York office.

In addition, Sal paid for bodyguards, often employing his own brothers, Victor and Mike. Business dinners at home and at restaurants brought his entertainment budget to at least $125 each month.

"Sudden money can make youngsters reckless," Josephine said. "They can throw it away foolishly. But Sal knew I'd done all the bookkeeping for my husband's business. He trusted me. I'm glad he agreed to let me handle his affairs. If he'd gotten into the hands of unscrupulous agents, he might have signed his life away. With me, he's free to change any time he wants."

It took Judge Triplett several days to review all the documents and hear testimony. Waxman's lawyer and Sal's agent pointed out to the court that Sal had other income in addition to the monies provided by the Waxman contract, which was nonexclusive and required only one picture a year. Triplett rebuked the attorney though and said it was only this contract that he was called upon to approve. He expressed concern that Sal was simply not being paid enough to cover his mounting expenses. Waxman agreed to pay Sal an increased amount of $35,000 for his next role plus 2.5 percent of the gross.

Sal volunteered to cover some of his expenses from other earnings and to appropriate 15 percent of the Waxman contract income to purchase additional government bonds, which could not be cashed in until he turned twenty-one years of age. With these new terms, the court approved the contract.

"We have a formula all worked out," Sal explained. "It's a long-range formula, and it'll remain more or less the same for many years to come. I got fifty thousand dollars for *Dino,* with five percent of the profits still to come. If I make money each year and the spending pattern remains constant, I should be ahead before long."

FEELING VIOLATED by the court hearing and embarrassed to have his personal business become a public matter, Sal kept a reasonably low profile for a couple of weeks after he returned to the Bronx. "I felt like somebody broke into my house and went through all my stuff," he grumbled. He also felt resentful that his mother had not assisted him in court. "I don't know anything about my business," he said. "She handles everything."

Sal's first big public appearance since the court hearing was on March 16, when he attended the 1956 Emmy Awards ceremony in New York. Josephine was noticeably absent as Sarina accompanied her big brother to the glamorous event. His appearance in the *Studio One* presentation of "Dino" earned him a nomination for Best Single Performance by an Actor. Sal was in good company with fellow nominees Lloyd Bridges, Frederic March, Red Skelton, and Jack Palance.

Once again, though, Sal did not take home a statuette. "When he didn't get the award we really weren't disappointed," Sarina said. "It just wasn't that important. Just being nominated was very wonderful."

A reporter thought Sal didn't look disappointed by the loss and asked the young actor what made him such a good loser. "I wasn't really a good loser," Sal answered. "I knew I wasn't going to get it. Jack Palance got his Emmy nomination for 'Requiem for a Heavyweight,' I was nominated for 'Dino.' So actually, I did it like an accountant. I figured the score and knew I didn't have a chance for a number of reasons. Palance was so great in that show that I just didn't even think about winning it. The same with the Oscar."

SAL ATTENDED the 1956 Academy Awards ceremony on March 27 at the Pantages Theatre in Hollywood. Two of Sal's films, *Giant* and *Somebody Up There Likes Me,* garnered numerous nominations. *Giant* was nominated for several awards, including Best Picture; Best Director for George Stevens, which he won; and Best Actor for James Dean. Sal was asked to accept the Academy Award posthumously for his friend and costar Dean, should he win. *Somebody Up There Likes Me* won two Oscars, for cinematography and art direction.

On March 28, the day after the Academy Awards presentation, young actors and actresses were in the Hollywood limelight. The fifth annual Milky Way Gold Star Award poll named America's ten favorite young stars. Sal, a first-time winner, placed third after youngsters Patty McCormack and Tommy Rettig.

# 11.

## "I haven't sung since my voice changed."

Sal Mineo Fan Clubs were popping up all over the country. With Josephine's shrewd encouragement and her willingness to provide fan club buttons, embossed membership cards, and picture postcards to approved fan club "presidents" to pass on to their eager members, membership soon numbered in the tens of thousands. When a new movie was set for release, fan club members mounted an aggressive telephone campaign to alert their friends to buy tickets at their local theaters. They flooded the Mineo household and movie producers with cards and letters espousing their devotion to the young star, clamoring to see him in more and more motion pictures and television programs.

"Teenagers sense their importance," Sal explained, "and now, when they want to idolize somebody they see on the screen, they pick someone who looks like them, acts like them, and talks like them. It's my good luck that they've found they can identify themselves with me."

A young girl named Mary Fitzgerald worked as a babysitter for Arnold and Elaine Maxin in Glenside, a small town outside Philadelphia, Pennsylvania. One evening in the fall of 1956, she excitedly told the Maxins that she had been given special permission to start a new Sal Mineo Fan Club in town for her favorite actor.

Arnold Maxin was the director of artists and repertory in the popular music department of Epic Records, a subsidiary of Columbia Records. The position gave him tight control of all the artists' song assignments for the company. He was intrigued by his babysitter's obsession with the actor. "I had seen Sal in a television show a short time before," Maxin said. "Since singing isn't too much different from acting, I felt sure [he] could project a song."

Soon afterward, Maxin contacted Sal and asked if he would be interested in recording for his label. Sal was taken aback. He loved playing the drums and enjoyed listening to music but hadn't sung or even considered singing since he appeared on Broadway in *The King and I*.

"I'd like to," Sal told Maxin, "but I don't know if I can. I haven't sung since my voice changed." Maxin was persistent, so Sal agreed to a test when he finished his film commitments in Hollywood.

In terms of business potential, Maxin's proposition was not improbable. Increasingly, young recording stars like Tommy Sands, Pat Boone, and Elvis Presley were lured into the movies by an industry hungry for more and more teenage market revenue. And conversely, many actors were tempted into recording booths to produce records. Robert Wagner, Ricky Nelson, and Tab Hunter had recently released singles that sold amazingly well.

When Sal returned to the Bronx after finishing *Dino*, Epic provided him with two coaches: Fred Steele, an accomplished vocal coach, and Otis Blackwell, who took charge of "style training." On April 16, 1957, Sal recorded "Start Movin' (in My Direction)" and "Love Affair" at a recording studio in New York City. He was enthusiastic but had some uncharacteristic self-doubts. Arnold Maxin, on the other hand, had no doubts at all. "You'd have thought he had been singing all his life," Maxin proclaimed.

DURING THE 1950s, Wednesday-evening television was dominated by *Kraft Television Theatre,* an award-winning and top-rated showcase for original and adapted dramatic and comedic plays. The programs were broadcast in color, live from New York. Recognizing an impressive demographic consisting of teenage viewers, youth-oriented episodes were more and more often presented by the producers. Mostly dramas, the story lines frequently revolved around popular music and starred young actor-singers.

In January of 1957, the producers of the series had approached Sal with a three-episode, fixed-salary contract offer. After a brief negotiation, the contract was changed to suit the Mineo family's demands. Sal would appear in one episode with an option to star in two further programs over the next eighteen months with substantial salary increases for each based on the show's television ratings.

In Sal's first *Kraft Television Theatre* episode, titled "Drummer Man," he played the part of Tony Russo, an ambitious young drummer. Sal's first single recording, "Start Movin'," was released by Epic Records in April. The teleplay "Drummer Man" was broadcast on May 1, and Sal sang his song on the program. No one was prepared for what came next. Though the critics were unimpressed by Sal's musical offering, his fans went wild. Within days, "Start Movin' " appeared on the *Billboard* chart.

The telephone at Wenner Place rang off the hook. Radio stations were inundated with requests to play the new record. Several days later, dressed in a slick leather sport coat, Sal appeared on ABC television performing his song for *Alan Freed's Rock 'n' Roll Revue*. Hosted by disc jockey Alan Freed, the special musical half-hour show was the first primetime network rock and roll program.

Epic Records placed full-page, color ads in *Billboard* magazine on May 13. *A new record GIANT is born! Over 484,000 records ordered in 11 days! You can't be without it!!!* Sal's first record climbed to number 9 on *Billboard*'s chart. The single earned him his first gold record after selling more than 1.2 million copies in less than two months.

The Mineos never imagined Sal's appearance on *Alan Freed's Rock 'n' Roll Revue* would cause such a furor, however. Most of the performers on the program were censured by many television critics and newspaper editorials. But it was Sal who bore the brunt of the attacks. Jay Tuck, the television columnist for the *New York Post*, led a vicious attack against "the boy with the soul in his eyes" (as Sal was referred to by his record label). Calling for a ban of his record and suggesting people now needed to take a closer look at his movie roles, Tuck classified the lyrics of Sal's songs as immoral and claimed one song, "Love Affair," which was not heard on the ABC program, was a "direct, unmistakable and passionate impersonation by Mineo of a boy attempting to seduce a virgin." Adults who had taken up arms against Elvis Presley and his lascivious gyrations now had a new target.

Sal was utterly bewildered. "I don't know what all the fuss is about," he said. "Why do people think this music makes kids bad?" Josephine Mineo came out swinging. She said she actually picked the numbers Sal recorded. "The song is really beautiful," she said. Referring to Jay Tuck, she continued, "I hope these two will get together and get to know each other, then he'll know the wonderful boy Sal is."

IN MID-MAY, Epic Records sent Sal on a promotional tour shortly after his first recording was released. Victor and two of Sal's childhood friends, Joe Cavallero and George Schwartz, accompanied him to Boston, Philadelphia, Cleveland, and finally Detroit. On the hectic trip, Sal was interviewed by reporters and radio stations in each city, met disc jockeys and fans, and appeared at record stores to sign photographs and copies of his 45 rpm single.

More than three thousand fans greeted Sal at the Boston airport. Several thousand copies of his record were sold in an hour the day of his personal appearance at a local theater. "I never had such a thrill in my life," Sal said. When the young star flew to Cleveland to appear on Bill Randle's local program, a special police detail couldn't contain the screaming fans who nearly overturned his automobile as it pulled up to the broadcast studio. But nothing could prepare Sal for his reception in Detroit. On Saturday afternoon, May 18, Sal was scheduled to appear on the popular radio show *The Bobbin' with Robin Show* on WKMH, starring the nationally known disc jockey Robin Seymour. The broadcast was advertised as a live appearance at Edgewater Park. Though Sal was not scheduled to appear until four o'clock, fans began to gather early in the rainy morning and eventually numbered nearly ten thousand.

"We parked the car only eight feet from the audio control booth," Arnold Maxin recalled, "but the kids hemmed us in. It was thirty minutes before we could get Sal out of the car." Twenty-five police officers couldn't contain the exuberant fans as they rocked Sal's car and jostled the remote broadcasting equipment, knocking the station off the air twice.

"I admit I was flattered that they would wait for me, but I was scared, too. In fact, I was petrified," Sal said. "Finally, my buddies decided to go for help, and together all of us formed a flying wedge and rushed to the trailer. Once inside I was shocked. The windows had been broken, the kids were crowded around outside, and I began to wonder just how long the trailer could remain right-side up. Even so I went on the radio and started to do my interview with the disc jockey. After about two minutes, though, I was told I'd better just forget the interview and get out. So out all of us went. It was a nightmare. I lost my coat, glasses, and lucky ring. But my brothers and the boys lost everything."

Hundreds of fans in caravans followed Sal's car to the Sheraton-Cadillac Hotel, where his party was staying. Again, extra security was called to get Sal from the car and into the hotel. In pursuit, hundreds of fans rushed the hotel lobby, overturning furniture and sending other guests running for cover.

That evening, Sal noticed his right eye felt irritated. It quickly became inflamed, and the pain kept him up most of the night. The promotional tour complete, they returned to New York the next morning. Sal was scheduled to be the guest of honor at the Music Operators of America convention in Chicago two days later. He was also preparing for the opening of his feature film *Dino.*

But Monday morning, Sal's right eye had swollen shut and the pain had become acute. Victor drove his mother and little brother to see a New York eye specialist. By the time they arrived, Sal's equilibrium was off and he needed help getting out of the car.

After carefully examining the eye, the doctor determined that the ulcer-like infection was a recurrence of the problem that had plagued him during his engagement in *The King and I.* Initially, the doctor felt corrective surgery was needed, but Sal begged him to wait. The doctor agreed to delay such radical treatment for a short time. He ordered Sal to stay at home, where he begrudgingly wore an eye patch and was confined to his darkened room to allow antibiotics to ease the infection. Sal was in constant pain and feared he would lose his vision permanently in that eye.

Sal's trip to Chicago was canceled. A further personal appearance tour to promote the record was rescheduled, and Josephine had to cancel scheduled television appearances on *The Perry Como Show, The Steve Allen Show, The Jackie Gleason Show,* and *The Arthur Murray Party.* Two recording sessions were postponed, including Sal's recording of "Dino," intended to be the theme song for his about-to-be-released film.

Sitting alone in a darkened room was the last thing Sal wanted to do. He was frustrated and very disappointed to interrupt his tour to meet fans and sell records, but he was most saddened to cancel a summer theater appearance in Clifford Odets's play *Golden Boy.* He was anxious to act onstage again and was especially interested in playing an adult role.

News of Sal's ailment spread quickly. The house was flooded with floral bouquets, candy, cards, letters, and telegrams. With the exception of family members and a couple of old friends, Sal was allowed no visitors. Josephine turned down reporters' requests for interviews, saying Sal could speak about his ordeal only after his recovery, but she did allow her son to be photographed for magazines wearing the eye patch.

Sal's mother thanked the fans but asked that they not send any more flowers or cards. Instead, she suggested they send record albums, since he could not read or watch television during his recovery. Within the first week, the Mineos had received more than five hundred records from fans across the country. Because he was so bored, Josephine eventually allowed him to be interviewed on the telephone by radio stations across the country, with preference given to the cities where he had been scheduled to appear in person. Sadly, Sal's mother told him that he couldn't attend the opening of *Dino,* scheduled for June 11 in Chicago.

Disconcertingly, Sal's eye condition worsened during the following week. On Monday, June 10, he went to the doctor's office as usual. "He gave me the usual sedation, treated me for a couple of hours, and when he put the patch in place, he said, 'All right, Sal, the operation's over.'

"Operation! No one told me!" Sal exclaimed. Having decided it was best if Sal was not told what was planned that morning, Josephine had authorized the procedure without her eighteen-year-old son's knowledge.

Though the doctor assured Sal he would recover, he told him he would need to wear dark glasses in the sunlight and cut back on reading for a couple of months. "The pain disappeared almost immediately," Sal recalled, "and on the very first checkup after the operation the vision began to return to my eye."

THOUGH SAL was unable to attend the Chicago opening of *Dino,* he had been able to attend an earlier preview of the film at the El Cortez Theatre in San Diego. Thousands of fans, including many Mexican teenagers who had crossed the border, overwhelmed Sal upon his arrival. Police on horseback were called in to control the jubilant crowd.

Reviews were favorable; the *Hollywood Reporter,* on June 11, 1957, wrote, "The success of *Dino* is in the playing rather than the writing. Sal Mineo gives a fine performance." *Variety,* on June 11, wrote, "Mineo gives the role both a hard finish and sympathy." *Cue* wrote on June 22, "The cast includes Sal Mineo, a good actor, as the boy, in a role that may type Sal as a perpetual juvenile Humphrey Bogart." *Variety West* on June 12 wrote, "Sal Mineo turns in one of the best bits of acting during a highly emotional scene that the screen has seen this year." And the *Los Angeles Times* wrote on August 8, "In a current market featuring all too many poor-taste, mediocre juvenile pictures of crime and violence, *Dino* stands out brightly and intelligently as a picture with a story to tell. Sal Mineo, as Dino, gives an outstanding performance. Director Thomas Carr had a lot of talent to work with in Mineo and obviously together, they worked out a bright, sensitive performance that at no times gets out of hand. Mineo's histrionics would certainly have overshadowed an actor with less ability."

The *New York Times* eloquently reviewed the film on June 22: "*Dino*, which opened yesterday, is as succinct, simple and fragmentary as the title. Mr. Mineo does a fine job in a difficult role."

Josephine proudly read the reviews to Sal and then pinned the clippings to the kitchen wall along with all the others. The doctor ordered Sal to take the summer to recuperate but did give him permission to appear on *The Arthur Murray Party* about ten days after the surgery. Sal's rehearsal time was limited, and he had to wear a patch to protect his eye from the bright television studio lights.

Sal sang his current hit, "Start Movin'," looking healthy and resplendent in a perfectly tailored silk tuxedo jacket. When Sal finished his song, he addressed the audience. "I want to thank you all for your wonderful get-well cards and Mass cards. I don't know what I would have done without them. I also want you to know that everything is going to be all right. I've been operated on and the surgery was successful." To drive the point home, Sal vigorously played the drums as the program finished.

On June 30, Sal appeared healthy and happy when he appeared as the "mystery guest" on the prime-time television panelist program *What's My Line*. Impersonating Edward G. Robinson when he spoke, Sal stumped the blindfolded celebrity panelists who tried to guess his identity. When asked if he was born in this country, he jokingly huddled with the host, John Daly, shrugged his shoulders, and whispered that he was born in the Bronx. But the question that stopped the show and collapsed Sal in laughter was posited by panelist Dorothy Kilgallen, who asked, "Are you the fellow who gets the girl in the end?"

THRILLED WITH the huge sales Sal's first recording was generating, Epic was afraid to be caught short should he get involved with a new motion picture, so they quickly scheduled more recording time. On July 3, Sal recorded three new songs for his label. "Lasting Love" and "You Shouldn't Do That" were scheduled to be released as flip-side singles in August. That same day, Sal recorded "Dino," though it was never released as a single.

Following his recording assignment, Sal rented a beautiful cottage on the wooded shore of Bayville, Long Island. This was his first family vacation that included everyone, even Bimbo the boxer, whom Sal said he missed the most when he was in Hollywood "'cause he can't write." The two-week respite gave Sal more time to recuperate and an opportunity to use the new sixty-horsepower, sixteen-foot Century speedboat he had recently purchased and christened *Dino*.

Without a television, and with an unobstructed view of Long Island Sound, this idyllic getaway not only provided Sal with time to rest but gave him the rare opportunity to spend quality time with his father. "My father has no interest in, really doesn't know anything about, show business," Sal explained. "So he stays out of it. He feels it's up to Ma and me. But that doesn't mean I'm any less close to him than I am to my mother. To me, he's the epitome of what every dad should be. Just because you don't talk about some things all the time doesn't mean you don't feel deeply about them. I look up to the guy!"

ON JULY 14, Sal sang "Start Movin'" on *The Ed Sullivan Show*, a Sunday-night variety show broadcast from New York. Buoyed by the success of *Dino*, which was still being shown in theaters; Sal's recording success; and the public's sympathetic interest in the recuperating young star, the studio launched a massive publicity campaign to promote the opening of what would be Sal's final big-screen portrayal of a troubled youth. The review in *Variety* on July 24 set the tone: "Film's chief asset is the performance turned in by Sal Mineo in the lead."

Opening in New York and Los Angeles on July 21, 1957, *The Young Don't Cry* promised to be a smash at the box office. Sal attended the

New York opening of the film. Thousands of fans choked the streets around the theater to catch a glimpse of their young hero, who was making his first official public appearance since his eye operation. Speaking to radio personalities and reporters outside the theater, Sal said he was feeling great and actually joked about his recent ordeal. When asked about his newfound success as a recording star, Sal said his sister was unimpressed with his record. "She's in love with Tony Curtis and Elvis," he joked. "She doesn't consider me a celebrity. I'm just her brother. She's still playing 'Don't Be Cruel.'"

On September 12, the *Los Angeles Times* wrote, "In *The Young Don't Cry*, America's favorite troubled teenager, Sal Mineo, is doing another slow burn at the world he and his pals didn't make . . . The cast is definitely grade A. Mineo is learning to shade his characterizations nicely."

*Time* magazine was less kind in the August 12 edition: "Sal Mineo—pouting, simpering, and rolling his eyeballs on the rocky road to manhood—is singularly unconvincing as a meek and mild sort of Michelangelo angel who is all set to inherit the earth."

Reviews aside, Sal was currently starring in two feature films playing nationally in theaters and drive-ins. Combined with his hit single and a new single about to be released, this time period proved to be what fan magazines were calling "the Summer of Mineo." Box office revenue for the combined pictures was more than impressive. With a negative cost of $350,000, *Dino* broke the million-dollar mark in only two months of domestic screening.

Though Sal put on a brave face in public, the possibility that he might have lost the sight in his right eye was a sobering realization to the handsome eighteen-year-old movie star. Thankfully, he recovered, but he did not regain complete sight in the damaged eye and needed to wear reading glasses from that point onward.

Without being disrespectful to his family, he determined to become more selective with his career choices, and he turned his attention to the future. "I have changed," he said. "My career used to be the most important thing in my life. My health now comes first."

Sal stayed close to home during the summer and began to read scripts again. He and his mother also began conferring with several architects, furniture makers, and interior designers as they made plans to begin construction of a new home. The project was beset with problems from the beginning. The land that was purchased straddled two different counties. Half of the house to be built appeared to be in the Bronx and the other half in Pelham Manor, which was a part of Westchester County. Building permits and construction restrictions were different in each. The house would have to be built in one county or the other to avoid a problem with dual property tax bills. Though the Bronx approved the Mineos' plans for a swimming pool in the backyard, the Westchester County Planning Commission did not. Unaware of the forthcoming financial ramifications of these issues, Sal joked, "The back part of the house, including my bedroom, will still be on the old side of the border. So, I'll remain what I've always been, a boy from the Bronx."

A DISC JOCKEY named Dick Clark took to the television airwaves in 1957 when he hosted *Bandstand*, a daily program created for teenagers and broadcast in the Philadelphia area. During the course of the show, one or two guest performers sang and chatted with Clark about their lives and careers.

*Bandstand*, originally syndicated locally, was picked up by ABC-TV in early August 1957. Renamed *American Bandstand*, it became a national sensation, drawing teenagers from all around the country to Philadelphia, where they tried to become a part of the live audience. *American Bandstand* was broadcast nationally for the first time on Monday afternoon, August 5. Sal's popularity was undeniable. Clark decided to create a "Why I'd Like a Date with Sal Mineo" contest to draw mail to prove the show's strength to ABC, which began with the first broadcast and led up to Sal's August 13 appearance on the show.

Several hundred thousand contest entries were mailed to ABC within the next few days. The premiere national broadcast was a hit, and one week later more than twenty million people were watching when the contest winner was announced. Sal sang his newest release, "Lasting Love," which was rapidly climbing the charts.

"There's no question," Clark stated, "Sal helped make *American Bandstand* an instant nationwide success."

With his promise to work a reduced schedule and with his doctor's permission, Sal was able to honor his personal appearance engagements that earlier had been postponed. Several days following his appearance on *American Bandstand,* he flew from Philadelphia to Flint, Michigan, for the first of several appearances in four Midwestern states. To help allay Josephine's concerns, Mike and Victor accompanied him with their mother's strict orders to keep an eye on their little brother.

When Sal walked to the microphone on the stage of the Palace Theatre before the matinee showing of *The Young Don't Cry,* fourteen hundred screaming fans nearly turned the ornate theater into a madhouse. After paying Josephine for exclusive rights to cover Sal's tour, *Modern Screen* magazine captured the triumphant return of the star.

The Mineo boys returned home on August 23, and before Sal had a chance to unpack his bags, he was rehearsing for his second appearance on *The Ed Sullivan Show,* to be broadcast two days later. Sal sang both "Lasting Love" and "You Shouldn't Do That" to a television studio audience filled with hysterical teenage girls. "Lasting Love" reached number 27 on the *Billboard* chart on September 9.

AFTER LENGTHY family conversations, Sal enrolled at Adelphi College in Garden City on Long Island. The sprawling seventy-five-acre campus was located close to Sal's home. With his less-than-stellar grades and unconventional schedule, few schools were receptive to his application. In addition, his fan base had become even more frantic since he began releasing records, and girls frequently chased him down the street. Hundreds of fans invaded the campus, some even entering classrooms in search of their idol.

Originally intending to pursue a degree in liberal arts, with an emphasis on writing, Sal signed up for a number of classes but could attend school only three days a week. Accustomed to the one-on-one attention and personal ministrations of a private tutor, Sal didn't respond well to the more conventional classroom environment. He wasn't disciplined enough to handle a college-level workload. His short attention span and his many professional distractions and commitments would soon make it apparent that a normal college life would not be available to the young movie star.

WHILE HIS singing career was taking off, Sal hadn't decided on his next film project. He and Josephine considered several offers. David Kramarsky, who had produced the successful *Dino,* was anxious to find another movie for Sal. The producer purchased *Lafayette Carter,* a novel about juvenile delinquency written by Melvin Levy. Negotiations began in earnest and a lucrative proposal was offered. Although Sal liked the book, Josephine was determined they should stay away from that type of subject matter and decided against the project.

Hedda Hopper reported that a producer named William Alland planned to begin shooting four feature films before the end of the year. "One will be *The Party Crashers.* It's about teenage violence, kids crashing parties and blaming their parents for not letting them have one of their own." Alland, Hopper wrote, was trying to secure a commitment from Sal to star in the picture. The proposal was rejected by the Mineos.

In September, the *New York Times* reported that director Arthur Lubin was planning a feature called *Sex and Miss McAdoo,* a romantic offering written by Adela Rogers St. Johns. The far-fetched story concerned a strict, old-fashioned schoolteacher whose life is completely changed by a young jockey who is one of her students. "I have an agreement with Joan Crawford and Sal Mineo to star in it," Lubin reported, "but that depends entirely on the script and production setup I can arrange." Actually, it depended on Josephine Mineo, who rejected this idea as well.

SHORTLY AFTER beginning classes at Adelphi, Sal took time off and slipped into the recording studio in New York to produce a few more songs for Epic. On September 24, he recorded "Too Young," set for a November release as a single, and "The Words That I Whisper" and "Party Time," set for release in October.

Again, school took a backseat when Sal began rehearsals for his first acting job since May. In "Barefoot Soldier," his second contractual appearance for *Kraft Television Theatre,* Sal played a wounded Confederate soldier who takes refuge with a Yankee woman and her daughter, with whom he falls in love. In addition to providing Sal the part of a young, romantic leading man, the program gave him the opportunity to sing his latest release, "The Words That I Whisper." "Barefoot Soldier" was broadcast on NBC-TV October 2. "The Words That I Whisper" reached number 45 on the *Billboard* chart on November 11, 1957.

That fall was a time of reflection for Sal. As his teenage years slipped away, he knew he had to move away from juvenile roles of any kind and focus on becoming a romantic leading man on the big screen. His first two starring movies were released back-to-back during the summer and reviews were mostly positive. Though the films were financially successful, due in part to his considerable fan base, both pictures played barely a week each on Broadway, where blockbusters could run for weeks and even months.

In the eyes of the public, Sal appeared to be a prosperous, well-established young star. However, he knew that if his career should taper off, he had no wealthy family to fall back on. In fact, he had slowly come to realize he supported his entire family. Not only had he helped his father secure a larger business space for the casket company, but he had subsidized his business losses for the last couple of years.

And the new family home he was building had become an albatross.

"We started hoping it would cost about fifty thousand dollars," Sal explained. "But you know how it is, you add something here, something there, then the house, without furnishings, ran up to a hundred thousand dollars."

Furthermore, Sal's recent eye trouble couldn't have come at a more inopportune time. It disrupted his professional schedule, threatened his career, and frightened him with the possibility of losing an eye. "I lost about two months," Sal said. "Two months of wondering if I'd ever see well again. Two months of worrying." He defended his mother's decision to keep him home during the summer months. "Mother was always a good businesswoman."

Josephine controlled the purse strings. She had always been Sal's manager. "I want the best for Sal," she had stated on many occasions. "If someone else should manage him, they might take advantage of him." Still, she cut herself in for 15 percent of her son's income. This was not an unusual amount of compensation for a professional manager, but many in Hollywood wondered if Sal was getting his money's worth since his mother lacked the know-how and business skill to guide the career of a film star. An experienced Hollywood manager would have known the inner workings of the show business game.

Sal never benefited from a long-term studio contract. The one offered by Universal International had been rejected by his mother. While he might not have been paid as handsomely as a contract star, the studio might have groomed him more carefully, lining up appropriate acting assignments to build his career into a lifetime of satisfying roles. With Hedda Hopper leading the charge, some gossip columnists wondered if Josephine wouldn't "lead Sal to ruin."

Mrs. Mineo never approved of or hired a publicist, relying instead on her own instincts. Without a press agent on the payroll, Sal never had the usual Hollywood publicity machine behind him. "Who needs a press agent to make up stories about Sal, or to take pictures of him standing on his head?" Josephine declared. "I want the public to know the *real* Sal, the one we love, not a character."

SAL WAS becoming a handsome young man with a smooth baritone voice, but he still stood at barely five foot seven and weighed a scant 135 pounds. His physical stature compounded the challenge of moving into mature, leading-man roles. His last two television roles had provided him the opportunity to play young leading men, and the public was responsive, yet he was still being offered mostly roles as a juvenile delinquent.

"I couldn't believe Sal was struggling to find the right parts," Perry Lopez recalled. "He was so popular, we'd go to clubs and the host introduced Sal. He'd stand up and wave and everybody shouted and applauded. But he wanted the right parts, and we talked about that a lot."

Magazine editors explored the professional dilemma Sal was facing as 1957 came to a close. A feature article entitled "Is Sal Mineo Burning Himself Out?" delved into the issue of fan appeal. The author, Henry Mitchell, wondered about Sal's future.

"His fan mail is staggering. Bobby-soxers screech at the mere mention of his name, and sit through his movies time and time again. Enthusiastic fan clubs have sprouted up all over the country. Teenagers buy his records. But these ardent admirers are aged 13 to 17. Will they be loyal in five years? Or will they be married leading lives of their own? Will they outgrow Sal?"

Sal was looking to the future. "Someday I'd like to have my own film company. Sort of an independent company but not necessarily with me in the starring roles. I would just help choose scripts and directors. I'd love to be a director. More important, I just want to stay in the business."

AFTER MONTHS of reading dozens of scripts, it appeared as though Sal had found just what he was looking for. "There's *Tubie's Monument*," he said excitedly. "I found this particular thing I liked—lots of comedy, a different plot."

To be based on the novel by Peter Keveson, *Tubie's Monument* told the story of a boy from the Bronx who, upon the death of his father, becomes a national singing sensation. "But there's a twist," Sal explained. "I don't become a singing sensation for teens, but for mothers!"

On October 8, the *Los Angeles Times* reported that work had begun on the screenplay and Jonie Taps would produce the picture for a 1958 Columbia release. Sal would sing three songs in the finished film.

Josephine wielded a heavy hand when she instructed her son's agent, Alec Alexander, to demand Sal's highest salary to date, including a percentage of the profits as well as director and cast approval. An executive at Columbia Pictures said, "In her sweet little way, Mrs. Mineo wheedles and connives until she gets every clause and every dollar she wants in Sal's contracts."

Based on continued strong record sales, Epic decided to produce an LP album of Sal's recordings. On October 11, backed by an orchestra conducted by Mark Jeffrey, Sal recorded "Deep Devotion," "Now and for Always," and the theme song from *Rebel Without a Cause*, "Secret Doorway." During the following week, Sal recorded seven additional songs.

Sal appeared again on *The Perry Como Show* on November 2 to promote his forthcoming album. He sang his current hit single, "Party Time," and accompanied himself on the drums.

On November 10, the LP *Sal* was released by Epic Records. The company also issued the soundtrack of the film *Dino* on a 45 rpm single, which included three musical selections from the movie and

Sal's recording of the title song. Both records jumped quickly onto the *Billboard* chart.

AFTER MONTHS of red-tape glitches and never-ending problems with county inspectors and building permits, the Mineo family scuttled their plans to build a new house. They were eventually able to sell the property but lost thousands and thousands of dollars on applications and plans, failed architects, useless permits, and, of course, lawyers. Sal had come to realize they had taken on a project that simply exceeded their experience and abilities. He was disappointed but told his friends he was also relieved.

But another disappointment presented itself in early December. The plot of *Tubie's Monument* was proving too thin to be effective on-screen. Josephine's unyielding demands now included her insistence that three of Sal's previously recorded songs be the three songs in the film. As a result, Columbia Studios decided to shelve the project and let the option expire.

With no acting assignments on the horizon, Sal appeared on yet another variety show on December 8. He sang a medley of his songs, including "Say You'll Be My Marie," "Too Young," and "Baby Face," on *The Steve Allen Show*. Rosemary Clooney, Peter Lawford, and Guy Lombardo and His Orchestra also appeared on the show. The finale was a production number featuring Allen, Clooney, Lawford, and Sal, who sang "Dixieland" backed up by the Lombardo orchestra.

With sales of the *Sal* LP holding strong, Epic brought Sal back into the recording booth for one last time on December 21, 1957. He recorded "Seven Steps to Love," set for later release as a single. He also completed "Little Pigeon" and "Cuttin' In," which were released on January 1, 1958.

On December 30, the *New York Times* reported, "Joanne Woodward and Andy Griffith, two screen newcomers, have been cited for the best acting of 1957 in the annual poll conducted by *The Film Daily*, a trade journal. Sal Mineo and Luana Patten were named best juvenile performers." Sal did not appreciate the honor. He was more determined than ever to find suitable material that would change the public's perception of him as a juvenile performer.

# 12.

"Sometimes I feel like I have a bomb inside me. I have to be on the go."

More and more, Sal had crept into the consciousness of the American public, and his name was becoming part of the lexicon of "hep cat" slang. Long a subject of movie and fan magazines, he was quickly becoming the darling of the mainstream media. He had been handsomely photographed by William Claxton for a profile piece in *Seventeen* magazine the previous year. In a February 1958 article entitled "Bronx Boy with Box Office" printed in *Coronet* magazine, Martin Abramson wrote, "On the strength of just a few important pictures and TV appearances, young Sal has shot up from absolutely nowhere to become a $200,000 a year star who draws a record-breaking 4,000 letters a week and gets more requests for autographed pictures than anyone you can name."

Not surprisingly, questions about girls and marriage plans were always posed to the single young star. "In case I'm ever in Detroit, or Chicago, or Memphis, I have a date just like that," Sal said. "I'm girl crazy now, but someday I want to settle down with some nice girl. If she's an actress, she'll have to retire, because a wife's place is in the home. I want to have a lot of kids." Sal said he didn't care if his future family was interested in show business, but he stated, "I wouldn't let them go in as kids."

As for the immediate future, though, he wanted to live his life to the fullest with no girls tying him down. "For me," he said, "every date is an incident. I'm the type of guy who plans everything, but somehow things never seem to work out the way I had in mind. I like to take advantage of my age, my youth. Sometimes I feel like I have a bomb inside me. I have to be on the go. Ever since I was a kid, it's been go, go, go! Tonight, for instance, if somebody like Sinatra was opening in Florida, I'd get a buddy and fly down. That's the way to do things. That's the way to live!"

———

DETERMINED TO find material that would take him in a new direction, Sal accepted his most challenging role to date. On November 22, 1957, the *New York Times* had reported that *The DuPont Show of the Month* agreed to pay Sal a staggering $25,000 to play the title role in a new musical adaptation of the classic story "Aladdin and the Magic Lamp." The half-million-dollar budget was unprecedented for a television special. Promising "an elaborate spectacle," CBS-TV scheduled a February 21, 1958, broadcast.

Richard Lewine, vice president of CBS-TV, was the executive producer of "Aladdin." Humorist S. J. Perelman agreed to turn the classic *Arabian Nights* story of Aladdin into a romantic comedy. True to the original tale, the script told the story of a poor Chinese boy who desires the hand of a beautiful princess. A rakish magician tricks the innocent Aladdin into entering a forbidden cave to retrieve a magic lamp, but Aladdin gets the lamp for himself.

Cole Porter, one of America's best-known songwriters, was collared to write the songs. In late 1957, Porter was ailing but agreed to do the show even though he said, "This is a sure way to destroy what little reputation I have left."

Italian-born Anna Maria Alberghetti was cast as Sal's leading lady, the Princess. She'd made her operatic debut at the age of fourteen at Carnegie Hall. In one of his first television appearances, Geoffrey Holder, a principal dancer with the Metropolitan Opera Ballet, was cast as the Genie. An unlikely pair, Sal and the Trinidad-born, six-foot-six Holder hit it off and became lifelong friends.

To help cover the staggering production costs, the sponsor partnered with Macy's, the venerable New York retailer, which was celebrating the one hundredth anniversary of their landmark store in Herald Square. A "TV and music festival," including in-store appearances by "world-famous stars," was planned to begin on February 10. A preview of the newest electronic products from RCA Victor and General Electric was scheduled in the TV and Hi-Fi Centre on Macy's fifth floor. To promote the upcoming broadcast of "Aladdin" and to introduce the newly recorded soundtrack album, Sal and Anna Maria were scheduled to appear there on Valentine's Day, at 2:30 in the afternoon.

On February 14, the *New York Times* warned fans to get to the store early to meet Sal and Anna Maria and get a free autographed picture of them from "Aladdin." But people had already formed lines around the block beginning at midnight. The young stars, coming directly from rehearsals, were whisked secretly into the building around noon. The fire department was called to help monitor and control the crowds as nervous employees opened the store doors.

Bedlam erupted. Thousands of kids rushed the electronics department to meet Sal. Racks and counters were knocked over, sending merchandise crashing to the floor. When some order had been restored, Sal was able, as planned, to pose for promotional photographs with the new Magic Genie TV antenna. As the photographers focused on Sal, the crowd surged forward, dislodging a massive display unit featuring new GE television sets and Webcor phonographs and tape recorders. The display wobbled and fell backward, destroying thousands of dollars of electronic merchandise.

Sal couldn't remember if he even had a chance to sign autographs before being swept away by security guards and police officers. In spite of the in-store riot, GE did honor their promise to Josephine for allowing Sal to be photographed with their product and delivered several new, state-of-the-art console televisions to the Mineo house.

WITH THE building project in Pelham Manor behind them, Sal now considered buying a house for the family. Victor saw a listing in the paper for a mansion for sale in Mamaroneck, New York. "They wanted three hundred thousand dollars," Sal said. "We knew it was impossible but just for laughs we drove out to look it over.

"It was a beautiful mansion with fifteen rooms overlooking Long Island Sound with a dock for our old boat. We looked at the guesthouse and the sixty-foot swimming pool and flipped. About one the next morning, we all got up and sat around just staring at each other. I said, 'Let's buy it!' "

On February 10, through his attorney, Sal made a counteroffer for the property. A price of $200,000 was agreed upon. "We're moving in on May 1," Sal told Fred Dickenson, a reporter for the *Baltimore Sun*. "As long as I can remember, I've thought of a place just like the one I bought. Now, it's really ours! I know it's going to work out. It's right, and it just has to!"

The stone and brick mansion, located at 1404 Flagler Drive, was more than Josephine and her husband could have ever imagined. Built on a high neck of land on Orienta Point in Mamaroneck, the house was erected in the late 1920s on the lot where D. W. Griffith had made such films as *Way Down East* in 1920 and *Orphans of the Storm* in 1921, starring Lillian Gish.

Perched on two acres of manicured gardens decorated with marble statuary, the three-story house had a sharply pitched slate roof with soaring chimneys at either end and peaked dormers at the front above rows of small-mullioned, white-framed windows. A second-level balcony with an ornate concrete balustrade topped a bay window on one side of an awning that protected the entryway.

At the rear of the imposing house, arched windows and a glass-enclosed sunroom looked out toward the sound, over an acre of shaded lawn and a swimming pool. There was a private boat dock at the shore. Gold faucets adorned the bathroom of a large second-level master bedroom suite, which included a dressing room the size of Sal's room in the old Bronx house. The mansion had three other bedroom suites and two maid's rooms in the main section. Below the first-floor living area was a large billiard room, which Sal would use as a home gymnasium, and a room that was finished like a rathskeller, including a wide fireplace. An east wing, appropriated by Victor and his soon-to-be-wife, Ann Drago, had separate living quarters, including a second living room and kitchen.

Josephine decided the time had come to put a little distance between Sal and his ravenous fans. The new Mineo telephone number, OW8-4055, would be unlisted.

"My home is in New York," Sal said. "I would never buy a home on the West Coast."

In the midst of buying a new house, coordinating the move, and grueling rehearsals for "Aladdin," Sal gave up his dream of being a "regular college guy" and formally dropped out of Adelphi College. Nevertheless, Sal managed to appear on three television variety shows.

Sal and Buddy Hackett were the guest stars on the January 3 broadcast of *The Patrice Munsel Show.* A few days later, Sal traveled to Philadelphia for another appearance on *American Bandstand.* To promote the release of his latest single on Epic, Sal sang "Little Pigeon" and

"Cuttin' In" on the January 10 broadcast. "Little Pigeon" reached number 45 and was his last single to chart on *Billboard*'s Top 100 List. On January 19, Sal performed on *The Big Record,* hosted by Patti Page, with Frankie Laine and Ray Anthony and His Orchestra.

On February 21, Sal reported to work at studio 72 for final dress rehearsals early in the morning. The studio had been converted to a labyrinth of elaborate sets. Broadcast live, the singing, choreography, and complex camera maneuvers would be tricky even for the experienced crew.

The ninety-minute telecast of "Aladdin" went off without a hitch. Despite the spectacular sets and costumes, the exaggerated theatricality and plump orchestration of the production challenged even the most ardent Mineo fan. The television special failed to attract a large audience and many critics dismissed the production as musically trite and slow moving.

The general consensus was represented by one New York critic who wrote, "Sal Mineo was fine as Aladdin indeed, once he devoted his vocal cords to dialogue, instead of singing, at which he is, frankly, hopeless though sincere."

Sal took a well-deserved couple of weeks off following his performance. Contract talks stalled about a proposed biographical film of renowned drummer Gene Krupa. While the family waited for a draft of the script, Sal returned to the studio on April 17 to record "A Couple of Crazy Kids" and "Souvenirs of Summertime." "A Couple of Crazy Kids" was released as a single by Epic later that month. "Souvenirs of Summertime" was scheduled for release later in August.

Sal appeared on *The Ed Sullivan Show* on April 27 to promote his latest recording and sang "A Couple of Crazy Kids" and "Baby Face." The review in the *Los Angeles Times* seemed to sum up the public's response to Sal's latest single. "Sal is slippin' . . . from here it appears that Sal Mineo has hit bottom with his newest, 'A Couple of Crazy Kids.' Let's face it; some can act, some can sing, but not many can do both."

Sal flew to Los Angeles days after his appearance on *The Ed Sullivan Show.* He shipped his Thunderbird to the coast by train and took a short-term lease on a small house in the Hollywood Hills, where Mike joined him.

On May 7, Hedda Hopper broke the news that Sal had been signed to star in Walt Disney's *Tonka*. "Mineo plays an Indian brave named White Bull in the story of the great cavalry horse [Tonka] and of General Custer's Last Stand in the Valley of the Little Big Horn." It had been sixteen months since Sal had stepped before a movie camera.

Though Sal's recording royalties had been appreciable, the purchase of the mansion and required costly deferred maintenance taxed his bank account. In public, he put on a game face, but in private he was mortified to be playing an American Indian brave in a Walt Disney movie. "How is anyone gonna take me seriously after this horse opera?" he complained. At his mother's urging, he had accepted the film role, but he felt he had been railroaded into the film for money.

Before Hedda Hopper officially broke the casting news, Sal had already been learning to ride bareback for the film. His first "barechested role" was about to be realized, and he renewed his membership at the Beverly Wilshire Health Club in Beverly Hills, where he arduously worked out with a personal trainer.

Shortly before leaving Los Angeles for location shooting for *Tonka*, Sal addressed reporters at a studio-arranged press conference at Frontierland in Disneyland. "This is the first time in three weeks I haven't seen the world from the back of a horse's neck," he said.

Sal wanted to talk about his new home in New York. "The folks moved in on the first of May. It's over the bay in New York and it's got a swimming pool. Boy, it's like a dream to know something like that is yours. This has really been my time. Do you know, almost a year ago I was blind. I thought the show was over just when it had begun."

# 13.

"What a place! Dust, horses, Indians — and no girls!"

L ocated in Central Oregon at the eastern foothills of the Cascade Mountains, and nestled in a curve of the Deschutes River, the city of Bend provided a home base for location filming for *Tonka*. The eight-week shoot would cover an area of more than 150 miles across Central Oregon and settle on more than a dozen locales, both natural and man-made.

Sal and Mike, who was hired to be his brother's stand-in, flew to Oregon on June 1, 1958. Tourists who had never before seen a movie being made came from miles around to watch the action and the realistic battle scenes, and to catch a glimpse of the star. The local sheriff struggled to control crowds of onlookers, who often interfered with the shooting by wandering in and out of shots and shouting during the battle sequences. Twice, Sal's hotel suite was broken into and all his clothing stolen.

In mid-June, Sal and Mike attempted to defy Sal's contract's "no-fly" clause and get away for two days to attend Victor's wedding in New York. Sal was supposed to be Victor's best man and Mike the head usher. "We put our heads together," Sal admitted, "mapped out a timetable, and figured we could sneak away the night before the wedding and before anyone missed us too much, we'd be on our way back." But shooting dragged on too long the day of the planned escape, and they missed their plane. Sal was very disappointed that he missed his brother's wedding.

The intense heat and dry, dusty earth around Bend made filming a challenge. As the fight and chase scenes were staged, one involving a stampede of fifty wild horses, great clouds of dust billowed and blotted out the scene in front of the camera, requiring tiresome and expensive retakes.

Sal was angered to feel responsible for the success of a $2 million movie he didn't want to do in the first place. Even before his injury, the mood was tense and expectations were high. Actors began to squabble. A situation prompted by petty jealousies developed between Rafael Campos, a young actor in the film, and Sal. The two nearly came to blows.

Three weeks into production, there was an important scene where Sal and Tonka are being chased by hundreds of mounted men. Something spooked the high-spirited horse, causing it to bolt down a hill, with Sal clinging to its back. "At the bottom of the hill he came to a sudden stop," Sal said. "I kept going. Right over his head." He hit the ground hard, driving his right knee into a large rock. His leg was severely sprained and badly lacerated, and his kneecap was broken.

Shooting continued around Sal as he spent several restless days in the hospital. "I didn't have to go on working," he explained, "at least not till my leg had healed, but I want to be a right guy with the whole company on location. Believe me, it was most uncomfortable working in one-hundred-and-ten-degree heat with a heavy cast on my leg."

Two production assistants carried Sal from place to place at the mountainous location. In spite of the help, working fourteen- and fifteen-hour days wore Sal out. Twice he collapsed on the set from exhaustion. By the time the location shooting was completed he had lost ten pounds.

It took Sal six weeks to completely recover; however, the long-term ramifications were considerable. The knee injury combined with his chronic eye condition made him medically ineligible for military service.

In mid-July, the film company moved back to Los Angeles for controlled interior shots and hours and hours of studio looping. While Sal was wrapping up his work on the film, the *Los Angeles Times* reported a new movie proposal from Philip A. Waxman. The producer had acquired the rights to remake the 1929 silent film *The Pagan*, which had starred Ramon Novarro. Metro-Goldwyn-Mayer tentatively agreed to finance and distribute the film based on Sal's commitment to star as the romantic hero. In the second of the three pictures Sal had contracted to complete with Waxman, he would again be cast as a "native," this time a sarong-clad South Seas pagan half-breed. Sal told Waxman he had no interest in the project.

The Mineo brothers returned to the house in the Hollywood Hills Sal had rented before leaving for Oregon. Sal spent a few weeks working with a physical therapist. He read scripts and lounged by the pool. This was the first time in his life he was actually living on his own. Mrs. Hoene visited him as often as she could, always bringing home-cooked food. It was difficult for Sal to find companions other than his brother during the long days confined to his house, and he felt lonely.

"It gets bad sometimes," Sal said. "I don't know why. I have my work, the work I've always wanted to do. I have friends. But still, sometimes it gets bad. I often feel like I'm searching for something. Like I'm missing out on something that's important in life."

Award-winning songwriter George Bruns, who had written the world-famous "Ballad of Davy Crockett," crafted *Tonka*'s theme song, "Tonka Wakan." Sal was asked to sing the title song, but he refused the offer. "I was very pleased with the success of 'Start Movin',' " he said, "and with the gold record I earned because the record sold over a million. But singing is a full-time job and acting is a full-time job. And at the moment, I'm acting."

While post-production and musical scoring of *Tonka* were put on the fast track, Sal was contractually bound to entertain the press and promote his upcoming picture. "You remember the sick boy in the street?" he asked Charles Stinson, a reporter for the *Los Angeles Times*. "The delinquent? Well, he's through."

Sal joked about his forthcoming film. "It's a love story," he said, "between me and a horse."

"The girls I met in Bend wanted to know if I was really from the Bronx, if I was actually so tough, did I carry a switchblade. So my career has, in this way, cut into my romantic life a little. I have had to live down my past, or something like that. What a place! Dust, horses, Indians—and no girls!"

He talked anxiously about his future plans, saying he hoped to begin work on *The Gene Krupa Story* very soon. He had suggested the biographical film to Waxman a couple of years before when he "was too young to do anything about it." Sal said he was practicing the drums every day. "I've driven my family crazy," he said.

"He's one of my heroes," Sal added. "The movie is going to be frank and tell everything. Gene will play all the soundtrack, naturally, while I do the drumming. But I don't do any faking, though. Gene made me learn all his routines." Sal said he had even traveled with the drummer and sat in on a few nightclub engagements.

Sal was looking forward to what he called his "first real adult role." He would play the drummer from late adolescence to full maturity.

WITH TIME on his hands, Sal considered his career options. Just nine-teen, he was straddling the fence between youth and adulthood. It was difficult for casting agents to know what to do with him. He had an ethnic look and, because of his small physical stature, still appeared very young. He was also perplexed by Hollywood's willingness to cast older actors in the parts he was now more suited to play.

He was exercising some independence, which in private meant his word was more frequently the last when it came to making profes-sional decisions at home. But he was publicly debating the problems of transitioning into adult roles, pointing his finger at "unimagina-tive" casting agents. This was a problem all young actors experienced, though rarely was the challenge explored within earshot of the public. Sal asked questions that were never verbalized before, and he bravely challenged producers and casting agents, speaking up for thousands of actors who faced the same dilemma he himself was facing. He felt the public's expectations, he said, but he also carried the weight of his own. The characteristically disarming young actor suddenly sounded assertive, determined, opinionated, and quite adult. Some attributed the "new Sal" to his recent career-stalling injuries, and some to his financial awakening, which had been embarrassingly public when the Waxman contract was challenged in a Los Angeles court. There were those who felt it was simply a young boy becoming a young man. But there were a number of Hollywood columnists who felt Mr. Mineo, as he now liked to be called, was not only feeling his oats but perhaps getting "a little too big for his britches."

SAL WAS cast in his only acting role all summer in the premiere episode of *Pursuit,* a one-hour drama series. After nearly a week of rehearsals, the episode, called "The Vengeance," was shot in early September and aired on October 22. The *New York Times* called it "a forceful drama, outstandingly performed and directed," and noted that "Sal Mineo as the boy and MacDonald Carey as the detective brought quality, vigor and humanness to their roles."

Sal and Mike took a leisurely train ride back to New York at the end of the summer. The boys had a private compartment, and so did Sal's Thunderbird. After making a few stops for his fan-club-scheduled personal appearances along the cross-country trip, Sal and Mike arrived back at the Mamaroneck mansion. Sal had barely spent a night in the house before traveling to Los Angeles several months before. "This house is a symbol of security to us," Sal said. "And it's going to be in the family until we all die. And besides, why put off owing tomorrow what you can owe today?"

Although he refused to sing, Sal agreed to appear with Dick Clark on his new prime-time series, called *The Dick Clark Saturday Night Beechnut Show*. Broadcast from the Little Theatre in Manhattan, Sal chatted with Clark about the imminent release of his film *Tonka* on the November 29 episode.

In anticipation of the Christmas Day opening of *Tonka*, the Walt Disney Company launched a massive advertising campaign utilizing print media, radio advertisements, and color previews of the film that were shown throughout the broadcasts of their own popular television series *Disneyland* and *The Mickey Mouse Club*. Sal's fears of being diminished by his characterization in the film were realized when he found himself costumed as White Bull on the covers of a Dell comic book and Little and Big Golden Books for children.

"SAL MINEO in a new kind of role!" advertisements proclaimed. The advertising campaign for the film featured a color photograph of a shirtless Sal in body paint, his long braids flying in the wind, wildly swinging a handcrafted hatchet.

*Tonka* opened on eighteen theater screens in Los Angeles alone. Generally, the reviews were positive: "Mineo handles his role nicely," said the *Hollywood Citizen News;* "From the juvenile delinquent which he has essayed in the past, Mineo makes quite a leap to portray this clean-limbed, young Indian, but he does it with ease and conviction," noted *Variety;* "Young Mineo, who over the past several years has developed a well-deserved reputation, plays the Indian lad with eagerness and vitality," said the *Motion Picture Herald.*

Howard Thompson was generous when he reviewed the film for the *New York Times.* "List *Tonka* as one of the better live-action features—at least for the youngsters, and especially for the young lads. With a nice leathery simplicity of tone and pace, the director guides a good, galloping little cast through some un-startling incidents that spell Mr. Mineo's approaching manhood."

But the *Hollywood Reporter* took a swipe at the film, writing sardonically, "Dialogue throughout is stilted and phony, including that of the horse, who emits the most protracted whinnies and neighs in film history."

# 14.

"If there's one thing I like, it's a swinging girl."

While Josephine busied herself supervising the decorating and furnishing of their new mansion, she took time to carefully plan Sal's twentieth-birthday party. More than a hundred friends and family members enjoyed live music, hearty Italian food, and the lavish surroundings of the newly nicknamed "big rock castle." But the Mineos' raucous party was tempered by the loss of a beloved member of the family. On the night of Sal's birthday party, their thirteen-year-old boxer, Bimbo, died. "We tried so hard to save him," Sal said. "I miss him. I used to talk to him, and he understood."

Talks resumed on the Gene Krupa project between the producer and the drummer. Sal enthusiastically prepared for the role while script issues were ironed out. Portraying the famed drummer on the screen had become a mission for Sal, who was certain the role would be just the part to enable him to make the transition from juvenile to leading man. He helped to secure the movie rights and befriended Krupa, who gave Sal a set of drums for his twentieth birthday.

When he wasn't practicing on what Josephine described as the "rubber drums" that followed him from New York to California and back, he carried a drum pad and sticks everywhere he went. He practiced on tabletops, chair backs, even the steering wheel and dashboard of his car.

COLUMBIA PICTURES reorganized their production schedule in early 1959. The film company's immediate projects included *Battle of the Coral Sea* with Cliff Robertson, *Ten Years a Counter Spy* with Ernest Borgnine, *Anatomy of a Murder* with James Stewart, and *The Gene Krupa Story* with Sal Mineo.

Hedda Hopper reported, "Sal Mineo is quite sharp in business. Besides being a good actor, he buys stories, then offers himself and the story as a package deal, and producers are buying." Sal was one of several actors, and by far the youngest, who explored film development and production and sought out and purchased scripts to develop and star in.

"There was a time when I'd get a script, learn it, and make a movie," Sal said. "Now it is so different. There is an idea first and for months I work with the writers on the script. For three years I worked on perfecting the drums for *The Gene Krupa Story* and for a year and a half I worked with the writers on the script. There is so much to do if you want to do things right."

Sal was disappointed, but not surprised, when casting issues and script problems concerning the representation of Krupa's drug use, incarceration, and womanizing further delayed the production of *The Gene Krupa Story* until the summer. The subject matter worried his agent and his mother, who was especially concerned with her son's public image. But Sal would not be deterred.

To appease his mother and generate needed revenue, Sal accepted another feature film role that he despised. At the end of March 1959, Sal agreed to play Luigi Maresi in *A Private's Affair*. Originally titled *The Love Maniac,* the story follows the misadventures of three young army inductees from very different backgrounds who form an unlikely friendship. Terry Moore, Barbara Eden, Christine Carère, Barry Coe, and Gary Crosby would also appear in the romantic comedy. Cameras were set to roll on April 1.

At a cost of $310 each, Sal and Mike flew to Los Angeles from New York on March 28 on their first transcontinental jet flight. Sal leased actor Scott Brady's modernist house on a hilltop in Laurel Canyon. For the rich and famous, the secluded area was an increasingly attractive respite from nearby civilization. The rustic nature of the canyon made one marvel that frenetic Sunset Boulevard was only five minutes away. Sounds of traffic and sirens were replaced by howling coyotes and screech owls. Brady's impressive house had a swimming pool, glass walls, sliding room dividers, and sweeping views.

Raoul Walsh, a hard-drinking man's man, directed *A Private's Affair.* The eye-patch-wearing curmudgeon had begun his career as a writer/producer/director in silent pictures. He worked with D. W. Griffith on *The Birth of a Nation* and directed more than 135 feature films, including *Klondike Annie, They Drive by Night,* and *They Died with Their Boots On.* An odd choice for a youth-oriented movie, Walsh was more interested in talking about his racehorses than providing any substantive direction to the film.

In between shots on stage 6 on the 20th Century Fox lot, Sal practiced fastidiously on the bongo drums in preparation for his Krupa role. Walsh soon banned Sal's rhythmic serenades, though. "It was bad enough that nobody could hear instructions or anything else that was said on the set," the director complained, "but when the actors began delivering their lines with a beat, those drums had to go."

*A Private's Affair* was shot in CinemaScope and DeLuxe Color. The score included three original songs, "Same Old Army," "Warm and Willing," and "36-24-36," written by the popular songwriting team of Jay Livingston and Ray Evans.

The staging of musical production numbers was tricky and painstaking. Walsh was completely out of his element and relied on his assistant director and the choreographer to properly capture the scenes. What should have taken a few days to complete often took weeks. Since child labor laws no longer applied, Sal was putting in twelve- and fourteen-hour days at the studio.

Filming proved to be tedious and disappointing. Sal smiled for the press but in private expressed his dismay about the film, which he felt would not be well received. On April 4, in the midst of filming *A Private's Affair,* the contracts and shooting dates were finally acceptable, so Sal signed on for *The Gene Krupa Story,* which was set to begin in mid-May. He told Hedda Hopper, "They're getting me married in this one and we have some babies. I feel so old now that I've reached the age of twenty and left my teens behind, but now I seem to have more problems."

Without a moment's hesitation, Sal packed his dressing-room items and happily drove off the 20th Century Fox lot when *A Private's Affair* wrapped on May 11. He was anxious to be done with it. Although his next film gave him something to look forward to, he lamented to his friends the unsatisfactory film roles being offered him.

Sal complained to his agent about "singing some one-note army drill and tossing sacks of potatoes back and forth and toe-dancing on a jeep" in his latest film. He instructed Alec Alexander to call on his old Broadway connections and find a suitable play. In early 1959, Broadway flourished with magnificent shows, including *A Raisin in the Sun* and *Sweet Bird of Youth*. Sal thought theatrical producers might offer him the type of serious, adult roles he struggled so hard to find in Hollywood.

In May, Sal dutifully appeared with his costar Jim Backus on the television program *Juke Box Jury* to promote the film. He also appeared with Terry Moore, his leading lady from *A Private's Affair,* on the premiere episode of columnist May Mann's television talk show *What's Your Problem?* Mann introduced Sal as the "money-back kid." She explained: "Make a movie with him and you're bound to get your money back." She and Sal talked about a recent gag that backfired. Several weeks before, Bob Hope had announced on a television show, "All the schools in the Bronx will be closed tomorrow because it's Sal Mineo's birthday."

"It was pretty funny," Sal said, "until the next day. None of the kids in the Bronx showed up for school."

"IF THERE'S one thing I like," Sal told journalist William Tusher, "it's a swinging girl. I mean she's a girl who can swing with the situation—who can be at ease and enjoy herself wherever you take her. I have a simple philosophy. I feel you ought to live and enjoy it while you can—live it up, do things on a big scale."

Women threw themselves, or were thrown, at Sal. His flirting skills and magnetism served him well. Women interested in a young movie star, and publicists wanting a good "photo op" for their female clients, provided easy pickings. But dating was a means to an end for Sal. Once he had slept with the girl, he quickly lost interest in her and moved on to the next. Sex ended the relationship rather than enhanced it. Part of this could be attributed to his age, but as much as he loved companionship, he had no desire for attachment. "Victor's marriage made me realize it's too big a step for me to even think about," Sal said. "It looks a little more serious than what I thought it was. Too much for little old Sal."

Sal's publicized dates and romances were mostly fabricated for public consumption. Some were overstated, and some were complete fantasies. Sal escorted actress Susan Cabot to the premiere of *The Diary of Anne Frank* at the Egyptian Theatre in Hollywood. "We didn't even know each other," he quipped. "We met in the car."

Singer Molly Bee, who had earlier met Sal at a USO function, enjoyed his companionship. She explained, "He acts like a typical New Yorker—smart, sophisticated beyond his years, flashy, witty, always trying to prove that he can hold his own with anyone."

Susan Kohner, Sal's costar from *Dino,* had a very different impression of the young man. "He's so interested in himself," she laughed, "he often doesn't know when I'm talking to him!" Susan enjoyed working with Sal and appreciated his intensity and determination. She appreciated his skills as a "smooth talker," which she attributed to his years running the streets in New York when he was a little boy. She explained, "I like the fact that he looks at the person he talks to. I can't stand fellows who seem to avoid a girl's eyes all the time."

Sandra Dee was sixteen years old when Sal asked her on a date. "Sal was a real pleasure to be with," she said. "He took the conversation over from the very beginning." One of Sal's best qualities was his ability to get along not only with his dates, but with their families as well. Sandra said that while he waited for her to get ready, he struck up a conversation with her mother and grandfather. "They didn't want him to leave," she laughed.

Agent Paul Kohner, Susan's father, was especially concerned about the boys who dated his beautiful daughter. But he admitted Sal was one of the nicest boys who ever came to his house.

On the other hand, actress Yvette Mimieux's parents feared for their fifteen-year-old daughter's well-being. Sal and Yvette met on a photo shoot orchestrated for a movie magazine. He expressed a definite interest in the delicate blond beauty. "His reputation scared my mother," Yvette said. "They didn't want him around and told me stay away from him."

Despite his constant denials in the press, Sal did see a girl more than once or twice. He began an affair with an aspiring actress and former Miss Kentucky, Marianne Gaba, in the spring of 1958. They met in Hollywood shortly before Sal went to Oregon to film *Tonka.* For a short time, Gaba had dated teen idol Ricky Nelson.

The two were introduced by actor Steve Rowland, a mutual friend with whom Sal had worked in *Crime in the Streets,* who warned her about the young star. "He told me, 'He's not your type of fellow,'" Gaba recalled. " 'Sal's real wild,' he warned me. 'He's a playboy, Marianne, a ladies' man. He swings too much for you.' "

The beauty queen was determined, though, and finally set a date to have dinner with Sal at La Scala. " 'You better be careful,' all my friends said," she recalled, " 'and watch your step.' I began to fear that dating him would be like waltzing with an octopus."

Marianne found Sal to be very self-assured. "He kissed me the first night we went out together, right in front of my door. And he didn't ask if he could, either."

They dated frequently until Sal left for Oregon but stayed in close contact by phone until he returned and they resumed their affair. One night, Sal called her at two in the morning and said he wanted to take her to the beach to look at the stars. "I thought it was crazy," Marianne said, "but you couldn't say no to him."

One day Sal and Marianne were swimming and she wore a flattering two-piece bathing suit. "He said, 'You know, Marianne,' " she recalled, " 'you really have a great figure. You should be a Playmate and pose for *Playboy*.' And I did pose for the magazine. I was Miss September."

Sal and Marianne carried on their affair through the fall, attending parties and premieres. A few times they ran into Ricky Nelson. "Sal loved that," Marianne said. "He liked to show me off. With him, nothing was ever ordinary."

Marianne found him to be exciting, unpredictable, and passionate. But there was also no mistaking that he had no serious intentions. " 'I just like to swing,' he told me. 'That's all.' Everybody warned me about him," she stated. "And they were so right. He was a playboy, but more like a Peck's Bad Boy."

JOSEPHINE WORRIED that Sal's demanding work schedule and frantic social calendar would take a toll on her son. She asked Mike to keep a watchful eye on his younger brother, but he was more interested in drinking and partying than Sal was. Many doors were open to the brother of a famous movie star, and Mike rarely missed a party or turned down an invitation. He charged thousands of dollars in Sal's name at a Beverly Hills clothier and thousands more in restaurant and bar tabs.

Over time, Mike's inability to find any work on his own in Hollywood manifested itself in self-destructive behavior. He did share Sal's money, but not Sal's good looks, charm, and quick wit, and most certainly not his acting talents. Living in the shadow of a *younger* brother was particularly difficult, and it began to take a toll on Mike's self-esteem.

The weeks between the conclusion of principal photography for *A Private's Affair* and the beginning of *The Gene Krupa Story* were filled with many late nights for the Mineo brothers. Josephine, feeling ever less in control of Sal, had cause to worry.

"Went to a party at Dean Jones's house," Sal said, "and, frankly, felt a bit uncomfortable about it. I took Marianne, Ricky Nelson's old girlfriend, knowing he would be there, too. I had the uneasy feeling that the main reason she asked me to take her to the party was to show off to Rick. The moment we walked into Dean's house, she made a beeline for Ricky, who was preoccupied with another girl. Rick and I hit it off quite well, though.

"I can't help wondering why some fellows like Rick, Elvis, and Brando suddenly hit it so big—and I just keep plodding along. Why doesn't my picture appear on the cover of magazines? What's wrong with me that I don't get fantastic salary offers like they do? I've certainly had enough chances. I guess I shouldn't feel sorry for myself; at least I'm working regularly."

Shortly after completing work on *A Private's Affair,* Sal had a chance encounter with his old friend Yul Brynner. They were stopped in adjoining lanes at a light when he noticed Brynner was driving the car next to him. Sal failed to get his attention, so he sped up alongside. "He finally cut me off and forced me to the side of the street," Sal recalled. "I was afraid he'd knock my block off. When he got out of his car, he yelled, 'I'm still big enough to beat the hell out of you,' then grinned. 'Where have you been, my son? My God, you've grown!' "

Without Mrs. Hoene to keep her posted about her son's comings and goings, Josephine worried when she didn't hear from either him or Mike. Once a week, she sent a large package of home cooking to her sons. "As usual," Sal remarked, "she's been worrying that I don't get sufficient sleep or enough to eat. I told her not to worry. After all, Mike's here and he's making darn sure I get enough food. Now, about sleep—frankly, that's a different story!"

Laurel Canyon provided a lush hideaway and Sal loved living in the canyon. The neighborhood was filled with young actors and artists.

He was most happy when the house was filled with guests, but the neighbors complained when his parties lasted into the early hours of the morning. Music was often blasting, and many evenings the police knocked on his door to send the revelers home. Sal never developed a taste for alcohol but did smoke marijuana, which Nick Ray introduced to him during the making of *Rebel Without a Cause*. Marijuana was expensive though easily accessible in the movie community, so Sal began to cultivate his own plants behind his rented house.

ON MAY 16, Hedda Hopper reported the surprising news that Sal would leave soon for a one-week concert tour of Australia. Though he had sung in public during personal-appearance tours to promote his recordings, he had never before performed a program of his music in concert. Despite his disenchantment with the recording aspect of his career, the offer to tour Australia could not be turned down by the actor. *The Gene Krupa Story* was not scheduled to begin for another month. The compensation, including a percentage of ticket sales, was staggering, and the proposal gave him his first opportunity to travel abroad, something he had long wanted to do.

"I've never been more happy," Sal said. Buying a new house for his family had always been a dream. "But more important, I've been working steadily now since I was eleven. Someone might say, 'What have you got to show for your constant years of working?' Actually, *this* is the only thing I can show . . ."

Music promoter Leo Gordon and Headliners Concert Programs, an Australian company, produced rock and roll touring stage shows in Australia and New Zealand. Gordon had introduced Little Richard, Buddy Holly, and Jerry Lee Lewis to Australian audiences, and his "Big Show" concerts were considered landmarks in Australian popular entertainment. By mid-May of 1959, Sal's recording career in America had peaked, but his Epic Records catalog of songs was just being released in Europe. His singles, released in Australia on the Philips label, were already at the top of that country's music charts.

Sal signed on to Gordon's 1959 concert tour relatively late but managed to secure top billing. He was joined by the Everly Brothers and Tab Hunter, another American film star who moonlighted as a singer, as well as several top Australian recording stars.

After layovers in Hawaii and the Fiji Islands, Sal and Mike arrived at the Sydney airport on May 28. They were mobbed by fans. "You'd think we were the first people ever to arrive from Hollywood," Sal said. "By the time we got to the Chelsea Hotel I had lost almost every button, had my tie torn off—don't know why I wasn't choked to death in the process—and had some girls' telephone numbers scribbled on my coat, in ink. Tab and the Everly Brothers didn't fare any better."

The first show in Sydney on Saturday, May 30, was a huge success. The concert program was a revue-style show, with each act doing a few signature numbers, then performing together at the end. The tour was frantic.

They played to sold-out audiences at the Melbourne Auditorium. Sal said, "It was like the Coliseum in Rome, like a fight arena. My tux was torn to pieces during the first show. For the second performance, our manager got five wrestlers to escort us to the podium. They thought Mike was me and lifted him on their shoulders—and while the crowd took off after him, I walked calmly behind them."

The final shows in Brisbane attracted more than fifteen thousand screaming teenage fans. Sal had difficulty adjusting to the time change and was suffering from exhaustion. Elated but worn thin, Sal left Australia on Monday, June 8. "The shows were a real gas," he said, "but I was glad they were over." On the flight to Fiji, their first layover, Mike and Sal played blackjack with Phil and Don Everly, Tab and his agent Dick Clayton, and a fellow passenger, the director Fred Zinnemann. At two in the morning, above shark-infested water and nearly three hundred miles from the plane's intended destination, one of the four jet engines caught fire and failed. Only a few months earlier, Buddy Holly, Ritchie Valens, and the Big Bopper had perished in a plane crash. "I was fifty dollars ahead," Sal said. "It was real quiet. We kept playing like nothing happened but I didn't do very well for myself. Within ten minutes I lost all my winnings." An hour and a half later, they landed safely at Nadi, the international airport in the Fiji Islands. "I can't remember when I was happier to step on solid ground," Sal said.

Tab and Dick had already planned to spend a few days resting at Korolevu, a remote village on Fiji. The plane was temporarily grounded, so Sal and Mike decided to stay on and get some rest. With lagoons, palm trees, white sandy beaches, fields of sugarcane, and wild mountains, Fiji seemed one of the most romantic spots in the world to Sal. He and his brother stayed in a hut with a thatched roof with all the modern conveniences inside.

The travelers had trouble again. Just minutes after taking off for Hawaii a few days later, the plane experienced engine trouble and had to turn back to Fiji. Tab and Dick returned to Korolevu, but Sal and Mike stayed in Nadi. They spent another day there, shopping and swimming. "But the beach there didn't compare to Korolevu," Sal said. "Then we took off again. By then we were all so jittery, we hardly talked to one another. We finally made it to Honolulu and stayed a couple of days to recuperate."

MONDAY MORNING, June 22, Sal, suntanned and relaxed, drove to Columbia Pictures Studios in Hollywood for some wardrobe fittings and to pick up the script for his next film. After more than two years of preparations and stalled starts, the cameras first rolled on *The Gene Krupa Story* on June 23. Produced by Philip A. Waxman, the film was directed by Don Weis and written by Orin Jannings, who also functioned as associate producer. This was Waxman's fourth feature film, and the second in accordance with his 1957 contract with Sal.

The story begins with Krupa's humble beginnings in Chicago. His early musical ambitions are thwarted by his father, whose unexpected death drives the remorse-filled young man to join a seminary. After a year, he abandons his unhappy life there and resumes his ambition to play the drums. He falls in love with a beautiful young woman named Ethel, though his career remains his primary goal. After the requisite struggles, including driving Ethel emotionally away, he begins to achieve success, only to lose it all after his reckless pursuit of women and drugs, culminating in a prison term for possession of marijuana. Following his release, he slowly rebuilds his life with Ethel and becomes the drummer in the Tommy Dorsey Band.

Sal was happily reunited with his former leading lady from *Dino*, Susan Kohner, for whom he had enthusiastically campaigned to play his love interest in the film, Ethel Maguire. Many real-life musicians were cast in the film, including Bobby Troup, trumpeter Red Nichols, jazz singer Anita O'Day, and bandleader Buddy Lester.

Susan Oliver took the role of a successful jazz singer who seduces Krupa with her wealth, connections, and sex appeal and introduces him to the world of "reefer madness." Sal enjoyed her bawdy sense of humor and developed an interest in astrology after spending hours talking with her mother, famed Hollywood astrologer Ruth Oliver. "She told me I had two lives," Sal laughed. "And she said my real life was more dramatic than any character I played."

# 15.

"I'm consumed by a tremendous, driving desire to prove myself, without knowing how to prove myself. I've got to know who I am and where I'm going."

Y ou live and learn in the picture business," Neil Rau wrote for the *Los Angeles Examiner* on August 9, 1959, "but it seems to me Sal Mineo has really done it the hard way prepping for the role of Gene Krupa. It's one of those ideal situations where a player is doing something he has wanted to do all his life."

Sal didn't just learn to play the drums the way Gene played them, he spent weeks with the writer and producer working out the "little things" in the script to accurately capture Krupa's life. "I thought things like this only happened in dreams," Sal recalled. "This has to be my best performance—even if it kills me."

After watching the daily rushes, Krupa admitted, "I myself couldn't have matched my own drumming as well. Sal did it so brilliantly—I could be replaced."

Temperatures sizzled during the summer of 1959 in California, breaking records from San Diego to San Francisco. The house Sal had rented in Laurel Canyon had no air-conditioning system. The soundstages at the studio were stifling. With the blazing lights and the ninety-plus-degree afternoon temperature, the mercury on the set often topped one hundred.

Columbia Pictures was gambling more than $1 million on the picture, and Sal gallantly assumed full responsibility for the film's success. "We're not losing any sleep," Waxman said. "Sal will draw them in. He always does."

The producer may have been sleeping soundly, but Sal was not. He had never worked so hard and so long to get a movie made. Fatigue and anxiety took a toll on the young man. One strenuous drumming session required four takes. At the end of the final take, Sal collapsed over his drums when he tried to stand. Stage hands rushed to him, ripped off his jacket and shirt, and rubbed him down until they revived him.

After investing money, creative input, and valuable time in the project, Sal felt more pressure than ever before during the making of this film. In order to stay awake and maintain energy while working, Sal took pep pills prescribed by a studio doctor. Reluctant at first, on the set he was soon gulping down as many as ten pills a day. Sal seemed to exist on cigarettes and coffee, and Mike became concerned when his little brother lost his appetite altogether.

For months, gossip columnists had reported that Sal was flirting with independence from his family. Some reports suggested that Sal had a falling-out with his mother and had been spotted drinking recklessly at Hollywood nightspots and cavorting with numerous starlets. Sal and his mother responded to the stories and vehemently denied that family relations were strained or that his personal conduct was unbecoming.

Despite the public denials, Sal *was* feeling his oats. He intended to take charge of his professional life as well as his personal life. And Josephine did have trouble dealing with Sal's coming-of-age. She felt her influence and control slowly slipping away. As direct communication with her youngest son lessened, she relied on Mike to keep her informed.

NEWS OF Sal's overwhelming work schedule, and thus his lack of sleep, loss of appetite, and severe fatigue, reached Josephine. She packed her bags and, with Sarina, flew to Los Angeles at the end of June.

"I think it's because they read about all the love scenes I have in the picture," Sal joked.

The "love scene" that worried Josephine the most was not being filmed at Columbia Pictures; it was the one that was reported to her by Mike and involved seventeen-year-old Tuesday Weld.

Dubbed a "beatnik bombshell" and "Hollywood's Queen of Teen" by the press, Tuesday Weld began her career as a child model. Reportedly, she started drinking alcohol at ten. As a fourteen-year-old, the vixen's measurements were 35-19-35. She had most recently created the memorable screen character Comfort Goodpasture, in the film *Rally 'Round the Flag, Boys!*

The young actress became a distraction for Sal. He dated the seventeen-year-old a few times before inviting her to his Laurel Canyon house. Sal told a male friend what happened their first night together. They decided to go swimming in his pool, but he told her he had no swimming trunks. They stripped to their underwear, and once in the water, kissing led to petting. They had sexual relations in the pool that evening, and began a short-term affair. Conscious of the possibility of bad publicity (something he could ill afford during the making of his film), and even worse, statutory rape accusations, Sal kept this relationship from the press. In fact, he admitted only to "barely knowing" the teenage actress.

When Josephine and Sarina moved into Mike's room in the Hollywood house, Mike bunked with Sal. "Seems like old times," Sal griped. Sarina was enlisted to answer the telephone and handle the mail, while Josephine took charge of Sal's daily calendar and cooked hearty meals, which were delivered to the studio for Sal's lunches and dinners. She also visited the film studio to watch Sal shoot a few scenes. It was the first time Josephine had seen her son on a movie set.

IN THE midst of filming *The Gene Krupa Story*, and with relief, Sal recorded the final four songs to satisfy his contract with Epic Records. To accommodate his Hollywood shooting schedule, the songs were recorded in Los Angeles. On July 9, he recorded "Make Believe Baby" and "Young as We Are," which were released later that month. "I'll Never Be Myself Again" was also recorded during that session and scheduled to be released in October. "Part of a Fool," never released, was the final song recorded that day.

A few weeks after recording the singles, Sal reluctantly flew to Washington, DC, and appeared with WJZ-TV personality Buddy Deane in Baltimore for the official release of "Make Believe Baby" and "Young as We Are." He returned to the West Coast within twenty-four hours. Neither song placed in *Billboard*'s Top 100.

After selling more than 1.5 million records, Sal was through singing, and there was no more time in his career for recording. "I'm no Pat Boone," he joked. "If I can't put my heart and soul into a thing, what's the point?"

*A Private's Affair* previewed at the Fox Wilshire Theatre on July 20, 1959, and opened nationwide several days later to lukewarm reviews. On July 22, *Variety* reported, "Mineo plays a beatnik type of G.I. as if he is aware there might be screeching teenager girls in the audience, and he must appear cute and lovable." The *Hollywood Reporter* stated, "Mineo good-naturedly underplays the part of a beatnik," and *Variety* wrote, "Mineo is good as a sort of modified beatnik type."

A. H. Weiler, writing for the *New York Times* on August 15, was less kind. He called it a "lightweight imbroglio" of "familiar, uninspired romances, mild comedy and a completely crazy marital mix-up." He saved the worst for Sal, describing his performance as "brash and callow."

SAL WAS relieved when production wrapped on *The Gene Krupa Story* on August 10. And he was proud of his effort. He felt this film represented his most important work in years. "I'm consumed by a tremendous, driving desire to prove myself," he said. "I've got to know who I am and where I'm going."

Mrs. Mineo, although genuinely concerned for her son's well-being, had an ulterior motive when she visited Hollywood. She was very concerned about his diminishing record sales and the poor reception of his latest film. As her son's business manager, it was her responsibility to talk with him about money. Aside from the funds appropriated by law for savings, Josephine had complete access to Sal's earnings. In the course of furnishing the mansion in Mamaroneck, all of Sal's earnings from *A Private's Affair* had been spent. She continued to funnel his money into the casket business, and Sal was paying Victor's college tuition bill. The mortgage, property taxes, and maintenance bills for the house were staggering. The payroll, including five secretaries, Sarina, Mike, and part-time assistants, drivers, and bodyguards, was another constant drain. After taxes and Josephine's and the agent's percentages, the $35,000 he was paid for *The Gene Krupa Story* had also been spent. He needed more work.

At his mother's insistence, Sal appeared in an episode of *The Ann Sothern Show*. The situation comedy was filmed at CBS Television Studios in Los Angeles. In an episode entitled "The Sal Mineo Story," Sal played Nicky Silvero, an up-and-coming young singer. He played the piano and sang "Chicken Cacciatore," "Take Off Your Shoes," and "You're Crushing My Duster" with Sothern.

For several weeks, Sal tried to relax. He returned to Columbia

Studios a few times to complete looping for the film but spent most of his days reading scripts. In July, Sal attended the premiere of Otto Preminger's film *Anatomy of a Murder*. The Columbia Pictures riveting courtroom drama was a critical and box office hit. He reiterated to his agent that he wanted to be considered for serious roles, and also said he was willing to buy the rights to secure the material he felt compelled to explore.

Sal's agent sent him a copy of Leon Uris's newest book, *Exodus*. Alexander told Sal that Otto Preminger was set to produce and direct the film version of the epic novel. Halfway into the book, Sal called his agent and told him he wanted to play the part of Dov Landau.

Sal felt that his next film would be a very important step toward establishing himself as an adult star and so was relieved when plans for the remake of *The Pagan* finally fell through. He told his friends it was wrong for him and he was very displeased that Waxman attached his name to the project. Word at Columbia Studios was that *The Gene Krupa Story* was going to be a hit. Sal felt Waxman was trying to secure him for a third film (only an option in their existing contract) before any new success made the actor's services more difficult to obtain.

Again, Josephine forced his hand. Sal resentfully accepted two more regrettable guest spots on television variety shows. On September 26, he appeared on *An Evening with Jimmy Durante*. The one-hour special was broadcast from NBC Studios in Hollywood. Sal performed in a comedy sketch with Durante and played the drums. The show was poorly received and reviewed.

Sal then made the most embarrassing television appearance of his career when he guest-starred on *The Big Party*. Bobby Darin's career-defining single, "Mack the Knife," had been released on October 5, 1959. The song jumped to number 1 on the *Billboard* chart and stayed in the top ten for nine weeks. Sal's last Epic single, "I'll Never Be Myself Again," was also released in early October. The song didn't chart. Sal was asked to sing Bobby Darin's hit on *The Big Party* rather than his own current release. *Variety* reviewed the show and wrote pointedly that "Mineo, who can't sing at all, sang 'Mack the Knife.'"

This became a seminal moment in Sal's career. He had gradually come to mistrust his mother's judgment, and he made it known that he would never appear or perform on a television variety program again.

THE ENTIRE Mineo family was home for Christmas. Sal was exhausted. He tried to rest over the holidays, but he was anxious about the reception of his newest film. He confided in his sister that he was confident, but he felt that his future depended on the success of this picture. In a revealing interview with May Mann, Sal said, "I don't think a writer can portray the real Sal Mineo when I can't even write about my real self. In order to be truthful, you have to detail all the little nuances that are important in your life. I don't think anybody knows me that well. And me, I couldn't reveal some of the things that I treasure in my life."

Sal began 1960 inundated with interviews promoting *The Gene Krupa Story*. On January 3, he and Krupa made a cameo appearance on *The Ed Sullivan Show*, where they introduced a short clip from the film and promoted the Verve Records release of an LP of the soundtrack from the movie. The album placed on the charts within days.

On January 10, Sal turned twenty-one years old. In spite of the momentous occasion, the family birthday celebration was restrained. Everyone, especially Sal, was anxious about the new film. What was most significant about the date, however, was the fact that Sal could legally lay claim to the nearly $150,000 that had been invested in savings bonds on his behalf from his earnings as a youngster.

*The Gene Krupa Story* premiered in New York on February 10. Immediately after the opening, Sal and Mike, accompanied by several family-hired bodyguards and publicists from Columbia Pictures, embarked on a grueling personal appearance tour that covered eleven states in less than three weeks. Gene Krupa was scheduled to join them intermittently.

Reviews were mixed but mostly complimentary of the star. The *Los Angeles Examiner* reported on February 11, "As a more mature Krupa, Sal seems a bit out of his depth, but his handling of the drums is something to see, and hear." The following day, the *Beverly Hills Citizen* review read in part, "I must doff my hat to Sal Mineo . . . this young man is one of the best young screen actors in the business today. His performance here is his finest to date by far, a really expert handling of a role almost too adult for him." *Variety* wrote, "The casting of juvenile looking Sal Mineo in the title role—and while this conception may pay off at the box office, weakens believability in the film. Not that Mineo isn't up to the role. He's excellent, fresh and alive, a frenzied whiz at the drums. As the Krupa of 18, he's real. As the Krupa of 34, he's asked to create too great an illusion."

On February 12, Charles Stinson wrote in the *Los Angeles Times,* "There's a lot of drumming which sounded good because, of course, Krupa does it. And it didn't look too bad either, because Mineo really learned the routines and shows a fair hand with the sticks. Young Mineo is a solidly talented performer and he manages to do a credible job despite the fact that he is just too darned young and healthy-looking to pass for a night club back room dissipant. The eyes are bright and there's not a stubble in a fortnight."

*The Gene Krupa Story* opened wide, simultaneously playing in thousands of U.S. cities. But the box office reception was mediocre. Sal enthusiastically supported the film, making many personal appearances at special screenings around the country. A few days of this grueling schedule sapped his strength. He knew he was overexerting himself, and the tension, pressure, and long hours finally caught up with him. His eye began to hurt him again.

Sal was devastated by the prospect of interrupting a publicity tour to promote an important motion picture for the second time in his career. He didn't want to return home despite his mother's telephone protestations. She had to put his doctor on the phone with her son. The eye specialist warned him that unless he went into seclusion for a month, wore an eye patch, and stayed out of the light, he would need another operation to relieve the pressure on his right eye. Sal went home to recover immediately.

In a telephone interview from his room, Sal told columnist May Mann, "It's just nervous exhaustion. It takes various forms in people, like headaches, collapse, and other nervous disorders. With me it affects my eyes. Once I get used to the pain, it isn't so bad. I lie here very quietly in the dark and think, and listen to music. And I make plans."

# 16.

"I didn't even ask about money. I'd have paid them for a part like this."

On February 25, 1960, the publicity department of United Artists Studios issued a press release to the Associated Press. "In one of the most off-beat castings in recent years, Sal Mineo was today assigned to play Dov Landau, 17 year old survivor of the Warsaw Ghetto and Auschwitz, in the film version of *Exodus*. Mineo, long a teen-aged favorite due to his films, records and TV appearances will be reverting to the kind of acting that made him the youngest performer ever nominated for a best supporting actor award for his role in *Rebel Without a Cause.*"

The long journey from *Exodus* the novel to *Exodus* the film began in May 1958 when Austrian-born director/producer Otto Preminger read Leon Uris's unpublished novel. The book told the sympathetic story of World War II's displaced Jews' determination to have their own state in Palestine, which put them in direct opposition to official British policy. But following World War II, a worldwide outcry led Great Britain (which occupied the Holy Land) and the United Nations to partition the country into Arab and Jewish states on May 14, 1948. The Jews, under the leadership of David Ben-Gurion, declared full independence and the creation of the new Jewish state, called Israel.

Otto Preminger's directorial skills earned him an Oscar nomination in 1944 for his film *Laura*. In 1955, he won the Golden Palm Award at the Cannes Film Festival for his film *Carmen Jones*. His other films included *A Royal Scandal, The Man with the Golden Arm,* and *Porgy and Bess.*

After nearly a year of negotiations, Preminger managed to buy the film rights to *Exodus*. He took the project to Arthur Krim of United Artists, who agreed to back the film with a budget of $3.5 million. Preminger revealed on January 19, 1960, that controversial author Dalton Trumbo had been engaged to write the script.

Casting for the film had already begun when Sal read the controversial bestseller in the summer of 1959. Paul Newman was the first principal player to be cast, followed by Academy Award–winning actress Eva Marie Saint. The international cast eventually included Sir Ralph Richardson, Peter Lawford, Lee J. Cobb, John Derek, Hugh Griffith, Gregory Ratoff, Felix Aylmer, Marius Goring, and David Opatoshu.

When news of his casting was announced in February 1960, Sal admitted that he had been trying for months to snag the role of Dov Landau. In fact, he had all but given up when Preminger called him in to read for it. "The next morning I read for him. He went out of the room for a few minutes and when he came back he said, 'I'll see you in Israel.' I didn't even ask about money. I'd have paid them for a part like this!"

Sal's reputation as a teen idol initially disturbed Preminger. He was reluctant to consider the young actor but was very impressed with his reading. Shortly afterward, Preminger screened *The Gene Krupa Story*. Halfway through the film, he yelled at the projectionist, "Stop! One more reel, and that boy'll be out of *Exodus*."

After a search that lasted more than a year, and just days before shooting was scheduled to begin, fourteen-year-old Sussex-born Jill Haworth was cast as Karen Hansen, Dov Landau's love interest. The five-foot-two-inch blonde won the part over thousands of young girls from around the world who auditioned for the role.

The film is set in 1947, and the story begins in Cyprus, where Jewish refugees have arrived from Germany. Young Dov Landau, an Auschwitz survivor, jumps from a truck transporting him and other refugees to a detention camp established by the British but run by Jews. He is wounded by soldiers and taken to the camp hospital, where he is tended by Karen, a young Danish girl, and an American nurse (Eva Marie Saint). A Jewish sympathizer, Ari (Paul Newman), obtains a ship to take the refugees to Palestine. The refugees, including Dov and Karen, board the *Exodus*, where they stage a hunger strike when a British blockade prevents the ship from departing. The British eventually relent and the ship sails for Palestine. On board, Dov tells Karen he plans to join an anti-British underground called the Irgun. When the *Exodus* arrives in Haifa, Dov seeks out the Irgun but is greeted with suspicion by the group's leader, Akiva (David Opatoshu). During his interrogation, Dov admits to being captured by the Nazis and confined to a death camp when he was barely thirteen years old. There, he shamefully admits, he removed corpses from the gas chambers and dumped them in shallow graves. As Dov weeps, he also is forced to confess that he, too, was brutalized by the Nazis. As he sobs, he says, "They used me. They used me like a . . . woman!" Following his emotional admission, he is accepted by the freedom fighters. Karen falls in love with Dov, who promises to marry her, but one night she is ambushed and killed by Arab militiamen.

In the few weeks between being cast in *Exodus* and leaving for Israel, Sal stayed home and nursed his ailing eye. In light of the lukewarm box office reception of *The Gene Krupa Story,* nothing could keep him from making this film. Josephine's excitement about her son visiting the Holy Land overshadowed her motherly concerns about his safety and the long flight. She arranged for Mike to accompany Sal on the trip. Sal promised to take photographs of Israel and keep a detailed diary of the sacred sites for his mother.

Wearing wraparound sunglasses to protect his right eye, Sal arrived with Mike at the airport on March 13, 1960. He and Eva Marie Saint, who were met by the press, christened the El Al jet *Exodus* with a magnum of champagne.

Eva Marie Saint said, "Back then it was a twenty-hour flight. It was awful. I had two little children with me and there was some kind of mix-up and Sal gave his bunk to us—for the kids. He was a real gentleman."

Their first stop was in London, where they picked up Jill Haworth. Sal was anxious to finally meet the girl who would play his love interest. He wrote to his mother, "I think she is beautiful and charming and only wish she were a little older than 14! She has the prettiest blue eyes I've ever seen. At first she was a little shy when she got on the plane, but I was able to gradually make her feel more at ease."

Jill asked Sal his age. When he told her he was twenty-one, she was crestfallen and said, "I didn't know you were *that* old!"

Despite publicity to the contrary, Jill had never heard of Sal Mineo before meeting him on the plane in London. "They said I was a big fan," she explained, "that I had photographs of him pasted on my walls. But it was a lie. I didn't know who he was. I'd never even heard .of him before. I literally met him on the plane."

After a thirty-minute layover in Rome, they took another four-hour flight to Lod, the international airport outside Tel Aviv. It was after midnight when they finally arrived. A crowd of two thousand people was waiting, and police were needed to escort Jill and Sal to the Dan Hotel.

No soundstages were used for the film. Instead, the film was shot on location or in sets built for the movie. As was Preminger's style, the day shots were shot during the day, and night shots were shot at night. A production office was set up, and an editing facility was constructed so the director could actually edit the film as production progressed. "Mr. Preminger knew what he wanted," Jill explained. "The script was completed before we started and I don't think one word of it was changed during the shoot."

For the next few days, the director rehearsed his actors, one-on-one, in a small dining room in the hotel. The work was intensive, and cast members took advantage of the evenings to unwind. Sal and Mike made the rounds of the nightclubs in Haifa, eventually settling on the Pica Club, a favorite hangout for local youngsters.

In 1960, there was virtually no television available in Israel, but the small country had more than two hundred busy movie theaters. Israelis were passionate about film, and the *Exodus* stars were chased by autograph collectors and mobbed by fans everywhere they went. "Whenever we step out of the hotel there are about two hundred fans waiting for us," Sal said.

The two-month shooting schedule began on March 27 in the ancient port town of Haifa, located ninety miles from Tel Aviv. Shot around Paris Square in the center of town, the relatively simple scene involved Sal as Dov Landau wandering through the town's narrow streets. Thousands of onlookers crowded the streets, rooftops, windows, and balconies and watched in awe as the plaza was dressed to look as it did in the spring of 1947—teeming with British soldiers and the Palestinian constabulary.

"When I got the role of Dov," Sal said, "I wasn't quite sure such a character really existed. But now I've met Dov not once but a hundred times over. You can meet him anywhere in Israel, a tough guy who thinks he can move mountains and who sometimes does."

A few days later, Sal filmed the love scene with Jill Haworth. Sal recalled, "Mr. Preminger can be so harsh at times, and so gentle on other occasions. 'I want you to be two real kids who forget all about the troubles you've had,' he told us before we went into the scene in which she offers herself to me in a ditch and I turn her down because I want us to get married first. He showed her how the scene should be played, and she reacted beautifully."

"Mr. Preminger could bark," Jill explained. "Sal was afraid of him. Very respectful of him, but fearful. He witnessed his temper and outbursts. I don't remember that Mr. Preminger ever yelled at Sal, but he was strong with him at times. And Sal worked so hard, he was so earnest and wanted to do his best."

Eva Marie Saint said, "Sal was a wonderful actor. Very hardworking and dedicated and completely prepared. He was concerned with every little nuance. He was very friendly and playful, and got along with everybody. Sal was a big surprise to me. I wasn't surprised at all that he stole the picture."

Israel's war for independence was still fresh in people's minds, and tensions were ever present between the Jews and Arabs in the area. *Exodus* the book was a big seller in the region and instilled a lot of emotion and agitation among the different factions. Throughout the production, Israeli forces had to increase security around the film company. When filming moved to the Gan Dafna village site, students in Nazareth tossed mimeographed protests and stoned the cast and crew as they drove to and from the dusty town.

Security was stepped up around the film company and bodyguards were assigned to watch over the stars. Sal was ordered to stop waterskiing in the nearby Sea of Galilee. "Syrian snipers on the shore were going to use me for a target," Sal said.

The political tensions and internal strife intrigued rather than frightened Sal. "Israel has been many things for me," he explained. "Reliving the Bible where it actually took place can be awe inspiring. Standing on a hostile border and knowing that one wrong step can get you into serious trouble spells excitement."

Sal's interrogation scene opposite David Opatoshu, a veteran stage actor, was shot in the old Acre prison, now used as a mental hospital. Shot in one day, the scene is a defining moment in the film and one Sal was especially proud of. Rehearsals had been grueling. "Everyone hoped Sal could keep up with David," Jill recalled. "And he did."

The subject matter of *Exodus* was sobering; so was the dictatorial director. There was no levity on a Preminger set. Still, the actors managed to eke out some fun. One evening, Sal joined Paul, Eva Marie, and fellow actors Michael Wager and Alexandra Stewart at a restaurant. A highlight of the meal was the cast's impersonations of Preminger. Eva Marie felt Paul and Sal were the best. Sal loved to impersonate the director's distinctive accent. "SOL!" Sal barked, "SOL! STAND!"

"The funny thing was," Sal said, "the next day on the set, Mr. Preminger very calmly said to us, 'Did you have fun last evening?' He always knew what was going on, even behind his back!"

Being on unfamiliar soil didn't hamper Sal's pursuit of beautiful women. Sal and Mike quickly earned the reputation of being after-hours Romeos with local young ladies. "But where Sal just talks about his conquests," Eva Marie said, "Mike is making all the progress."

The few times Jill was allowed to watch the proceedings on the set, she watched Sal in action. "I could see him flirting with so many girls," she said. "And I heard the girls standing nearby saying, 'He went home with her last night,' or 'He went home with another girl the night before.' Mr. Preminger kept us apart.

"Mike just hung around the set," she added, "and sold Sal out to the press for a price." Jill told Sal she missed her dogs back home. He bought her a little wobbly-legged donkey at an Arab market in Beersheba. "Sal put the donkey through a car wash before he gave it to me," Jill explained. "I called it Buddy. Mike set up a photo shoot with us and the donkey for a movie magazine. He was always mucking things up. I had Buddy for two days in my suite but the hotel people took it away from me when Mike spilled the beans."

THE FILM cast stayed at the King David Hotel for the last twelve days of shooting in Israel. "Sal and I had tea with Prime Minister Ben-Gurion at the hotel," Jill recalled. "In the middle of it all, some men in suits came up and whispered in Ben-Gurion's ear. His face went white, and he excused himself and left. That was the day the Israelis captured Nazi war criminal Adolf Eichmann in Buenos Aires."

On June 1, the company flew to Cyprus for the final scheduled three weeks of shooting. With telephone communication very difficult, Josephine relished her son's telegraphed travel stories. Without Sal's knowledge, she edited his tales and sold the "Israel Diary" to *Silver Screen* magazine for later publication.

# 17.

> "I wasn't really happy anymore, and I was
> frightened by all the responsibilities."

In the midst of film production in Israel, Sal won his most sardonic award. *The Harvard Lampoon,* published in Cambridge, Massachusetts, by the university's students, printed its annual tongue-in-cheek selections for "movie worsts of the year" on April 1, 1960. Sal and Lana Turner won the so-called Hasty Pudding Award as the worst actor and actress of the year.

The *Lampoon* reported that Sal was "honored" for his performance as an American Indian in *Tonka,* and Turner for her appearance in *Imitation of Life.* Sal was delighted with the irreverent award. For days, his friends and fellow actors ordered pudding for his dessert when dining out in Israel.

SHOOTING RESUMED on June 4, 1960, in Famagusta, Cyprus. The company moved into the Constantine, an oceanfront hotel in the old city, located on the east coast of Cyprus.

"I had more freedom in Cyprus," Jill said. "Peter Lawford had the room above me and we managed to have fun. We went sightseeing and had dinners with Sal after shooting during the day. It was looser than in Israel, less security concerns I believe."

One of the most important "castings" had been done by Preminger in Cyprus. He chartered a run-down Greek freighter called the *Olga* for the role of the ship *Exodus.* The 1,700-ton vessel had a rusty hull and a wheezing engine. It was exactly the type of small, neglected craft the Jews had bought or chartered for their attempts to run the British blockade and reach Palestine.

"Most of our work was done on the ship," Jill remembered. "It was shot 'boat to boat.' Mr. Preminger and the cameras were on a boat next to the one we were on. It was over one hundred degrees. It smelled so bad. There were just two bathrooms on the boat, and it was awful.

"I began to feel terrible that the movie was coming to an end. Everyone else was looking forward to going home. I wasn't. I wanted to stay there with all my new friends. I was afraid I'd never see them again.

"The last shot done was of me and Sal. I was talking about the king of Denmark. Sal was afraid I would cry on camera. He was stamping on my foot all the time so I wouldn't cry and when I looked at him in the corner of my eye *he* was actually tearing up."

When production of *Exodus* ended in mid-June, Sal and Mike flew to Italy for a short vacation. The Italian paparazzi dogged the young star everywhere he went. Accustomed to the discriminating coverage afforded by the American press, Sal was mortified by their aggressive tactics.

Sal had become increasingly concerned with his brother's heavy drinking and subsequent embarrassing behavior in public. Mike had caused several unpleasant incidents in Israel and had charged hundreds of dollars' worth of bar tabs and restaurant checks to his brother. The situation reached a critical point one evening in Rome.

Mike and Sal had a late-night dinner on the Via Veneto. Mike met thirty-three-year-old Eva Bartok, a Hungarian-born actress, at the restaurant bar. They both proceeded to get drunk. Mike made a scene, scuffling with a man who flirted with Bartok. Sal angrily put his brother in a cab and instructed the driver to take him back to their hotel. Bartok was too inebriated to drive, so Sal took her keys, helped her to her car, and graciously attempted to drive her home. The paparazzi were in hot pursuit. The actress made Sal stop along the way at a nightclub, where she drank even more and became unruly. Sal finally managed to get her out of the club. Fed up with her antics, he gave a parking attendant a handful of cash to drive Bartok home.

Preminger was outraged when photographs of Sal and a disheveled Bartok slouched in the front seat of her sports car appeared on the front page of European newspapers, the actress's three-year-old daughter's booties dangling from the rearview mirror. Bartok, twelve years Sal's senior, had recently divorced her fourth husband, actor Curd Jürgens. She had spent a few years in a German concentration camp as a young girl. At fourteen, she had married a Nazi officer. The flap was especially compromising since Sal was portraying a Jewish freedom fighter in *Exodus*.

Sal and Mike flew to Madrid on the way home. They spent several days there while Sal discussed a role in *El Cid* with some European producers. "It just didn't work out," he said. "I turned it down. I'm still undecided. I suppose people will think I'm crazy, but I'm afraid to do just a lot of pictures. I just want a good part."

Laden with gifts for his family and, according to Sal, "a dozen $250 Italian suits and silk ties" for himself, Sal returned to New York in mid-July 1960. His feeling of professional satisfaction after a couple of years of less-than-satisfying work was tempered by the news that greeted him in Mamaroneck. Financial obligations had overwhelmed the young star's bank account in his absence. Josephine told her son his earnings from *Exodus* had been consumed by debt, and monetary resources were at an all-time low. In addition, the money previously released to him on his twenty-first birthday, which Josephine could then access, had nearly all been spent during his absence.

In spite of the disheartening news, Sal told his mother he would not let financial needs influence his choice of work from then on.

Shortly after returning home, Sal was a guest on Mike Wallace's interview program. He told Wallace he considered the role of Dov in *Exodus* "the first great part I've had since *Rebel Without a Cause*. In between, I made commercially successful movies—a couple were good. But now," Sal told the reporter, "I'm determined to accept only the choicest roles even if it means choosing unemployment."

For the next several months, Sal stayed in Mamaroneck. His unwieldy debts and familial responsibilities consumed him. Federal and state tax liens were served against him for failure to properly report and pay withholding and social security taxes for the monies paid his family members for the four preceding years. As a result, he owed tens of thousands of dollars to the Internal Revenue Service and the state of New York.

Despite his dire financial situation, Sal still felt responsible for his parents, who had come to depend upon his earnings. No matter how hard he had worked, though, there didn't seem to ever be enough money. And other than the mansion his family occupied, he had little to show for his efforts. He took long, solitary walks on the beach near his house. Nightmares woke him in the middle of the night.

"It seems," Sal said, "that when one thing goes wrong, everything does. My life had been so simple before. Now it was like a sweater that had started to unravel. I had been happy before. I wasn't really happy anymore, and I was frightened by all the responsibility."

"I HADN'T seen or heard from Sal since we left Cyprus," Jill explained. "My only contact was through Tom Ryan, who worked for Mr. Preminger. He'd tell me, 'Sal sends his love.' "

Accompanied by her mother and father on an El Al flight from London, Jill arrived at New York's Idlewild Airport at four in the morning on December 9. Preminger had asked her to attend the *Exodus* premiere. This was her first trip to America. In spite of the early hour, photographers and press representatives from United Artists were waiting. "Sal met me at the airport. He had white roses, and I was exhausted after the long flight," Jill said. With only a few days before the premiere, Sal promised to "help [her] grow up" and make her as "American-like" as anybody else.

Jill and her parents joined Sal in a waiting limousine and were driven to the Gotham Hotel on Fifty-fifth Street in New York. Sal had moved out of the Mamaroneck mansion and taken a room in the hotel shortly after the Thanksgiving holiday. He explained to his parents that he was accommodating a hectic upcoming publicity schedule. He would never live in the mansion again.

The days leading up to the premiere were filled with interviews and photo sessions. "We were driven all over the place," Jill said. "It was exhausting. I didn't even know where I was most of the time. We were taken to radio stations and television studios. Usually, Sal and I were interviewed together."

The December 12, 1960, issue of *Life* magazine featured a beautiful color photograph of Sal and Jill from the film *Exodus*. They gazed into each other's eyes as their foreheads touched. "We were recognized everywhere," Jill said, "people looking and pointing at us."

By mid-October, the advertising campaign for *Exodus* launched six months before the opening had generated $1 million in advance ticket sales. Screenings in New York were already sold out for the first several months of the run. The invitation-only world premiere of *Exodus* attracted thousands of people at the Warner Theatre in New York City on Thursday, December 15. Sal attended with Otto Preminger, Peter Lawford, David Opatoshu, and Jill Haworth.

Jill recalled, "That was the first time I saw the film. I didn't think it was me up there on the screen. I remembered the making of the film, but it was a bit like watching home movies. By that time, Sal was bigger than life to me, but that was because I thought he was *my* Sal."

Sal and Jill flew to Chicago for the opening at the Cinestage Theatre on Friday evening, December 16. They spent one afternoon and evening at the Drake Hotel overlooking Lake Michigan. "Don't think we even saw the lake," Jill said. "We worked on interviews every single moment there."

They arrived in Los Angeles on December 17 and took rooms at the Beverly Hills Hotel. Mike Mineo shared a room with Sal, and Jill shared a suite with her mother and father. The next evening, Sal and Jill attended a Hanukkah banquet to benefit the Jewish National Fund at the Beverly Hilton Hotel in Beverly Hills and accepted an award on behalf of Otto Preminger.

The days were filled with press conferences. "There was barely time to eat," Jill added. "But afterward, in the evening, we did have fun and laughed together about all the things going on."

*Exodus* premiered at the Fox Wilshire Theatre in Beverly Hills on Wednesday evening, December 21. Sal, Jill, and her parents took a red-eye flight to Miami following the screening. *Exodus* premiered in Florida on the evening of Thursday, December 22, at the Sheraton Theatre in Miami Beach. "We were interviewed by Larry King there," Jill recalled. "He had a radio program. That was one of our busiest days. We were to dance together at a dinner following the premiere. I had to pick out a gown, and we had waltz lessons just before leaving for the evening. Sal couldn't dance."

"I TOLD Sal I wanted to see snow," Jill recalled. "There had been none in London when we left and I wanted to see snow. He said, 'Don't worry, you'll see plenty in New York.'

"When we got back to New York, it had indeed snowed. It was freezing cold. People were going down Fifth Avenue on skis. We spent Christmas at Mamaroneck. The house was huge. It was filled with so many people, cousins and uncles and aunts. I'd never seen such a big family. Sal gave me a gold bracelet made of entwined hearts from Tiffany. It was beautiful. He drove me back to Manhattan and he scared me to death. His driving was awful. He drove so fast.

"There was no work, no publicity to do between Christmas and New Year," Jill explained, "so we had time to be together in Manhattan. He showed me around. We took a hansom cab ride in the snow through Central Park. He was always holding my hand. It was beautiful.

"We had Italian dinners in restaurants in Manhattan, and we went to the Copacabana nightclub. It was the most perfect five days of my life. Mike drove my parents to Mamaroneck for New Year's Eve. They actually stayed there a couple of days. Sal took me to actress Ina Balin's apartment for a party on New Year's Eve. It was a nice, small party, but Ina wasn't too nice to me. She might have resented me. She and Sal had had an affair before. We left her place before midnight and went to my suite at the Gotham Hotel."

That night, fifteen-year-old Jill lost her virginity to Sal.

"It was just a natural progression. Sal had become more and more affectionate with me since I arrived in America. We laughed at the same things. We were in on it together in a way. He was very affectionate with me in private, but very gentle, as if he was afraid of me. In public, he was very gregarious and held my hand and threw his arm around me for the press. He had kissed me in Los Angeles and Miami in the evening, before going to his room. With his mouth open, and I was shocked. I'd never done that before.

"We stayed in my room that night. Sal was very passionate, but nothing happened against my will. He was so sweet and protective of me, I could have said no. And I didn't. He did not take advantage of me. I was young, but it just progressed to that stage. After intercourse, Sal carefully checked the bed for blood. I didn't know a thing about sex and didn't fully understand what he was doing or why. I guess he wanted to make sure he was my first lover, which was ridiculous. I was fifteen; I don't know what he was used to.

"The next morning we had breakfast in bed. Sal ordered room service. We had four days without anyone bothering us. I talked to my mother and asked how she was. She said my father and Mike were drunk, and the house was so big she got lost finding her room."

WITH A production budget of $4 million, *Exodus* grossed $21,750,000 in U.S. rentals within months of release. Sal garnered the greatest reviews of his career. The *Los Angeles Times* wrote, "Mr. Mineo demonstrates impressive resources of emotional power. Preminger raved to me particularly about Sal Mineo's portrayal." The *Los Angeles Mirror* concurred: "Sal Mineo is the acting surprise of the film with his touching portrayal of the tempestuous youth named Dov." The *Oregon Journal* wrote, "Winning honors for himself is Sal Mineo as Dov Landau, the hate-filled teenager who makes use of experience forced on him while a victim of Nazi brutality and horror in concentration camps." The *Hollywood Citizen* singled out Sal's work: "Sal Mineo, who at times gets carried away with his meaty role, has moments of illumination." And *Newsweek* reported, "Preminger has got generally good performances from Newman, and Eva Marie Saint, and a fine one from Sal Mineo, as a haunted, hate-filled survivor of Auschwitz."

The entertainment trade papers praised Sal's work. The *Hollywood Reporter* wrote, "Sal Mineo is very moving." *Variety* added, "Sal Mineo is excellent."

Bosley Crowther wrote in the *New York Times* on December 16, "The character of Dov Landau, played superbly by Sal Mineo, is absolutely overwhelming." On December 25, Crowther included *Exodus* as one the year's top ten best films in his annual list for the *New York Times*.

The *New Yorker,* however, took a dim view of the film, and Sal's performance in particular. "We are asked to believe that Sal Mineo is a terrorist capable of blowing up half of the King David Hotel; to me, he doesn't look old enough to have mastered a zip gun."

ON JANUARY 3, 1961, Sal was a guest on *The Jack Paar Show.* Broadcast live on NBC-TV from New York, the late-night talk show was hosted by Joey Bishop, who filled in for a vacationing Paar. Jill watched the broadcast from her hotel room as Bishop asked Sal what he'd done for New Year's Eve. Sal said, "I rang it in with a bang!"

Sal read from chapter 5 of Exodus from the Bible on *The Ed Sullivan Show* on January 8, and on January 10 was interviewed by Barry Gray on radio station WMCA in New York. Sal and Jill then traveled to a number of cities, beginning with Pittsburgh, to promote the film. "We were big in Oklahoma," Jill remembered. "We got keys to all the cities, plaques, citations, and rubber-chicken dinners everywhere. It was one big blur."

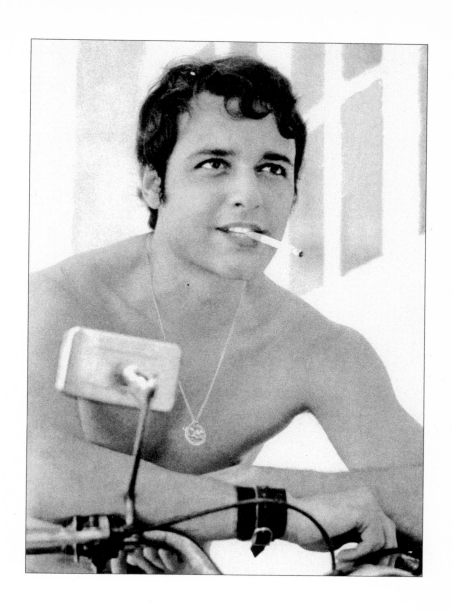

# PART THREE

# FREEDOM

Sal, France, 1965

# 18.

"That was *my* fucking Oscar."

Sal wasted little time taking control of his career choices. He arrived in Hollywood in early February 1961 and tested unsuccessfully to play opposite Rossano Brazzi in the MGM production of *Light in the Piazza,* and turned down the starring role in *The Mickey Cohen Story.*

In a bold move, Sal canceled a production development deal he had with 20th Century Fox. The deal was fashioned as an inducement to secure his 1959 appearance in *A Private's Affair* for the studio. During the following two years, the studio had rejected every idea Sal proposed. "They saw me only as a teenage cutup," he complained. He also refused a lucrative offer to star in a Western-themed television series playing a "good outlaw."

"I'm not a good businessman," Sal admitted. "I'm an actor, and I have to do what I feel, especially now. And if that means being self-unemployed until the right role comes along, then that's what I'll do."

Sal admitted that all his decisions weren't foolproof, though. "I made one mistake—records. I let myself be talked into singing. It was the worst thing that could have happened to me. I cut down on my movie work and found myself doing something I really didn't care about. What I did care about—acting—was neglected. I wish I'd never made a record at all."

The acting experience from *Exodus* was stimulating and transformative for Sal. "I'm determined to prove to people and myself that I'm somebody," Sal said to reporter Don Alpert of the *Los Angeles Times.* "I think the most important thing is for a person to respect himself before others will respect him. Until *Exodus,* I hadn't made a picture I was really proud of since *Rebel.* Now I hope people give me back the respect I want as an actor."

Sal told the reporter what his biggest goal was. "I guess to be very happy someday. It will probably take many years to find out what it will take to make me happy. I haven't found that intangible thing."

---

DURING THE winter, Sal appeared in an original dramatization written by Robert Crean and produced for NBC-TV by Robert Alan Aurthur, *Cry Vengeance!* He was paid $5,000 for the one-hour special.

*Cry Vengeance!* was set against the last days in the life of a tormented Sicilian bandit. Sal was cast as Andrea, a member of a Sicilian gang of outlaws who betrays his gang leader. The television play was directed by Sidney Lumet, who had been nominated for an Academy Award for Best Director for the 1957 film *12 Angry Men.*

"Andrea is a role an actor can really get his teeth into," Sal explained. "Good dramatic impact, good writing, good character development. That's important. I don't like to play a guy who never changes."

*Cry Vengeance!* was the first dramatic television appearance Sal had made in three years. Like *Dino,* which was originally broadcast on television and later produced as a feature film, *Cry Vengeance!* suggested the same potential to Sal.

As he prepared for *Cry Vengeance!* his performance in *Exodus* continued to generate a positive buzz in Hollywood. Critics and journalists declared his performance one of the best of the year. There was talk about an Academy Award nomination. Otto Preminger did not campaign for awards, so Sal hired a publicist to promote him for nomination.

SAL WAS staying full-time at the Gotham Hotel in New York City as he searched for a Manhattan apartment. "Sal wanted to be independent," Jill recalled. "He wanted to be on his own, which was funny because he didn't really like being alone."

Jill joined Sal on Sundays when he drove to Mamaroneck. "He hated to go," she said. "We drove out there for a big dinner. He didn't want to be there but felt obligated to spend some time with his family. He told me he didn't like that house."

Being an only child raised by rather reserved English parents, Jill was unaccustomed to loud, demonstrative families like the Mineos. "They were overwhelming," Jill explained. She noticed that the topic of family conversation had nothing to do with Sal's professional life or experiences. Table talk concerned more ordinary, mundane subjects that did not interest Sal.

"Sal seemed very uncomfortable being around his family," Jill recalled, but his love for his father was very apparent. "He told me his father was an artist," Jill said, "a wood-carver. He could whittle figures and characters from little pieces of wood. He carved me a Minnie Mouse once. He was everything a person could want in a father."

Sal's mother was another matter. Jill found Josephine to be "almost frightening." There was no doubt who ran the household. "It made your skin crawl the way Josephine treated Sal's father," Jill explained. "She demeaned him all the time. It bothered Sal very much, but he never talked back to his mother. He took his father's attitude: just ignore her. For him, it would go in one ear and out the other. He smiled a little but didn't listen to her at all."

AFTER COMING to terms with his staggering debt, Sal made the difficult decision to transfer the management of his career and finances to a New York–based lawyer named Louis Harris. Harris immediately pulled in the reins. Sal continued to cover the costs of the Mamaroneck house, but he no longer directly supported his siblings. No further monies were funneled into the casket company. And Josephine was no longer able or entitled to tap 15 percent of her son's earnings. Though she tried, she was never involved in Sal's business dealings or choices again.

Sal never talked about the overwhelming nature of his financial problems in public. What hurt him most, he told his closest friends, was the disappointment he felt that his family had not protected him from financial ruin. "I was a kid," he said, "and I depended on them to take care of things."

Critics who had placed Sal's performance on the short list for Oscar contenders proved correct. On February 28, 1961, Sal received his second Academy Award nomination for Best Performance by an Actor in a Supporting Role for *Exodus*, making him the youngest performer in history to receive two acting nominations. Surprisingly, the film received only two other nominations: one for Best Music/Scoring, and one for Best Color Cinematography. Sal's fellow supporting-actor nominees included Peter Falk, Peter Ustinov, Chill Wills, and Jack Kruschen.

Sal returned to Los Angeles in early March. "Even before *Exodus* was released," he told Erskine Johnson, a reporter for the *Los Angeles Mirror*, "I had a good idea that this was 'it.' "

On March 16, Sal won the Best Supporting Actor award for his performance in *Exodus* at the annual dinner of the Hollywood Foreign Press Association Golden Globe Awards in Beverly Hills. First presented in 1944, the Golden Globe Awards had since been presented annually to television and motion picture actors and actresses. Sal attended the glittering and star-studded banquet in the International Ballroom of the Beverly Hilton Hotel with actress Joan Staley, *Playboy* magazine's November 1958 Playmate centerfold.

"First I was America's favorite juvenile delinquent," Sal joked, "now I'm all things Jewish." In late March, Sal was honored by the Valley Chapter of Hadassah at Temple Beth Hillel in North Hollywood, California. As part of the celebration, Sal was presented a plaque for his portrayal of Dov Landau. In addition, Sal narrated a program of music and interviews for radio station WNBC to celebrate Israel's thirteenth anniversary as a nation. The program aired on the evening of Sunday, April 23.

The day before the Academy Awards presentation, *Los Angeles Times* entertainment reporter Philip K. Scheuer predicted that Sal would win the Oscar for his performance in *Exodus*. He was not alone in his belief. Industry insiders considered it "a given" that the young actor would be recognized by his peers and awarded the prized statuette. The first Academy Awards presentation in thirty-three years to take place outside the city of Los Angeles happened in the sleek Santa Monica Civic Auditorium on Monday evening, April 17.

Sal attended the awards celebration with actress Tuesday Weld. He was anxious, filled with celebratory optimism, and confident he would win an Academy Award. But the first and only real surprise of the evening came with the announcement of the Oscar for Best Supporting Actor. Peter Ustinov won for his performance in *Spartacus*. Sal was dumbstruck. He said he remembered nothing more of the ceremony.

With a hollow smile frozen on his face, Sal posed for photographers while he stood numbly beside Weld, who found herself answering questions on his behalf. Reporting from the festivities, Dick

Kleiner said that Sal looked glum over losing to Ustinov. Sal told the reporter that his friends in New York had bet several thousand dollars that he'd win. "Even a chic and smiling Tuesday Weld on his arm failed to lift his spirits," Kleiner wrote.

Following the presentation, Sal made a token appearance at the Governor's Ball but decided to skip the formal dinner. After returning Weld to her home, Sal was driven to his hotel in Beverly Hills. Alone, Sal walked the deserted city streets for several hours.

"Mr. Preminger did not want me to be with Sal," Jill explained, "so I didn't go with him to Los Angeles for the awards. He didn't want us socializing together at all. He didn't approve, and I was under personal contract with him. He told me that Sal was too old for me. But this didn't discourage Sal in the least, and it certainly made him more appealing than ever to me.

"Sal called me at five in the morning after the awards. I was in New York. 'Did you watch?' he asked me.

"I said, 'Yes. You looked beautiful.'

"He said, 'No I didn't. And can you believe the one thing that won was the music! Did you see me lose?'

" 'You didn't lose,' I told him.

" 'I lost. Oh, well. Next time.' Then he said, 'Did I really look good on camera?'

" 'Yes, you did,' I said."

BROADCAST THE night after the Academy Awards presentation, Sal's return to television drama with *Cry Vengeance!* was critically disappointing. John Shanley of the *New York Times* called it "disjointed and obscure, handicapped by acting that was too intense and production that was artificial and cumbersome."

Cecil Smith of the *Los Angeles Times* was kinder. "The play profited by some lusty acting—by young Sal Mineo—the kind of acting you rarely see on the little tube anymore."

It was an innocuous comedy that brought the young actor back to the stage. Sal accepted the starring role in the play *Operation Mad Ball* at the Casa Manana Theatre in Fort Worth, Texas, for a week, beginning April 26. Still stinging from his Oscar loss, the play provided a slight distraction. His foray into theater-in-the-round took him out of town and away from the watchful eye of critics. Sal said, "I've never done a comedy so I'm doing it in Fort Worth and no one will know how bad I am. I won't even be nervous there."

Sal flew to Texas on April 19 to begin rehearsals for *Operation Mad Ball*. The play, written by Arthur P. Carter, told the story of Private Petrelli (Sal), who schemes to produce a madcap dance to celebrate the closing of an army surgical hospital at the end of World War II while evading his controlling commanding officer and winning the heart of a beautiful nurse.

The theater, located about forty miles from Dallas, employed a resident company of actors. Mr. America 1960, Gene Shuey, was a member of the company and had a role in the play.

"For about a week we rehearsed in the evenings in the theater," Shuey recalled. "Sal had a good, approachable presence. It was like he was everybody's little brother there. I thought there was a lot of the Plato character in Sal. I would say that he was unsure of himself. There seemed to be something missing in his personal life. He was looking for a friend, somebody he could confide in."

The producers launched an aggressive and very successful advertising campaign in anticipation of Sal's appearance. The play ran from Wednesday, April 26, through Saturday, April 29, to sold-out audiences. Sal had hoped *Operation Mad Ball* would be a vehicle he could take to Broadway, but the play proved to be dated and too weak.

SAL WON a Laurel Award, decided upon by industry insiders, with the results published in *Motion Picture Exhibitor* magazine, for his role in *Exodus*. Hedda Hopper wrote, "He has a highly individual face, dark beauty with a reservoir of power behind it. Directors who've worked with him say he has a versatility which usually comes much later in an actor's career. He can be cruel, deliberate, pathetic or naïve, but sometimes has the smile of a child. He has been acting since he was eleven. He's 22 now, the youngest actor to have two Oscar nominations."

Neither the award nor her kind words appeased Sal's bitter disappointment at losing the Oscar that he felt he had earned and deserved.

"That was *my* fucking Oscar," he griped.

# 19.

"By the adult roles I have played I hope I'm convincing my fans that I'm no longer a child star."

On May 4, 1961, the *New York Times* reported from France, "The gala opening of the fourteenth Cannes Film Festival included the feature presentation of the American entry, *Exodus*, shown out of competition. Otto Preminger, its producer and director, headed a twenty-five-man delegation representing the film at its first screening outside the United States."

Sal and Jill accompanied Peter Lawford and his wife, Patricia Kennedy Lawford, on the flight from New York to France. They arrived in the Mediterranean resort city several days before the film festival began.

"I was kept in my room at the Carlton Hotel out of the public eye," Jill said. "Sal stayed on another floor. We were not seen together except at the opening."

The famed film festival drew journalists and photographers from around the world. The public's fascination with the newly elected President Kennedy made his sister Patricia as popular as the film's stars.

"The press hounded Pat Lawford as well as Peter," Jill recalled. "I was terrified at the opening. Sal held my hand so tight. People were hanging off the roofs. We were all overwhelmed by the attention and the photographers."

After several days in Cannes, Sal, Jill, Peter and Patricia Lawford, and the Premingers flew to England to attend the London premiere of the film on May 9 at the Astoria Theatre. Their reception in Britain was nothing less than raucous, and the film received rave reviews.

Jill and Sal found themselves on magazine covers on the London street stands. *Films and Filming,* a British film review, featured a romantic photograph of the two young stars embracing. "Mr. Preminger tried to keep his eye on me, but it didn't always work," Jill said. "Sal and I still managed to find time to be together."

From London, the Preminger party returned to France for the Paris premiere. On May 17, *Exodus* was shown in two large-screen theaters on the Champs-Élysées. Jill recalled, "Photos of Sal and I were plastered all over the newsstand in front, on the cover of *Paris Match.*"

Before Sal and Jill returned to America, the *New York Times* reported on May 24 that Sal had signed to star with his old friend Yul Brynner in the film adaptation of the novel *Appointment in Zahrain,* written by British author Michael Barrett. The adventure novel centered around condemned prisoners in a strife-torn Middle Eastern country who narrowly miss their scheduled execution by escaping in a stolen ambulance with a nurse as hostage. Robin Estridge was hired to write a script, which he completed on March 16, 1961. The newly titled *Zahrain* was purchased by producer and two-time Academy Award nominee Ronald Neame.

Sal was in need of a job. Earlier in the year, he had contacted Brynner for professional advice. Sal had always credited Yul with helping him understand the art of acting. Soon afterward, Sal was offered the role of a young Arab outlaw in *Zahrain.* "Sal was cast at Yul's insistence," Brynner's son, Rocky, recalled. "My father said Sal was desperate. He badly needed a job and his romance with Jill Haworth, who was so young, was top-grade gossip."

Though filming of *Zahrain* had begun on May 15, Sal was not scheduled to begin work until early June. He found a small, furnished one-bedroom apartment below the Sunset Strip at 8577½ Holloway Drive, rented a sports car, and quickly fell into the daily routine of moviemaking at Paramount Studios.

Sal's searing portrayal of Dov Landau made a lasting impression on audiences but came at a cost. He found himself typecast again and felt he lost a part he coveted in *Lawrence of Arabia* because casting agents wouldn't accept him as an Arab after seeing him as a freedom-fighting Jew. He even told journalist Marcia Borie that he had been accosted in the carport behind his newly rented Los Angeles apartment by a group of thugs wearing swastika armbands.

Being able to play the part of an Arabian freedom fighter in this film, retitled *Escape from Zahrain,* made an otherwise mundane project a little more interesting for Sal. "By the adult roles I have played I hope I'm convincing my fans that I'm no longer a child star," he said.

Despite the exotic locale depicted in the film, all the interior shots were completed on soundstages at the studio. On June 15, the film company moved to the Mojave Desert for location work. Sal said the weather there couldn't have been more searing if they had been on location in Arabia. There was little fun to be had in the crippling heat, so the actors took refuge in their tiny motel rooms at night. Sal listened to records he had brought along and talked with Jill every night on the telephone.

While filming in the desert, Sal was injured when he and costar Madlyn Rhue tripped during a scene, setting off a string of detonating caps used to simulate machine-gun fire. Sal was burned and taken to a local hospital. He was urged to take a few days off but soon returned to the set.

"I first met Yul in Los Angeles," Jill recalled. "Sal had time off the film and I had some time off from Mr. Preminger, so I snuck away. Sal flew me in and I stayed with him in a room he took at the Beverly Hills Hotel. We spent our time with Yul, who was also staying there, and had dinners together and relaxed by the pool."

Production on *Escape from Zahrain* wrapped in mid-August.

ON SEPTEMBER 18, 1961, the *New York Times* reported in an article entitled "Schary to Direct Military Drama" that Sal was considering the starring role in a new play to be produced on Broadway by Dore Schary. He would portray an eighteen-year-old inept but highly articulate soldier, "a precocious, balky, often exasperating boy in his brief but spirited relationship with the Army."

Dore Schary had a long and successful career in motion pictures before turning his attention to Broadway. In 1958, he won the Tony Award as author and producer of the Best Play winner, *Sunrise at Campobello*. The new play, *Something About a Soldier,* would be based on the novel of the same name written by Mark Harris, a respected novelist with several very popular novels to his credit, including *Bang the Drum Slowly*. Ernest Kinoy was hired to adapt the Harris novel to the Broadway stage.

"All the action takes place in an army camp during World War II," Schary explained. "A cast of twenty-five is to unfold the story in fourteen scenes, utilizing highly impressionistic scenery. It's an unusual and what I think is a wonderful story of man's decency even in times of great crisis. The story is told in wonderful comedy terms plus a suddenly moving and warm dramatic tension."

Sal seemed assured of a successful return to Broadway, something he had pursued for the last few years. His career began on the stage, and he felt a return to the theater might reinvigorate his stalled motion picture career. He was very excited by the prospects posed by *Something About a Soldier,* despite the fact he was cast as a teenager, as he had been in *Exodus* as well.

In October 1961, Sal sublet actor Farley Granger's Manhattan apartment. Rehearsals for *Something About a Soldier* began in Manhattan on Wednesday, November 1. Sal looked forward to working with Kevin McCarthy and Ralph Meeker, actors he had admired. The direction, however, was weak ("directionless," Sal complained), and lines were still being written each day as they rehearsed.

Sal had little time to be with Jill in New York. Otto Preminger could not find an immediate project for her, so, exercising the rights provided in their contract, he lent her out to a French production company to star in *Ton Ombre est la Mienne* (*Your Shadow Is Mine*).

"The movie was *in* French," Jill said. "And I couldn't speak French. I think Mr. Preminger just wanted to get me out of New York and away from Sal." Jill and her mother flew to Cambodia for location work. "As far from Sal as we could be," Jill said.

HOW DO you plead?" asked Judge Louis Wallach in Manhattan Traffic Court on November 10.

"On the first speeding offense, guilty," Sal answered. "On the second, not guilty." Sal's reckless driving had finally caught up with him when he was ticketed twice in one hour, and his days of charming his way out of speeding tickets were over.

Immediately, the court levied a $50 fine on Sal's guilty plea. The punishment was severe because it was his second offense. The second speeding charge, which Sal contested, was remanded to a trial set for January 16, 1962.

"I was guilty the first time, but not the second," Sal explained outside the court following his appearance on November 10. A reporter wondered if the double brush with the law soured Sal on New York cops. "I like cops," Sal said. "As a matter of fact, I appeared only recently at a Patrolmen's Benevolent Association affair in New York City. I get along fine with cops—except the ones who are out to get me!"

*Something About a Soldier* opened in Wilmington, Delaware, for one week on December 1, 1961. The play then moved for a one-week engagement to the Forrest Theatre in Philadelphia. On December 18, the military drama opened at the Colonial Theatre in Boston for two last weeks of out-of-town tryouts.

Although the reviews during tryouts were enthusiastic about Sal, in general they were mixed about the play. Nevertheless, the public was responsive, and the box office statistics were encouraging to the producer. *Something About a Soldier* opened on January 3 at the Ambassador Theatre on Broadway.

"Sal and my father called me around New Year's Eve," Jill said. "Sal didn't talk about the play when I asked him, so I knew things weren't going well. Later, he told me there were a lot of problems with that production. On the road, they were writing and rewriting all the time, right through opening night. He was terribly disappointed. Sal was expecting the worst, I think, and that's what he got."

Howard Taubman reviewed *Something About a Soldier* for the *New York Times* on January 5: "Despite its decency of spirit and its literary grace, *Something About a Soldier* is a halting, discursive play. Mark Harris' novel may have made one of its pivotal characters, Pvt. Jacob Epp, a youngster of flesh and blood. In Mr. Kinoy's play he remains a two-dimensional figure. Sal Mineo, who plays him with disarming simplicity and sincerity, cannot make him more than a good basic idea that lacks definition and inflection."

Jack Gaver wrote for United Press International, "The good things in *Something About a Soldier*—humor, sensitivity, perceptive acting—don't add up as effectively as they should. Mineo, who started on Broadway as a child, returns for his first grownup stage role in this, and he is extremely effective. His is a warm and knowing interpretation of a role that could misfire easily in the wrong hands."

Robert Coleman's review in the *New York Mirror* proved to be prophetic. "Episodic, often amusing and often moving. But the over-all effect is not cumulative. There is no real mounting of dramatic tension . . . it sets a fast and funny pace in its first strikes but falters in the stretch. This judge doubts that it has the stamina for a winner."

*Something About a Soldier* failed to draw an audience and closed on January 13, 1962, after only twelve performances.

# 20.

"The part of the Israeli terrorist in *Exodus* did wonders for me. But I wonder if it typed me as a fighting man."

Nervous exhaustion and a deep feeling of disappointment side-lined Sal for days following the premature close of *Something About a Soldier*. His eye condition recurred, which necessitated his wearing a patch over his right eye again. On January 16, 1962, he was convicted in Bronx Traffic Court of speeding for the third time in eighteen months. Judge Maurice Downing found him guilty, imposed a $50 fine, and revoked his New York driver's license for six months. Sal resigned himself to the sentence but was angered by the headline in the *New York Times* on January 17 that read, SINGER'S LICENSE IS REVOKED FOR SPEEDING IN THE BRONX.

"Jesus," he complained, "I haven't sung in three years!"

WHEN FILMING for *Ton Ombre est la Mienne* was completed in late January, Jill and her mother returned to their newly rented Fifty-first Street apartment in Manhattan for a few weeks. Sal and Jill resumed their affair.

"Sal was staying in Manhattan at Lou Harris's apartment on Fifty-fourth Street," Jill recalled. "We spent our time together in the city. It was romantic," she recalled. "We loved to eat at Downey's and Danny's Hideaway. And the Clique on Forty-ninth Street actually put us on the menu. We were an 'item.' The 'Sal Mineo Omelette' included cheese and herbs, and the 'Jill Haworth Omelette' had sweet white grapes and powdered sugar."

Accompanied by her mother, Jill returned to Paris to begin her next French film in February. A short time later, Sal flew to France for a World War II–themed role. With a budget of $10 million (making it the biggest-budgeted black-and-white film in history), *The Longest Day* had begun production in August of 1961 with location shooting in Corsica and Normandy Beach. The film, based on Cornelius Ryan's bestselling book *The Longest Day*, told the story of the D-day invasion of France during World War II from both the Allied and German points of view. The Daryl F. Zanuck production for 20th Century Fox starred more than fifty internationally known actors and actresses. Sal played the role of Private Martini, a member of the Eighty-second Airborne Division. These heroic troops had parachuted behind German lines just hours ahead of the landings by Allied forces on Normandy Beach.

Sal stayed at the Hotel George V in Paris. His three scenes in the film were shot on stages at the Studio de Boulogne, the largest movie studio in France. Two of his three scenes included Richard Beymer, a handsome six-foot-two-inch actor who had appeared in several films, including *The Diary of Anne Frank* and *West Side Story.*

Sal and Beymer, exercising completely different acting techniques ("I have one, he didn't," Sal said), did not get along well on the set. Once their work together had been completed, the two men were scheduled to be interviewed by European newspapers at the hotel. A reporter wanted Sal to play the drums that were set up in an adjacent room and appear to be teaching Beymer how to play. Beymer refused. Then Sal glibly asked him, "How about me giving you a few *acting* lessons then?" Beymer did not appreciate Sal's sense of humor. He angrily stormed out of the room.

With no professional commitments calling Sal back to New York, he decided to stay in Paris for a couple of weeks. "I was staying at the Hotel le Belmont in Paris," Jill explained. "I had a double suite. Sal came to stay. I worked all day, from eight in the morning till five in the afternoon. Sal was bored, I think. He had no work and nothing to do. He was in no hurry to go home, and besides, he didn't really have a home anymore."

In spite of the success of *Exodus,* Sal's celebrity was minor in France. "I had learned to speak French," Jill said. "Sal didn't, and he didn't try. And he felt out of his element there." He was barely recognized in the Paris streets. Newly turned twenty-three, professionally and personally liberated from his family, there was a lot for him to contemplate. He had never been completely responsible for his professional choices before. He was deeply in debt. And the romantic relationship that had developed with Jill was one he had always believed he would avoid.

"Sal would spend time shopping and sightseeing," Jill said, "and he spent a lot of time with my mother when I was busy or too tired to socialize after work. That's when he met Harold Stevenson."

Stevenson, a flamboyant, Oklahoma-born painter, gained a reputation for his large-scale homoerotic paintings and drawings. In early 1962, the diminutive painter became infamous, and, as he has referred to himself, an "expatriot American darling" with Paris society, when his show *Le Sensuel Fantastique,* which featured twenty-four erotic paintings of his male lover, opened at Galerie Iris Clert.

Stevenson said, "I had a large studio in Paris. I had some French friends who met Sal and they brought him to me. They thought he would like to meet another American in Paris. I vaguely knew who he was. I knew he was a movie star, but I didn't really know his films.

"He was wonderfully proportioned. I needed a well-proportioned model for a large-scale painting I was undertaking. It was a tribute to my friend, who couldn't pose because he was too large a man. And a tall man would not be ideal. I asked Sal, 'Would you like to pose for me? It is in the nude?' "

Although Sal liked the low profile he was keeping, he also missed the attention he was accustomed to back home. He was flattered by the request and intrigued. Sal expressed an interest in Harold's work and was shown numerous paintings and drawings of nude male models.

"We talked the rest of the day," Harold recalled. "I think he was struggling to find the truth in his life. To figure out who he was as a person and as a performer. He seemed to be experiencing some sort of identity crisis. He became more and more comfortable with me, though, and finally said yes to my request."

The prospect of shedding his clothes was profoundly symbolic. The fact that he was far away from home helped him decide. He would never have done such a thing in New York. He had truly taken control of his life in a liberating manner. He knew posing nude was something Josephine would never have approved of.

The next morning, Sal returned to the studio. "He took off his clothes and laid on a posing bench," Harold said, "and after a short time, he suddenly went blind!"

Jill's mother took Sal to American Hospital in Paris for treatment. He was given an eye patch to wear over his right eye and told to return to his hotel and rest.

"That chronic condition was brought on by emotional things," Jill recalled. "If something weighed on him or upset him emotionally, he had trouble with his eye. Although he never spoke in detail about his family rift, I knew he was troubled."

Jill's chauffeur drove Sal to Harold's studio each morning, where he posed for hours. He told Jill that Harold was doing sketches of him and undertaking a large painting, but he never told her he was posing nude.

The painting that Stevenson eventually finished was called *The New Adam*. It was a sensual, graceful, seven-and-a-half-foot-high-by-thirty-nine-foot-long nude portrait of Sal lying on his right side. It was painted on linen and mounted on nine panels.

"Sal laid his arm across his face for the painting," Stevenson explained. "I did several sketches before undertaking the actual painting. I drew him frontally nude as well. He was quite comfortable being nude. I did many paintings of Sal in Paris . . . his body, his navel, his eye, his ear . . . and numerous preliminary sketches. He was amazed to see what I had done when he eventually regained his full sight."

"At the same time he did the reclining nude of me," Sal said, "he also did one for me to own. It's about five feet square, just of my navel and below, that general area. And they stopped it at customs because my pubic hair showed."

SAL RETURNED to New York in late March to film a television play for the NBC television series *DuPont Show of the Week*. Written by Oscar-winner Harry Brown, "A Sound of Hunting" told the story of an eight-man rifle squad stationed during World War II at an advance U.S. Army position in Italy. Sal played the role of PFC Charles Coke.

This was Sal's first television appearance in nearly a year, though his film *Tonka* had been serialized into two parts and presented on the Sunday-night series *Walt Disney's Wonderful World of Color*. Retitled *Comanche,* the film had been.broadcast on February 18 and 25, 1962. Sal had politely refused requests by Walt Disney Productions to promote the television broadcast, which nevertheless earned very high ratings.

In an interview to promote "A Sound of Hunting," Sal spoke with reporter Jack Gaver. "The part of the Israeli terrorist in *Exodus* did wonders for me," he said. "But I wonder if it typed me as a fighting man. Last winter I was an American soldier in *Something About a Soldier* on the Broadway stage. I fought again in this television play and I'm under contract to start a movie in July that has me in the Korean conflict." Sal had been cast in a new war-themed film starring Rod Steiger called *They Had to Kill.* The film, written by Steiger and Stanley Shpetner, was set for summer production at Allied Artists.

SAL RETURNED to Paris in early May. By that time, Jill had begun work on her third French film, a swashbuckler costarring Jean Marais, called *Les Mystères de Paris* (*The Mysteries of Paris*). "Sal was a little stunned that I was beginning my third starring film within one year," Jill said.

Though not entered in competition, *Ton Ombre est la Mienne* was scheduled to be shown at the Cannes Film Festival, which opened on May 7. "Sal wanted to be with me at the screening," Jill recalled. "The airline lost his luggage, so he arrived at the hotel with nothing. No clothes but what he was wearing.

"There was no time. He wore white jockey shorts, which he couldn't find in Paris. He actually climbed over the railing of our balcony at the Carlton Hotel to steal a man's underwear on the clothesline on the next balcony. But it was Spyros Skouras's room. He was head of 20th Century Fox Studios. The shorts were too big. Sal actually wore my silk panties to the movie screening at Cannes. His luggage never did arrive, so he shopped for all new things and finally found some jockey shorts."

Following the screening, Sal and Jill returned to Paris. They stayed at the Palais D'Orsay Hotel while Jill returned to work. In the evenings Sal and Jill dined together and sometimes went to the popular Élysées Club. "I went to bed early because I had an early call for the movie," Jill said, "but my mother and Sal would go out late at night. They'd be creeping in when I'd be getting up to go to work in the morning."

Jill became good friends with a man named Sigmond who worked with the costume director on *Les Mystères de Paris.* Jill explained, "Sigmond was gay and a lot of fun, and before Sal came back to Paris, Sigmond and I went out often. We'd have dinner and go dancing."

Sigmond introduced Jill to the popular French singer Gilbert

Bécaud, whose 1961 English-language release "What Now, My Love?" brought him international fame. "Gilbert took me to see Charles Aznavour," Jill said, "and we went to Chez Regine. He was very charming, and he gave me a beautiful bracelet."

One day after work, Jill returned to the suite she shared with Sal at the D'Orsay and noticed that her jewelry box was empty. "The bracelet Gilbert had given me *and* the Tiffany bracelet Sal had given me on our first Christmas were gone," she said. "I asked Sal where my things were. And he said, 'Oh, I guess you were robbed.' I know Sal got rid of them. He was very jealous of Gilbert. He said he was just being protective."

Earlier, Jill had learned that Sal lived by a different standard. "He could come and go as he pleased," she said, "but I couldn't. People didn't notice him in France. He wasn't as popular there as I was at the time. Everyone was falling over me and not him, and he was increasingly uncomfortable with the attention that I got."

One night at the club, Sigmond came to Jill and Sal's table and knelt on the floor to talk with her. He introduced her to his gay friends. They were a flamboyant group and seemingly unimpressed with Sal. "Sal took offense and actually grabbed Sigmond around the neck and strangled him for an instant," Jill recalled. "I couldn't believe it. I was shocked. Sal had a temper. Though he never directed it at me, I witnessed it a few times. But that night I couldn't believe what he was doing."

# 21.

"I like very, very young girls, with small breasts and flat chests."

With his earnings from *The Longest Day*, Sal rented a small, furnished house at 1448 Benedict Canyon Boulevard in Beverly Hills in June 1962. He also rented a new convertible Cadillac. Unfortunately, though, the Rod Steiger film project that brought Sal to the West Coast fell through soon after he arrived in California.

*Escape from Zahrain* was released on June 14. Paramount launched an aggressive advertising campaign, but the general moviegoing public ignored the film. Sal's teeny-bopper fans had outgrown him. The critics, too, were unimpressed. *Variety* dismissed the film in a review on May 30: "Sal Mineo, shirt carefully unbuttoned to show just enough pectoral for he-man stature, rides along with Yul Brynner as an Arab student patriot."

*Escape from Zahrain* moved from first-run movie theaters to drive-in double bills within two weeks of release.

JILL FLEW to California in early July after finishing her films in France. Her mother agreed to the visit on the condition that Jill stay with Sal's friend, producer Marvin Schwartz, and his wife.

"I was trying to stay under Mr. Preminger's radar," Jill explained. "My mother called each Sunday, so Sal would drive me to Marvin's house and we would wait for the call. She never knew if I was really staying there."

Actually, Jill stayed with Sal in the cozy house he had rented on Benedict Canyon. Tucked into the woods in the rustic canyon not far from the Beverly Hills Hotel, the furnished, ranch-style house seemed dwarfed by the massive mansions nearby.

"It was a spooky little house," Jill said. "It had a pool, but it was so filthy I don't remember anyone ever using it. One of the first things Sal did was take me to a gynecologist to get a diaphragm. I didn't know anything about those things. My mother never talked to me about sex.

The first night, I ended up in tears because I couldn't put it in. It was slipping all over the place. Sal had to help me."

Sal and Jill had never spent so much time alone together. "We went out for most meals," Jill said. "At that time, he didn't pay for anything. The restaurant would always pick up our check because they wanted him there."

MICHAEL ANDERSON JR. was truly a child of show business. His father, Michael Anderson Sr., was the Oscar-nominated director of *Around the World in 80 Days*. In 1958, Michael Jr. began his film career in *The Moonraker*, followed by *Tiger Bay* and *The Sundowners*.

In early 1962, he accompanied his father from London to Los Angeles for what he thought would be a short vacation, but he got a part in George Stevens's new film *The Greatest Story Ever Told*.

He took a small apartment while he waited for the film to begin. Originally set for the early summer, the start date was delayed time and again. Eighteen-year-old Michael had nothing to do and knew no one, so an acquaintance of his father suggested he meet Sal. They drove to Sal's house in Beverly Hills. No one was at home, so they waited.

Michael recalled, "Finally, Sal drove up in a white convertible Cadillac with Jill Haworth in the front seat. We heard the car radio playing before they turned the corner. She was just sixteen, but she looked much older, and very beautiful, looking like a real movie star, her blond hair in a ponytail. Sal looked like a movie star, too. I'll never forget what he was wearing . . . a bright red shirt and white pants and sunglasses. We got on like a house on fire."

The three young actors spent the day together, talking and hanging around the house. "Sal wouldn't let me go," Michael said. That evening they went to dinner at Cyrano, a popular gathering spot for the entertainment crowd on Sunset Boulevard. A table set for four was waiting when they arrived at the restaurant. They were seated and handed menus. Another menu was left at the fourth place setting. "We were looking at the menu, and Sal made some suggestions," Michael recalled. "I glanced at the fourth place at the table a couple of times and finally said to Sal, 'Is someone joining us?' Sal looked over his menu at me and casually said, 'No, that's for Jimmy.' I waited a minute and asked, 'Jimmy who?' Sal looked at me with a straight face and said,

'Jimmy Dean.' I looked at him a moment, and then he fell apart laughing. He was a prankster."

After dinner, they returned to Benedict Canyon. "Sal wouldn't let me leave," Michael said. "I told him I had to get back to my place, and Sal said, 'Why? You don't have anything to do there. Stay here with us.' So, I did. I ended up staying for days.

"He was magnetic and very engaging. When he talked with you and looked at you he made you feel like you were the only person in the world. I believe he usually got whatever he wanted. 'Oh, don't go,' he said to me after spending days there. 'Stay . . . please stay. We love you here.' I finally went home to get my clothes and moved in with Sal and Jill."

Though they shared a common profession, Michael said, "We really didn't sit around talking about business or the past. Sal didn't dwell on the past. He lived in the moment. There was no hint of a deprived childhood. He was very bright, but he said he regretted not having more formal school."

Sal and Michael quickly bonded. They spoke freely to each other, but Sal never talked about his family or the circumstances of their growing apart. Sal spoke to his sister and parents by telephone occasionally, but they exchanged only common pleasantries; serious subjects were never broached. "I didn't even know he had a brother named Michael," Michael said. He recalled the only person Sal spoke about with fondness was his father.

"He was fascinated that I had danced ballet," Michael said. "He liked my legs. He was in great shape. He was proud of his body and took care of himself but he thought his legs were skinny. Mine were muscled from dancing and he was very curious about that. He was very aware of his body."

Sal cultivated a seductive style that suited his interest and need for sexual gratification with no strings attached. His sex appeal and the sway it had over others was something he could control, and claiming that power was another step in taking control of his life. He was also obsessed with the topic of sex and sexuality. He loved to talk about sex and delighted in shocking people with sexual innuendo and dirty jokes.

"When we first met," Michael said, "Sal said, 'Oh, the English all are homosexual.' I said, 'No, we're not all homosexual.' And Sal said, 'I was talking to my psychiatrist and he said the British are more sophisticated about sex than Americans. British men get hung up on cock for a short time when they are boys. Americans get hung up on cock forever.' "

Michael and Jill also had something in common. They were both British. "We got along at once," Jill said. "I adored Michael. We had such fun. We made up our own language; Sal thought it was some kind of cockney. We talked and laughed about Sal and he didn't know what we were talking about. I was sixteen and Michael was eighteen. At twenty-three, Sal was the oldest person in the house. Michael and I called him the 'old man.' The three of us had a wonderful, wonderful time."

It was truly an idyllic few months. In spite of his state of affairs, Sal lived with abandon and spent money freely on himself and his friends. He was a popular figure within the industry and attended the most coveted parties in Hollywood. "He seemed to know everyone in Hollywood," Jill said. "I think he was very happy then. In a way, he was Peter Pan . . . he never really grew up."

"He was very comfortable with himself," Michael remembered, "very self-assured. And almost buoyant. He didn't seem to have a care in the world."

Sal developed an interest in the occult, séances, and Ouija boards. "He loved supernatural and paranormal things," Michael explained. "He loved the idea of ghosts." His interest in the paranormal, though, had more to do with perpetrating jokes on unsuspecting friends rather than a real interest in the spiritual world. The Ouija board was a party favor in his house. "He'd say, 'Jimmy Dean is coming through,' " Michael said. "Everyone would fall on the floor. Sal didn't talk very seriously about Dean, he kidded a lot."

"Sal could pull the wickedest stunts on people," Jill recalled.

"One night," Michael said, "Brandon De Wilde came over. Sal brought out a Ouija board after dinner. He was also a practical joker, which always made me suspicious. But this night, we all sat around the Ouija board playing around, Jill, Sal, Brandon, and I. So, we sit at the board and Sal says, 'Let's ask it how we'll die.' First we asked about Brandon. And the board spelled out 'CAR ACCIDENT.' We thought Sal was moving the board, but it was a little odd and spooky.

Then Sal said, 'Let's ask about Jill.' And she would have none of it. She said she didn't like the game and got up and left. Then we asked the board, 'How will Sal die?' And the board spelled out 'SAL WILL BE MURDERED.' Sal had an amazing sense of humor. A real dark sense of humor, really. But it was so strange that night. Then Sal asked about me. I said, 'No, no, I don't want to know,' but he went ahead and it spelled out 'DIE AS AN OLD MAN.'

"It was misty that night. When Brandon was getting ready to leave, Sal slipped out and ran to Brandon's car and wrote with his finger in the misty windshield 'DON'T DRIVE.' When Brandon left the house, after a minute, he ran back and pounded on the door. He was frightened to death and was stammering about the writing on his windshield. Sal collapsed, and we had a great laugh. That was Sal's sense of humor."

Sal liked being a little secretive at times, too. One morning, he left the house for a business meeting. He told Jill and Michael it was very important but wouldn't explain. In the afternoon, he returned and told them he had lunch with George Stevens. "He said it very casually," Michael recalled, "sort of tossed it off. Then he said he'd been cast as Uriah in *The Greatest Story Ever Told*!"

"Well," Sal said to Michael, "now it looks like we'll be working together, too."

During Sal's relationship with Jill, Michael said he never saw Sal with another girl. He loved to flirt, though. When they drove around Los Angeles in Sal's convertible, he'd slow down when he saw a pretty girl to take a better look. "He talked the talk," Michael said, "but I think Sal was true to Jill. She was so young, and I know he felt responsible for her. And they had a hot and heavy sex life. He was a very sexual, very sensual person. And he'd play it up, too, to play with people and shock them. He'd say something so forward and outrageous just to see their expression. And he loved to catch people off guard and ask intimate questions about their sex life."

"I had no experience with sex before Sal at all," Jill said, "but he was certainly experienced. He gave me a 'sex contract.' He wrote it in his hand with all the little misspellings. It was a list of what I could do and what I couldn't do. He signed it and he expected me to sign it, too. One of the rules was I couldn't perform fellatio on any man except him. I thought it was a joke, but I was never sure if he did."

———

AFTER BEING coddled by his mother all his life, Sal possessed no domestic skills. "He couldn't boil water," Michael said. "He lived on coffee and Salem cigarettes. There was no food in the house." Once in a while a guy named Mario who worked as a waiter at Sal's favorite restaurant, La Scala, dropped in to cook. Sal loved good food. Jill and Michael accompanied him out for most meals, beginning with breakfast. At night, they went clubbing at Pandora's Box, the Interlude, Ciro's, the Rendezvous, and P.J.'s. Michael remembered, "Sal would be asked to sit in on the drums often when we were out. They would always announce him in the audience, 'Ladies and gentlemen, Sal Mineo is here this evening.' They would applaud and yell. He loved it. And he loved to play. He'd punch a cigarette in his mouth and get up there and pound away."

Periodically, Sal drove to Hollywood Ranch Market on Vine Street and bought barbecued chicken and a big stack of movie magazines. Back home, he and Jill and Michael sat on the floor to eat and looked for pictures and news about each other in the magazines. "It was a joke," Michael explained. "But Sal got a little annoyed if there wasn't anything about him in the periodicals."

IN EARLY September, Sal gave up the lease on the house in Benedict Canyon in anticipation of going to Utah to work on *The Greatest Story Ever Told*. Michael Anderson Jr. had been called to work earlier for the film, and Jill and Sal returned to New York.

Hillard Elkins was a Broadway producer who befriended Jill in Manhattan. His Weimaraner dog birthed six puppies. He gave Jill one of the puppies. "I named it Dove, because it was dove-gray colored, not after Dov Landau," Jill said. "Sal wanted it so bad."

The puppy tormented Jill. "The dog would bite me, playfully, and pull my hair and wouldn't leave me alone," Jill recalled. "It would pull me out of a chair and pull me out of bed in the morning." She finally called Sal and told him to come and get the dog.

Sal attended the October 4 premiere of *The Longest Day* at the Warner Theatre in New York City. The $10 million production opened nationwide on October 14 to overwhelming international critical acclaim.

*The Longest Day* was included in the list of the top ten films of the year by film critics in more than fifty cities throughout the United States. The National Board of Review named it Best Picture of the Year 1962. Before the end of the year, the film earned more than $39 million in U.S. box office rentals, making it the most successful black-and-white picture in the history of motion pictures.

With so many stars sharing the screen, no one actor was singled out for his performance. The movie itself was truly the star. Nevertheless, Sal was happy to be included.

GEORGE STEVENS purchased the film rights to Fulton Oursler's best-selling 1949 book, *The Greatest Story Ever Told*, in 1960. Oursler had written several bestselling religious-themed books and the popular biography *Father Flanagan of Boys Town*.

Stevens and James Lee Barrett completed the script during the summer of 1962. The renowned poet Carl Sandburg made uncredited, though highly publicized, contributions to the dialogue. According to Stevens, little remained of Oursler's novel in the final script. The soap-opera style of the book was abandoned for a less sentimental one.

Stevens organized his own independent production company and raised his own capital. United Artists committed several million dollars to the venture. To ensure the huge investment and attract other potential investors, the cast included more than forty international top box-office stars. In total, Stevens employed thirty Academy Award winners in front of and behind the cameras. The film had 117 speaking parts and provided five thousand man-days of work for the principal players and thirty thousand for extras.

*The Greatest Story Ever Told* was budgeted at $15 million, making it the most expensive film ever shot in the United States at that time. The Technicolor film was a financial extravaganza, and an albatross. Forty-seven major sets were built on location in Arizona, Nevada, Utah, and at Desilu Studios in Culver City. Wahweap, a tiny town near the Colorado River in Utah, was the home base for the film company. Complete villages of tents, trailers, dressing rooms, production offices, and prefabricated two-bedroom aluminum bungalows were erected to accommodate the film company.

Sal joined Michael Anderson Jr. in Utah in mid-October. Before shooting began, Stevens had prophetically told the press that he was unconcerned with production costs, and he intended to take as much time as he needed. "We sat around doing nothing for weeks," Michael said. "We were bored to death. We played bridge and poker endlessly. Sal kept to himself. He had his own cabin, and he had his dog, Dove. Roddy McDowall showed us pictures he'd taken of Elizabeth Taylor nearly naked in a bathtub on the set of *Cleopatra*. He'd just finished working on that film. We three became chums. To kill the boredom, Roddy took a lot of beautiful photographs of Sal on location."

"Sal called me in New York and said, 'Come to Arizona,' " Jill remembered, " 'it's really boring here.' So I snuck out of town. It was supposed to be our secret. I hardly left his cabin. But Sal got some costume for me and I mingled with a crowd of extras for a shot in the film. We didn't think anyone knew I was there."

Jill quickly returned to New York, though, when Hedda Hopper reported in her November 20, 1962, column in the *Los Angeles Times,* "Sal Mineo won't get lonely on his picture location in Arizona. Jill Haworth flew over. That romance started when they worked together in *Exodus.*"

"I wasn't afraid of a scandal," Jill said. "I was afraid I'd get in trouble with Mr. Preminger."

Stevens had hoped to finish in Wahweap before Christmas, but bad weather scuttled his plans. Many vital scenes remained unshot as the holiday drew near. Occasional snow flurries played havoc with the shooting schedule, and the director feared an unpredictable blizzard might end location shooting. Concern began to mount in Hollywood, as well. United Artists, the distributing company for the film and one of its primary backers, had one eye on the massive, uncontrolled outflow of cash and the other on the small inflow of finished film. In addition, studio executives who observed both the actual shooting on site and the screenings of portions of the film felt that it lacked tension. A pointed memo to Stevens warned that "the picture is on a flat, unemotional level."

The film company broke for a three-day Christmas holiday.

Stevens paid for more than five hundred cast members and personnel to fly to their respective homes, including Sal, who flew to New York to be with Jill.

"Sal brought me a white beaver coat for Christmas," Jill said. "And we went to see *David and Lisa* when it premiered." Sal and Jill had originally been considered to costar as young lovers in the film. "Mr. Preminger vetoed that idea," Jill remembered.

After the short holiday break, Sal returned to camp in Wahweap, newly christened "Fort George Stevens" by disgruntled members of the group. The thermometer dipped to zero at night and reached a high of fifteen degrees during the day. Four inches of snow fell on January 3, 1963, covering the massive Jerusalem set. The following day, a blizzard shut down the location shoot for good. On January 9, Stevens and company returned to Desilu Studios in Culver City.

Studio executives confronted Stevens and forced him to reorganize. Filming progressed at a faster pace at the studio. At the end of February, Sal returned to Wahweap with the film company for additional shooting, but snow and rain continued to plague the production.

Stevens then moved to Pyramid Lake for another three weeks. Located in northwest Nevada, Pyramid Lake is about thirty-five miles from Reno. "One night in Pyramid Lake," Michael said, "Sal and I and Shelley Winters were in the mess tent. We were eating and talking about dating. Sal was sexually insatiable; all he ever thought about was getting laid and talking about body parts and sexual positions. Playing around, Sal said in a husky voice, 'I like very, very young girls with small breasts and flat chests.' And Shelley said, 'Yeah, and the next thing you'll like is really young boys with little *tiny* dicks!' Sal fell on the ground laughing. She had him on that one."

Location shooting dragged on at Pyramid Lake. "One day," Michael said, "Sal went up to Stevens and asked him, 'When do you think you'll be finished with me?' and Stevens said, 'What are you still doing here?' They released Sal, but he had been paid a thousand dollars a day for weeks and weeks and weeks, long past his release date, because no one told him he was finished. Not that he complained about the money."

Sal had actually worked in front of the camera a total of nine full days. He was paid more than $93,000.

## 22.

"Jill is a beautiful girl. She looks like an innocent
devil. She always has the devil in her eyes, and yet
she's very pure."

In January, Sal had rented a small, one-bedroom house in the hills
above Sunset Boulevard at 8564 Hillside Avenue. With his pock-
ets overflowing with cash, he leased a red Corvette convertible
and bought a Harley-Davidson motorcycle, which he parked in the
living room.

He enjoyed the nightlife the Sunset Strip offered, and he relished
the attention his celebrity attracted. "He'd bring home a magazine,"
Jill said, "and he'd say, 'Look, it says here we were at such and such a
club. Well, I guess we better go there tonight.' And we would!"

The Interlude nightclub became a favorite hangout for Sal. It featured a hypnotist, Pat Collins, who quickly became the hottest attraction in town. One evening, a young aspiring journalist named Elliot
Mintz went to the club to interview Collins. He met Sal at the bar.
Elliot recalled, "As I walked into the club I saw this figure, bearded,
with black leather pants, black leather jacket, sunglasses, cigarette out
of the corner of his mouth, and a lot of people were glancing his way.
It was the first movie star I had ever seen. He looked like a star. Sal
said to me, 'She's hypnotized me every night for the past five nights
and I'm under hypnosis now.' I asked him if he would do an interview
under the influence. He said, 'Sure.' " Sal invited Mintz to his house.

Elliot was worshipful and affable. His pseudointellectualism impressed Sal and the two struck up a fast friendship. "That night we spent
talking," Elliot said. "I slept upstairs on a couch; he went downstairs."

JILL HAD spent a couple of weeks in late February and early March in
Boston filming *The Cardinal* for Otto Preminger. When she was finished, she flew to California to accompany Sal to the Academy Awards
ceremony, despite Preminger's displeasure.

*The Longest Day* had received five Academy Award nominations.
Sal represented the film at the Oscar ceremony. Frank Sinatra hosted

the presentation on Monday evening, April 8, 1963, at the Santa Monica Civic Auditorium.

Jill said, "Sal was asked to accept an award for an actor who wasn't there, should he win. He didn't really want to do it. He was so nervous. And when the guy didn't win, Sal was so relieved. Standing up there and accepting an award for someone else was the last thing he wanted to do."

In the spring, Sal leased a house at the beach. The rambling, two-story Spanish adobe-style house was located at 637 Pacific Coast Highway in Santa Monica. Within walking distance of the Santa Monica Pier to the south and the Santa Monica Beach Club to the north, the beachfront estate was a couple of doors south of the massive home owned by Peter Lawford and his wife, which President Kennedy used as a vacation spot. Sal liked to tell people that onetime Hollywood glamour queen Carole Landis had committed suicide in the house he rented, though it wasn't true.

Sal told his friends the house was haunted. "He had dinner parties," Michael recalled, "and during dinner, all of a sudden, he'd say, 'Did you hear that?' And there'd be this moaning sound. He'd have everybody running around and you could hear this ghostly groaning. It was a tape recorder he'd hidden. He had an audiotape of a man and woman having sex. It lasted about twenty minutes. He was an imp. So full of it."

The house was filled with heavy oak antique furniture. High-backed chairs, heavy couches, and imported Italian baroque wall cabinets filled the living room. Wood-framed centuries-old Italian tiles covered the high ceilings. Large, unframed photos of Jill, and a picture of Sal's Weimaraner, were displayed on the mantel above the fireplace. The enclosed, west-facing backyard was fifty yards from the Pacific Ocean.

"It's got three bedrooms upstairs," Sal explained, "the living room, dining room, kitchen, servants' quarters, and it's got a bar downstairs that's built like a yacht, and the fenced-in beach property. It's real groovy."

"When Sal leased the house at the beach," Michael Anderson Jr. recalled, "I took over the little house on Hillside. The place was a mess. I think he trashed every place he ever lived in. There was dirt and oil from the motorcycle on the living room carpet. And dog shit all over the place. Sal didn't clean up. I would say he was the worst tenant."

The first day Michael moved into the house, he found a letter on the table by the front door. Someone had typed, "There is evil in this house. Light a candle. There is no love in this house. Get out, get out. One A.M., one A.M.," and the words dribbled off the page.

"I was getting crank calls there at all hours of the night," he recalled. "Sometimes there was no one on the line, but once a voice said, 'I know who you are. I can see you.' That place was so dark at night you couldn't see a thing in the house. It was spooky, but it was Sal up to his tricks. When I told him about it, he couldn't help but laugh."

THOUGH SUBSTANTIVE job offers were few, Sal was still an in-demand celebrity on the social circuit and in the gossip columns. Occasionally, and reluctantly, he worked as a "celebrity for hire," appearing at select public functions and theater openings for a fee. On June 18, accompanied by a local high school marching band, Sal officiated at the opening of the Capri Theatre in West Covina, California, which premiered the soon-to-be hit musical film *Bye Bye Birdie*.

A few nights later, Sal hosted a party at his beach house for pianist Peter Duchin, who had arrived from New York to appear in the film *The World of Henry Orient* with Peter Sellers. Sal knew Duchin from New York.

On June 26, Hedda Hopper reported in her column, "First night here, Peter Duchin went on a grunion run with Sal Mineo; never saw one. It was a dark night; the grunions appear only during the full moon."

Michael recalled, "Elliot Mintz was there, and Jill, and Jane Fonda. Also Jill Banner, a seventeen-year-old groupie who hung around Sal, and a young, gay actor named Marc Rambeau. After the run, Elliot and Jane and I ended up in the upstairs bathroom washing tar off each other's feet. Sal yelled, 'Makeup!' "

"Someone brought marijuana," Jill said, "and joints were passed all over the place. I smoked it for the first time, and I swore the green carpet in the bathroom was growing like grass."

Hopper concluded the reportage in her usual droll way. "After his visit here," she wrote, "Duchin will tour the Greek Islands on a sailboat with a guy pal and three Greek sailors."

DURING THE making of *The Greatest Story Ever Told*, Sal deposited his paychecks into his personal account in California rather than sending the money to Louis Harris, his New York business manager. As funds in Sal's trust account dwindled, Harris frantically wired Sal and asked, "Must know immediately what you came away from film with." Sal wired back, "Religion."

Sal relished his freedom and took control of his spending with a vengeance. In addition to leasing the beach house for $900 a month, he purchased a new green Bentley. And he hired a husband-and-wife team to work as housekeeper and butler. Michael recalled, "We called the butler Dunbar. He was in his sixties and dressed formally, like he was *playing* the part of a butler. It was hysterical."

"Mabel was wonderful," Jill said about their housekeeper. "She was like a second mother to Sal. She adored him. She was a wonderful cook and took such good care of him. We loved her."

SAL WENT through money like mad," Michael said. Sal was a gracious host and generous friend. "He would rather give you the shirt off his back and go cold himself." Sal had never learned how to manage money, always relying on his mother. Earning and losing a fortune didn't seem to have taught him a lesson. His philosophy was a simple one: money was meant to be spent. He spent his own and his friends' as well. "He was the reason I foolishly bought a Rolls-Royce," Michael explained. "I went with him one day when he got his Bentley serviced. I had finished a job and had some money, and he pushed me to buy a damned Rolls-Royce! He had a way of talking you into *anything*."

Sal's business manager flew to the West Coast to meet with his extravagant client. "Lou told him he was spending too much money," Michael recalled. "He told him to stop spending and go back to work. Sal said okay, but he didn't change a thing."

With no work on the horizon, Jill and Sal spent several leisurely weeks at the beach house before she had to return to New York for some personal business. "We'd troll the beach and go to the Santa

Monica Pier for fun, and walk to Pacific Ocean Park near Muscle Beach," Jill said. "It was like Coney Island. Sal loved being recognized and loved the attention."

Sal spoke more seriously about stepping away from acting and becoming more involved behind the camera. Directing was no longer a dream but a determination.

Sal was very interested in the latest electronics. He bought tape recorders, sound recording equipment, and the newest home-movie cameras. "He liked to make home movies," Jill explained. "He'd invent these little scenarios and we'd act them out and he'd direct and film the scenes. We'd do them in the house, on the beach, all over the place. He'd record his parties, too."

Sal's interest in "home movies" was nothing new. Using an 8mm camera, he often filmed theatrical rehearsals when he was a kid. From the wings, he shot actors on the stage in *The Rose Tattoo* and *The King and I*. He also made behind the scenes movies on his film sets.

Rudolf Nureyev and Margot Fonteyn performed for the first time in Los Angeles in June 1963. "I had a party when Nureyev was making his debut in Los Angeles," Sal said. "And it was during the days when the twist was so popular. He said, 'Teach me what they are doing.' And I said, 'You're putting me on! You want me to teach you how to dance?' "

Jill said, "Sal asked me to teach him how to twist. So, I taught Nureyev the twist."

To his closest friends, it seemed as though Sal was truly living his life, exploring his independence and his options. No longer supporting his family, though spending his money on friends, Sal was relaxed and happy. "It was a halcyon summer," Michael recalled, "the most carefree, most fun time of my life. There was no responsibility and no end to fun or money."

"Sal was the ringmaster," Jill said, "and life was a real circus."

Elliot Mintz remembered the first time he visited the beach house. "Sal said, 'Welcome to the end of America,' when he showed it to me." The young journalist was debating whether to pursue his college education. He shared his dilemma with Sal. "He said it was dumb for me to go to school and that I should move into his house at the beach. That beach house, summer of 1963, was the best time of my life. Parties with everybody. He knew how to spend money better than anybody I know. We would sit up all night laughing and playing music. Thanks to Sal, I dropped out of college."

Mabel ran the Mineo household in Santa Monica. She coordinated Sal's schedule, kept the house and laundry clean, and meticulously cooked for Sal. Periodically, she'd cut off certain of his friends and hangers-on from the dinner table, refusing to serve them. One day she took Michael aside to complain.

"She said, 'I'm worried about Mr. Mineo,' " Michael said, " 'there's bad people around here taking advantage of him. You don't, but Mr. Elliot takes advantage of Mr. Mineo.' " Sal genuinely liked Elliot, but Mabel was suspicious of Elliot's motives. She felt he was using Sal as an entry into the world of show business and movie stars.

"Sal could be a bit of a snob," Michael recalled. "He was aware of his common background and lack of education, and liked to collect people he thought knew more than he, or were more sophisticated, so he could learn something. So he appeared to be in the know."

Sal had a way of finding people and bringing them into his circle. Once he took a liking to a person, he was very loyal, sometimes mistakenly. "If Sal liked you," Jill said, "he'd say you're a keeper."

I TOOK walks on the beach all the time," Jill said. "Several times I saw a young guy hanging around in the sand near the house. Once he was playing volleyball. But he was alone, usually. He was always wearing a bathing suit. Finally, I said hi. We talked a few minutes and I thought he was leading-man material for Sal and his home movies. I said, 'Why don't you come to the house for dinner?' And he said, 'Oh, you mean the Mineo house?' At the time, I didn't stop to wonder why he knew whose house it was. I took him over to the house, and Sal said bring him in."

Michael remembered the day distinctly. "I remember clearly when Sal brought him into the house," he said. "There were a few people around and Sal said, 'Hey, everybody, this is . . . what's your name?' And the kid said, 'Bobby Sherman.' "

Bobby Sherman was a nineteen-year-old native of Santa Monica. He was a fresh-faced, blue-eyed athletic boy with music aspirations. He played guitar and a few other instruments. "I sang a couple of songs at a party at Sal Mineo's house," Bobby said. "Jane Fonda, Roddy

McDowall, and some other stars were there. Sal asked me if I had an agent; I hadn't, and he arranged for his manager to rep me."

"I'm sure Sal was attracted to him," Michael remembered. "It was obvious. I don't know why, but when I saw Sal with him, I thought, 'Oh, oh, this can't be good.' " Sal quickly, and surprisingly, became infatuated with Bobby. Sal was drawn to his young friend's youthful abandon, something Sal never had the chance to experience, and Bobby was interested in show business, which gave Sal a way to ingratiate himself.

"Sal wanted to be a star maker," Michael explained. "He wanted to promote Bobby. He told him he could help him. Before long, Sal signed him to a personal contract and took to managing his music career. That was a turning point. Something happened with Sal from that time forward. He changed."

AFTER SPENDING a few weeks in New York, Jill returned to California at the end of July to prepare for her first television role. "Sal met me at the airport," Jill recalled. "He was holding this little white fur ball. It was a miniature poodle. Sal gave him to me for my eighteenth birthday. I named him Joey."

Although in private he was trying to understand his newfound feelings for another male, Sal spoke about his relationship with Jill for the first time in a candid interview with a journalist friend shortly after her eighteenth birthday.

"It's frankly nobody's business," he said, referring to his romance with the young actress. "It's Jill's and mine, that's all. If people want to know do we love each other—sure we do. But it's not anybody's business what our personal, intimate feelings are for each other. Jill has one of the most important qualities that a man looks for. That is the respect and complete living for the man! Her way of life, her whole way of living is for one man, and that's it. The thing that I detest—*detest*—is the dominating woman. I'm very uncomfortable with people when I see the wife putting down the husband or some chick putting down her boyfriend.

"Jill is so feminine that there's not an inch, not even the slightest sign of any masculinity. She's completely feminine in everything she does, her whole way of life. Jill is a beautiful girl. First of all, she's the complete opposite of me, physically. You know, in coloring. Very fair. Blue eyes. White skin. Very small. She's delicate and fragile and exceptionally beautiful. She looks like an innocent devil. She always has the devil in her eyes, and yet she's very pure.

"I know that basically I'm a very eccentric person and always have been. It's a marvelous life. How long it will last I'll never know. But I have never gauged myself. I have never said maybe I'd better slow down because ten years from now, things will be bad.

"I live day to day. Every day is a new day and that's it. My love of freedom is fantastic. Even with Jill we don't plan what we're going to do until we do it."

Sal admitted that marriage had crossed his mind lately. "I don't know what 'engaged' means, actually," he said. "I really don't. I don't know what it entails. If it's supposed to mean a decision or commitment to get married, we have that. But we're not saying we're engaged. We don't feel we have to follow the prescribed ritual for a relationship, hell no."

Sal, Jill Haworth, and Jimmy O'Neill, Pandora's Box, Los Angeles, 1962.

*Collection of Jill Haworth*

# 23.

"I think that son of a bitch is trying to wreck my career."

Sal secured the largest salary of his career when he agreed to play the part of Red Shirt, a young Cheyenne Indian, in a film by veteran director John Ford. Warner Bros. Studios paid the young actor a quarter of a million dollars. Sal accepted the role in August 1963.

The screenplay, based on the historical novel *Cheyenne Autumn* by Mari Sandoz, was written and rewritten by James R. Webb. His other screenplays included *How the West Was Won, Cape Fear,* and *Trapeze.*

John Ford began his motion picture career in 1917. With more than 120 films to his credit, Ford was one of the most respected directors in Hollywood. He won a record six Academy Awards for *The Informer* (1935), *The Grapes of Wrath* (1940), *How Green Was My Valley* (1941), *The Quiet Man* (1951), and two documentaries made during World War II. He was especially adept at making Western-themed films, which made him the perfect choice to direct *Cheyenne Autumn.*

The novel recounted the horrible treatment received by a band of dispossessed northern Cheyenne Indians who were transported to barren land in the Oklahoma Territory in 1877. One year later, most of them had died from malaria and starvation. The three hundred surviving men, women, and children fled Oklahoma and tried desperately to return to their Yellowstone homeland, nearly fifteen hundred miles away. This treacherous journey, during which they were pursued by nearly ten thousand U.S. troops, was the story of the film.

Enthusiastic about the project, Jack Warner committed $5 million to shoot the film in Technicolor and Super Panavision. At the age of sixty-nine and suffering from various ailments, the eye-patch-wearing Ford was ecstatic. "Every time I make a Western, they say, 'There goes a senile old John Ford, out west again,' but I just don't give a damn!"

————

IT WASN'T long before Sal's interest in Bobby Sherman extended beyond a professional one. He catered to the nineteen-year-old and courted his companionship. Sal's closest friends thought his behavior was excessive and obsessive, and a little disturbing. "Sal was so taken with him," Michael Anderson Jr. recalled.

Bobby began to stay at the house, at first sleeping on the couch and eventually staying in one of the upstairs bedrooms when Jill was away. Sal hired a photographer to take professional photographs of his protégé, bought him a drum set, and hired a music teacher to give him lessons.

Jill had introduced Sal to her English friend Eric Williams a year earlier. Eric, at first a friend of her mother, occasionally accompanied Jill as a chaperone from New York to Los Angeles. Eric was a charming rogue, and Sal befriended him at once.

Eric recalled, "There was a picture of Jill in the beach house and Sal took it down when she wasn't there and replaced it with Bobby's. Mabel would come up behind him and switch it back. She didn't approve of what was going on at all."

SAL ARRIVED in Monument Valley in early October to begin work on *Cheyenne Autumn*. The film company numbered 865 during their stay in the picturesque but remote area nearly 180 miles northeast of Flagstaff, Arizona.

*Cheyenne Autumn* was the seventh film John Ford made in Monument Valley. A paved highway and proper mobile homes replaced the dirt roads and army tents Ford dealt with during his previous location work in the area. Sal, along with Ford and other stars of the picture, stayed at the historic Gouldings Lodge, with few amenities. Telephone service was spotty and mail had to be picked up in Flagstaff every few days.

Jack Woods, one of the director's assistants, said, "It's a typical Ford company with no levity and 'yessir' and 'nosir'! We never know when he's nice or will blow his top!"

The natural beauty of the location did nothing to ease Sal's miserable experiences on the film, however. In addition to a weak script and an impatient and ailing director, the casting of certain actors appeared ludicrous. Ricardo Montalban, Dolores del Rio, Gilbert Roland, Victor

Jory, and Sal all being cast as Indians was a colossal exercise in dramatic license. "Whoever had an accent," Sal said, "had a feather stuck in his head and was cast as an Indian."

Ford actually wanted the two main Indian roles to be played by Native American actors. Warner Bros. had a different idea. The studio wanted Montalban and Sal for the leads. Sal, they explained to Ford, had marquee value and appealed to a young audience.

Ford had argued against it, saying Sal did not resemble an Indian and he spoke with a Bronx accent. The studio had not backed down, and Ford was forced to accept their casting demand. Unaccustomed to being overridden, Ford harbored a deep resentment, which manifested itself in the way he treated Sal, whom he addressed as "Saul."

Pat Ford, the director's son, said, "My father and I agreed that the Cheyenne should not speak English in the picture. They should serve, in his words, as a 'Greek chorus.' Red Shirt [Sal] and Little Wolf [Montalban] should speak some English but in a rather stilted, traditionally Indian manner." Consequently, Sal spoke barely a word of English in the finished film.

Sal rarely watched the dailies being shown in the mess tent at night and was never invited to join Ford's after-dinner game of Twenty Questions. Instead, he chose to spend time alone in his room at Gouldings Lodge, where he listened to jazz records played on his phonograph.

One night, Ford entered his room and asked him to play his records more quietly. "Well, you see, sir," Sal answered, "this kind of music has to be played at that volume. Otherwise, one can't get complete satisfaction out of it."

Ford took a knife from his pocket, flipped it open, and placed it on the table beside the phonograph. "Play it a little softer, Saul," he said.

"Yes, sir, I can play it real soft," Sal replied.

Ford picked up his knife. "That's what I thought," he said as he walked out.

People on the set felt that Ford quickly became bored with the project. The director's poor sight and hearing, as well as other health problems, caused one of his assistants to say, "He's no longer operating at full capacity." The director also started drinking heavily.

An assistant director said, "There were problems between John and some of his actors. His relationship with Sal was terrible. The young actor was intimidated by John's gruffness and his performance wasn't what it might have been."

Ford insisted that Sal do his own riding without the help of a professional stuntman. In one scene, Sal ran and stumbled, failing to jump on his horse. After an awkward few seconds, he managed to mount the horse and ride off. He was shocked when he heard Ford yell, "Cut. Print." He asked for a second take so he could do the scene properly.

While dozens of cast and crew members watched, Ford stared at Sal for a moment, then asked, "Do you wanna do it again with an empty camera, Saul? You were angry. And you missed. I like it. Completely in character. I don't want it to look perfect like a circus. But you can do it again, if you want, with an empty camera, Saul."

Sal stepped on a nail during one scene and injured his foot. The wound became infected and required medical attention. He insisted on working, and when Ford saw him hobble slightly to take his position for a shot, he notified the studio that Sal was "a problem to work with." The unfair comment found its way into the trade papers.

"This son of a bitch is trying to wreck my career," Sal complained to Eric Williams.

IN OCTOBER, a young writer named Peter Bogdanovich who wrote articles about film for *Esquire* magazine arrived in Monument Valley to interview Ford. He was a little distressed to find that Sal was one of the stars of the film. "The prevailing winds around Sal in the early sixties were anything but favorable. The old established snobs in Hollywood could never quite forgive him his teenage popularity."

Sal was happy to see a contemporary on the set. Both young men were twenty-four years old. The majority of the cast and crew were at least twenty years older. Bogdanovich and Sal sat next to each other for a meal and Sal immediately struck up a conversation. "I have never met anyone quite so instantly disarming as Sal could be," Bogdanovich recalled. "No one took himself less seriously than Sal, which is not to say he was frivolous; he'd just drop off into that funny snore of his at any hint of pomposity in himself or others."

Bogdanovich admitted that he did admire some of Sal's earlier films but said, "I never saw a picture that even remotely captured his essential sunny and easygoing qualities, his quick wit and infectious self-mockery."

In mid-November, the company moved to Moab, Utah, near the Colorado River in the northern extremes of Monument Valley, for another two weeks of filming. Sal remembered the day his character, Red Shirt, was killed in the film. "You know what day they killed me?" he told Peter Bogdanovich. "The same day as Kennedy—November 22. We're up there in Monument Valley—and the Old Man [Ford] likes the weather. So he says, 'Let's kill Saul.' He always called me Saul . . . and they get the shot set up and old Ricardo Montalban shoots me. I fall down. Ford says, 'That's swell!' and they do something else. A couple of hours later we hear Kennedy's been murdered and Ford calls a wrap for the rest of the day. Somebody figured out that at the same time Ricardo was shooting me, Oswald was shooting Kennedy."

With his role completed in late November, Sal happily left the rugged, frozen beauty of the Utah desert and the insults of his irascible director and hurried back to his luxurious house on the Santa Monica beach.

Michael Anderson Jr. saw Sal shortly after he returned to California. "He was exhausted," Michael said. "We were sitting in the back of the house and Sal showed me the paycheck he just got for his work. I told him how excited I was for him, but he was disgruntled. The work experience had been the worst in his life, he told me. 'I'm never doing a picture like that again,' he said. 'I'm never working on anything unless it's just what I want. I don't care.' "

IN EARLY December, Sal finalized plans to incorporate a production company and ultimately assume full responsibility for his career choices. He felt this would give him more latitude in reviewing offerings and provide him with the ability to option film properties for future development. Hollywood producers seemed less and less interested in working with him. "It was the prevailing mood," Bogdanovich observed. "Sal was an anachronistic reminder of the teenage fifties the chic people preferred to forget; that he was also a talented actor seemed beside the point."

Before flying to the East Coast for business, Sal hired songwriters and musicians and rented a recording studio in Los Angeles to produce two songs for Bobby Sherman, "Nobody's Sweetheart" and "I Wanna Hear It from Her." On December 10, Sal Mineo Productions Inc. was incorporated in Albany, New York, by Sal's business manager/attorney Louis Harris, who told the press the main reason for the incorporation was the fact that Mineo had produced a record for his discovery, Bobby Sherman.

Unwelcome at the New York opening, Sal stayed in California to attend the December 19 West Coast premiere of Jill's newest film, the Otto Preminger–directed *The Cardinal*, at the Egyptian Theatre on Hollywood Boulevard.

"I was in trouble with Mr. Preminger," Jill explained. Despite the director's warnings and ominous tone, Jill continued to see Sal. "Mr. Preminger was angry at me and called me in to see him in New York."

"Do not let the publicity get to you," the director told her. "I want you to know you will outgrow Sal. He is not right for you. He will stifle you. He will hurt you as an actress."

Jill was banished from the West Coast premiere of *The Cardinal*. "I was being punished for my relationship with Sal," she said. "Mr. Preminger knew I still saw him and that I slipped away to California, too. I think he had me followed. I do think I was being watched."

While the other stars of *The Cardinal* traveled to Los Angeles and to European cities, Jill was required to stay in Manhattan for the New York premiere on December 20, 1963. "I went to Boston," she added, "and Scranton and Poughkeepsie. I had been a bad girl."

SAL FLEW back to New York to spend Christmas with Jill. The three-ring-circus atmosphere of the Santa Monica beach house ironically found its way into Sal's only 1963 television acting role, a circus-themed drama called *The Greatest Show on Earth*. Sal starred as an aerialist in an episode called "The Loser," broadcast on ABC-TV on New Year's Eve. "Me in tights," Sal huffed.

Peter Bogdanovich convinced *Esquire* magazine editor Harold Hayes to allow him to do a feature about Sal. Jill said, "Sal liked Peter very much. He and Peter talked and talked about the business, movies and directors and things, and where the business was headed." Sal was impressed with Bogdanovich's knowledge about show business and his opinions on life. He looked up to the writer, even though they were the same age.

And then, Sal did something he had said he would never do again. He recorded a couple of songs, "Take Me Back" and "Save the Last Dance for Me." One of the conditions of securing a recording contract for Bobby Sherman was that Sal record a new single for the Fontana label. Sal had not recorded since the summer of 1959. His recordings had disappeared as quickly as they had become hits and rarely merited radio play during the past several years.

Sal returned to Los Angeles in January 1964 to work on another television program. He was cast as Carlos Mendoza, a young man who illegally practices medicine in his depressed neighborhood, in an episode of *Dr. Kildare* called "Tomorrow Is a Fickle Girl."

But Sal had another, more interesting reason to hurry back to California. Harold Stevenson's nude painting of Sal, called *The New Adam*, was supposed to have been included in a show that introduced pop art, organized by Lawrence Alloway for the Guggenheim in 1963. Alloway wrote to Harold saying he couldn't show the painting because it would create an "imbalance" in the exhibition.

Not to be deterred, Harold proudly exhibited the painting at the Richard Feigen Gallery in New York and Chicago later that year. In January 1964, the gargantuan painting was shown at the Feigen-Palmer Gallery on La Cienega Boulevard in Los Angeles. "Sal attended the opening and participated in the publicity and press," Harold said. The massive paneled painting was a sensation. Never before had an Oscar- and Emmy Award–nominated actor posed nude for such a work of art. Sal loved the attention.

Jill returned to the Santa Monica beach house in mid-February 1964. Jill and Sal enjoyed a leisurely break. The house was peculiarly quiet, except for the comings and goings of Bobby Sherman.

On February 14, Sal gave Jill a gold heart pendant for Valentine's Day. The delicate heart was lovingly engraved, "Forever, Sal."

## 24.

"I prefer men. I like it. That's the way I want it.
That's what I want. I'm attracted to boys."

Jill had spent the morning on the beach. She came into the house after a few hours in the sun, said a passing hello to Mabel, who was in the kitchen, and hurried upstairs to change her clothes.

"I walked in on Sal and Bobby Sherman in our bed," Jill said. "It was in *our* bedroom. They were buck naked in our bed. Doing it. Sal was the aggressor. I was absolutely shocked." Sal looked over at Jill while she stood in the doorway. "But he didn't stop," she said. "He kept going at it."

Jill had the presence of mind to find Sal's address book, call Michael Anderson Jr., and tearfully plead with him to come and pick her up. She knew Bobby had been spending a lot of time with Sal at the house. "But I had no idea what was happening," she said. "I didn't have a clue. I was completely shocked."

Michael arrived with some flowers. Sal had never come downstairs all the while Jill had waited for her ride. "Jill," Michael recalled, "was so deeply hurt. It was clear that her heart was broken. I drove her away and she said it was over. It couldn't work out."

Jill left the house with only her purse and flew to New York. She told her mother she had broken up with Sal but didn't explain why. Jill recalled, "Sal used to talk about the swinging sixties and free sex. A short time after meeting Bobby, Sal actually asked me if I was interested in going to bed with Bobby. He said, 'Aren't you curious? How could you go to bed with just one person all your life? How do you know what you're missing?' I was disgusted. And I wasn't interested in Bobby Sherman one bit."

Beyond the horrible experience working on *Cheyenne Autumn*, the reckless spending, and Bobby Sherman's ever-increasing presence, Michael had sensed a change in Sal. "Something inside," he explained, "some profound realization that challenged his sense of self and made him oddly defensive. He couldn't handle all those feelings, and, I think, he wanted it over with Jill and didn't know how to do it. He did love her in his way."

Michael never saw Jill again. A couple of days passed before he called Sal. Michael told him he had picked Jill up at the house. "He said he knew," Michael recalled. "And I asked him what happened. 'Why did you let Jill go?' I asked. And he said, matter-of-factly, 'I prefer men. I like it. That's the way I want it. That's what I want. I'm attracted to boys.' And I thought, 'Aha.' I had heard rumors about him before but never thought anything of it. But I wasn't that surprised. And I was mad at him, but not for that. I didn't care about that. I was mad because he hurt Jill so badly."

Sal, having had no previous sexual experience with another man, had asked for help. During a haircut appointment, Sal had confided to his male hairdresser his sexual interest in Bobby. He actually asked the man, who was homosexual, "I don't know how to do this. What do guys do?" His hairdresser said, "Well, come home with me and I'll show you." And Sal had.

Sal's determination to be "himself" gave him the courage to explore his sexual impulses. Since Bobby Sherman was younger, Sal did not feel vulnerable and could control the course of their relationship. Still, he understood the revelation of such a relationship would destroy his career, and trying to internalize those feelings was difficult.

Michael said, "Sal was very open and the life of the party, but there was something guarded about him. Around that time he was outed in some rag tabloid. There was a piece about him being gay. Pure speculation, as those stories persist in Hollywood all the time, but Elliot told me Sal was very hurt by that."

One day Sal called Michael and asked him for help with a home movie he planned. He wanted Michael to be his cameraman. "I went out to the beach," Michael recalled, "and Sal and I were in the backyard area, and Bobby Sherman was lying on his back in the sand wearing a little brief bathing suit. And I'm holding the movie camera and Sal is directing. Sal says, 'Now get in close. Focus in on his nipple.' And I said, 'What are you talking about?' He said he wanted it to look like a sand dune or some damn thing. So he says, 'Focus on his nipple and then slowly pan down to his stomach.' And I said, 'Sal, what kind of movie is this?' He laughed. He always laughed when you caught him when he was up to something. It was like some sort of teenage fantasy. I said, 'You don't need me for this.' I handed him the camera and went home."

Michael said one night he and Sal went to the Interlude to see Pat Collins. They were joined by other acquaintances and most people were drinking. When the evening was over, they left through a back door and went down a steep flight of stairs to the parking lot. "Sal was several steps ahead of me," Michael remembered. "A gay guy, he was sort of feminine, and very drunk, said something to Sal, and suddenly they went for each other. Fists were flying. Two people had to hold Sal back, and he was furious and yelling, 'Let me at him!' Later in the evening, when things calmed down, I asked the people who were with us what happened and they said the guy called Sal a fag."

Michael said, "All these pieces suddenly fit together."

WITH THE money he earned from *Esquire* magazine for the article he had proposed to write about Sal, Peter Bogdanovich moved to Los Angeles in the spring of 1964. He interviewed Sal numerous times and completed the article. The editor of the magazine actually had the article set in type and had pictures taken of Sal for the piece but decided not to run it. "After several postponements," Bogdanovich said, "he finally admitted to me, 'I just couldn't stand the idea of having Sal Mineo in the magazine.'" Times had changed and the leather-jacketed rebel, an image Sal found so difficult to shake, was considered passé.

On March 10, Sal presented Tippi Hedren a Golden Globe Award for her performance in Alfred Hitchcock's film *The Birds* at a ceremony at the Cocoanut Grove in the Ambassador Hotel in Los Angeles. He was accompanied by a nineteen-year-old dancer/actress named Joey Heatherton. During their red-carpet entrance, he coyly dodged questions about Jill's absence.

Bobby Sherman was staying at the beach house almost full-time. Sal was determined to secure a recording contract for his young protégé, but American popular music had been turned on its ear by the Beatles and other British musical imports. Sal's distaste for the music business and his own brief time as a teenage recording star made it even more difficult for him to be taken seriously as a record producer.

Sal and Jill's business manager Louis Harris invested a sizable amount of Sal's *and* Jill's money (unbeknownst to her at the time) in an independent label called Dot Records, which released Bobby's single "Nobody's Sweetheart." Shortly after singing at Sal's house party the previous summer, Bobby had received a call from an agent who introduced himself as Dick Clayton, Sal's friend. He told Bobby he had been recommended to him by Sal and offered to book some auditions on his behalf. Bobby began to make the rounds.

Sal had known Clayton for several years. After years of representation, Sal left his childhood agent, Alec Alexander. For a time, he was represented by the William Morris Agency, which had handled his recent "all-star epic" film assignments. Clayton occasionally helped Sal when he was between agents, which became a more frequent and career-threatening circumstance.

In late March 1964, Sal took Bobby to New York, where Bobby recorded a few demos for Cameo Parkway Records. The songs didn't sell. Sal did not see Jill while he was in Manhattan.

"It took me almost a year to talk to Sal again," Jill said. "He was in contact with my mother all the time on the phone, asking what I was doing and who I was seeing. Mr. Preminger was finally pleased with me. He said to me, 'He is not for you. He is into men.'

"Yul Brynner came to New York," Jill explained. "He called me and said he was passing through town and wanted to come by to see me. I thought that was a bit strange, but he came to my apartment.

"He said, 'Sal is a homosexual.' And I said, 'No, I don't believe it!' I didn't know what to think, and I didn't know why he was telling me this. Apparently, everyone had known but me!"

It was not surprising that Sal had confided in the man he considered a second father. And it was not uncommon that he had someone else act on his behalf in the midst of an uncomfortable situation. Sal didn't like confrontation and used the services of attorneys and managers to handle conflict.

Despite his help and willingness to invest money in Bobby's singing career, Sal's fawning attentions made the young man uncomfortable. Eric Williams joined Sal and Bobby for dinner at the Brasserie in Manhattan one evening. "Sal was so besotted with Bobby," Eric recalled. "He actually traveled with a picture of Bobby in his suitcase.

He'd set it on the table by the bed wherever he was staying." Eric was taken aback by Sal's behavior in the restaurant. "Sal was nearly crying at the table," Eric explained. "He left to go to the bathroom and Bobby said to me, 'I love Sal but he wants me to do something I can't do.' "

Bobby's interest in Sal had to do with the advancement of his own singing career. Sal's interest was more personal. He was unused to anyone spurning his advances, which only made Bobby more appealing to him. "I knew," said Eric, "there was trouble ahead."

BEFORE RETURNING to California from the East Coast, Sal taped five episodes of the daytime game show *The Match Game*. With no other television or motion picture offers at hand, Sal decided to accept a limited-run engagement in Clifford Odets's play *Awake and Sing!* at the Theatre by the Sea in Venice, California. Sal would star as Ralph in the role created on Broadway by his childhood favorite John Garfield. Under the direction of Max Miller, rehearsals for *Awake and Sing!* began in June.

On July 7, Sal's West Coast stage debut was attended by many notables, including his friends and coworkers, Eva Marie Saint, Gary Crosby, Elliot Mintz, and Michael Anderson Jr. The play received good notices. The *Los Angeles Times* said, "Sal Mineo plays young Ralph with authority and evidence of increasing ability as an actor." Sal's appearance drew large audiences to the theater, and *Awake and Sing!* was extended for two additional sold-out weeks.

Eric Williams had moved to Los Angeles in mid-1964 and spent considerable time with Sal. Sal's circle of friends had tightened since Jill's departure and Michael's burgeoning acting career. In public, Sal appeared with female dates, but Bobby Sherman remained a fixture at the beach house. Sal craved Bobby's companionship, though Bobby then openly discouraged any romantic overtures. Sal had a wandering eye and didn't believe in denying himself sexual pursuits. He was emboldened and curious and invited other boys to the house as well. "Mabel did not approve of all the boys in the house," Eric added. "Once she put together a breakfast for Sal and me, and there was a boy there. And Sal told her to fix his guest something to eat, too. When she left the room, she rolled her eyes and said, 'Guest . . . more like a pest . . .' "

———

IN AUGUST, Sal finally realized his dream when producer David Fulfort invited him to direct *End as a Man* at the Canal Fulton Summer Arena in Canal Fulton, Ohio, about thirty miles southwest of Akron. Sal did not want the burden of his celebrity to impact his first such effort, and the remote location of the theater virtually guaranteed little press scrutiny. The engagement was reported in the show business trade papers after the fact. The production opened on August 11 and ran until August 16.

Sal chose a provocative work for his directorial debut. *End as a Man,* written by Calder Willingham, concerned a handful of young men in a Southern military college. A hazing incident has a disastrous effect, and the unrepentant sociopath who engineered the event terrorizes his reluctant coconspirators to keep them silent. The story of the bizarre "rite of passage" to "end as a man" was a classic struggle for power among headstrong, testosterone-driven young men.

The play was first performed at the Actors Studio in New York in 1953. Ben Gazzara played the part of Jocko, the villainous young man at the center of the story. James Dean played a young cadet. When director Jack Garfein announced plans to film the play, newly retitled *The Strange One,* in 1955, James Dean heavily lobbied for the lead. He had talked with Sal about the project, even suggesting he read for a part in the film, and lent him a copy of the play to read. The story was particularly interesting because it contained a homosexual character who has an obvious crush on the handsome and conniving Jocko. The play included a shower scene with the young men in the school, especially surprising considering the time.

In addition to directing the play, Sal played the role of Jocko. Actors George Reinholt and Kenny Solms joined Sal onstage. Reinholt recalled, "Sal did a marvelous job. I loved working with him. I fell in love with him, really. He had a wonderful, natural instinct. I thought Sal was a pioneer in a new genre of Hollywood actors. He had a wonderful vulnerability. He could effectively play a sensitive young man and still appear very masculine. He could split that hair down the middle. He established himself as a new type of actor, and I loved working with him."

Yul Brynner and Sal, *The King and I*, New York, 1953.

Sarina, Sal, Mike, and Victor, Wenner Place, the Bronx, 1952.

Above: Sal's first professional headshot, New York, 1954.

Right: Sal, *Six Bridges to Cross*, 1955.

Sal and James Dean (above), with Natalie Wood (below), *Rebel Without a Cause*, 1955.

John Cassavetes,
Mark Rydell, and
Sal, *Crime in the
Streets*, 1956.

Sal and Caryl Volkman,
*Rock, Pretty Baby*, 1956.

Sal Mineo Fan Club official
button, 1956.

Sal, *Crime in the Streets* premiere,
New York, 1956.

Sal, the "problem photograph," November 1956.

Sal, *Dino*, 1957.

Sal following eye surgery, summer 1957.

Sal recording,
New York, 1957.

Sal, Will Rogers Beach,
Santa Monica, 1957.

Josephine, Sal,
and Sal Sr.,
Mamaroneck,
New York,
1958.

Top left: Sal,
*Tonka*, 1958.

Top right:
Sal, *Aladdin*,
1958.

Left: Sal,
Los Angeles,
1959.

Terry Moore and Sal, *A Private's Affair*, 1959.

Sal and Gene Krupa, *The Gene Krupa Story*, 1959.

Sal, *Exodus*, 1960.

Above: Sal and Jill Haworth, *Exodus*, 1960.

Left: Sal wins the Golden Globe Award for *Exodus*, 1960. Presented by actress Martha Hyer.

Below: Unknown, Yul Brynner, and Sal, *Escape from Zahrain*, 1962.

Above: Sal, *The Longest Day*, 1962.

Right: Jill Haworth and Sal, Paris, France, May 1962.

COLLECTION OF JILL HAWORTH

Below: Michael Anderson Jr., Jill Haworth, and Sal, Los Angeles, 1962.

COLLECTION OF MICHAEL ANDERSON JR.

Sal and Jill
Haworth, Santa
Monica, 1963.
COLLECTION OF JILL
HAWORTH

Sal and
Dolores del
Rio, *Cheyenne
Autumn*, 1964.

Sal, *Who Killed
Teddy Bear?*, 1965.

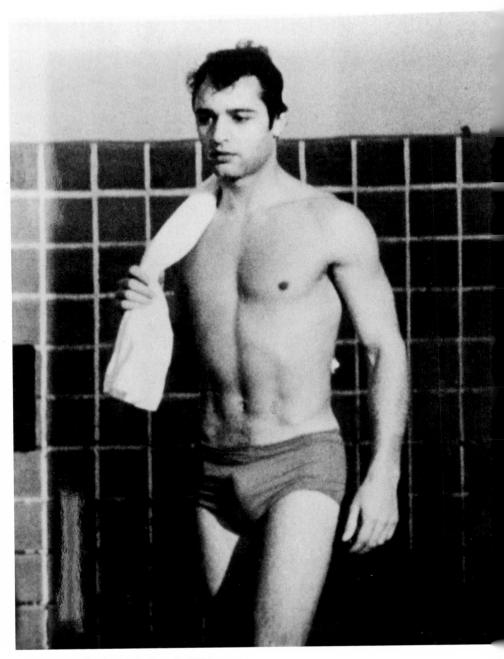

Sal, *Who Killed Teddy Bear?*, 1965.

Sal, Santa Monica, 1965.

Sal and Bobby Sherman,
*Shindig!*, January 1965.

Don Johnson, Sal, and Don's sister and mother, Los Angeles, 1969. Premiere of *Fortune and Men's Eyes*.

PHOTO COPYRIGHT FRANK EDWARDS

Left: Sal and Don Johnson, Cinerama Dome, Hollywood, 1969.

PHOTO COPYRIGHT FRANK EDWARDS

Below: Sal and Don Johnson, *Fortune and Men's Eyes*, Los Angeles, 1969.

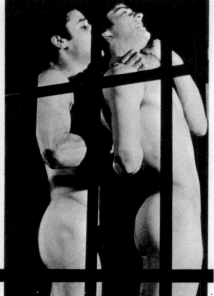

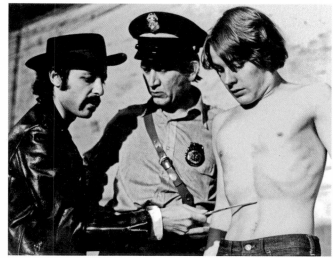

Sal and Courtney Burr III, *Fortune and Men's Eyes*, San Francisco, 1970.

Sal and Michael Anderson Jr., *In Search of America*, 1971.

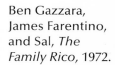

Ben Gazzara, James Farentino, and Sal, *The Family Rico*, 1972.

Sal, *P.S. Your Cat Is Dead,* San Francisco, 1975.

Above: Courtney Burr III, Jeanne Jarvis, and Sal, Florida, 1975.

Right: Sal and Courtney Burr III, *The Tender Trap,* Florida, 1975.

Emerson Batdorf reviewed *End as a Man* for the local newspaper, the *Plain Dealer*. He praised Sal's "vigorous direction," though the play had "an air of decadence." He additionally praised Sal's acting, writing that he fit the role of the bully and had "a haughty air with a surly lip."

"Sal was wonderful," recalled Alex Gildzen, a writer and theatrical archivist who reviewed local productions for nearby Kent State University at the time. "It was a jolting production."

"The play was a little tough, though, for summer stock audiences," Reinholt added. "It involved sadism in a Southern military school. Audiences might have been a little put off by it, but the theater was full."

Upon his return to Hollywood, Sal told columnist Dorothy Manners that on the strength of his work in Ohio, he hoped to get film and television directorial assignments.

"But I'm by no means giving up acting," Sal explained. "I should be satisfied just making movies, but I've always been ambitious. I've always wanted to spread my wings and fly a little higher. Directing is the next step and I hope I don't fall flat on my face.

"I'm working so hard these days because frankly I need the money. I live above my means most of the time and travel the expensive route. So I always need the green stuff. I'm not hanging my head in shame about this. A lot of people do it—but are embarrassed to admit it. I think if you're a movie actor, you should live like one—not like a plumber. I must admit, though, plumbers probably have more money.

"My father was a coffin maker back in New York. He used to tell me, 'Son, one day you'll be wearing one of these—we all will—so get all the fun out of life you can because that time comes a lot sooner than we think.' "

AFTER *AWAKE AND SING!* closed in early August, Sal was forced to downsize his living expenses. He gave up the house in Santa Monica. Bobby Sherman had moved into his own apartment, and Sal leased a compact, modernist house at 2700 Krim Drive, on a hillside not far from 20th Century Fox Studios.

At about the same time, Dick Clayton arranged for Bobby Sherman to audition for a new television program called *Shindig!* created by Sal's friend, disc jockey and nightclub owner Jimmy O'Neill. Taped in front of a live audience at ABC Studios in Hollywood, the program featured the popular music hits of the day. Bobby nervously auditioned for the show's producers, Jack Good and Selig J. Seligman. Seligman was the executive producer of the hit series *Combat!*

Bobby felt he did poorly, but his connection to Sal proved to be very useful. Sal asked O'Neill, the show's creator and soon-to-be on-air host, to intercede on Bobby's behalf. In addition, Sal committed to appear in three episodes of *Combat!* for Seligman's production company should Bobby land the job. Within days, Bobby was hired as a "house singer" on the program with a twenty-six-episode contract. The first episode of *Shindig!* aired on September 16, 1964. At a salary of $750 a week, he was earning more money than Sal.

"Sal was living hand to mouth during those days," Eric said. "The glory days of big money were over. And it was hard for him to accept that." Sal's management company finally took all his credit cards and gave him an allowance. He still managed to find places that would allow him to run up tabs, though.

Universal Casket Company could not continue to operate without infusions of capital from Sal's earnings. Months earlier, Sal had stopped paying the bills for the mansion in Mamaroneck. His father did not earn enough money to maintain the property. The business and the house were sold, and Mr. and Mrs. Mineo moved to a small apartment in nearby Harrison, New York.

Josephine occasionally called Sal in California and asked to visit, but Sal always discouraged her and said he would see her when he was back in New York. "Sometimes," Eric recalled, "Sal didn't even tell his family when he was coming into New York. Sal had grown to hate his brother Mike and didn't talk to him anymore. Sal had very little contact with his family; he was a little embarrassed by them. And he actually felt he had been ripped off."

IN SEPTEMBER, Sal shot the season-premiere episode of *Kraft Suspense Theatre* for NBC-TV. In "The World I Want," Sal played a deaf-mute apprentice cabinetmaker who is framed for the murder of his boss. Cecil Smith favorably reviewed the drama for the *Los Angeles Times:* "The best recent television premiere was the *Kraft Suspense Theatre . . .* a finely tuned melodrama in which Sal Mineo gave [an] extraordinary performance."

*Combat!* was a one-hour, war-themed drama that dominated its time slot on Tuesday evenings and depicted the harrowing exploits of a U.S. Army platoon fighting its way through Europe during World War II. Bernard McEveety directed Sal in an episode called "The Hard Way Back," which aired on October 20. Sal turned in one of his finest television performances to date.

Several days later, Hedda Hopper prematurely reported that Sal, Nick Adams, and singer Johnny Mathis were cast in a proposed film called *Rebel in the Streets*. Mathis would play a Puerto Rican living in New York's Spanish Harlem. Richard Bernstein was set to produce the motion picture. Nothing came of the idea.

Forced to accept any job offer at the time, Sal appeared as a celebrity guest on another daytime game show, *What's This Song?* The thirty-minute program, patterned after *Name That Tune*, aired on November 16.

CHEYENNE AUTUMN opened in Los Angeles to the general public on Christmas Day at the Pantages Theatre. With few exceptions, the reviews were dismal. Following the initial press preview of the film in October, the *Hollywood Reporter* cheerily wrote, "Sal Mineo adds youthful appeal to the film." *Box Office* was a little less enthusiastic: "Sal Mineo gives an adequate performance."

Ford said, "This is the best-photographed picture I ever made in my life." When a reviewer commented that *Cheyenne Autumn* looked like a silent movie, Ford snapped, "It's still a silent medium." The film *was* a silent movie for Sal. The two-time Oscar nominee hardly spoke a word of English in the finished film.

One major review spoke of the film as one of John Ford's "biggest disappointments," and another called it "far and away the most boring picture of 1964."

Stanley Kauffmann, reviewing for the *New Republic*, found the cast "beyond belief." "*Cheyenne Autumn*," he wrote, "is a pallid and straightening version of the best Ford, with no new visual ideas and, what is perhaps worse, fumbling use of the old ones. Sal Mineo, as a proud Cheyenne brave, acts like a reject from a road company of *West Side Story*."

*Newsweek* magazine's assessment, though, was the harshest. "Ford has apparently forgotten everything he ever knew, about actors, about cameras, about Indians, and about the West. The performances of Edward G. Robinson, Carroll Baker, Karl Malden, and the rest are uniformly terrible. Sal Mineo, the worst of all, walks with a pelvic lead, as if he were playing the first Cheyenne female impersonator."

*Cheyenne Autumn* was an embarrassment and a flop, losing Warner Bros. millions of dollars.

# 25.

"When I started in films, I was fifteen, sixteen, and I had this baby face that made me look like a wheat flour dumpling or something. And my fucking name didn't exactly help."

Rejoice!" the *Los Angeles Times* announced rather cynically on January 6, 1965. "Sal Mineo is making a TV singing appearance after an absence of many years on *Shindig*. Why not?"

In a few short months, *Shindig!* had become a very popular rock and roll television show. Bobby Sherman was enjoying his newfound stardom with millions of teenage girls, who flooded the network with loving fan mail.

Sal reluctantly fulfilled a professional obligation to appear on the show and sang two numbers, "The Girl Across the Way" and "Save the Last Dance for Me," which were later released as a flip-sided single on Fontana Records.

I CAME home," Jill said, "and Sal was sitting in the living room with my mother drinking tea. I was shocked. My mother said, 'Sal will be staying here for a few days. He needs a place. He'll take your room, and you'll stay with me.' "

Sal came to Manhattan in mid-January to make a film. "He stayed with us for a few days until he moved into Lou Harris's apartment on Fifty-fourth Street," Jill explained. "It was very difficult, but I was happy to see him. We never talked about what happened in California. He never apologized. Never referred to it. He never mentioned Bobby Sherman's name to me, and I never saw Bobby again."

Sal's unexpected reappearance after an awkward parting was not out of character. He'd behave badly and then just show up again when he was ready, with a smile on his face like nothing untoward had ever happened. Sal thought his return was apology enough.

"Aside from the intimacy," Jill said, "we sort of picked things up where we left off. We were friends now."

Sal coaxed Jill into their first public appearance together in more than a year when they attended the New York opening of *Cheyenne Autumn* in late January. The staid New York film reviewers were no less unkind than their West Coast associates had been.

SAL'S PURSUIT of substantive film roles continued to be a challenge. He weighed the few film offers he received but wanted to move away from conventional, big-budget movies and become involved with more edgy independent films. He had compromised himself and broken a promise to never sing professionally again when he appeared on *Shindig!* And, as a favor to his friend, director Don Weis, he appeared as himself in an episode of *The Patty Duke Show*. Sal took little comfort when the episode, "Patty Meets a Celebrity," won its time slot when it aired on ABC-TV on January 20.

In an attempt to reach a mature audience, he accepted a role in a low-budget film that was not only extraordinarily adult in nature but downright perverse. On January 25, Sal began work on his next feature film, *Who Killed Teddy Bear?* Costarring Juliet Prowse and Elaine Stritch, the film was produced by a new independent company, Phillips Productions.

Prowse had appeared in a few films, including *GI Blues* with Elvis Presley and *Can-Can*. She enjoyed success as a dancer and nightclub performer and was briefly engaged to Frank Sinatra.

"I was a lesbian owner of a disco who fell in love with Juliet Prowse and got strangled on Ninety-third Street and East End Avenue with a silk stocking by Sal Mineo," Elaine Stritch said. "Jesus, who's *not* going to play *that* part?" Stritch, a two-time Tony Award nominee, had starred in numerous Broadway hits, including *Pal Joey, Bus Stop*, and *Who's Afraid of Virginia Woolf?*

Joseph Cates directed *Who Killed Teddy Bear?* Cates, nominated for a 1959 Emmy, directed and produced game shows, including *The $64,000 Question* and *Can Do*, on which Sal had appeared in 1956. He produced the hit Broadway musical *What Makes Sammy Run?* in 1964.

*Who Killed Teddy Bear?* was written by Leon Tokatyan, a television writer, and Arnold Drake. Drake's other "exploitation" B films included *The Flesh Eaters* in 1964 and *50,000 B.C. (Before Clothing)*, a 1963 "nudie" B film.

*Who Killed Teddy Bear?* tells the story of Norah (Prowse), a disco hostess who is victimized by an obscene telephone caller. Her only friends are Lawrence (Sal), a waiter at the club, and Marian (Elaine Stritch), the club owner, who has sexual designs of her own on Norah. When Norah learns the caller has actually been tailing her, her annoyance turns to terror. She voices her fears to a new acquaintance, a police detective who specializes in sexual crime. The detective finds evidence pointing to Lawrence, who lives with his maladjusted teenage sister in a nearby apartment house that has a view (aided by binoculars and a dressing mirror) into Norah's apartment.

Realizing he is the suspect, Lawrence goes in search of Norah. He mistakenly attacks Marian and is forced to kill her for fear of being discovered. He eventually finds Norah, who tries to run from him, but he brutally rapes her. The detective arrives too late to stop the attack but beats Lawrence, who eventually breaks free and runs into the street, where he is shot by the police.

*Who Killed Teddy Bear?* presented provocative and, at times, lurid subject matter. The black-and-white photography and on-the-street location shooting in the grimier parts of Manhattan, including Times Square, created a tawdry, sordid atmosphere.

Journalist George Hatch wrote, "*Who Killed Teddy Bear?* bolstered the tail end of an exploitation invasion that, for nearly a decade, had been aggressively insinuating a darker and more subversive element into the local drive-ins and neighborhood theatres. Several cuts above the usual grind-house fare, but still falling far below major release standards, this handful of scrappy and rather eccentric B-films, each imbued with a disturbing subtext that played upon emotional imbalance and compulsively destructive sexual behavior, attempted to smuggle a more potent dose of eroticism past the Hollywood censors. *Teddy Bear* came along, creating what is, in effect, a skewed and savage portrait chronicling the perverse underside of a swinging sixties subculture."

*Who Killed Teddy Bear?* begins with a slow burn. The audience is thrust into the role of voyeur, watching as a muscular young man (Sal) climbs out of bed wearing only a pair of briefs. He lights a cigarette, admires his body in the mirror, then fondles himself while making an obscene phone call to a woman who is pictured in snapshots taped to his dresser mirror.

The scene was riveting and shocking. "I played a telephone freak," Sal recalled, "and we were having this hassle with the censors. In some of the shots while I was on the phone they wanted to sorta suggest that I was masturbating, but I couldn't be naked. So I was just wearing jockey shorts. It turned out that was the first American film where a man wore jockey shorts on-screen."

During a tirade, Sal's character paces a room wearing a muscle shirt and a pair of white chinos. The pants are so tight that the outline of his genitals is clearly visible. The film contained no outright nudity and only a few shots of the shapely Prowse in a bra and half slip. However, an unusual amount of attention is lavished on Sal's physique, from the opening sequence through a later scene in a health club. As Norah rests in the water of the pool after swimming a lap, Sal makes an entrance wearing a Speedo-style bathing suit that leaves nothing to the imagination. "Nice body," Prowse's character mumbles.

By combining explicit visuals with controversial subject matter, *Teddy Bear* introduced to the screen sexually profound images and ideas that Hollywood would not acknowledge for many years to come.

Sal was given top billing although he had only a third of the screen time. Many scenes were shot on location in the streets of New York City, including the seedier parts of Times Square. Elaine Stritch enjoyed working with Sal, finding him to be "a real actor." "He loved to discuss scenes," she said. "He loved the process."

Sal began an affair with Juliet Prowse during the making of the film. He told Michael Anderson Jr., "I was going where the 'Chairman of the Board' had been. I asked her what Sinatra was like in bed, and she said he couldn't cut the mustard. I didn't want her to say anything about me, so I really got into banging her!"

A FEW weeks after its New York premiere, accompanied by actress Ina Balin, Sal attended a special screening of *The Greatest Story Ever Told* at the Music Hall Cinerama Theatre in Manhattan on March 9. The gala event was a benefit for the United Nations Association and the Eleanor Roosevelt Memorial Foundation.

Despite a running time of nearly four hours, *The Greatest Story Ever Told* opened to good business and generally good reviews. In the end, the film grossed more than $15 million in the United States. The combined receipts for *The Greatest Story Ever Told, The Longest Day,* and *Exodus* placed Sal at number 80 on a list of the top one hundred stars at the box office in the 1960s.

IN THE late spring, Sal rented a small house in the hills near Laurel Canyon when he returned to Los Angeles to film an episode of *Burke's Law* called "Who Killed the Rabbit's Husband?" Sal was reunited with director Jerry Hopper, who had directed Sal's second feature film, *The Private War of Major Benson.*

On June 6, Sal hosted a colossal benefit "on behalf of freedom from hunger," as the *Los Angeles Times* stated, at the Shrine Auditorium in Los Angeles. Produced by Jack Good (the producer of *Shindig!*), the event, called "Rock, Rock for Sweet Charity," was cosponsored by Los Angeles radio station KRLA. Sal introduced some of the biggest popular-music acts at the time, including the Byrds, the Crickets, Jackie DeShannon, the Everly Brothers, Gary Lewis and the Playboys, and Sonny and Cher.

Eric Williams recalled, "Sal was mobbed. He couldn't believe it. He didn't think the kids would know him anymore."

Beginning at 6:30 in the evening, the powerhouse show, broadcast on KRLA radio, played for hours. "I drove the car around and around until he ran out and jumped in," Eric recalled. "He found a very cute boy there and brought him home. Sal never slept with anyone older than he was."

Though Sal had no interest in singing, he was very attracted to the rock and roll scene in Los Angeles. There was a sense of urgency and freedom expressed in the music, and Sal liked the excitement. He was also attracted by the abundance of attractive and sexually liberated young men and women who frequented the Strip.

"Sal was trying very hard to be relevant," Jill explained. "He was trying to be a member of contemporary, working Hollywood. He wanted to fit in. He wanted a place at the table. But in a way, he was an anachronism. He represented the past, and many people saw him as a leftover or reminder of the fifties. And he hated that."

Recently graduated from high school, Susan Ladin met Sal in the summer of 1965. Sal took her dancing at the Trip and the Whisky a Go Go on Sunset Boulevard. Susan was seventeen and impressed by the special celebrity treatment Sal got at the clubs. She found him "cute, a little weird, but very charming." Later, Sal brought her back to his place, where they chatted, listened to records, and smoked pot.

Sal and Susan began to casually date. During that time, she did not have a clue he was interested in men, though he frequently brought men home when Susan wasn't around. People told her he was homosexual, but she considered herself to be his girlfriend. Still, the gossip persisted.

Sal's homosexual curiosity had become an obsession. His taste in men was particular, however. Though he was amused by effeminate gay men, he was attracted to straight-appearing homosexuals. He often set his sights on men who were, in fact, dating or involved with women. Sal liked the challenge it presented and was confident he could get almost anyone he wanted.

Since Sal could not bring a male date to public functions, Susan served the purpose. She was pretty and she loved the attention. Whatever her feelings may have been for Sal, he had a need and she unwittingly played the part of his adoring date for the cameras.

One day Sal told Susan he was going out of town and asked her to stay and watch his house. He told her Bobby Sherman would be staying there as well. Though Susan and Bobby flirted, nothing ever happened between them. When Sal returned, though, he was convinced they had slept together and he insistently questioned Susan.

At first, Susan thought he was jealous, but she realized he was just trying to figure out if they had, in fact, been together. She finally decided to lie about it and admit to sleeping with Bobby while Sal was away. But Sal was not jealous. Actually, he was anxious to hear all the intimate details. Later, when she told him she had made it all up, he thought it was very funny. "He had a motto," Susan said. " 'Fantasy is better than reality,' a key phrase of his."

David Cassidy began to hang around the house a lot during that summer. David's stepfather had directed Sal in "The World I Want" months before. The two had become friendly, and Sal gave David the drum set he used in *The Gene Krupa Story*. Sal was teaching him how to play the drums, and the teenager crashed at the house and got stoned with Sal often. David said, "Sal took a genuine interest in me. He was a very caring and wonderful person, someone who made an effort to try and support people who were creative and talented."

David was straight, and Sal encouraged Susan to sleep with the fifteen-year-old. Susan and David actually fell for each other, though, and got involved. But whenever Susan saw Sal after being with David, Sal grilled her for all the details of their sexual trysts.

Susan realized this was Sal's way of "being sexual" with David, since there was no chance the two men would ever be physically intimate with each other. Sal wanted to see David "in action," to experience David's lovemaking skills vicariously through Susan. The couple sometimes had sex in Sal's room. Unbeknownst to the lovers, Sal hid in the closet and watched them to satisfy his own curiosity.

Susan said Sal was an interesting, intelligent person with a great sense of humor. Because of his obsessive interest in the guys she slept with, she began to suspect Sal might be bisexual and kept her around for publicity's sake so nobody could accuse him of being homosexual. It was imperative that Sal put forth a heterosexual image to preserve his career. "His career was not doing well and I don't think coming out of the closet was going to do anything for him," she said.

SAL WAS unsatisfied. The year was proving to be one of transition for the actor. He had effectively distanced himself from his family, actually banning his brother Mike completely. His sexual interests isolated him as his socializing habits took a turn, and his choice of friends changed. Once interested in professionally beneficial acquaintances, he was more attracted to younger people who interested him sexually and satisfied a need to experience the abandon of teenage years that he himself had missed. Though he had reestablished a relationship with Jill, he saw Elliot and Michael Anderson Jr. less frequently. Juggling two different personas, that of a straight man in public and homosexual in private, Sal compartmentalized his life and friends. His personal battle with image versus reality resulted in a certain amount of emotional chaos.

His friends felt he was searching for a sense of self—was he an actor, a writer, a director, a rebel, an iconoclast, a curiosity, or a has-been? Michael Anderson said, "It was the old Hollywood joke. Who is Sal Mineo? Get me Sal Mineo. Get me a Sal Mineo type. Get me a young Sal Mineo. Who is Sal Mineo?"

With acting roles in short supply and bills ever increasing, Sal was forced to cash in on whatever celebrity value he maintained and "play himself" on television. Earlier in the year, he had appeared as a celebrity contestant on the prime-time game show *The Match Game.*

*The Celebrity Game* was another prime-time game show filmed in Los Angeles. The show was directed by Seymour Robbie, who had previously directed Sal in *The DuPont Show of the Week.* Three contestants guessed how each of nine celebrity guests would answer posed questions. Written for an adult audience, the format of the entertaining show allowed the celebrities to joke, interact, and make funny responses.

Sal appeared on the episode broadcast Thursday evening, August 19, at 9:30 P.M. He shared the stage with Lee Marvin, Connie Stevens, Gypsy Rose Lee, and Mickey Rooney. Sal was asked, "Do romantic screen heroes tend to make wives *dissatisfied* at home?" He answered, "No. I don't know about other screen heroes but I tend to satisfy a lot of wives."

Sal became a regular at Canter's Deli on Fairfax, which was a popular after-hours hangout for young people and musicians. "Sal felt comfortable around younger people," Jill said, "and emotionally, he connected."

Sal met music producer Phil Spector at Canter's and they became friends. When Jill was in town, she often accompanied Sal there for late-night coffee. They celebrated her twentieth birthday at Canter's and Sal gave her an art book illustrated with the work of Salvador Dalí. In it, he wrote, "For Jill, Hello 'Dali'—Goodbye 'Teens,' Happy Birthday Pussycat! I love you, Sal."

During the summer, Sonny and Cher's recording "I Got You Babe" hit number 1 on the music charts and stayed there for several weeks. "We had a late breakfast one night with Phil and Sonny and Cher at Canter's," Jill recalled. "They all talked about doing some sort of movie project together. Nothing became of that, but Sal and Cher became friends."

However, Spector did offer Sal a job as the host of a rock and roll special called *Live at T.J.'s.* The program introduced the popular

British band the Dave Clark Five to American television audiences. The syndicated thirty-minute program was part of a series of music specials produced by Jimmie Baker and directed by rock music promoter and impresario Steve Binder. Phil Spector, who also appeared on the show, was the musical director.

IN AUGUST, Sal and his personal manager Mark Mordoh formed their own motion picture production company, SalMar-Co. Productions, and signed Robert Kane to write the screenplay for an original modern-day drama based on a treatment Sal had concocted. Kane had written the screenplay for *Kisses for My President.*

Sal liked to tell people he had ridden with the Hells Angels, some of whom he met during his motorcycle day trips. It's unlikely that he actually traveled with them, but he did meet up with some Angels on a trip he made to Bass Lake, near Yosemite National Park in California.

"Long before they started getting all the publicity," Sal explained, "I got interested in Hells Angels. They seemed like they'd be good material for a screenplay, and I like to write, and I wanted to try a script about the Angels. I knew, though, that the only way I could do it would be to get to them myself.

"I spoke to some of the guys and I told them what I wanted to do. There had been a lot of shit written about them, and I was objective. They let me ride with them, and I did everything that they did. I went to one of their initiations, and it wasn't nearly as hairy as the publicity makes it out to be. The whole thing reminded me of a gang we used to have in the Bronx when I was a kid."

Based on Sal's one-page film proposal, simply titled *Hell's Angels,* Robert Kane created a script called *Devil's Angels.* Sal was pleased with it. "It has a great plot," he said. "I'll play the lead."

Michael Anderson Jr. felt that the making of *Cheyenne Autumn* had been a professional turning point for Sal. "His career faltered after *Cheyenne Autumn*," Michael said. "It was a terrible professional experience. It wasn't good for him, and he changed after that. He became more picky . . . he was interested in other things. He acted as though he had been let down by everyone around him. His image was becoming darker and he wanted to make independent films but he didn't have the name to pull it off. The money and the 'things' didn't seem to matter to him. He seemed almost resigned to his financial mess. It was about the art for him. That was primary."

Movie producers, however, weren't interested in Sal. He was respected for his professionalism, but casting agents couldn't seem to find appropriate roles. "When I started in films, I was fifteen, sixteen, and I had this baby face that made me look like a wheat flour dumpling or something," Sal said. "And my fucking name didn't exactly help."

The phone just stopped ringing. Sal couldn't understand why one minute he had more offers than he could handle, and the next, no one seemed to want him. "I went through a time when my name was mud in Hollywood," Sal explained. "I'd always played a certain kind of role. I was getting older, and nobody wanted to give me a chance to try anything else. I found that when I wasn't working, I wasn't on the best party lists either. I had a choice to make. I could sit back and feel sorry for myself, blaming Hollywood for having exploited me, or I could live. I decided to live and to forget about self-pity."

Sal's physical appearance changed in concert with the emotional and intellectual issues he dealt with. Gone were the tailored suits and expensive imported Italian shoes. His black curls now touched his shoulders and he grew a mustache and sideburns. And he dressed himself in motorcycle boots and black leather pants.

"Once Sal came to visit me in hospital," Michael recalled. "I had an operation. It was the talk of the hospital. He was decked out in biker clothes, leather and a vest, and had a bunch of rough-looking guys with him. In 1965! I just laughed at him!"

IN THE summer of 1965, a private nightclub called the Daisy opened on Rodeo Drive in Beverly Hills. The club immediately became a celebrity favorite. Jill recalled, "It didn't start swinging until after ten in the evening." She had met producer Aaron Spelling when she was filming an episode of *Burke's Law*. The forty-one-year-old producer was newly divorced.

"He was a real gentleman," Jill said, "and we dated casually a few times. He was really a very nice man. Sal was always jealous, which was odd, considering everything we had gone through. He could exhibit a temper. It would blow and then pass very quickly. And then it would be over.

"One night, I was at the Daisy with Aaron. Sal came in, and stormed over and actually punched Aaron in the face! I was shocked. He didn't have enough trouble getting work, he has to punch the biggest television producer in the face? Sal yelled, 'Do you know how old she is? What are you doing with her at your age?' "

Jill stayed in Los Angeles during the summer to fulfill several television engagements. While she was filming an episode of *Rawhide*, there was an accident on the set. "The horses bucked in a scene," Jill recalled, "and I hurt my back." Publicists for the program used the dangerous on-set accident for publicity. "I was booked on *Girl Talk*," Jill said. Hosted by Virginia Graham, *Girl Talk* was a nationally syndicated daytime talk show filmed in Hollywood.

"I was there to talk about the incident on the set of *Rawhide*," she recalled. "I was shocked because Sal was also on the same show, and I didn't know that. We both just sort of looked at each other on the couch.

"Then Virginia Graham asked, 'Now why did you two children break up?' I was shocked. I said, 'Well, he left me for another man.' I didn't even think about my answer, it just slipped out. Sal turned white. But it seemed to go over everybody's head. There was a studio audience, too. And nothing. There was no follow-up.

"When it was finished, I went back to the dressing room and the guy who was helping me there said, 'Do you know what you said?' I did know what I said. I felt bad. I regretted saying that, but I don't think anyone really understood, or if they did, they figured I was making a joke."

IN OCTOBER, Sal taped a guest shot on Juliet Prowse's new television series, *Mona McClusky*. The show, professionally reuniting Sal and Prowse, was scheduled to air in December to coincide with the general theatrical release of *Who Killed Teddy Bear?* He also filmed another episode of *Combat!* playing a reckless young soldier in a compelling episode called "Nothing to Lose."

*Who Killed Teddy Bear?* was previewed at a rented Los Angeles screening room in early October. At best, the reviews were mixed. *Variety* wrote, "Mineo as the moody discotheque busboy who falls in love with Juliet Prowse plays a downbeat role which probably won't progress his career but is convincing." The *Hollywood Reporter* was un-impressed: "Mineo does what he can with the role, which isn't much." *Box Office*'s review said, "Mineo is convincing in his most adult—and certainly most unpleasant—screen role to date." And the *Los Angeles Herald Examiner* wrote, "Mineo's performance in an unsavory role is superior to the tone of the picture."

*Who Killed Teddy Bear?* opened nationally on December 8, 1965. Josephine Mineo was dumbstruck by her son's film and mortified when the Catholic Church condemned *Teddy Bear* and instructed millions of followers to boycott the movie. Two weeks after its initial release, Sal's film was doubled-billed as drive-in fare with *The Ghost*, a B thriller starring Barbara Steele.

Even though Sal's performance was generally praised, *Who Killed Teddy Bear?* was not the kind of film that would persuade Hollywood that Sal Mineo was still a worthwhile property in the motion picture business.

After the release of the film, Sal joked, "I found myself on the weirdo list."

## 26.

"I won't be a loser, I won't accept that."

Freezing temperatures greeted Sal when he arrived in Toronto from New York late in the evening on December 16, 1965. Accompanied by his dog Dove, Sal was driven to the Carriage House, where they would stay during his engagement at the Royal Alexandra Theatre.

The next morning, Sal began ten days of rehearsal for his starring role as Sammy Glick in *What Makes Sammy Run?* Joseph Cates, who directed Sal in *Who Killed Teddy Bear?* staged the original Broadway production of *Sammy.* The successful show had closed earlier in the year, and a national touring company was assembled. Cates encouraged Sal to take the leading role in the first post-Broadway, out-of-town production of the hit musical. The role of a singing, dancing leading man was admittedly a departure for Sal, but he liked the challenge and desperately needed the $1,000 weekly salary.

Sal's star power appealed to Michael McAloney, the Canadian producer. As soon as Sal's appearance was formally announced, advance ticket sales validated the producer's suspicion that he could draw a crowd. Still, McAloney, a wily businessman, elicited a professional promise from Sal to seal the deal. In exchange for allowing him the opportunity to star as Sammy Glick, Sal had to commit to a future, mutually agreed-upon production at the landmark Toronto theater.

"Sal hit the ground running," said Gino Empry, the theater's publicist. "He was easy to work with and always cooperative with the press."

Sal managed to find time to explore the city. "Sal wanted to go to a gay bar, which surprised me," Empry said. "He didn't appear gay to me at all. It caused quite a scene. We went out to gay clubs two or three times a week, after hours."

"I really dig your Village," Sal told reporter Sid Adilman of the *Toronto Telegram.* "You know, man, I had forgotten what it was like to be in this kind of place with so many teenagers." Sal had been mobbed on Yorkville Avenue when he first arrived in Toronto. Police were called to rescue him from an enthusiastic crowd of young autograph seekers. Sal said he wondered at times what it may have been like to be an ordinary teenager. "It all sounds romantic," he said, "but those are experiences I haven't the vaguest idea about."

In an interview with Frank Morriss of the *Globe and Mail* newspaper, Sal complained about the lack of good roles available to him. "I don't dig boy-next-door roles," he said. "They're always such boring things. I don't believe in that kind of person anyway. [But] play a juvenile delinquent and you keep on playing juvenile delinquents. I'm going to do a film about the Hells Angels, next, and I'm playing a part, too."

When the reporter asked Sal if that type of part didn't follow the stereotyped pattern he objected to, Sal said, "No. I want to take a group of so-called outlaws and show how they react to the image that has been created by the press. They try to live up to it!"

On Monday evening, December 27, *What Makes Sammy Run?* opened to a sold-out audience at the Royal Alexandra Theatre. Reviews were disappointing. On December 28, in her review for the *Toronto Daily Star* titled "Sammy Should Keep Running," Rae Corelli wrote: "The revival can only be described as disastrous. The lead is played by one-time teenage idol Sal Mineo. There is no denying that Mr. Mineo, nominated for Academy Awards for *Rebel* and *Exodus,* has major dramatic talent. But he hasn't a singing voice applicable to the musical stage, either in strength, clarity or quality, and his performance naturally suffers for it. Still, there are moments when he struggles free of the cloying ineptitude surrounding him to demonstrate a sensitive understanding of the unpardonable Mr. Glick."

Ronald Evans's review, "Sal Makes Sammy Stroll," was especially harsh. "Mr. Mineo, who must be ironically classed as an aging matinee idol at the tender age of twenty-six . . . is a movie performer; he is not a singer, and certainly not a dancer. And he's really not much of an actor either, at least not in this show. Played in Mr. Mineo's light and sardonic way, Sammy becomes as soft as boiled noodles and the show collapses on its centre with a dreadful sighing sound."

Despite the bad reviews and savage winter weather, *What Makes Sammy Run?* drew large audiences. "A star is a star is a star," reviewer Dennis Sweeting said on his television broadcast praising Sal as a top performer despite his shortcomings in the role. And, as another reviewer wrote, "Sal Mineo sells."

"I won't be a loser, I won't accept that," Sal told reporter Michael Sherman. "This is a good vehicle for me."

Sal was most anxious to talk about his latest venture, though. "There must be more to life than just acting," he said. With his newly formed production company, he said he wanted to produce "honest" films, not just ones a producer felt the "mass" audience wanted to see. And, he stated, he wanted to open his executive door to young, untried talent.

In three months, Sal explained, he hoped to begin his first movie production about the Hells Angels motorcycle gang. "If this doesn't work out, and my business manager had reservations about it, then I'll try something else. I've blown money before."

*What Makes Sammy Run?* closed on January 8, 1966. Though he was disappointed by the critical reception he had received in Toronto, Sal was looking ahead. "When my first film is completed," he said, "I'll be the youngest executive producer in the business, and that's just the beginning!"

THOUGH MARKED by disappointments, 1966 was the busiest professional year Sal had enjoyed in more than four years. However, before Sal could line up additional financing for his feature film *Devil's Angels*, director Roger Corman began work in March on his own film at American International Pictures about the Hells Angels motorcycle gang, called *The Wild Angels*. After months of planning and thousands of dollars spent on a screenplay and development, Sal's proposed film was scrapped.

With creditors at his door, small-claims court suits from coast to coast, and overwhelming storage bills in New York for the Mamaroneck mansion furnishings, Sal decided to aggressively pursue television work and contracted the Hugh French Agency to represent him.

Over the next few months he would appear in a two-part episode of the hit television series *Run for Your Life*, starring Ben Gazzara, and an episode of *Court Martial*, a drama filmed in London, starring American actors Bradford Dillman and Peter Graves.

As Bobby Sherman's television career had taken off and his need for Sal's professional guidance waned, he quickly distanced himself from Sal. Besides, Bobby was not interested in the type of romantic relationship Sal had in mind. Although he credited Sal with his "discovery," the whisperings in the industry about Sal's private life and sexual interests drove a wedge between the two men. Sal had grown bored with the situation and sold the personal management contract between himself and Bobby to Louis Harris for one dollar. For the next several years, Sal had a photograph of Bobby hanging over his toilet.

Sal never invested his money outside of failed show business projects. What little money he had was spent on living expenses. Mabel, his beloved housekeeper from the beach house, helped organize his things whenever he moved into a new rental house. Though he couldn't afford to pay her any longer, she still visited regularly to tidy up and prepare meals.

Often he struggled to pay his rent. For a while, Sal and Jill shared the same business manager. Sal was too proud to ask anyone for money. "Sometimes Sal would mention his problems," Jill said, "but always making a joke about his situation. I had money at the time and I would tell our manager to transfer money to Sal's trust account to pay his rent, but we never told him."

"Sal had no business sense at all," Michael Anderson Jr. said. "He had the chance to buy the beach house for seventy or eighty thousand, and he had the cash from the movie at the time. But he didn't want any more responsibility. He owned nothing but his clothes. If he had a dime, he'd spend a quarter."

Elliot Mintz recalled the pressure on Sal to spend money in order to keep up appearances. If Sal went out to dinner with a large group of people, some of whom may have been strangers, he paid the bill. "He even signed for bills he couldn't pay," Elliot said. To counter any negative talk about him in Hollywood, Sal felt he had to maintain the lifestyle of a movie star, even if he couldn't afford it.

On May 27, entertainment trade papers reported that Sal was about to leave for Mexico, where he would costar with Ralph Meeker and Fernando Lamas in a feature film called *Deadly August*. Lamas was set to direct. The production never materialized. But Sal had been working on a made-for-TV movie since mid-April. Produced as a pilot for a prospective series that failed to sell, *The Dangerous Days of Kiowa Jones* was basic Western fare. Sal played a killer trying to elude a bounty hunter. The film was shot on the Culver City back lot and stages of MGM Studios, and on location in nearby Vasquez Rocks State Park.

Pressed for cash, Sal begrudgingly accepted the role of Doctoroff, a psychopathic beatnik, in "The Cool Scene," a segment of the *Bob Hope Presents the Chrysler Theatre* series. The segment was eventually renamed "A Song Called Revenge." The special presentation was broadcast many months later, on March 1, 1967.

In September, Sal signed a contract to portray Peter Van Dam in an NBC-TV production of *The Diary of Anne Frank*. His fee was set at $5,000, and shooting was scheduled at the NBC studio in Brooklyn, New York. The *New York Times* reported on September 19 that a young, unknown actress named Diana Davila would portray the title role in the television adaptation. The stellar cast included Max von Sydow, Lilli Palmer, Viveca Lindfors, Donald Pleasence, Theodore Bikel, and Marisa Pavan. Produced by David Susskind, the two-hour production was directed by Alex Segal.

Sal was very excited to at last be involved in a prestigious project and to work with such respected actors and actresses; however, after several days of rehearsal, creative differences developed between Sal and the director. Susskind had second thoughts as well. Sal was replaced by a younger actor named Peter Beiger.

"The actors had already been rehearsing for a few days and there was only one week left before the show was shot live," Beiger recalled. "When I stepped in, no one knew Sal had been replaced. I just showed up that day. No one spoke about Sal at all, except some people said he didn't read 'young enough.' I was ignored by the entire cast."

Sal had never been fired from a job before. He appeared dumbstruck to Jill, with whom he was staying in New York. "He never told me what happened," Jill said, "but he could do that, just shut things out that were unpleasant."

Instead of appearing in *The Diary of Anne Frank*, Sal taped five episodes of *The Match Game* with Jane Anne Jayroe, the newly crowned Miss America, before leaving Manhattan for Los Angeles. "He did it for the airfare," Jill said.

While Sal's career stalled, Jill's had taken off. In the summer, she had been cast as Sally Bowles in a new musical called *Cabaret*. With music and lyrics by the writing team of Kander and Ebb, and produced by Harold Prince, the musical was based on Christopher Isherwood's book *The Berlin Stories*. There was a three-week tryout in Boston before the show opened on Broadway.

Sal surprised Jill when he attended the opening night of the show at the Shubert Theatre in Boston on October 10. "Sal was terrified for me. He was white as a sheet and actually shaking, he was so afraid for me. But he loved the show. He couldn't believe I pulled it off. He didn't know I could sing. He was very proud of me. There was no jealousy at all. He came to the party afterward, then flew out the next day."

Sal was not able to be in New York when *Cabaret* opened at the Broadhurst Theatre on November 20. Mr. and Mrs. Mineo, who considered Jill "the girl who got away," telegrammed their best wishes. Sal sent a telegram, as well, that read, "Hope you have a warm hand on your opening tonight." Jill recalled, "Sal never saw the show in New York, but David Cassidy showed up backstage one night. He said Sal told him to see the show and come backstage to see me. Sal loved those teenyboppers."

In late October, Sal worked in Hollywood on what the producer called an "adult Western." Costarring Henry Fonda and Anne Baxter, *Death Dance at Banner* (later renamed *Stranger on the Run*) was produced by Universal Studios for an NBC premiere television broadcast.

The original story was written by Reginald Rose, the writer who had provided Sal with two of his finest teenage film vehicles, *Dino* and *Crime in the Streets*. Dean Riesner wrote the compelling screenplay based on Rose's story. And Sal was reunited with Don Siegel, who had directed him in *Crime in the Streets*. Sal played the role of George Blaylock, a posse member. With a six-week shooting schedule, the movie was filmed at Universal Studios and on location in the California desert.

*The Dangerous Days of Kiowa Jones* was finally broadcast on Christmas Day, December 25, on ABC-TV. The reviews were dismal. In his review titled "Blue Christmas for *Kiowa Jones*," Paul Henniger wrote in the *Los Angeles Times*, "This celluloid wasteland, passed off as a Western, was, as they say in the trades, a bomb! In all probability it will now be shipped out of the country to become the lower half of a double bill at Lowes Singapore. Caught up in this travesty . . . [is] Sal Mineo, still playing juvenile delinquents, this time as a cackling killer in chaps."

# 27.

"Hugh French found me a shitty picture, but the money's okay."

Sal turned twenty-eight years old on January 10, 1967. Marking a particularly low point in his career, *The Dangerous Days of Kiowa Jones*, a television flop, was released as a drive-in B film on February 7.

Since Sal had become less interesting to the press, it was easier to keep his private life and dating habits under wraps. He continued to be photographed in public with women. The legitimate press never asked about his sexual preference, and he never talked about the issue in public. In fact, he had casual sexual relations with both women and men at the time, though his closest friends believed he was more interested in men.

"He led his life the way he wanted," Eric Williams said. "He had sex with whomever he wanted. He wasn't public about it, but all his friends knew. He didn't make a bold proclamation, and he was not interested in being anyone's poster boy."

Despite his close relationship with Jill, Sal never came out to her, but he didn't hide from her his feelings for men. "Sometimes he'd introduce me to some guy he was interested in," Jill said, "but we never talked about his sexuality."

Still, the pursuit of his sexual impulses and attractions caused him undeniably conflicting feelings. His career ups and downs, his upbringing, and his family's intolerant religious beliefs all weighed heavily on him. " 'There are no gay Italians,' he used to say," Jill recalled. "And I said to him, 'What about Michelangelo?' " Jill found a T-shirt in New York that was imprinted with the names of famous gay Italians, including Michelangelo, da Vinci, Botticelli, Caravaggio, and Sal. She sent him the shirt as a joke. "He was infuriated," Jill said. "He'd didn't get it at all."

Sal's private life was splashed in front of the public, though, when Susan Ladin tried unsuccessfully to commit suicide. The newspaper headlines were unwelcome publicity. On February 21, the *Los*

*Angeles Times* reported that Susan was found semiconscious in the bedroom of her apartment by her roommate. Authorities reported she had taken an overdose of tranquilizers after writing a suicide note to her father in which she said, "This has nothing to do with my boyfriend Sal."

Sal told the sheriff's deputies that he had dated Susan but had recently told her that their relationship should become less serious. Sal expressed surprise that she would attempt to take her own life.

Later, Susan explained that she had gone to Sal's house to drop off two cases of dog food her father had purchased for him since he was experiencing monetary problems. Sal seemed unappreciative, she said, so she told him that she didn't want to see him again. The next day, Susan decided to confront Sal. She drove over to his house and told him she was in love with him but didn't think he was committed to her.

Sal told her he was bisexual.

Devastated that her suspicions had been confirmed, she drove home and took a handful of sleeping pills. Susan called Sal and told him she had taken an overdose. He rushed to her apartment as the ambulance was pulling away.

This was actually the first of two suicide attempts Susan made.

"I felt terrible the first time," Sal said. "Really down. It's a terrible thing to think that somebody, some human being, tried to end his own life because of you. The second time she tried it, though, I got bored with it.

"When you play the same game twice, it loses some of the excitement. The whole idea of suicide, of that kind of self-destruction, really turns me off more than anything else. After that, I think, I cooled it with having a steady chick."

JON PROVOST met Sal on the Sunset Strip in early 1967. The blond, blue-eyed seventeen-year-old had starred as Timmy, the boy companion and master of Lassie, the most famous canine television star in history. The beautiful, delicately featured young man was trying very hard to shake his teen-idol image and make the transition from child star to adult actor.

Shortly after they met on the Strip and began a friendship, Sal offered Jon a part in *The Flower Children,* a film Sal was set to costar in and coproduce with Nancy Sinatra and her independent film company, Boots Productions. General Artists expressed an interest in packaging the project, which was based on a fifty-page treatment that Sal had written with Russell O'Neil. On March 14, Sal had purchased O'Neil's interest in the treatment and completed a first-draft screenplay.

"*The Flower Children* is a very significant project," Sal told a journalist. "There are a lot of young people in America involved in massive demonstrations to protest the war in Vietnam. I have participated in real marches against the Vietnam War, and I have shared and understood their problems. Are they rebels, with or without a cause? It seems like that's the question."

Jon went to several production meetings at Nancy Sinatra's house. Most of the people there, including Sal's entourage, were nearly ten years older than Provost. Jon thought it was all very exciting, and he felt a million miles away from *Lassie.* Though many of Jon's friends thought Sal was a "has-been," he didn't think of Sal in those terms at all.

As their friendship developed, Jon learned that Sal was bisexual, though he only saw him with Susan Ladin. Jon didn't care about Sal's preferences, nor did he care what other people thought. "He was so charismatic," Jon said. "Sal was striking and could draw all eyes to him when he walked in. The way he carried himself, his whole image, he lived for that, for people to say, 'Look, there's Sal Mineo.' "

After a few months, plans to film *The Flower Children* were abandoned, but Jon maintained his friendship with Sal. Jon knew that Sal was not rich, but when they went out to clubs and restaurants, Sal never had to pay. They were always given the best seat in the house, and people rushed to attend to him. Jon loved being a part of the scene.

Sal had moved to a small, Spanish-style bungalow in West Hollywood. He drove an old, black Cadillac convertible, and everything in the house was black on black. There were always a lot of young people there. David Cassidy and some of his high school friends spent many after-school hours with Sal, talking about music and jamming with their guitars. Sal liked to "hold court," controlling the conversation and listening to everyone talk. David knew that Sal had girlfriends and boyfriends, but he didn't care, either. "Sal was one of the most incredibly warm, gentle, sensitive, funny, and hip people I'd ever met," he said.

Jon spent a lot of time at Sal's house, too, playing music, drinking coffee, and smoking pot. Sal well understood the challenges a child star faced when growing into adult roles, and Jon felt a true connection to him. Fueled by marijuana, their conversations were philosophical and often quite intimate. Sal didn't like taking drugs that might interfere with his ability to control himself, or to control others. Sometimes he gave the impression he was taking drugs, but he really wasn't. He wanted to watch everything that was going on. Marijuana and "poppers" were Sal's drugs of choice. He told Jon he used poppers when he was having sex. He said he'd break open a capsule and inhale just when he was about to have an orgasm, and it made him feel as if his head was going to blow off.

ON JUNE 16, 1967, the Monterey International Pop Music Festival rocked Southern California and set the tone for a summer that would come to define a generation. Colored by war, civil disobedience, and racial unrest, the summer of 1967 came to be known as "the Summer of Love." For many people, it was more appropriately called "the Summer of Sex." And Sal's one-bedroom, black-draped bungalow in West Hollywood was a part of the action.

Ever since Susan became fully aware of Sal's sexual preferences, he had engaged her in an interesting game of cat and mouse. With her own flirting, she helped him procure handsome young men. Susan enjoyed the game, but her interest changed when Jon Provost came into the picture. The teenage actor was awestruck by Sal. He was very impressionable and tried to keep up with the fast lane Sal was living in. Susan and Jon began a sexual affair, which Sal encouraged from the sidelines. She knew people could get hurt, but she was still very influenced by Sal. Other participants seemed to be able to take care of themselves, but she felt Jon wasn't prepared, and she tried to keep them apart. When Susan warned Sal to stay away from Jon because he wasn't gay, Sal said, "I'll show you that I can change anyone."

Sal encouraged Jon to enjoy life and to experiment. From the beginning of their friendship, Sal liked to talk about sex in detail and wanted to hear about Jon's sexual experiences. At first, Jon thought the interest was like that of a big brother and younger brother, but he never realized how calculated the conversations were.

One sunny June day, Jon stopped by Sal's house and he was surprised to find Sal uncharacteristically alone. Sal and Jon smoked a joint, stripped, and hopped into Sal's hot tub. Once again their conversation turned to sex.

Though Jon knew that Sal had sexual experiences with men, he only talked about heterosexual experiences with him. On that summer day, Sal talked about orgasms. Sal told Jon that he liked to get close to orgasm but stop and hold out. He'd repeat that for several days until finally giving up to an explosive climax. The seventeen-year-old boy marveled at such unbelievable self-control.

While Sal was talking so animatedly about orgasms, Jon noticed that he was intimately stroking his dog, Dove, in front of him. "I knew he was trying to shock me," Jon said, "so I pretended it was no big deal, but I was shocked."

BACK IN 1965, on the heels of his successful films *The Thin Red Line* and *Battle of the Bulge,* producer Philip Yordan had proposed to several studios a feature film idea about the historic volcanic blast on Krakatoa Island in Indonesia between Java and Sumatra. In 1883, a volcanic eruption there destroyed more than 150 villages and killed over 36,000 people. Work had begun on the $10 million production in October 1965. Not only was there no script, but there was no story as well. Art director and special effects master Eugène Lourié only had a title, *East of Java,* and a list of proposed special effects. "There were many different ideas on how to handle the script," he recalled, "as a somber tragedy based on the disaster, a travel adventure à la Jules Verne, or a musical comedy."

While the script was being prepared, work slowly progressed at Cinecittà Studios in Rome. Lourié shot special-effects scenes and began the construction of delicate miniatures. Cinerama Releasing Corporation committed to distribute the film, which would be shot using the Cinerama format, a wide-screen process that allowed the simultaneous projection of images from three synchronized 35 mm projectors onto a huge, curved screen. This technique, first invented in the 1950s, provided for an extra-wide screen image in a movie theater.

When the script written by director Bernard Kowalski, his secretary, and his brother finally arrived, Lourié was disappointed. In the rewriting, the adventurous aspects of the story were lost and it had become a mishmash of scenes.

In the late nineteenth century in the Dutch East Indies, Captain Hanson of the *Batavia Queen* prepares to embark on an oceanic treasure hunt. His mistress, Laura, knows the location of the wreckage of a ship that belonged to her late husband. On board the sunken vessel was a priceless cargo of rare pearls. The shipwreck lies dangerously close to the erupting volcano on the island of Krakatoa, where Laura's young son attends a convent school. The climax of the picture is the eruption of the Krakatoa volcano, which was actually located *west* of Java.

On May 8, 1967, Sal signed a contract to appear in *East of Java*. Eric Williams recalled, "Sal told me, 'Hugh French found me a shitty picture, but the money's okay.' " Sal's guaranteed compensation was $12,000 for a minimum of twelve weeks' work.

In order to avoid paying the many creditors' claims filed against him, the contract provided that his compensation be payable to the order of Madrin Enterprises Inc., an offshore company that acted as Sal's agent.

After eighteen months of pre-production, the cast finally arrived in Spain in July 1967. No one had read a script. "But each," Lourié recalled, "had been promised 'the best part of your life.' "

Sal was cast as Leoncavallo, an improbable balloonist reduced to performing in carnival shows. Rossano Brazzi played his father. Shooting was scheduled in Madrid, Spain, at Samuel Bronston Studios and the Sevilla Films Studios. Location filming was done on Spain's largest island, Majorca, in the waterfront village of Denia. The village of Sóller, a municipality near the northwest coast of Majorca, was the home base for the film company. The cast was flown to the location by helicopter and the crew arrived by boat.

The actors stayed at the exotic El Molino Hotel in Majorca during location filming. Eric Williams kept Sal company during most of the time he spent in Spain. "There was an actress in the film," Eric said, "playing the part of a missionary nun. Sal said he always wanted to fuck a nun. He took the girl back to the hotel and fucked her on the balcony while she was still wearing her nun costume. When they finished, they got a round of applause from the people who were watching from below."

When location shooting was finished, the company moved back to Madrid. "When we were in Madrid," Eric said, "Sal rented this tremendous penthouse apartment at the top of the Tora building. The other actors had apartments there, too. One day, I got a bit tired of standing around the studio, and Sal gave me the key to go to his penthouse. I let myself in and there was this beautiful young blond Swedish boy sleeping in his underwear on Sal's bed. Sal told me he had met him in the public lavatory in the building."

When principal photography was completed in Spain, Sal decided to fly to Amsterdam for a short holiday before returning to the United States.

"Sal called me," Eric recalled. "I joined him in Amsterdam. He was staying at a gay hotel, which I'd never heard of before. He had run short of money and told me he was selling dope in the town square. He may have been kidding with me, but he always managed to have pot, which he called 'boo.'

"We went to a famous club there called the DOK Club. We went downstairs to a basement and we stopped dead on the steps. There were two hundred formally dressed men dancing a Viennese waltz. The male couples were waltzing about. It looked like a cotillion . . . what a sight!"

The two men stayed long enough to have a beer. "Sal and I took a walk that evening," Eric recalled, "and we were talking. We never openly talked about his sexual interests, though I was well aware. But I told him I was gay. He didn't say anything to me, but he hugged me."

SAL FLEW to New York and stayed in Manhattan for a short time and visited Jill before heading back to California. Jill's starring vehicle on Broadway had become an enormous commercial success, and she was the toast of the town.

Jill said, "I'd get home late from working in *Cabaret* and sleep in. When I got up, Sal would be there with my mother drinking tea and talking. My mother absolutely adored him. Everything that ever happened between me and him was *my* fault, according to her. He couldn't do anything wrong in her eyes. And he knew it.

"Sometimes, after the show, I'd go out to late-night clubs," Jill explained. "I'd go to gay bars with my chorus boys and with Lotte Lenya; who was in *Cabaret* with me. One night we went to the Penthouse, a gay after-hours club, and Sal was there with my mother! Lenya walked up to them and said, 'Ven are you two gurls going home?' "

Jill said, "Sal didn't exactly fit the gay stereotype. I actually introduced boys to Sal at those places. He wasn't really the aggressor at that time, but he did have a good sense of who could be had in the club."

Eric Williams recalled, "Sal really knew how to work a room. When he talked to you he never took his eyes off you. And he would look around and find someone who looked lonely or alone and he would seek them out to talk with them."

IN OCTOBER, Sal returned to Los Angeles. Before he had left for Spain in July, he had narrated an educational documentary film about LSD. Produced by the General Telephone Company, the fifteen-minute film was designed to aid in the fight against illegal drug use and addiction and was made available to California schools, colleges, and other educational organizations. *LSD: Insight or Insanity?* included appearances by doctors from veterans' hospitals and UCLA, who explained what was known about the drug and its effects on users. On October 1, 1967, the *Los Angeles Times* reported, "Police officers who have previewed the film say it is an excellent documentary on the drug problem."

Drugs were not a "problem" in Sal's personal life, however, and he spoke willingly with the press about his occasional use. His honesty was refreshing but counterproductive to a career already in trouble. Sal was involved with the hippie scene and found himself at parties where the Sunset Strip crowd experimented with LSD, as well as other drugs. "I took LSD about fifteen times," Sal said. "It was kind of trippy—I got into this whole intellectual thing. I tried mescaline, too, and it was pretty scary. I saw that I wasn't going anywhere with it, so I stopped it. Now I can get higher *without* drugs. I can groove on my own thing.

"Stuff like LSD can be dangerous, I guess, but our attitude about pot is ridiculous. We know it doesn't hurt the body, and it's still illegal. Liquor can ruin your liver, really mess you up, but for some reason, that's okay. We should face the facts. Pot should be legalized."

———

THE TELEVISION FILM *Stranger on the Run* was broadcast on October 31. The *Hollywood Reporter* reviewed the telecast enthusiastically: "Sal Mineo fleshed out his supporting role in a fine performance." *Variety* wrote, "NBC-TV's 'World Premiere' movie, *Stranger on the Run,* got the highest rating of any NBC movie aired thus far in the current season." Several months later, the film was successfully released as a theatrical feature in Europe.

Sal rang in the New Year a few days early when he attended the star-studded opening in Los Angeles on December 28 of Arthur, the West Coast replica of the glittering Manhattan discotheque. The Los Angeles nightery was owned by Sal's friends Roddy McDowall and Natalie Wood, among other Hollywood celebrities.

"Everyone was there," wrote Joyce Haber, a gossip columnist for the *Los Angeles Times.* "Sal Mineo looked playfully menacing in leather, and Natalie Wood glowed in a silver and black checkered military mini."

# 28.

"My agents told me, 'You're not a hot property anymore.' And they were right."

Without the benefits of long-term, exclusive contracts, actors and their representatives had to maneuver through job offers and determine which projects were legitimate and which were not. On March 15, 1968, *Variety* reported a problem Sal had experienced in an article titled "Sal Mineo Burned by Backfiring Foreign Film Deal." With little protection offered by their union and European producers reluctant to sign firm contracts or provide money up front, American actors often encountered problems with overseas-based productions.

After signing a rather vague letter of intent for a film called *The Last of the Gunfighters,* to be shot in Italy, Sal said, "It sounded interesting enough for me to make the trip to Rome to close the contract and start the picture." The film was scheduled to begin in February 1968. Sal said, "It never got off the ground."

He explained, "When I was working in *East of Java* in Spain last summer, an Italian gentleman, Federico Topal, came to me and proposed a two-picture deal. Everything seemed fine until I returned to California in October. Telegrams kept promising the money was being sent, but it didn't arrive."

After numerous phone calls and wires, Sal decided to go back to Rome after Topal sent him a round-trip ticket. "But still no contract or money in the bank," he added.

He was provided with a $50-a-day suite at the Excelsior Hotel in Rome, limousine service, and $350 a week for expenses. "I actually thought that after three days everything would be settled. But three weeks went by and still no contract, no picture, and after not being able to contact Topal, a bill for $2,500 was presented to me," Sal said. After trying, without success, to contact the producer through his Italian agent, Sal returned to Los Angeles.

In the months since his return from Spain in the fall of 1967, Sal had not had any film or television offers. His representative at the Hugh French Agency was unable to arrange any auditions for him, either.

"All of a sudden," Sal said, "my agents told me, 'You're not a hot property anymore'. And they were right, I wasn't. I wasn't getting any offers. Before, when I *was* getting the offers, they were just more than I could handle, and then when things started to cool off, I couldn't get *anything* I wanted. The roles I wanted most went to new people."

In 1960, Sal was angered when Horst Buchholz got the part that he had coveted in the Yul Brynner film *The Magnificent Seven*. A few years later, Buchholz again landed a role Sal had lobbied for, that of the assassin of Mahatma Gandhi in *Nine Hours to Rama*. Sal's friend Eric Williams recalled his friend was bitterly disappointed. "Sal said, 'First that goddamn German was in a Western and now, he's playing a fucking Indian.' "

Sal wanted to play the part of Perry Smith, one of the murderers in the film *In Cold Blood*, based on Truman Capote's bestselling nonfiction novel. Though the producers told Sal that they wanted an unknown actor for the role, they eventually cast movie veteran Robert Blake.

"Sal tried to get the rights to *Midnight Cowboy*," Eric said. "He told me he took the book to Joseph E. Levine to sell him on the idea. There was no script yet. Sal told Levine to read the book, and Levine said he never read books and asked what it was about. And Sal said, 'It's a leukemia love story between two guys.' He couldn't get it done." When the project finally got off the ground, Sal anxiously read for the part of Ratso Rizzo, a homeless cripple. Dustin Hoffman got the part.

Written and directed by Peter Bogdanovich, *Targets* was filmed in Los Angeles in early 1967 for Paramount Pictures. It was Bogdanovich's first movie and the last film appearance by Boris Karloff, whom Sal wanted to meet. He hung around the set for a day and did a walk-on in the film, but the shot was eventually cut out.

Sal had been the first person to offer Bogdanovich a job in movies. He had wanted them to write a script together based on *The Folded Leaf*, a novel by William Maxwell about a young, sensitive boy whose mother's death forces him to question the past and his own deep sense of lost childhood. But he couldn't get the rights.

"Somehow Sal managed to scrounge up the money to buy the rights to *The Last Picture Show*," Eric said, "but he could never get it made." The successful 1966 novel by Larry McMurtry was about the coming-of-age of two young men in a small Texas town in the early 1950s. One day Sal gave the book to Peter Bogdanovich and told him he had tried in vain to produce it but still believed it would make a great film. Sal felt he was too old to play the lead. The director recognized the cinematic potential of the novel, quickly obtained the film rights when Sal's option expired, and eventually directed the film.

For a short time, Sal shared the same business manager, Andy Morgan, with his friend Michael Anderson Jr. Sal had earlier been paid $5,000 for *The Flower Children*, the scuttled screenplay he had worked on for Nancy Sinatra.

"One day," Michael said, "someone expressed an interest in it, and Sal called Andy to buy it back from Sinatra, and her representative told him it would cost one hundred thousand dollars! Sal couldn't believe it. Sal told them, 'I'll pay you back the five grand I got for it,' but Sinatra's people said no. The poor guy couldn't catch a break. It was that way for him all the time. People wouldn't even return his phone calls anymore. And he told me some actually hung up on him."

"My agents were frank with me, for which I'm grateful," Sal said. "Anybody with whom I have any dealings or any kind of relationship must lay their cards on the table. I don't dig the salesmanship thing, 'Stick around, baby, it's going to be cool,' because it's not going to be cool; when I saw that I wasn't getting good offers for good roles, I knew things weren't going to get better for a while."

IN MARCH 1968, Sal made the first of two sloppily packaged and poorly written made-for-television movies at Universal Studios. The first film, called *The Challengers*, concerned race car drivers who competed in the Grand Prix. Sal played the small role of Angel de Angelo. After numerous delays, it was finally broadcast to dismal reviews on CBS-TV in March 1970 and released overseas as a B feature film.

In April, Sal made his first television appearance in months with Jon Provost on a teen show produced by Dick Clark called *Happening '68*. Throughout the spring, Jon and Susan continued their casual but heated affair. Before long, they were having sex at Sal's place, and Sal asked if he could watch. Jon thought the request was a little weird, but the idea was exciting to the teenager. Susan and Jon made love in Sal's bed, while he smoked a joint, sat in a chair at the foot of the bed, and watched.

These sexual shows happened numerous times and Jon came to feel very secure there. Susan experienced the excitement of a young lover and the vicarious thrill of being watched, though she knew Sal was really interested in Jon.

It didn't take long before Sal and Susan invited Jon into bed with them. Jon left his innocent past behind and jumped at the opportunity to try something he'd only read about in magazines. Susan lay between the two men. At first, Jon enjoyed the experience and Sal respected Jon's boundaries.

Susan enjoyed the liaisons with the energetic eighteen-year-old, but she began to worry. She warned Sal that he wasn't going to have his way with Jon.

"You're wrong. You're wrong. You're wrong," Sal told her.

Susan said, "Sal had to be in control of every situation and it would drive him crazy when he didn't have control. And he'd find another way so that he *would* have control."

One night, Sal, Susan, and Jon got stoned and Sal suggested they all move to his bedroom. They undressed and lay on the bed, Susan again between Jon and Sal. They smoked another joint, and Jon, feeling relaxed and comfortable, rolled onto his back. Susan lay across his chest and assured him everything would be okay. While the threesome shared a popper, Sal slid closer to Jon and began to grope him. As Jon struggled to get up, Sal pinned him down on the bed. When Susan finally moved aside, Jon jumped up, grabbed his clothes, and ran out.

"It's okay," Sal said, "let him go."

Sal and Susan had a terrible argument after Jon left. Susan was tearful and regretful. She angrily asked Sal what was wrong with him.

Sal said, "What's wrong with *you*? Can't you hang with the big boys?"

Several days later, Jon, still upset, called Sal, who was nonchalant on the phone. Jon told him he was angry and disappointed about what had happened. Sal remained calm and said, "It just seemed so natural. I thought it was cool with you." Jon continued to see Sal around town but never socialized with him again.

DURING THE SUMMER, Sal made his second made-for-television movie at Universal Studios. Shot in July, the film was originally titled *Only One Day Left Before Tomorrow.* Retitled *The Scavengers* and later *How to Steal an Airplane,* Sal played Luis Ortega, the vicious and autocratic son of a South American dictator, who steals a jet. Upon completion, the film sat in the vault at Universal Studios for more than two years before eventually being shown on NBC-TV.

In the midst of filming at the studio, Sal participated in a meet-and-greet event for fans at Universal Studios' Hollywood theme park. "Sal was mortified," Eric Williams recalled. "He said he stood in a booth and tourists could come up to take his picture and get an autograph. People gawked at him and if they weren't interested, just turned their backs and walked away. He said he was surprised the studio didn't have him selling tickets to the amusement park."

Sal flew to Hawaii in August to appear in an episode of a new police series called *Hawaii Five-O.* In an episode called "Tiger by the Tail," Sal played Bobby George, a young rock and roll singer who decides his career needs a publicity boost, so he plans a phony kidnapping stunt with two pals. The episode was a ratings winner.

AFTER LIVING A FEW YEARS in California and New York, Eric Williams had moved back to England in 1967. "I was in London," Eric said, "and Sal called. He heard about a play called *Fortune and Men's Eyes* that was playing in London. He said he thought he should see it. I bought a ticket for him to fly to London."

Sal recalled, "I found the play in Martindale's bookstore in Beverly Hills. I was trying to find a play that dealt with young people."

Eric explained, "Sal came over to London for a few days and we went to see the show. He was interested in it but said he was glad he saw it so he knew what *not* to do with it. For such a provocative play about men in prison, it was a bit dull. He wanted to bring it back to the U.S. and direct it himself. Then he set about obtaining the rights."

On October 18, 1968, the show business trade papers *Variety* and the *Hollywood Reporter* posted the same news item. "Sal Mineo is casting for the West Coast premiere of the off-Broadway play *Fortune and Men's Eyes* by John Herbert. Mineo, making his directorial debut, is casting tomorrow at the Meredith Repertory Theatre."

## PART FOUR

# THE EROTIC POLITICIAN

Sal, Los Angeles, 1969

# 29.

"To me, anything and everything has some kind of a sensuous overtone to it . . . I don't see in any given situation where there isn't a spark of erotica."

Sal explained, "I didn't have the thousand dollars I needed to buy an option on *Fortune and Men's Eyes*. So, I did what I often did when I came close to being broke: I flew to Las Vegas."

Sal had a specific system for gambling in Las Vegas. He flew in on a round-trip ticket for a weekend. He gambled all day, beginning with roulette and then playing chemin de fer with his winnings, and whether he was winning or not, he never missed his scheduled flight back to Los Angeles. "I have literally lived off it for months in this town," Sal said. "It isn't much fun to go to Vegas this way, but I wasn't going for fun; I was trying to make the option money—and I made it!"

Frustrated with his inability to find substantive roles, Sal reorganized his professional representatives. While he was in Europe in August 1968, Sal left the Hugh French Agency. Lawrence Kubik of the Robert Raison Agency became his new agent. In September, Sal hired Phillip B. Gittleman as his personal manager. Gittleman, who also managed actress Corinne Calvet, had once worked as an actor's agent and had been in the restaurant business in Southern California.

*Fortune and Men's Eyes* was written by Canadian author John Herbert. The sensational and provocative play was first produced in Ontario in 1965. It opened off-Broadway at the Broadway Actor's Playhouse in 1967 and ran nearly a year. The play concerned homosexuality in prisons. The lead character, a naïve young student named Smitty, is sentenced to jail for six months for a minor offense. He is incarcerated with three cell mates. Queenie is a flamboyant homosexual who exploits every situation to his own ends. Mona is a boy whose only coping mechanism is his ability to mentally separate himself from his surroundings. Rocky is a manipulative, opportunistic bully. During his time behind bars, Smitty is harassed, beaten, and violated by fellow prisoners. The theme of the play was the transformation of

Smitty, who is essentially a good person, into a hardened prisoner, even more callous than his fellow cell mates. His transformation was principally the result of a homosexual rape, played offstage. Toronto-born Herbert had actually served time in the Canadian penal system when he was a young man. Herbert found the title for his play in a sonnet by William Shakespeare: "When in disgrace with fortune and men's eyes, I all alone beweep my outcast state, and trouble deaf heaven with my bootless cries."

It was difficult to cast the challenging play. The subject matter and the required onstage nudity were problems for most young, established actors in Hollywood. Sal cast Tom Reese, a veteran character actor with whom he had previously worked, as the prison guard. A twenty-five-year-old actor named Michael Greer was cast as Queenie. Greer, who towered at six foot four, had appeared in the film *The Gay Deceivers*. Roger Garrett was cast as Mona, and James Oliver was cast as the antagonist, Rocky.

The role of Smitty proved to be particularly problematic. The play called for the young actor portraying the character to strip onstage and be sexually violated by Rocky.

IN THE late summer of 1968, the successful Broadway rock musical *Your Own Thing* opened at the American Conservatory Theatre in San Francisco. A handsome, dark-haired young actor named Richard Markell played Sebastian, the lead character. He'd previously toured in the national companies of *Bye Bye Birdie* and *Gypsy*. Sal saw him in *Bye Bye Birdie* on the road in Las Vegas and went backstage to meet the eighteen-year-old. Richard said they became lovers. Though long since broken up, they remained friends and got together now and then.

Two weeks before *Your Own Thing* opened in San Francisco, an eighteen-year-old aspiring actor named Don Johnson arrived in town from Kansas. He had been referred to the resident director of ACT by one of his teachers and hurriedly arranged for an audition.

"Don arrived on the last day of auditions," recalled Walter Willison, another cast member. Though all of the roles had been cast, Don managed to get the part of "general understudy." One of the lead actors broke his ankle shortly before the opening, and Don opened with the show in that role.

"We were all surprised when Richard became friendly with Don, who most of us thought was an opportunist," Walter explained. "Richard heard Sal was casting *Fortune and Men's Eyes,* and I guess he thought Don would be Sal's 'type,' so he really surprised us all one day when he took Don to Los Angeles for a long weekend to meet Sal. They smoked dope and did mushrooms and had a pretty wild weekend at Sal's place. Sal conducted a séance, and they told us James Dean's ghost appeared to them, actually walking into the house through a window or door."

When they came back to San Francisco, Don had the part of Smitty in *Fortune.* Don was very interested in *Fortune and Men's Eyes,* but he was a little apprehensive and curious about first meeting Sal. "I'd heard of Sal's reputation," Don said not long after *Fortune* premiered in Los Angeles. "I mean, he has a monstrous reputation. And I was super-naïve at the time. I didn't know anything about all that. I mean, I wasn't so much turned off by the thought of homosexuality—after all, back in the Midwest, on the farms, it's more or less taken for granted that boys will be boys, and while they're growing up they're going to start checking out each other's wee-wees and see what each other looks like. So that sort of thing didn't turn me off as much as the lecherous way everybody looks at it out here. So I got down to L.A. and I played it really super-butch, you know? I told Sal, 'Look now, if you think I'm letting anybody fuck me for this role, you're out of your bean.' I really brought down the law to him. I said, 'Forget it. I'll just forget my career and the whole damn thing, because I'm not getting involved in that shit.'

"And that just put Sal on the floor. Rolling on the floor, laughing. 'Cause I was really serious. And he said, you don't have to do any of that. No legitimate producer is going to make that sort of a thing a prerequisite for a part. And so I said, 'Great, then I'll walk through shit a quarter of a mile, I'll do anything you want me to do, but don't get involved with me in a sex scene on any level, 'cause I can't deal with it.'

"You know, Sal was great—he was really great. Of course, there were some wild stories that went down about us, which is fine, because they helped sell a lot of tickets and everything. And there have been some outrageous stories about us! God, God, God!"

Shortly after arriving in Los Angeles to begin rehearsals for the play, Don, with little resources or connections, shared an apartment in the Montecito Apartment Hotel in Hollywood with Sal and his dog Dove. Located on Franklin Avenue in a then seedy part of Hollywood, the imposing art deco building built during Hollywood's golden age had seen better days.

On December 8, 1968, the *Los Angeles Times* reported that *Fortune and Men's Eyes,* with Sal set to direct, would premiere on January 9 at the Coronet Theatre in Los Angeles. Moe Weise and Sal's business manager, Phillip Gittleman, were the executive producers. The newspaper wrote, "Due to the blatant approach of its subject matter, no one under 18 will be admitted to this engagement. The iconoclastic drama has been continuously under fire since its premiere in New York, and has been prohibited from production in many parts of the world."

Despite lurid newspaper ads highlighting the scandalous subject matter of the play, advance ticket sales were disappointingly slow. The producers decided that Sal needed to act in the play as well as direct if there was any hope of a financially successful engagement in Los Angeles. The decision was made to dismiss actor James Oliver, who had been cast as Rocky. Sal assumed the role. In press releases, the producers explained that Oliver had developed nodes on his vocal cords and needed to leave the production for medical reasons.

In addition to the bold casting change, Sal decided to take certain liberties with the script. He felt it needed more edge to effectively portray a realistic prison environment. Days before the play opened, while he nursed a recurrence of the chronic infection in his right eye, he told Margaret Harford, a reporter for the *Los Angeles Times,* that he cast young, unknown actors, some still in their teens. He wanted to be as realistic as possible, and he said he was very influenced by the New Wave cinema of such directors as Michelangelo Antonioni and Franco Zeffirelli. "I want to tell it like it is," he said.

Because of his criminal conviction in Canada, Herbert could not enter the United States. Sal sent Herbert his newly altered script of the play. "While he didn't agree with everything I was doing," Sal said, "he didn't forbid my doing it my way. I've added scenes."

Sal decided the homosexual rape scene in the prison shower should appear onstage rather than offstage as in previous productions. The intention, he said, was not to titillate the audience so much as it was to depict the deplorable conditions within a prison that dehumanize men.

Sal actually visited local jails and a prison with his fellow cast mates. They all went through "receiving" as new prisoners, were handcuffed, fingerprinted, showered, deloused, and issued prison clothing. He visited Greenlands in Westchester County, New York, an incarceration facility for young criminals. The experience gave him nightmares.

"None of us will be the same after this play," Sal told the reporter. "I'm interested in the treatment of prisoners. Physical brutality will probably always exist. I'm concerned with mental brutality. Some of those guys come out more warped than when they went into the joint."

Los Angeles theater audiences had had a taste of full-frontal onstage nudity when the Broadway hit musical *Hair* opened at the Aquarius Theatre in Hollywood several months earlier. In *Hair,* the entire cast disrobed in dim light at the first-act curtain. But Sal had different plans for his production of *Fortune.* To begin the dramatic rape scene, Sal decided to strip at stage left and walk across the stage with just a towel tossed over his shoulder. His character, Rocky, then grabs Smitty, pushes him into the shower, tears off his clothes, shoves him against the prison bars, and begins to sodomize him. A prison guard's whistle blows as the lights fade to black and Smitty painfully screams. Theater audiences had never seen anything like it before, and they had *never* seen a famous American actor (especially one twice nominated for an Academy Award) appear nude in a film or onstage. The stage director was terrified that the theater would be raided and all the actors would be arrested. Sal told him, "If they raid us we'll run three years!"

The nudity was not a problem for the actors. Don Johnson recalled, "I never really thought about it at the time, frankly. I said this is a real good thing—this play—and the nudity in it, well . . . fine. And it's a very new thing. Nobody was doing it in films really. A little chick nudity, maybe—tits and all that—but no male nudity."

Don had little reluctance in regards to the staged homosexual rape, either. "It was a whole, heavy, heavy number to go through, especially when you're eighteen years old and fresh out of the sticks. I really didn't stop to think about it. I felt this is right, what I'm doing, and so I just forged right on. When the play opened and we got rave reviews, shit, it was easy then. I had proved my point—that I could do something with style and class, and meaning to it, and not be put down for the way I made that statement. That was a big thing in my life. It turned my whole life around."

The Los Angeles production of *Fortune and Men's Eyes* opened on January 9, 1969, to a specially invited audience. The reviews for the show were sensational. On January 13, *Variety* wrote, "A boy's reformatory, where homosexuality is spawned and nurtured by the biological needs of the inmates and the apathy of the guards, is not the most desirable environment in which to make the transition from the innocence of youth to the responsibilities of manhood. But such a setting is fertile ground for the stinging comedy and stirring drama of *Fortune and Men's Eyes* magnificently mounted by Sal Mineo, who is making his directorial bow. The controversial piece is handled with such good taste that it rises far above the somewhat objectionable subject and results in an entertainment that should assure tingling thrills through a long run. His inventiveness marks an auspicious initial directing effort and stands him as an exciting new directorial talent." Frederic L. Milstein wrote in the *Los Angeles Times*, "Intense theatre . . . it shocks—vividly, and brutally. Beautifully staged. Sal Mineo's direction is excellent."

In early March, Sal took a few days off from performing and flew to Honolulu, Hawaii, to attend a special preview screening of *Krakatoa, East of Java*. Sal had not seen the film, which had been in postproduction for more than a year. He was appalled by what he saw. Halfway through the screening, he blurted out, "This is the worst piece of shit I've ever seen!" He walked out of the theater, to the dismay of the film's attending producers and Cinerama officials.

Sal rejoined *Fortune* on March 8. As long as Sal was appearing in the play, standing-room audiences turned out. Many celebrities attended the show and visited Sal backstage, including Richard Chamberlain, Roddy McDowall, Richard Deacon, Chita Rivera, Paul Lynde, Rip Taylor, and Jim Nabors, among many others.

Jon Provost saw the show, and so did David Cassidy, who occasionally had an early dinner with Sal at the counter of the Rexall drugstore just a block from the Coronet Theatre. Jon Provost and Don Johnson were about the same age and shared the same blond, rather "pretty" features. Still trying to shock Jon, Sal had told him he planned to rape Don for real onstage. Jon remembered the play as very dark and very heavy. He hadn't seen Sal very often since Sal had forced himself upon him. Now, six months later, here was Sal starring in a play that Jon felt featured a similar attack. Jon said Sal, cast as the bully, "was able to live out this scenario—forcing himself on a straight, naïve, eighteen-year-old boy—night after night."

In an interview for *In* magazine, a gay publication, Sal talked at length about the artistic choices he made. "My intention was not: where can I put a nude scene. I didn't believe the kid's transition from a typical nice boy into a boy-slave—just like that—with no sign of it at all. I mean, they don't show anything in the original play—not one moment of physical violence.

"I just can't understand censorship at all in any media in any form of any kind. I don't understand what censorship means. Who has the right to determine what is pornographic, what is lewd, perversion? What is perversion? It's when one forces someone else, and in many cases even that's not perversion, because the person being forced really wants to be forced. So anything we deal with in our fantasies—and I'm sure we all have some groovy fantasies—should be acted out on the stage or on film or in books. I just can't go with any kind of censorship.

"To me, anything and everything has some kind of a sensuous overtone to it . . . I don't see in any given situation where there isn't a spark of erotica . . . Even though it's horrible, tragic—à la *Fortune*—within that, there is tremendous love, tremendous passion, tremendous sensuality.

"I like Rocky. For all his hang-ups and his weaknesses, he's kind of a pathetic kid. Not the brightest kid you'd want to meet, and yet I find it very moving that he is affected by another kid. He could never be a Smitty. Maybe that's what hurts him so much in being rejected by Smitty—is that for the first time in his life he was able to make contact with an unknown kind of image. It's kind of sad that he realized he could never be that—and never really understands why, either."

The subject matter complicated the advertising campaign for the play. The *Los Angeles Times* carried a small block ad, without illustration, daily. It was difficult for the producers and the show's publicist to appeal to most mainstream publications.

Elliot Mintz wrote Sal's biographical notes for the program of *Fortune and Men's Eyes:* "Sal Mineo is an erotic politician . . . Mineo hates boundaries . . . He is an anarchist of the arts." A full-page, pensive photograph of James Dean graced the program. The inscription printed on the photograph read, "Jimmy: In memory of your friendship and inspiration, I dedicate this production to you, Sal." The producers felt the press would seize upon the "personal" dedication and that Sal's professional association with Dean would provide good publicity.

Instead, publicity targeted a predominantly homosexual demographic. One publicity stunt suggested by Elliot Mintz proved embarrassingly wrong and only fanned the fires of gossip surrounding Sal's private life. Elliot convinced Sal to pick up several gay street hustlers on Santa Monica Boulevard and take them to dinner at Nate 'n Al Delicatessen in Beverly Hills for the publicity. No one got the joke.

A decision was made to grant interviews and provide provocative photographs from the play to "throwaway" periodicals and gay-themed magazines. In-depth interviews of Sal appeared in such magazines as *In, Avanti,* and *After Dark.* These magazines covered the world of entertainment—especially experimental, independent, and underground productions—and also filled their pages with pictorials of nude men.

In a revealing interview with *Avanti* magazine, Sal discussed the theme of homosexuality in the play. "I don't consider it a play about homosexuality. Homosexuality is definitely a part of it and motivates so much of it. But that's not the problem; the problem is a mental thing. In this particular case, homosexuality is a tool, used as a kind of weapon."

Sal admitted that the play had two prevailing themes: an exploration of the penal system, and homosexuality. "I think it's all together," Sal explained. "The point I'm trying to make is kind of a soul-searching thing. For instance, will a so-called straight man sitting in that audience look at what's happening to Smitty, the new boy? Will he be able to be honest enough with himself and identify with that kid as a kid who's straight, who's moral, who comes from a fairly middle-class home and yet because of survival—that's the point . . . What does one do, how far does one go for survival? And we see the kid submitting to an act. The act happens to be a homosexual act."

The "homosexual act" that Sal referred to—actually a violent rape—was integral to the story. In fact, there was nothing about prison life *aside* from homosexual activity that was presented in the play, though Sal felt there was a larger issue. "Because in this case homosexuality is such a dominant force in a prison," Sal explained, "this is what we use to show the transition, also the brainwashing, the conditioning. But the play as a whole deals with a much larger situation, and that is survival.

"I think a lot of emphasis, the wrong kind of emphasis, has been placed on homosexuality, not only in my play, but in books and articles and things like that. And in my dealing with this kind of subject matter, I expected, of course, other connotations. Why would I do a play dealing with homosexuality?"

When Sal was asked if he was homosexual, he responded, "No. And I don't think it's in any way prevented me from having an honest understanding of the situation.

"The point is that one does not have to be involved to understand. That's what the homosexual is crying for, not sympathy, but simple understanding. How different really is the true homosexual relationship from the true heterosexual relationship, when you come right down to it?"

The subject of homosexuality was more and more frequently being represented in motion pictures, books, and theatrical productions. "I think a lot of films are cashing in on the laxity of censorship," Sal explained, "and are cashing in on the sensationalism. A lot of people really don't know what homosexuality is."

In Sal's version of *Fortune and Men's Eyes*, the characters' sexuality and motivations become blurred. "I tried to open up that whole taboo," Sal said, "that we can't really and shouldn't put labels on people. I'm exposed to all of those labels: heterosexuals, homosexuals, all of that nonsense. But I believe it's wrong and that's why we do a play like this, because it throws them right out the window.

"Even bisexuality is a label. You do your thing and you go where your heart takes you and that's where you should go. But if it's in any way forced on you, that's perversion. If you want to make it with your dog and the dog digs it and you dig it—that's not perversion. That's why I hope, if anything, that there is better understanding of homosexuality and when people come to see the play that they don't see it as a horrible disease as everybody is making it out to be. It is a form of life and there are all kinds of forms."

Though the project was artistically satisfying, Sal's monetary problems followed him to work. After three months performing in *Fortune and Men's Eyes,* he hadn't yet taken a salary. The stage manager recalled that a process server wandered into the theater one afternoon during a rehearsal. He had a summons for Sal. Sal took the summons, shook the guy's hand, and told him not to worry about it. Then he gave the man two passes to see the show.

Jill was in Los Angeles for television work in March. "I was staying at the Beverly Wilshire Hotel," she said, "and Sal would just show up and sometimes spend the night on the couch. I had a suite there. He'd order room service after I'd gone to work and just charge it to the room. He had no money at all. Sometimes he left clothing for the hotel to launder for him."

In May, Sal worked five days on *80 Steps to Jonah.* The feature film was produced by Steve Broidy, who had been introduced to Sal by their mutual friend Cher. Broidy had recently produced the film *Good Times,* starring Sonny and Cher. Sal played a drifter who dies in the first few minutes of the film. *80 Steps to Jonah* was released by Warner Bros. on October 29. Critics and moviegoers paid no attention to the film.

*Krakatoa, East of Java* had its American premiere on May 14 at Pacific's Cinerama Dome in Hollywood. The star-studded red-carpet event was carried live on a local Los Angeles television station and hosted by Steve Allen. Despite Sal's disgust with the finished film, and the fact that the timing of the event overlapped his own curtain time at the theater, he decided to attend the festivities. He concocted a publicity stunt to promote the play.

Sal hired several off-duty Los Angeles police officers and rented a nondescript white van. Actor Tom Reese, who played the prison guard in the play, joined Sal, who was handcuffed to Don Johnson. Fellow "prisoners," actors Robert Redding and Gary Tigerman, completed the group. Michael Greer and Roger Garrett had previously left the production. All the actors, dressed in their prison costumes from the show, climbed into the van and went to the Cinerama Dome. The actors got stoned during the ride.

On a television set in the bar next to the Coronet Theatre, the stage manager and his friends watched Sal's arrival. The van slowly pulled up to the red carpet, accompanied by a police escort. The actors spilled out of the van and walked the red carpet handcuffed together as Tom Reese, in character as their prison guard, barked orders. Steve Allen was nearly speechless. Sal danced around any questions to do with the film and instead spoke about the play. After several minutes, they turned and paraded back to their waiting van.

By that time, the audience had assembled in the Coronet Theatre for that evening's sold-out performance. The stage manager explained the delay. After almost thirty minutes, the van finally pulled up in front of the theater and the actors entered through a side door that opened directly into the auditorium. The stage manager held the door open and yelled, "They're coming! They're coming! He's bringing 'em back!" Tom Reese led the handcuffed cast through the audience and onto the stage, where he pushed them into their "cell" and locked the door. The show began.

Kevin Thomas, writing for the *Los Angeles Times*, felt *Krakatoa, East of Java* was a terrific film. "*Krakatoa* is one of the best movies ever made in Cinerama. With its erupting volcano and terrifying typhoon, it makes full use of the giant screen's potential for spectacular effects." Thomas was virtually alone in this enthusiasm, however.

The *New York Times* review was scathing. "Its most breath-taking panoramic shots are of things like shoes and foreheads. The ads for the movie quote a Los Angeles reviewer praising a 'terrifying typhoon,' which is not in the movie. Sadly, Maximilian Schell, Rossano Brazzi, Brian Keith and Sal Mineo are."

Shortly before taking a break from the play, Sal appeared on *The Joe Pyne Show* on May 24, 1969. Hosted by Pyne, a controversial "shock jock" on Los Angeles radio, the thirty-minute talk show was broadcast locally in Los Angeles on channel 11. Their frank conversation about sex prompted the station manager to ban Sal.

Stephen Lewis interviewed Sal for the May issue of *After Dark* magazine. The entertainment monthly often profiled gay artists. In an article entitled "Sal Mineo: Rebel with a New Cause," Sal spoke about his experiences with the play and his hopes for the future.

"Some directors work on a show, then once it opens, they're done," Sal said. "I don't believe in that. If I hadn't taken over the role of Rocky, I'd have been at the theater every night anyway. I'm looking for a replacement now, and as soon as I can, I'm going to start watching the show from out front."

Sal said he was looking forward to directing films. He said, "Film is a director's medium. With the stage, you have some control. You work, you try. But the curtain goes up, and that's it. You're powerless. With films, you have complete control. You can really do what you want, the way you want, and you can say, that's mine."

When Sal's agent approached John Herbert about obtaining the rights to a film version of *Fortune and Men's Eyes* that Sal would direct, the playwright refused. Herbert was mortified by the changes Sal made to the original play. The sensationalism and nudity certainly helped the box office success of the Los Angeles engagement, but the playwright felt the changes undermined his intent and defined his work in a completely new, and unwanted, way.

BY JUNE, all the original actors had left the play and been replaced by understudies. About six weeks before the show closed, a young couple from New York attended a performance. Kenneth Waissman and Maxine Fox, both still in their twenties, were forming a production company. For their first production, they were interested in bringing Sal's version of *Fortune and Men's Eyes* back to New York City. With Sal's revised script in hand, they returned to New York after a couple of days to find backers for the show.

In early July, Sal flew to New York to meet with Waissman and Fox and finalize plans for their upcoming production. Jill was appearing at the Westport Country Playhouse with William Shatner in a summer stock production of *There's a Girl in My Soup*. Before returning to California, Sal drove to Connecticut to see Jill. They were both lonely, and Sal, though buoyed by the upcoming New York production of *Fortune,* was feeling especially overwhelmed by the state of his acting career. In a moment of weakness, they slept together that night. "I don't know what we were thinking," Jill said. "It just happened. Maybe he was trying to prove something to himself. Or to me. I don't know. It was confusing for both of us, all very awkward, and over as fast as it started. We actually finished it up laughing."

On July 7, 1969, the *New York Times* reported, "The Sal Mineo production of *Fortune and Men's Eyes,* which has been running at the Coronet Theatre in Los Angeles since January, will open here October 22 Off-Broadway."

The *Los Angeles Times* followed the story on July 9 with a report that Sal would not appear in the play but would continue to direct *Fortune and Men's Eyes* when it opened off-Broadway at the three-hundred-seat Seventy-fourth Street Theatre in October. "*Fortune*'s local producer, Moe Weise," the paper reported, "said it failed once Off-Broadway so he dropped the rights to it."

Weise had actually been influenced not to take the play to New York by a pending criminal case in the state that centered around the arrest of three cast members and the author of a play called *Che!* A fifty-four-criminal-count indictment had closed the show on May 7, 1969. *Che!* was the first theatrical depiction of heterosexual and homosexual sex acts with a nude cast. Days after its opening, the cast and crew were charged with public lewdness, consensual sodomy (though simulated), obscenity, and conspiracy to commit such acts under the New York State penal code. Moe Weise had no interest in risking similar charges or, worse, actually ending up in court. Rather than give Sal pause, however, the controversy enticed him.

In mid-July, the *New York Times* reported that Sal was set to direct his first motion picture, *Midnight and the Moving Fist,* written with the help of his friend Elliot Mintz. "The film," Sal said, "will be made by Hilltop Productions, a new independent company, after I stage *Fortune and Men's Eyes* off-Broadway this October."

The publicity and praise that resulted from *Fortune* was a welcome surprise to Sal. He also appreciated the notoriety. He thought he had finally put his finger on the kind of entertainment product that could jump-start his career. Not deterred by John Herbert's refusal to sell him the film rights to *Fortune,* Sal had decided to write a similar-themed work to direct and produce.

*Midnight and the Moving Fist* also dealt with prison life. "It's about a young guy who refuses to kill and is therefore jailed as a draft dodger,"

Sal explained. "When he comes out of prison, after being tortured by his fellow prisoners, he is more a threat to society than many hardened criminals." Sal said he would not appear in the film. "I'll be behind the camera calling the shots," he added.

Moe Weise and Phillip Gittleman closed *Fortune* on July 29. Don Johnson, Michael Greer, and Sal returned to their original roles for the last week of the engagement. Enthusiastic audiences filled the theater.

# 30.

"I wasn't trying to build an image . . . I was trying to build a life for myself."

The provocative nature of *Fortune and Men's Eyes* provided Sal with the most publicity he had experienced in years. The disturbing subject matter of the play, his effective portrayal of a predatory homosexual, his onstage full-frontal nudity, and his willingness to be interviewed by and appear in numerous "gay" magazines and papers was a professional coming-out for the actor (despite his public denials regarding his personal sexual preferences). It didn't take long for Sal to realize the downside of his successful effort. He got what he wanted, but he lost what he had. For many producers and casting agents, it was the last straw and effectively ended his career as a leading man in motion pictures.

Michael Anderson Jr. said, "The transition from child star to adult is very tough. It is a little easier on girls, but boys, when they are child stars, they have to be sensitive and asexual. That is hard to grow out of, and Sal was sensitive all right, but he was *not* asexual at all. He was the complete opposite."

Sal was most effective when he played a vulnerable boy whose aggressive behavior was a self-defense mechanism, as evidenced by the three roles—Plato, Dino, and Dov—that earned him the most acclaim. Many thought Sal had simply outgrown the roles he was most suited to play.

The rise and fall of his acting fortunes caused him no bitterness, Sal said in an interview with *After Dark* magazine. "It would be easy to blame Hollywood," Sal explained, "to say that I was typed and forced to play the same role over and over. For a while, I did. But the truth is that I knew what I was doing. I was enjoying myself. I was making money. I suppose that it had to stop. I made some good pictures, and I made some bad ones. I wasn't trying to build an image, though; I was trying to build a life for myself. But being able to do what I want now is what I really care about. I always felt that way. I went where it was happening. I haven't made a dime off *Fortune,* but it's what I want."

Sal's lack of money was the primary reason he left the Los Angeles production and was replaced by another actor. He needed to find a paying job. His friends tried to convince him to collect unemployment benefits, but he couldn't bring himself to do it.

Phillip Gittleman said he took Sal to the unemployment office in Hollywood after arranging for his claim to be processed quickly. "But Sal was too proud," he said. "He took a look around that place and then he had to leave."

With a weekly salary of only $100 for his acting in *Fortune*, Sal was put on a weekly allowance of $25 by his business manager. The $3,000 Sal had earned for *80 Steps to Jonah* were spent in two weeks. Amicably, Gittleman severed his business ties with Sal early in the summer of 1969.

Sal had not paid rent for the apartment he shared with Don Johnson at the Montecito in Hollywood. He had told the owner that he was interested in buying it. The ruse lasted for several months before the owner realized he was being conned. Sal owed thousands of dollars in back rent. When the owner pressured Sal to close the deal or pay the rent, Sal and Don escaped through a window in the middle of the night.

Seemingly unfazed, Don moved in with a beautiful, red-haired aspiring model named Kristine Clark, whom he had begun dating. He had met Clark through Sal's friend Susan Ladin.

For a short time Sal rented a second-floor duplex on Lasky Drive in Beverly Hills. The building was near a grade school a couple of blocks south of Wilshire Boulevard. One day Michael Anderson Jr. dropped in on Sal. He ran into Don Johnson's sister, Jamie, who was coming down the stairs. Michael recalled, "She said, 'I've had sex before, but never like that!'"

Gossip and innuendo publicly defined Sal and Don's relationship. In private, there was no question that Sal was charmed by the young actor. Sal didn't completely reveal the nature of his relationship with Don, though he told some of his friends that he and Don had sex on the set of the play at the Coronet Theatre late one evening. Sal did, however, recognize Don's talent and appreciate his appeal. He genuinely tried to help Don find his way professionally in Hollywood.

Veteran casting agent Marvin Paige recalled, "I was living in

Hollywood and Sal brought Don Johnson over one day. He wanted to introduce him to me for castings."

Sal decided to leave the Robert Raison Agency in August. With no prospects for another agent, Sal engaged Don's agency, Hyland-Chandler, to represent him.

"For Sal," Michael Anderson Jr. remembered, "art was more important than business. He had really fallen on hard times. I know he slept on friends' couches at times. During those dark days, Elliot Mintz would call around and find an Italian restaurant in Long Beach or some other remote place and they would go there and Sal would regale them with Hollywood stories, and then when the bill came, they would never let him pay. It was on the house. Sal did that a lot of the time."

A friend who owned Arnie's Budget Rent-A-Car on Sunset gave Sal an unrented car to drive when he couldn't afford to rent one. When Sal earned some money, he'd rent a nice place but often wasn't able to maintain the payments. He'd wait it out until the landlord evicted him.

Michael explained, "There was a guy we called Crazy Nate who rented anything. You could rent a television for ten dollars, tables, chairs, and even silverware. Sal would call him when he moved into a new place and Nate would show up to furnish it."

"Sal would lease a bed for nine dollars," Elliot recalled, "twenty-five cents for the topsheet and twenty-five cents for the bottom. He'd get crates from the supermarket, or wooden boxes, and he'd cover them with marble contact paper and use them for end tables. He'd use candles, and he'd say, 'If we keep the room dark, who's going to notice the difference?'

"Everything I learned about finances, I learned from Sal," Elliot said. "And he was not a hustler or a thief. He just believed that certain things were owed to him."

THE GODFATHER, written by Mario Puzo and published in 1969, was a critical and commercial success. Sal read the novel about a New York Mafia family and saw himself as Michael, the young son of Don Corleone. Sal believed his own heritage as a native-born New York son of a Sicilian immigrant qualified him for the role over any other actor mentioned. He campaigned earnestly for the part. Unfortunately, Francis Ford Coppola, chosen to direct the film, was looking for an unknown actor. Sal was bitterly disappointed.

"What difference does it make if the audience knows me?" Sal said. "I'm a good actor and I'm hearing that 'new face' bullshit."

IN LATE JULY, Sal was cast in the season-premiere episode of the hit NBC television series *The Name of the Game*. Michael Anderson Jr. costarred in the episode, titled "A Hard Case of the Blues." The story concerned a blues singer whose thieving business manager is accidentally electrocuted. Dripping in oversized rings and jewelry and wearing a flowery silk blouse and metallic purple suit, Sal's characterization of a music mogul resembled an effeminate Sammy Davis Jr. Michael recalled, "Wardrobe actually called us at home and asked us to bring our own clothes to wear!"

*The Name of the Game* starred veteran film actor Robert Stack, best known for his portrayal of legendary FBI agent Eliot Ness on the television series *The Untouchables*. Sal's friend Eric Williams said, "Sal told me he got Eliot Ness stoned! He gave Robert Stack a joint and they smoked it together at the studio!"

The ninety-minute show, which aired on September 26, 1969, was the most highly acclaimed episode of the series. Sal's appearance on the show provided him with his only television acting role in 1969. He had appeared as a celebrity contestant with Buddy Greco on *Oh My Word* earlier in February and as one of three bachelor contestants on the prime-time game show *The Dating Game*.

DON JOHNSON did not want to re-create the role of Smitty in the New York production of *Fortune and Men's Eyes*. Instead, he accepted his first starring role in a motion picture. He flew to New York in August to begin work on *The Magic Garden of Stanley Sweetheart* for producer Martin Poll, who had seen him in the Los Angeles production of *Fortune*.

The New York production of *Fortune* was very different. A new soundtrack was created for the show, and the new set, painted industrial green, was brightly lit and featured new mechanically controlled prison bars and locking doors. The rape scene at the end of act I was rewritten. Sal decided the thirty-second scene would be extended to last three minutes. The attack now began with a naked struggle in the shower and ended with Smitty being pinned and raped by Rocky against the cell bars—facing the audience.

When Sal arrived in New York in late August, he contacted a casting agent named Mark Fleishman. At the time, Fleishman represented nineteen-year-old actor Armand Assante. Sal desperately wanted Assante to play the part of Rocky in the New York production, but he wasn't interested.

Bart Miro Jr. was eventually cast as Rocky. Miro had played a tribesman in the New York production of *Hair*. Smitty was played by Mark Shannon. Jeremy Stockwell, a young man with little acting experience, was cast as Mona. A respected character actor named Joe Dorsey was cast as the guard. And Michael Greer re-created the role of Queenie.

The company fell into a hectic rehearsal schedule. Ten- and twelve-hour workdays were not uncommon. Ken Waissman and Maxine Fox launched an aggressive advertising campaign to promote their first production. The decision was made to rename the play *Sal Mineo's Fortune and Men's Eyes*. Since Sal was not appearing in the play as an actor, the producers felt they needed to exploit his name for maximum attention. In addition, a silhouette drawing of Sal's face was used in all the print advertisements.

The renaming of the play was the last straw as far as the playwright was concerned. John Herbert wrote a letter to the trade paper *Variety*, which was printed shortly before the show opened in New York. The author distanced himself from the production and slammed Sal for the "scandalous" additions to his original script. Further, Herbert wrote that he had neither been asked permission for the changes nor approved of any changes to his play.

IN THE final days of touring in *There's a Girl in My Soup*, Jill began to feel ill. When she returned to Manhattan from upstate New York in September, she discovered she was pregnant. The only man she had slept with in months had been Sal.

"We were both shocked," Jill recalled. "And upset. Obviously, we couldn't have a baby." Sal arranged for Jill to go to England for a legal abortion. He wanted to go with her but was in the midst of working on the New York production of *Fortune.* Jill flew to London alone. She paid for the trip and the medical procedure herself. She recovered at Eric Williams's flat.

"We couldn't tell anyone it was Sal's baby," she said. "My mother was the only other person who knew. It was not our finest hour." They even lied to Eric and told him Jill had become pregnant by her last boyfriend, whom she had broken up with many months before. Jill suffered severe bleeding following the abortion. "I bled on Eric's couch," she said. "He laid plastic everywhere. It was a terrible mess, and I was in such pain. And then Sal sent an enormous bouquet of long-stemmed red roses. The room was awash in red."

Sal and Jill never spoke about the pregnancy again.

PREVIEW PERFORMANCES of *Fortune and Men's Eyes* began at Stage 73 in New York on October 10, 1969. The provocative play attracted enthusiastic and appreciative audiences during the previews.

In October, Sal's version of *Fortune and Men's Eyes* was not the only gay-themed play on a New York stage. *The Boys in the Band, And Puppy Dog Tails* by David Gaard, Robert Patrick's *The Haunted Host,* and John Osborne's *A Patriot for Me* enjoyed varying degrees of critical and box office success. On October 31, *Time* magazine printed an extensive article titled "The Homosexual: Newly Visible, Newly Understood." Sal made his New York directorial debut in an atmosphere of anxiety and confusion but also at a time of heightened sexual freedom, expression, and awareness. He believed his timing could not have been better.

Word of mouth was very good, but the official opening-night performance on October 22 was a disappointment. The audience seemed unmoved by the show and sat in stony silence. The after-party was on the second floor of Sardi's. Sal, the producers, and the cast were joined by friends and family members. Elliot Mintz had flown in from Los Angeles and Eric Williams from London. Mr. and Mrs. Mineo seemed a little out of their element, and when asked about her son's debut as a director, Josephine was at a rare loss for words.

"The thing I worried most about doing that play," Sal recalled, "was what my parents would think. They're not theatergoers, and they see only the things I do. I almost hated to see my folks after the show, but when I asked them what they thought about it, my father said, 'Very well directed, Sal. Very well directed.' "

Jill had returned to her apartment in Manhattan a couple of weeks earlier. She could not attend the opening-night performance, but she joined the party later in the evening. "It was horrible waiting for reviews," Jill recalled. "I was afraid for him; I knew how hard he worked." The local television review was not very good but paled in comparison to the withering review by Clive Barnes in the *New York Times*.

> Mr. Mineo's version of this play is pure and tawdry sensationalism. I am not sure what kind of reputation Mr. Mineo has—he is a minor Hollywood player I believe—but I am perfectly certain of what reputation Mr. Mineo deserves.
>
> The first production was fundamentally a serious indictment of the North American prison system. Mr. Mineo's version, which I saw at a preview, is neither so well plotted, nor so well acted, nor so well directed as the original. The actors are rather too pretty to be particularly acceptable as typical prison inmates—a circumstance that presumably must offend Mr. Mineo's highly calculated taste for verismo realism. They are permitted to act by Mr. Mineo in a range between hysteria and sensitivity.
>
> I consider that the changes Mr. Mineo has made in this play have been made in the interest of sexual titillation—chiefly of the sado-masochistic variety—rather than in the interest of drama.

Despite Clive Barnes's scathing review, New York business was brisk.

"The play is real," Sal said in response to unfavorable New York reviews. "I've done my best to keep it real and powerful."

SHORTLY AFTER *Fortune* closed in Los Angeles, Sal met a boy working for a clothier in Beverly Hills. "I was fourteen when I met Sal," Michael Mason explained. Sal spotted Mason at Lenny's Boot Parlor in Beverly Hills. He approached him and asked for assistance. "He started calling me at the store and coming back," Mason recalled.

Mason finally accepted Sal's invitation to dinner. They joined two women at the restaurant. He saw a friend at another table, who said to him, "Michael, what are you doing with Sal Mineo? Don't you know he's a fag?" After dinner, Mason went home with Sal. He was surprised to find the house decorated with prison bars, a ball and chain with spikes in one corner, and the words "fuck" and "hate" written on the walls.

With the money he earned from *The Name of the Game,* Sal had rented a small house at 1438 North Beverly Drive, off Coldwater Canyon in Beverly Hills. The house, on a dead-end street, was tucked between two imposing hillsides. Sal had no furniture and few belongings. He used set pieces and props from the Los Angeles production of *Fortune* to furnish the house. The *Life* magazine cover with the photograph of Jill and Sal was framed and hung over the tiny fireplace in the living room.

Michael Mason remembered, "Sal and I got to the bedroom real fast." Sal closed the bedroom door and Mason thought they were going to have a serious conversation. "Sal walked toward me," Mason said. "He said, 'Swing with me. Swing with me.' All I saw were those big dark eyes. We fell onto the bed, boom, boom. This was my first sexual experience. Of course, the next morning I ran away. I mean, it took me months to have another scene with him. I couldn't deal with it."

When he finally spoke with Sal again he told him it had been his first time and he didn't really enjoy the sexual experience. A month passed while Mason thought about what had happened. He and Sal had a few more sexual interludes, but they became friends over time. The young man cooked for Sal and house-sat for him when he went out of town.

Mason quickly embraced his newfound sexuality but thought that Sal was actually sexually repressed despite his aggressive behavior. Occasionally they went to an area frequented by gay men on the beach in Santa Monica. Sal was uncomfortable and sat in the sand in his pants and T-shirt for a couple of minutes before wanting to leave and walk in the sand.

"He did love to put people on though," Mason recalled. "All the stories and rumors about him after *Fortune.* There were even rumors about S and M, but he wasn't into that at all. He loved to put people on. If somebody was talking about something strange, something sexual, he'd get a sly smile on his face, lick his lips, and pretend he was getting all hot and bothered."

A production of *Fortune and Men's Eyes* opened in Honolulu in late November. Sal directed the play, which Waissman and Fox produced in a small venue that primarily functioned as a gay bar.

The Los Angeles Bah-Humbug Theatre Awards, chosen by resident drama critic Dan Sullivan, were printed in the *Los Angeles Times* on December 28, 1969. One of Sullivan's carefully chosen awards went to "Sal Mineo, director, for interpolating several scenes into his production of the prison drama, *Fortune and Men's Eyes*, undreamed of by playwright John Herbert, but very big with the audience that flocked to see the show at the Coronet." The playwright himself earned an award as well: "John Herbert, for disavowing Sal Mineo's production when it went to New York; but not to the point of turning down royalties."

Sal, Maxine Fox, and Ken Waissman, New York, 1969.

# 31.

"Now that I know you like playing games, I wonder
if you're up to playing with the big boys."

Despite the critical vilification of the play, New York audiences
lined up to see the provocative show. *Fortune and Men's Eyes*
had become the proverbial talk of the town. *Women's Wear Daily*
writer Martin Gottfried editorialized in the *New York Times* on January 18, 1970, about nudity and sexuality being depicted onstage. Gottfried wrote,

> *Fortune and Men's Eyes* is a powerful production of a weak play.
> The power lies in Sal Mineo's violent, physical and extremely
> theatrical staging. Mr. Mineo exactly fulfilled the directing function, not merely stressing the play's strengths and minimizing its
> weaknesses, but materializing his idea. It proves that nudity and
> explicit sex can be used in the theater in a valid and effective way.
> *Fortune and Men's Eyes* received some rough notices, but its
> business has been excellent. Its business has been excellent because homosexuals have been flocking to it. There's no sense
> resenting a predominantly homosexual audience. If you feel uncomfortable, it's the price you pay for your prejudices.

COURTNEY BURR III was a twenty-one-year-old actor working in two
vastly different shows in New York: a children's theater production
of *Little Red Riding Hood,* and an underground theater production of
a play called *Nude Gymnastics.* The young actor had a privileged upbringing. His grandfather, Courtney Burr, was a renowned Broadway
producer with more than twenty-five productions to his credit.

One evening, a friend invited Courtney to see *Fortune and Men's
Eyes.* Courtney recalled, "To this day, that night was one of the most
exciting I have ever spent in a theater. The tension was palpable. When
the play ended, the audience sat in the dark in stunned silence, which
continued as the lights came up and the actors came out to take their
curtain calls. I was a walking, throbbing nerve. There was nothing at

that moment that I wanted more, or that seemed equally unattainable, than playing the role of Smitty in the play as I had just seen it."

A short time later, Courtney heard the producers were looking for replacements in the New York production and for planned productions in San Francisco and Toronto. On Friday, January 16, 1970, Courtney went to the Manhattan Theatre Club to audition for the role of Smitty.

The producers were impressed and told Courtney he was selected for a callback audition for Sal, who would make the final decision. Sal was scheduled to arrive in New York City sometime in February.

Courtney said, "In the meantime, rumors were rampant about the show, about Sal, about what the final selection process might really get down to. Sal had a curious reputation. I listened to it all because I had no knowledge of him whatsoever. Whenever I mentioned I had a final callback for *Fortune*, people's eyes would widen; they would cluck their tongues, take me aside, and warn me of what was probably ahead. Had I heard that Sal was 'into young boys,' that he was heavily into sado-masochism, that he had slept with everybody who had ever played in any of his productions because that had been a requirement to get a part, and that I should be prepared to find out that my final audition would involve my having to put out for the director like all the other Smittys before me? At the same time, my not knowing who he was, and most of the people not knowing that much about me, the rumors added another level of suspense to the whole process."

On Valentine's Day, Courtney proposed marriage to his long-term girlfriend, Jessica. She accepted, moved into his New York apartment, and began to plan their May wedding.

Ten days later, the producers asked Courtney to again pick up "sides," the script excerpt he'd perform for his audition, so he could read for Sal the following day. "I was relieved to learn that the audition was to take place in the theater," Courtney said, "and not in his hotel suite."

Sal arrived in New York on February 11 and moved into the spare bedroom in Jill's apartment. After many anxious days, Courtney finally auditioned for Sal on February 25. "I had never seen a Sal Mineo movie," he said. "I had never seen a photograph of him. I really had no idea what to expect when I arrived at the theater. I remember being a little stunned by his appearance. Shaking my hand was a man barely five foot eight, with well-tanned, olive skin, a horseshoe mustache worthy of Pancho Villa, long wavy black hair almost to his shoulders, an earring in his left ear, and tight purple levis tucked into brown leather Spanish cowboy boots. He also had on a flat Spanish cowboy hat and dark glasses on his broad, obviously once-broken nose."

Courtney did the same scenes he had done before for the producers. Sal made a few suggestions and Courtney read again. When the reading was over, Sal asked him questions about his feelings for the character, the story line of the play, and how—if at all—he related to prison life.

"I told him that what had affected me was the jockeying for power between the inmates," Courtney explained, "as well as the brutality and the mental cruelty that especially young, inexperienced males inflict on each other when they are forced to live together. I had experienced that kind of treatment firsthand when I attended an all-boys prep school."

The conversation turned to the issue of the nudity required for the rape scene. "Do you have any scars, or missing, or additional, or disfigured parts that might alarm an audience?" Sal asked.

"No, everything's in perfect order," Courtney answered. Sal then asked him to remove his shirt. "Sal's eyes stared briefly at my torso, then he reached out to shake my hand."

"Thank you," Sal said. "We'll be in touch."

As Courtney started to leave the stage, Sal added, "Oh, congratulations."

"For what?" Courtney asked.

"Your engagement," Sal answered. "Ken and Maxine said you just got engaged to be married. This must be a pretty exciting time for you."

"Oh, thank you," Courtney said. "Yes, I'm excited . . ." That night, Courtney took his fiancée to see *Fortune and Men's Eyes.*

Before returning to Los Angeles, Sal traveled to Philadelphia to tape an appearance on *The Mike Douglas Show,* a daytime talk show. Maxine Fox called Courtney at 5:30 that afternoon and told him he would be playing the part of Smitty in a new production of *Fortune* scheduled to open in San Francisco on April 22. Plans for a Toronto production were canceled due to financial considerations and anticipated problems with the play's author, who lived in Canada.

Courtney flew to San Francisco on March 8. The following day, rehearsals lasted eight arduous hours. Courtney found an apartment and prepared for his fiancée to join him.

A few days later, after rehearsal, the cast went to Sal's apartment for a get-together. Eric Pierce, the young actor playing Mona, had been discovered in Los Angeles by Sal. They had actually flown together to San Francisco. The meeting ended late, and someone suggested that Eric, who had yet to find accommodations, spend the night at Courtney's apartment. Courtney and Eric ended up in bed together that evening.

The next day at rehearsal, Eric told Courtney, "Sal wants to see us after the show."

Courtney was concerned that Sal was unhappy with his work at the rehearsal, but Eric explained with a smirk, "I told him about last night. He was so pissed!"

Courtney was dumbstruck. "Why would you do that?"

"Don't sweat it," Eric said, to reassure him. "He'll get over it."

That evening at Sal's, Courtney found out that Sal had "discovered" Eric one evening standing in the shadows on the steps of the Baptist church on Selma Avenue in Hollywood, hustling. Sal had picked up Eric and taken him home for the night. He and Sal saw each other several times before Eric told Sal he was interested in acting. As a favor, Sal let him read for the role of Mona and was surprised to see the young man had talent. With no professional acting experience, Eric was given the role in the San Francisco production.

Sal and Eric admitted to Courtney that they had wagered on which of them could get him into bed first. Sal was angered that Eric had won their bet. "Sal was very competitive sexually," Courtney said. "His feelings of self-esteem were closely associated with his sexuality."

That evening, Sal castigated Eric and Courtney for a poor rehearsal, accusing them of not concentrating on the work. "But this was not the case," Courtney admitted. "I was petrified and Sal was regaining authority over territory he felt he had lost.

"As a director, I found Sal to be smart, insightful, caring, patient, certain, knowledgeable, and authoritative. In the more personal social associations he seemed less comfortable, more of a poseur, displaying more of a persona than revealing himself. After his tirade, Sal seemed more at ease. He turned to me just before I left and smiled."

"Do you like chess?" Sal asked Courtney.

"Yeah, sure. Why?"

"Now that I know you like playing games," Sal said as he looked from Courtney over to Eric, "I wonder if you're up to playing with the big boys. The high stakes. If you're up to it."

Courtney was quick to answer. "Maybe, but when I play, I only play with ivory pieces."

For the next few days, long rehearsals kept the cast and director busy. Eric Pierce stayed at Courtney's apartment and began to develop a romantic interest in him. On March 16, Sal was diagnosed with hepatitis and confined to bed. The entire cast was given gamma globulin shots as a preventative, and five-hour daily rehearsals were scheduled, with the stage manager stepping in for an ailing Sal.

Courtney's fiancée, Jessica, arrived from New York on March 22. The next day during rehearsal at the theater, Eric and Courtney had an argument. Eric, jealous of Jessica, had broken off his sexual entanglement with his fellow cast mate. Later that day, the cast went to visit Sal, who was slowly recovering at his apartment.

"Sal was getting stronger," Courtney recalled. "He wanted to keep in touch with us. When he appeared from out his bedroom, he tried to strut as usual and he tried to look casual and in good spirits. I watched him closely as he lit his cigarette and sat slowly on the sofa. His complexion was sallow and it took all his effort to appear energetic as he questioned us about our recent visit to San Quentin prison. The meeting was short. Sal smiled warmly at me as we left."

On the drive back from Sal's apartment, one of the cast members remarked that Sal looked good. Other actors agreed. Suddenly, Courtney yelled out, "He's afraid he's going to die! Can't you see that?! He's afraid he's going to die!"

The outburst startled Courtney as well as his cast mates. He didn't bother to explain. "I had not felt particularly close to Sal in our brief association," Courtney remarked. "But at that moment, I realized I felt something deeply about him. There was some sudden glimmer of understanding about him, a revelation of some common understanding. I had witnessed his fear, his sense of being alone, and I understood.

There was also the chilling awareness that what I felt I recognized in him was really a fear and separateness I had within myself."

George Ryland, the stage manager of the New York production, flew into San Francisco to help direct the blocking while Sal was recovering. On March 24, Sal returned to the theater to watch the progress. Before he left, Sal took Courtney aside and told him, "I need a B$_{12}$ shot," which was his way of telling Courtney he was sexually interested in him.

With only one week before the first preview performance, Sal fired two cast members. Tom Reese arrived to replace the actor who had been playing the guard, and James Wigfall replaced Bob Patterson, who had originally been cast as Queenie. Wigfall came to *Fortune* following a six-month run in the San Francisco production of *Hair*.

"Patterson was fat," Courtney recalled, "and Sal couldn't stand him touching me. That might not have been the best reason to fire the guy, but there was no sensuality there."

After days of twelve-hour rehearsals, *Fortune* first previewed on April 9 to a full and appreciative house. The next day, Sal and Courtney stole a few hours to have lunch together and stroll around the UC Berkeley campus.

One evening after a preview performance, Sal approached Courtney with some notes. "How about that game of chess?" he asked with a smile.

Courtney answered, "Huh . . . oh, right. You sure you're well enough?"

"The doctor says it's time," Sal said. "I'm no risk, and it's just the sort of B$_{12}$ shot I need."

"Maybe you should wait," Courtney remarked. "The producers won't be too pleased if the experience proves too much for you and you perish before the play opens."

Sal laughed. "I'll take my chances."

The next afternoon, following the morning rehearsal, Courtney went to Sal's apartment. After some small talk and nervous moments, they had passionate sexual relations. Courtney spent the night with Sal. The next morning, Sal became complicit in the deception of Jessica when he called her and told her the rehearsal had run very late the night before, and Courtney had fallen asleep at his apartment.

———

SAL, KEN, and Maxine did a flurry of radio interviews to promote the play on Saturday, April 18. Mark Shannon flew into town to see the evening performance. Courtney struggled with his feelings for his fiancée and his newly developing feelings for Sal. And he was surprised to discover that he was jealous of Mark Shannon and the night Mark had spent with Sal before returning to New York.

On their day off, Sal and Courtney drove to Carmel to visit Courtney's grandmother. They then drove to Pebble Beach and walked on the misty shore. They were mostly quiet, but Sal confided in Courtney.

"He admitted that he had been having difficult financial times, the aftermath of his own ineptitude with money and also high-costing professionals he had hired to handle his affairs during his successful years in Hollywood," Courtney said. "He saw my family as a much more typical type of upbringing, and one he envied. He was fascinated by the idea I had attended top prep schools in this country and gotten an education. His lack of conventional education seemed to haunt him and made him self-conscious. It ain't all what it seems from the outside, I reminded him. He envied my knowledge of books, music, opera, and dance. I warned him that he overestimated my credentials. I took a little knowledge and expounded elaborately on it. He said he liked the way I did that.

"In contrast, I told him I looked at the unconventionality of his life as far more interesting and probably more worthwhile in learning what life is really about, seeing the world, meeting interesting, productive people. Sal was amused but unconvinced by my point of view."

Courtney added, "We both admitted our surprise that the other found us attractive or appealing."

"I wouldn't go out with me," Sal laughed. "I'm not attracted to my type, whatever that is."

Courtney watched Sal walk over to the landmark lone cypress tree at Pescadero Point in the cloudy mist. "I realized that I cared really deeply for this man," Courtney said, "that I loved him. This was a part of the equation of life I had never figured upon. It had never occurred to me that I might *love* another man. I was also aware that the man I was having these awakening feelings about might not be in love with me. I kept my feelings to myself as we headed back to the car."

"This is an exciting time for you," Sal suddenly said. Courtney didn't know what he was referring to. "You're starring in the lead role in your first professional production," Sal stated.

"Oh, yes," Courtney said. "I am excited . . . nervous, but excited."

"And you're getting married," Sal added.

"I'm a little confused about all that right now," Courtney admitted.

"You'll work it out."

Inside the car, Courtney turned to Sal and said, "There is one thing that I regret. My mother had been an aspiring actress. She died when I was nine. I just wish she could be here. I wonder what she would have thought of all this."

Sal didn't say a word. They drove back to San Francisco in silence. That night, Courtney made some excuse to Jessica about going over production notes and returned to Sal's apartment, where he spent the night. The following day, Courtney celebrated Jessica's birthday by taking her to dinner.

*Fortune and Men's Eyes* opened on Wednesday night, April 22, at the Committee Theatre in San Francisco. Sal's friend Susan Ladin had flown in from Los Angeles at his request to attend the opening and to meet Courtney. The cast and a few close friends had a midnight dinner at Sal's apartment.

"I received a stack of telegrams from family, friends, Jessica, and the producers," Courtney said. "One arrived separately later. I couldn't figure who was unaccounted for as I opened it. 'She would have been as proud as I am tonight. Peace and love. Sal Mineo.' I couldn't believe he had remembered our conversation at Pebble Beach."

Critics were generally receptive to the show. George Mendenhall wrote in a gay publication called *Vector*, "It may be that Mineo's wish to lose his 'movie star' image and be recognized as a talented direc- tor will now be realized. He does not let the San Francisco audience down. It is all there—and more. Every performer in this production is a stand-out."

In the *San Francisco Examiner*, Stanley Eichelbaum wrote, "Sal Mineo has done a lot to improve *Fortune and Men's Eyes* . . . [his pro- duction is] considerably better and more gripping than the orthodox version we saw two years ago at the Encore." Paine Knickerbocker of the *San Francisco Chronicle* concurred. "In this version of the prison drama the pluses outweigh the minuses."

Box office sales were steady. The dramatic machinations on the stage paled in comparison to what was going on behind the scenes, though. For the next few days, Courtney, Jessica, Susan, and sometimes Sal had lunch or breakfast together. One night after the show, they all went to the Purple Onion, then to actor Michael Greer's apartment for a late-night party. As Sal prepared to return to Los Angeles, his affair with Courtney intensified. While Jessica stayed alone at Courtney's apartment, he shuttled back and forth between her and Sal until Sal left San Francisco for Southern California. Courtney continued to lovingly attend to Jessica. Being a performer, she understood the rigors of appearing in a show and if she suspected a love triangle had developed, she kept it to herself.

Sal rented a VW Beetle and a trailer, which he and Courtney carefully packed. Courtney and Jessica originally planned to ride with Sal to Los Angeles. "Jessica thought she might find some work in Hollywood," Courtney said. But perhaps sensing something was awry, Jessica told Courtney she had changed her mind and actually wanted to return to New York. Courtney gave her some money, and early Monday morning, April 27, he and Sal began their road trip to Southern California. They stopped for lunch at Nepenthe in Big Sur, and Courtney first experienced Sal's love of speed when they were stopped by the highway patrol and Sal was issued a speeding ticket.

They arrived at Sal's small house at 1438 North Beverly Drive in Beverly Hills late that day. Courtney was appalled. "The house was awful," he explained. "I'd never seen anything like it—no furniture, mattresses on the floor. All the interior doors had been removed and replaced with the fake prison bars from the set of the L.A. production of *Fortune*. Some S-and-M-type ropes were hanging around, but that was just for effect. He just had that stuff to shock people. And there were large gothic-like candelabras around. It was really weird. I said to him, 'This is awful. How can a grown man live like this?' I embarrassed him."

On Sal and Courtney's first night together in Beverly Hills, Don Johnson and his girlfriend dropped in at one in the morning. They seemed at home, Courtney recalled, but an exhausted Sal was not interested in entertaining company. "He kept cool with them," Courtney said.

"That *was* a very strange place," Jill recalled. "Sal had a few groupies hanging around there. We called them the 'fellatio fillies.' I didn't like most of them. And Susan Ladin was awful. She hated me. Susan said to me, 'If it wasn't for you, I'd be the first Mrs. Mineo.' And I said to her, 'If it wasn't for Bobby Sherman, you'd be the *second* Mrs. Mineo."

Courtney flew back to San Francisco the next afternoon. Jessica had not left for New York City as planned. The following few days were emotionally wrenching as he attempted to reconcile with Jessica and understand his developing feelings for Sal, whom he deeply missed. Finally, he told his fiancée he had been sleeping with Sal and he was not willing to continue his relationship with her. The next day she returned to New York.

On Sunday, May 3, Courtney flew to Los Angeles on the midnight flight following the performance that evening. This began a practice of spending his off days with Sal throughout the run of the play. Sal picked him up at the airport on a new motorcycle, purchased by Susan Ladin's mother. Courtney was surprised to see that during the past week, Sal had cleaned the house, and furnished it. "Sal had taken his things from storage and had furniture in the house. Clunky old Italian stuff, but still, real furniture," Courtney recalled. "And he had moved a baby grand piano in for me to play."

THE CAST grew disconcerted by the gradual decline in audience attendance. Though word of mouth was generally good, many people wanted to see Sal in the production. In an attempt to draw new crowds, the producers took a large advertisement in the *San Francisco Chronicle* with a headline that quoted a reviewer's cryptic line, "My God, Mary, guess what I saw in San Francisco!" Rather than enticing the public, the line offended many people in the city's large homosexual community. Others, who knew little about the show, thought it was strictly a homosexual play, and they, too, stayed away. "That was a very stupid move," Courtney said.

While the San Francisco production struggled to find an audience, the New York production was faltering as well. In late spring, Bart Miro, who had played Rocky, left the show. Miro's understudy, a twenty-three-year-old Texas-born actor named Tommy Lee Jones, assumed the role. Jones stayed with the show until it closed on May 10.

On May 12, when Courtney and the rest of the cast assembled at the theater in San Francisco, they were given two weeks' notice by the producers that the show would close. Courtney commiserated with Sal on the phone. The earlier publicity faux pas that alienated both gay and straight theater patrons and the absence of Sal acting on the stage proved fatal to advance ticket sales. Neither man was overly surprised by the premature closing of the show.

*Fortune and Men's Eyes* closed on Sunday night, May 24. Shortly after, Courtney packed his few belongings and moved into Sal's Los Angeles home. "He and I talked about it. He never told me what to do. He never encouraged me to leave Jessica. He said it was up to me."

They soon fell into the nonrhythms of Los Angeles life. "Our days were spent lying around," Courtney remembered, "having sex, doing drugs. Doing nothing. At first, it was very relaxing."

IN EARLY June, Sal began work on a new television movie, *In Search of America*. He hadn't appeared in a television role for nine months. *The Challengers,* the made-for-television movie he had completed two years earlier, was finally broadcast on March 28. It was then released as a feature film in Europe.

*In Search of America* was written by Obie Award–winning playwright Lewis John Carlino. The story concerned an upper-middle-class white American family who buys an old school bus, refurbishes it as a mobile home, and sets out with their teenage son to travel the back roads of America. The teenage son was played by Jeff Bridges in one of his first major roles. Sal and Michael Anderson Jr. played hippies encamped at a music festival.

"I remember the first reading, the table read," Michael recalled. "I got there and everyone was there, and Sal said, 'Oh, you must be the name.' And I laughed and said, 'What?' And Sal said, 'I tried to get your part for Don Johnson, but they told me no, they had a name.'"

Initially, the network engaged in a serious discussion about the original story becoming a pilot for an ABC-TV series, but the producer could not secure a commitment to a series from the principal players, so the idea was dismissed.

While Sal worked, Courtney often spent time with Susan, and Don Johnson and Kristine Clark. "We'd go to the beach, have lunch, lay around," Courtney recalled. "There were two existences in L.A. for me: sitting around waiting, or spending time with Sal's few friends, with whom I had very little in common. I was always so busy in New York, going on auditions all day, and in Los Angeles, I had nothing to do. All people ever did was lay around in the sun. I wasn't pursuing anything. I felt like I was wasting my time."

In early June, *Variety* reported that Courtney had been cast in a new film written by Sal and Elliot Mintz called *Fallen Dove* (originally titled *Midnight and the Moving Fist*). Sal would direct the motion picture, which would also star Sammy Davis Jr. and Don Johnson.

Later that month, Sal and Courtney flew to Las Vegas and checked into an impressive suite at the International Hotel. "Sal knew I was restless," Courtney explained. "He was trying to entertain me, and I think trying to show off his exciting lifestyle to me. And I had just gotten a small inheritance from my grandmother, so I had some money." That evening, they attended Andy Williams's opening performance at Caesars Palace. Sal and Courtney then saw Sammy Davis Jr. perform at the Sands. Backstage, Sal gave Davis the script for *Fallen Dove* and introduced him to Courtney. Sal and Courtney played roulette into the early morning hours. And lost.

The following evening, after Sal lost more of Courtney's inheritance at the baccarat table, they attended Perry Como's opening-night show. "Everyone seemed to be there that night," Courtney said, "Bob Hope, Johnny Carson, Jackie Cooper, Don Adams, and Hedy Lamarr. Sal seemed to know them all." Before going to bed in the wee hours of the morning, they lost still more money in the casino. Courtney was shocked to have lost so much, but Sal said, "Yeah, but we had fun, right?"

After the Las Vegas weekend, Courtney had little to do in Los Angeles. With what remained of his inheritance, he bought an old red MG. "Susan and I went to Disneyland," Courtney said. "Twice. But I had come to be with Sal. Life in Los Angeles was excruciatingly slow and unproductive for me. I would have left in a New York minute were it not for my intense feelings for Sal."

Still, there was fun to be had in the City of Angels. Both men surrendered to the romance and passion of their deepening relationship. And Sal's determination to be true to himself and his own impulses sometimes bordered on recklessness. "I remember careening through Beverly Hills on Sal's motorcycle," Courtney said. "We were both stoned and shirtless, and I was sitting behind him—actually riding the bike backward!"

Sal had an insatiable sex appetite. "We were physically opposite," Courtney explained, "but we were completely compatible sexually. We'd go at it for the longest time, take a twenty-minute break, and do it again. When we had the chance, we'd do it all day. I discovered his fetish for navels. He loved mine. And he had a strange recurring dream that he was being chased and then stabbed in the navel.

"Sal was attracted to young blond guys, especially in white jockey shorts. That's all it took to really get him going. He told me when he was very young, he liked to draw pictures of boys in jockey shorts. He laughed about that and said, 'I should have known . . .' Our relationship developed into a very open one. I quickly perceived Sal's limits, perhaps because they were my own. I observed his friends and those who remained had to accept Sal's independence. I wasn't the jealous type, and he was intrigued by my lack of displeasure with his antics. It might have provoked him to test me even more. And he loved to hear about my early sexual experiences with boys. He never had that.

"It was pure calculation on my part to not lose the relationship. I didn't want to make what I saw would be a fatal mistake and say to him, 'Only me.' I knew that would have ended things because he just wasn't capable of such exclusivity. My calculation was put to the test one day when Jay North came to the door. He looked familiar to me. It took me a minute to realize he played Dennis the Menace on TV." North had earlier read for the role of Smitty in the New York production of *Fortune*.

Sal took Jay into the front bedroom. "He asked if I wanted to join," Courtney recalled, "but I said I wasn't interested. I watched them for a moment, but when Jay took off his clothes, he was wearing little yellow jockey shorts. He was a skinny, cute, blond kid, but he still looked like a vulnerable little boy to me. I feigned indifference and left."

———

COURTNEY WAS surprised by Sal's small circle of close friends. One day, Sal decided he wanted to visit Natalie Wood and her husband, Robert Wagner. He called them and they invited him over for the afternoon. "Sal told Natalie he wanted to bring me," Courtney recalled, "and he listened and said, 'Oh, oh, all right, well, some other time, then.' When he hung up, he said, 'Fuck them.' They didn't want him to bring me there."

The few friends Sal had seemed to come and go as they pleased at the Beverly Drive house. "Sal and I had gone out to lunch one day," Courtney said. "When we got back to Sal's place, Don and Kristine were coming from behind the house. He had actually broken a window to get into the house to get some pot. I was incredulous. I asked him what he thought he was doing. Don said, 'I'm part of the family.' I snapped back, '*Not* anymore. I live here now, too. And you call when you want to come over.' Sal didn't say anything. He slipped into the house. He just didn't like saying no to people. And they took advantage of him."

That's how Sal lost his dog, Dove. Don Johnson had stayed at the house while Sal had been away for a few days, and the dog ran away. Eric Williams recalled, "The dog ran away once and for all. Dove was always running off, usually to Jack Benny's house down the road, and they would call. Sal went there one day to pick up the dog and it didn't want to go with him because it was playing with Benny's grandchildren. Sal's feelings were hurt. The dog would run away to the Beverly Hills Hotel nearby all the time, too. Sal said once the hotel called early in the morning and said, 'Mr. Mineo, your dog is here.' Sal said, 'What's his room number?' "

One day in early July, Sal and Courtney had lunch at the Old World Restaurant on Sunset Boulevard. "There was nothing going on with *Fallen Dove*. Just talk," Courtney explained. "I thought I could be working if I was in New York. I felt I had no life anymore. I was living Sal's life. I told him I had to get back to New York."

In Courtney, Sal had met his match. Courtney was strong willed, opinionated, and ambitious. And Sal soon discovered that Courtney could give as good as he got. Sal decided to have a Fourth of July party. Tension had been building between the two men. Sal had enrolled in a film class, taking further time away from Courtney. "He was pissed that I was leaving," Courtney said. What started out as a just another get-together ended in a terrible fight.

"I was moody," Courtney admitted. "Sal was busy away from the house all the time. And I wanted to be with him, not Susan. The film wasn't getting done. Sal was the center of attention, something he enjoyed and cultivated. We got into a terrible argument when everyone left. Sal ripped mirrors off the wall and threw them across the room. They were glued to the wall and they shattered all over the floor.

"I was outraged. I said, 'How dare you?' Sal was very regretful he had gotten so mad. I said, 'If you ever do anything like that again, you'll never see me again.' His eyes filled with tears. He was trembling with regret. He said, 'I'll never do that again.' "

Courtney packed his things in his 1954 MG and left Los Angeles bound for New York on July 9. The night before, Sal treated him to dinner at Dino's Restaurant on the Sunset Strip. "He bought me a beautiful pocket watch," Courtney said.

During the next few months, Courtney tried to secure representation and work in New York. He stayed in constant contact with Sal by telephone. And Sal began a hectic schedule of eclectic television appearances.

Sal filmed a guest-starring role on a new detective series called *Dan August,* appearing as an unsavory character named Mort Downes, an accused rapist, in an episode that concerned child molesters, extramarital affairs, and the investigation of the rape-murder of a young woman who had been receiving obscene telephone calls.

In early August, Sal filmed another episode of *The Name of the Game.* The third-season premiere episode, called "So Long Baby, and Amen," was written by Steven Bochco. He followed that up by playing a drug dealer in "Flip Side," an episode of *Mission: Impossible,* a one-hour drama series about international intrigue.

That same month, Sal secured enough financing for *Fallen Dove* to rent a production office at 8833 Sunset Boulevard. Unable to find work in New York during the summer, and with the renewed promise of a starring role in what would be his first motion picture, Courtney moved back to California. He rented an apartment in the Halifax Building on Franklin and Cahuenga in Hollywood. "I wanted to protect myself," Courtney said. "I wanted a separate apartment to at least give me a sense of independence." He also financed a Bentley. "I loved that car. But it was ridiculous. No job and driving a Bentley that Sal talked me into."

Sal filmed two additional guest spots for television in October. In an episode of *The Immortal* called "Sanctuary," Sal played an American Indian. He then appeared as Jim Bell, a hippie childhood friend of one of Fred MacMurray's television sons on the situation comedy *My Three Sons*. Looking like something straight out of *Easy Rider*, Sal rode into the story on a motorcycle. Appealing to his newly married friend's wanderlust with his tales of freedom, travel, and adventure, he encouraged him to leave his wife and join him on a road trip.

Since MacMurray separately filmed all his scenes that would later be edited into each finished episode, the regular scheduled filming required the other cast members to act opposite stand-ins. Sal was disgruntled. Don Grady played the eldest son, Robbie, and worked with Sal in the episode. "He was great to work with," Grady said, "a unique actor. Moody, but controlled."

Grady was a very young-looking twenty-six years old. He had been an original Mousketeer on *The Mickey Mouse Club* and had become a teen idol in a short time. Though the job was unsatisfying to Sal, he likely found his costar appealing. "Sal invited me to his pad and offered to coach me in acting. He claimed he had a workshop on the weekends, but I wasn't interested in Sal's style of coaching, which involved a lot of yelling, screaming, and 'tearing out your hair.' All improv. Sal was a very emotional guy and he could go there easily, many times a day."

"Life in L.A. fell back into a familiar pattern," Courtney recalled. "Despite all his work, Sal was broke. He was embarrassed by not having money and being in debt," Courtney remembered. "Not outwardly, but internally, it bothered him very much. His new agent, Tom Korman, helped him a lot. He helped manage his money and gradually pay off some old debts. Tom was a good friend to Sal, while most of the others were there for the ride.

"When Sal and I went out to dinner with others, when the check came, everyone sat on their hands," Courtney added. "The check sat on the table and everyone just looked at it. Sal always felt like he was supposed to cover the bill somehow. Elliot would invite people to dinner and then give Sal the bill to sign for. I stopped that. One night, we went out with Elliot and Don and the usual hangers-on, and when the bill came, I said, 'I'll take that.' I said, 'Now, do you want me to divide this up equally, or should I tell each person what they owe?' Sal just looked down and fiddled with his fingers, and Elliot and the others just stared at me. They hated me, and I had no respect for them."

After disassociating himself from Sal, Bobby Sherman had enjoyed a successful show business career. He had starred in the television series *Here Come the Brides,* which ended a two-year run in September 1970. Beginning the year before, he had several million-selling pop-music singles, including "Julie (Do You Love Me?)" and "Easy Come, Easy Go." Courtney contacted Sherman's manager and asked for the newly crowned teen idol to reimburse Sal for the drums he had purchased for Bobby years before. "Sal helped so many people," Courtney said, "and once they hit it, they'd back away from him. But he got the money back for the drums. Sal got three thousand dollars from Bobby's manager."

FINANCING AND film start dates kept changing for *Fallen Dove.* In the meantime, at the recommendation of his friend Roddy McDowall, Sal was offered an unusual role in a motion picture that was set to begin production at 20th Century Fox Studios. On November 27, 1970, the trade papers reported, MINEO PLAYING CHIMP! "Sal Mineo will play a chimp in Arthur P. Jacobs's 20th Century Fox production, *Escape from the Planet of the Apes.* For the new film (third in the series), producer Jacobs has added a new ape character who, in a switch in casting, is played by filmdom's longtime favorite juvenile delinquent, two-time Oscar nominee, Sal Mineo."

The story of *Escape from the Planet of the Apes* begins when three talking apes (Cornelius, Zira, and a new ape character named Milo) escape the cataclysmic explosion of their planet and travel in a space capsule to the Earth of the past—1973. Roddy McDowall and Kim Hunter returned as Cornelius and Zira, the roles they had created in the first two *Planet of the Apes* films. Sal was cast as the third intelligent chimpanzee, Milo.

Sal discovered that his discomfort with the elaborate makeup rapidly escalated to terrible claustrophobic panic attacks. Roddy McDowall said, "A lot of people had psychological trauma with the makeup because their ego was in danger somewhere. Sal had trouble." Roddy went to the makeup room to watch Sal being made up. After nearly two hours of makeup application, Roddy saw near terror in Sal's eyes. He went to the director and told him he was going to have trouble with Sal. The prosthetics and makeup were suffocating, and Sal panicked.

Milo's death scene (strangled by a gorilla in the zoo) was shot on a soundstage on the 20th Century Fox lot on December 22 and 23. Courtney recalled driving Sal to and from the studio. "Sal hated that job," Courtney recalled. "He was disgusted. He felt it was the worst moment in his acting career. He said, 'I'm playing a fucking monkey. It could be anybody in there. I'm covered up. Anybody could play a fucking monkey.' He did it for the money, but he was embarrassed and he hated it."

Sal soon accepted another job that challenged his distaste for artistic anonymity. In 1970, *Jonathan Livingston Seagull,* a novella written by Richard Bach about a seagull learning about life and flight, hit the *New York Times* bestseller list and remained on top for thirty-eight weeks. The story was awkwardly adapted for the screen by Hall Bartlett. Starring mechanical seagulls, the motion picture utilized the voice-over talents of numerous well-known actors. In a pinch for cash, Sal lent his vocal talents. Happily for Sal, his voice-over contribution (along with the other actors') was uncredited in the film. The movie was finally released in October 1973 and was a box office disaster.

SAL AND Courtney spent a mostly uneventful Christmas holiday in Los Angeles. "We saw three movies on Christmas Day," Courtney said. But the on-again off-again interest in *Fallen Dove* was wearing thin on both men. The challenge to raise production money proved much more daunting than anyone had expected. On January 8, 1971, Sal flew to Vancouver to meet with potential investors. The following day, Courtney and Mabel cleaned the Beverly Drive house in preparation for Sal's surprise thirty-second birthday party. Sal returned with little more than a flicker of interest in his film. More than thirty guests surprised him when he returned home, including Roddy McDowall, Tom Korman, Susan Ladin, Don Johnson and Kristine, Holly Near, Mabel, and Ken Waissman and Maxine Fox.

On January 14, after months of trying to raise the capital to film

*Fallen Dove,* all the promised financing fell through. The project was permanently shelved. Courtney picked up a disappointed Sal at his Sunset Boulevard production office, and they had dinner at Kelly's Steak House. That evening, Courtney told Sal that in light of the failed film project, he was considering returning to New York.

After spending a weekend alone in Carmel to ponder his options, Courtney met with his Los Angeles agent at Hyland-Chandler, the agency that once represented Sal. "I was looking for an excuse to stay in California with Sal, but I couldn't get any work in Los Angeles," Courtney said. "I just couldn't get an audition. I just couldn't figure it out, and I asked my agent what the problem was. She said simply, 'Everybody knows you're Sal Mineo's trick.'"

Courtney was mortified. He couldn't believe his ears. "That was it," Courtney said. "I had to get out of Los Angeles. I thought I'd never have a career."

The next day, Sal drove Courtney to the airport for his flight to New York. "I was so anxious to get away from there," Courtney said, "I just left my Bentley on the street in front of my apartment. Elliot moved it to a gas station, and from there it was repossessed."

# PART FIVE

# THE WRONG PEOPLE

Sal, Los Angeles, 1971

# 32.

"I spent the last five days of my father's life with him in New York, and what I learned from him in those five days was how important the moments are every day and how quickly time goes."

In the course of looking for film-worthy projects, Sal came upon a notorious novel that had been published in 1956. *Giovanni's Room* was written by James Baldwin, a black, homosexual American author. The novel explores homosexual love, homophobia, misogyny, and the cultural gaps between America and France. The plot concerns a young, white American man who is left alone in Paris when his girlfriend goes to Spain to contemplate their upcoming marriage. While he waits in France, he begins a torrid affair with an Italian man named Giovanni.

Eric Williams recalled, "Sal called me one day and asked me, 'Have you ever read *Giovanni's Room*? I want to make a picture of it.'

"I went to the London Playboy Club shortly afterward and James Baldwin happened to be there. I followed him to the bathroom and stood at the pisser next to him and actually told him about Sal and his interest in making a movie. Baldwin said, 'I think that's the most brilliant idea I've ever heard.' I called Sal and told him the news. I told him he must come to London to meet Baldwin."

Disconcerted by his inability to produce *Fallen Dove*, Sal flew to England, and he and Eric met with Baldwin. "Everything seemed wonderful and a go," Eric said, "then, after Baldwin went back to the United States, I got a letter from his agent, who said no way, Baldwin had no right to negotiate such a deal and they wanted millions for the project."

A few days later, Eric called Courtney and invited him to a belated surprise birthday party for Sal in London. "I was ready to go," Courtney said. Choosing between pounding the pavement in search of an agent and the swinging London scene was easy. "I bought a new suit," Courtney said, "and left!"

Courtney arrived in London on February 2. That evening, they celebrated Sal's birthday at a pub that Eric managed called the Bull and Gate. "Then," said Courtney, "we disappeared for forty-eight hours at Eric's flat on Baker Street."

The idyll in London was a perfect respite for the two men. They were able to rest and enjoy time together away from the watchful eyes of Hollywood and New York. The anonymity London provided Sal was a welcome relief. With no acting offers on the table, the time away from America and his creditors gave Sal the opportunity to personally regroup. Sal and Courtney decided to pursue a business relationship with Eric and form a production company in England to acquire and produce movie projects.

Sal and Courtney returned to New York City on February 10 and moved into Tom Korman's East Side Manhattan apartment for a short time. They were photographed by Kenn Duncan, Courtney for his modeling portfolio and Sal for play, posing in black briefs and a mink jacket.

VALENTINE'S DAY 1971 was a big day. "I met the parents," Courtney recalled. Mr. and Mrs. Mineo lived in a one-bedroom garage apartment on High Street in Harrison, a town adjacent to Mamaroneck. Visiting from their home in Massachusetts, Sal's sister, Sarina, and her husband were there as well. Courtney was introduced by Sal as his "friend and business associate." The family was cordial. "Mr. Mineo was very nice," Courtney said, "a nice, quiet man." Josephine prepared lunch and packed some food for Sal and Courtney to take back to Manhattan when they left that evening.

The next day Courtney and Sal drove back to Mamaroneck, picked up Josephine and Sarina, and took them to lunch at Theatre Bar in Manhattan. They then saw a matinee performance of the long-running musical *Man of La Mancha* at the Martin Beck Theatre. It was an awkward afternoon. Sal hadn't spent very much alone time with his mother or recently married sister in a very long time.

"Sal didn't care for the production," Courtney said, "and his mother and sister just didn't understand it."

---

SAL AND Courtney relished their alone time together and socialized with Sal's friends occasionally in the evening. After attending a matinee performance of *Tarot* at Circle in the Square Theatre, Sal and Courtney met Nicholas Ray walking on the street. Ray had fallen on tough times. They went to the director's house on Twelfth Street in Greenwich Village. Ray's wife, Susan, recalled, "I remember Sal wore very pale clothes, beiges, very slick clothes. He looked very pretty. He was smooth featured. I remember Nick making a comment to the effect that Sal was a little lost."

Sal and Courtney stayed at Ray's apartment for several hours, reminiscing about *Rebel Without a Cause* and James Dean. Ray had had some homosexual experiences and they talked about that. "Sal said he had no idea he was interested in guys at that time," Courtney recalled, "and he wouldn't have known how to handle it then if he was."

On Friday, March 5, Courtney took Sal to the airport to catch a plane to Los Angeles. Sal would settle his affairs there and give up the Beverly Drive house. He planned to ship some things back to New York and put the rest of his belongings in storage before returning to the East Coast.

Sal and Courtney spoke frequently on the phone, and on March 12 Courtney sent Sal a telegram to commemorate their one-year anniversary. "The stakes were high. We used ivory for luck. Now a year has passed. Check, you fuck!"

Sal returned to New York on March 20 and moved into Courtney's Eighty-fifth Street apartment. While Sal worked with an attorney to form his new London-based production company, Courtney earnestly auditioned for modeling assignments and acting roles with limited success.

"It was very, very difficult," Courtney said. Both men were passionate and opinionated. "It was the reverse of Los Angeles. Instead of me feeling out of place, Sal had little to do. It was not his turf. Now we were spending time with *my* friends. He was bored, and it showed. There was little money. I finally got a job at Le Drug Store as a waiter. I was wondering if the London plans were really going to happen or was it a repeat of the *Fallen Dove* business. Tension was building again, and it was tough."

Sal's television movie *In Search of America* was broadcast on

March 23. The film won its time slot. *Escape from the Planet of the Apes* premiered on May 26 in Los Angeles and New York City. Sal did not attend the opening in New York and did not participate in any promotional publicity. Though the film was a box office success, quickly earning more than $12 million in domestic rentals, the critics were unimpressed. Not only was Sal unrecognized and unnoticed by the critics, but the new moviegoing demographic of youngsters no longer knew who he was.

SERPENTINE PRODUCTIONS was incorporated in the United States with the help of an American attorney named Conrad Shadlen who worked for a law firm with offices in New York and London. Sal, Courtney, and Eric Williams were the corporate officers. "Serpentine Productions was named after the lake in Hyde Park that we used to walk along," Eric recalled. "Sal enjoyed walking around there in the evening unnoticed."

There were a couple of ideas that Sal considered for possible film projects, including one based on the Chicago Seven and another on a concept album released in the United Kingdom called *Out of Borstal.* Eric explained: "It was a collection of pop songs telling the story of a boys' reformatory. He liked that idea a lot and really wanted to make a film or play of it. He wanted it all to happen where all the boys slept. He wanted to explore the seamy side of that, but we couldn't get the rights."

When Sal was in London earlier that year, he came across a novel called *The Wrong People,* written by British author Robin Maugham. The distinguished author was the nephew of W. Somerset Maugham. Robin Maugham, who described himself as "overshadowed, queer and alcoholic," began his career as a novelist in 1948 and went on to publish eighteen novels.

Maugham's provocative, pederastic novel was originally published in the United States in 1967 under the pseudonym David Griffin. But only after enjoying surprising critical and commercial success was *The Wrong People* published three years later in Britain under Maugham's own name.

*The Wrong People* is centered around the character of Arnold Turner, who finds sexual fulfillment in a young Moroccan boy named Riffi, procured by a self-exiled American named Ewing Baird. But Baird expects his favor to be returned, and after bribery and threats of blackmail, Turner agrees to kidnap a young boy from the reform school where he works in England and smuggle him into Tangier. Set in Morocco, the novel strongly portrayed the sexual exploitation of young boys.

In August 1971, when the incorporation papers for Serpentine Productions were finally in order, Sal moved to London. "Sal was interested in obtaining the rights to make a movie of *The Wrong People*," Eric explained. "We flew to Ibiza for a couple of days to meet Robin Maugham, who was an English lord."

Robin Maugham lived in a three-story, bougainvillea-draped villa outside the town of Santa Eulalia. Eric said, "He had a party for Sal. It was a glamorous night with champagne and beautiful people. Sal sold himself very well. He had such a talent for charm. He chatted up Lord Maugham and got the rights from him."

SAL ENJOYED the personal freedoms London offered. He took advantage of the nightlife and of a country, unlike America, where homosexual activity in private was no longer forbidden by law due to the 1967 Sexual Offences Act.

He sought out a few young actors whom he found attractive and who, as they were told, were potential candidates to appear in his film. He met Martin Potter, a beautiful blond young man who had starred in Federico Fellini's *Satyricon*, and met several times with Leonard Whiting, an angelic-faced twenty-year-old actor who had starred as Romeo in the 1968 Franco Zeffirelli–directed film *Romeo and Juliet*.

"Sal met an actor at my flat," Eric remembered, "John Moulder-Brown. At the time he was seventeen years old. Sal was mad for him. He wanted him badly."

John Moulder-Brown, a startlingly handsome, blue-eyed brunette, had starred with Jane Asher, ten years his senior, in a creepy film about teenage lust called *Deep End*. Moulder-Brown played a low-class youngster who works at a British public bath where he fixates upon and stalks his flirtatious, older female coworker.

"Sal and I saw that film," Eric said, "and it reminded him of the film he did, *Teddy Bear*, though more overt. He was so interested in John."

Moulder-Brown was not interested in Sal, though, or *The Wrong People*.

COURTNEY WORKED through the summer as a waiter at Le Drug Store in Manhattan. He considered a recording contract offer from Paul Murphy, a wealthy businessman he had met at Kenn Duncan's photography studio, but turned down the lucrative deal and flew to London to join Sal in September.

Sal and Courtney stayed in an apartment on Baker Street arranged by Eric Williams. In the evenings, they dived into the cultural milieu of London, attending a number of plays in the West End. After some leisurely time in the city, they spent a weekend in Mevagissey, a picturesque Cornish fishing village on the channel. "We bought each other a ring on Portobello Road," Courtney said. "We were going to exchange rings seaside. Sal fumbled with his ring and it fell into the harbor. Talk about being nervous about making a commitment. He was mortified, though. I tossed mine in after his."

When they returned to London, they met with Robby Lantz and several other agents as they began their search for a screenwriter who could adapt *The Wrong People*. Initially, they contacted both Peter Shaffer and David Sherwin. Shaffer had written several plays and screenplays, but his greatest successes were ahead, including *Equus* in 1973 and *Amadeus* in 1979. Sherwin was a British screenwriter who collaborated with director Lindsay Anderson in 1968 on the film *If*... Neither writer was interested in Sal's project.

With the help of Conrad Shadlen, Eric solicited potential investors to fund the film project. "I raised the first five thousand pounds to pay for the film option of *The Wrong People*," Eric said. "When Sal got to London in August, I had to spend two thousand pounds to buy him presentable clothing. He had absolutely nothing to wear. He looked like an urchin."

ON OCTOBER 1, Courtney returned to New York to put his affairs in order, close out his apartment, and arrange storage for his belongings. He sent a few copies of the American edition of *The Wrong People* to

Sal in London and delivered some of their belongings to the Mineos' apartment in Harrison for safekeeping, including an antique baroque chair Sal had given him as a gift. Josephine was friendly and interested in—though worried about—Sal's move to England. Courtney was a little disconcerted to find Mr. Mineo ailing. Josephine assured him it was nothing to worry Sal with, that her husband was merely suffering from a bad bout of the flu. In fact, she told Courtney not to mention it at all.

Courtney returned to London, arriving in the morning on October 27. Sal had already moved into a beautiful flat on Westbourne Terrace on the north side of Kensington Gardens and Hyde Park. Sal welcomed Courtney to their new London home with a champagne lunch. "The flat was beautiful," Courtney recalled. "It was like a romantic garret with a huge bay window that looked out over the London rooftops. It was walking distance to Eric's flat on Baker Street and just two blocks from Hyde Park." They furnished their new flat with odd bits of furniture and antiques they purchased on winding Portobello Road in the nearby Notting Hill district.

Their social network soon included certain show business power brokers. Interestingly, it was a small club dominated by homosexuals. Sal enjoyed the community and the breezy, glib nature of British wit. He and Courtney relished their time together in England, and this began the most peaceful and satisfying time they had yet spent together. "It was the most relaxed we had been," Courtney said, "and we had the most fun. For the first time we really started to have fun together as a couple. And our daily life became quite domestic."

ERIC RECALLED, "It was my responsibility to raise the money for *The Wrong People*. Some forty thousand pounds in all. This paid operating bills. We had no real office except my own, and we rented Sal the flat at Westbourne Terrace and actually put him on a meager salary to live." With no working papers, Sal could not legally work in England.

"People were buying shares in the project, but there was no guarantee of a return," Eric explained. "It was their risk, though we really did intend to make the picture with Sal directing. We had prepared a fine promotional package with the photograph of an older man's hand upon a younger man's hand. Very provocative.

"But people who were investing were really just buying time with Sal. They were paying money to keep company with him. We socialized a lot and really worked to get this project off the ground. But people did want Sal to act in the picture, as well. For some, it wasn't enough that he was simply directing."

Jill Haworth, working in England at the time, invested a small sum in the company. "I didn't have much money then, but I did have a bit more than Sal. The idea sounded very good."

Eric's biggest catch, though, was a financier and show business heavyweight named David Shaw who was Robert Stigwood's business partner. Shaw became a primary investor.

Robert Stigwood, an Australian-born entertainment tycoon, managed the Bee Gees and produced the rock opera *Jesus Christ Superstar* on Broadway in 1971. Stigwood was an influential part of London's gay showbiz establishment, which included music producer and manager Simon Napier-Bell; Kit Lambert, who managed the Who; Brian Epstein, who managed the Beatles, Donovan, and Petula Clark; music publisher Joe Parnes; recording engineer and music producer Joe Meek; *Oliver* composer Lionel Bart; and Sir Joseph Lockwood, the managing director of EMI, the largest recording company in the United Kingdom. This so-called Pink Mafia dominated British show business and could make, or lock out, acts, performers, and productions.

In the late sixties, after experiencing some financial setbacks, Stigwood took on a powerful London banker named David Shaw as his business partner. Though Shaw was married and had several children, he, too, was gay. He led a double life, keeping his family ensconced in Henry VIII's rustic hunting lodge, which he had purchased, and living his own decadent, independent life in London.

Shaw purchased an impressive house off Kinnerton Street. Celebrities, power brokers, the rich and famous, international jet-setters, the infamous, and even British royals clamored for an invitation to one of his parties.

To celebrate their reunion and new business venture, Sal and Courtney had drinks in the evening on October 27 with Serpentine Productions' new accountant, Michael Glover, then they went to their first David Shaw party.

"It was unbelievable," Courtney said. "It was the wildest thing we'd ever seen! Downstairs was very refined, but upstairs was a different story. In the bathroom, the tub was filled with champagne and ice, and a variety of couples were having sex in the sauna. People would wander in, grope someone, and wander off! It was a wild night! Sal and I loved it."

SAL EARNESTLY looked for a screenwriter he could interest in *The Wrong People*. In October, novelist Simon Raven's agent, Diane Crawford, notified Sal that her client was not available. Sal thought Raven was a good choice since he had adapted two of W. Somerset Maugham's short stories for British television. In addition, he was as famous for his debauched lifestyle as his considerable writings. "But Raven's reaction was like a [paralyzing] palsy," Courtney recalled.

Early that same month, Glyn Jones met with Sal and Courtney at their flat at Westbourne Terrace. Jones was an actor and director, and a prolific playwright. He had written for the BBC television series *Dr. Who*. He had also penned several gay-themed plays that had been produced in London.

Over the next few weeks, Glyn met with Sal several times and finally began work on *The Wrong People* on October 29. "We got on well from the beginning," Glyn said. "And it was by no means a rush job, but I finished the treatment of *The Wrong People* on twelfth November." The following evening, to celebrate the completed treatment, Sal, Courtney, and Glyn had dinner. But the celebration was premature. Sal turned down the script, telling Glyn that "like a curate's egg, it was only good in parts." In fact, Sal had a different idea altogether about the direction he wanted to pursue. He felt that Glyn had soft-soaped the material. Sal wanted an edgier approach, according to Courtney.

"Sal was a charmer and the socializing and friendship continued even after the work was done and rejected with no hard feelings," Glyn said.

Through the end of the year, Sal considered numerous screenwriters. Though actively involved in the search, Courtney began to feel stagnant again. Sal knew Courtney had turned down a recording offer in New York in order to join him in London. He thought Serpentine

Productions could branch out into the music business and produce recordings for Courtney, so meetings were arranged with Kenny Young, a popular American songwriter living in London. Young had written the classic song "Under the Boardwalk" for the Drifters and had written several hit songs for the British pop group Herman's Hermits. Courtney recorded a couple of songs but wasn't interested in pursuing a recording career. Nothing came of the project.

Though American-based, Serpentine Productions, once approved by authorities, could conduct business in Great Britain provided the company hired Brits. To satisfy that requirement, Eric drew a meager salary. Courtney was eventually paid by the company to keep the books and manage the daily business.

"That was my deal before I ever left New York," Courtney explained. "I wanted to be working and engaged in the creative process of the company in London. I wanted to be paid for my work. I negotiated the deal with Sal and Eric very carefully. I did not want a repeat of the *Fallen Dove* escapade if I could prevent it. Sal was paid a flat producer fee by the company, which he had already spent by the time I got there. We both ended up living on the small salary I drew. I bought the food, our dinners, and I paid for our theater tickets."

Courtney was determined to maintain a sense of order in their new life together in England. "I was keeping house, keeping our schedule," Courtney said, "and a routine developed. One day I was working on our schedule, trying to plan our time, and Sal said flatly, 'Courtney, I don't need another mother.' I was just trying to bring some structure into our lives, and I was too earnest. Sal was right, and I felt ashamed of myself, actually.".

With scant resources to work with, they had to be clever with their spending. "Sal actually borrowed money from me to buy me a Christmas present," Courtney said. "He knew I loved opera, and he found antique mother-of-pearl opera glasses somewhere and bought them for me. It was funny; they were so nelly. I was a little taken aback but I was also deeply touched and I used them at the opera."

Sal and Courtney spent a cozy Christmas with Glyn and his lover, Christopher Beeching, at their home on Richmond Road. Jill returned to London following the Christmas holiday after appearing in the touring company of *Abelard and Heloise*. At the time, she was experiencing problems securing a working visa for the United States. Sal, Jill, and Courtney pondered an interesting, though peculiar, remedy. "Jill and I considered getting married," Courtney explained. "That way, I could work in England and she could get her papers together more easily for work in America. We talked about it a lot."

Jill agreed. "We really considered it. Can you possibly imagine? It sounded fine to me, then. I don't know how Sal would have dealt with it, though. He was usually playing Courtney and me against each other. He'd tell me, 'Courtney said this about you,' and then he'd tell Courtney something else. He made it all up. Sal loved to stir the shit pot."

AT 4 A.M. on Monday morning, January 3, 1972, Sal and Courtney were awakened by a telephone call from Josephine. She told Sal he had to come home because his father's health had worsened. Courtney drove a morose Sal to the airport for a 3 P.M. flight to New York City.

While Sal was away, Courtney continued the search for a suitable screenwriter. Colin Spencer, an English novelist and playwright whose rather eccentric novels often portrayed the more baroque aspects of homosexual life, was contacted. Spencer, who would later write *Homosexuality in History* (1996) and *The Gay Kama Sutra* (1997), was not interested in the project. Acclaimed Irish novelist Edna O'Brien, who was experiencing censorship troubles with some of her books due to their frank depictions of their characters' sex lives, was considered. Her agent, Robin Dalton, politely refused the offer.

Since the Mineos lived in a small one-bedroom apartment, Sal stayed at Tom Korman's apartment in Manhattan. Courtney spoke with Sal every day. On Sunday afternoon, January 9, Sal called Courtney to tell him that his father had died at 4:30 that morning. Salvatore Mineo Sr. was fifty-nine years old. Sal was controlled but melancholy. In spite of the issues Sal had with his family, he had a deep love and respect for his father, of whom he always spoke lovingly. He was profoundly saddened by Sal Sr.'s death.

Courtney wrote a poem for Sal to read at his father's funeral and sent it by telegram to him early the next morning. "Sal said he was so glad to have it," Courtney recalled. "He said he hadn't known what to say and read it at the funeral."

A couple of days later, Sal's father was buried in the Gate of Heaven cemetery in nearby Hawthorne, New York.

"I spent the last five days of Father's life with him in New York," Sal said, "and what I learned from him in those five days was how important the moments are every day and how quickly time goes. Being in the same room with him and looking at him—he couldn't move but we had eye contact—I realized that one day I would be in the same position as he, facing death. Before it happens, I want to do the things I want to do. I don't want to end saying, 'I wish I had.' "

## 33.

"I can't imagine that this project wouldn't work out. I never even think in those terms. It's going to work. It's going to happen. I won't think negatively now under any circumstances."

Sal quietly celebrated his thirty-third birthday in Manhattan on January 10. Meanwhile, Courtney met with their accountant, Michael Glover, and Eric Williams to discuss Serpentine Productions' dwindling capital. Sal and Courtney were living off the pre-production money that had been raised to produce their film, and the funds were running low. Glover contacted an English investor named Simon Rueben who had expressed an interest in Sal's project. Courtney called Sal and gave him contact information for other potential investors he knew in New York. They reached out to anyone who might be the slightest bit interested in their film.

Before returning to London on January 14, Sal had several meetings, with no success. While the search for investors and writers continued in England, Sal and Eric planned a location-scouting trip to Morocco (the setting of Maugham's novel) in May to coincide with the Cannes Film Festival. They thought they might generate additional interest in the film there. In the meantime, Sal contacted his agent, Tom Korman, and asked him to find him some work in America. The little bit of money Courtney had earned for a toothpaste commercial he had earlier filmed in Switzerland was hardly enough to live on, let alone sustain their flat in London.

On Friday, February 4, Conrad Shadlen received Robin Maugham's proposed contract to write a screenplay from his novel. That evening, Sal and Courtney discussed their concerns about Maugham's monetary demands over dinner at the restaurant April and Desmond's. The proprietress, April Ashley, was Britain's most famous transsexual. Courtney recalled, "Sal loved it there. Lady April made a grand entrance at eleven o'clock each night. She'd come down the stairs and sweep through the dining room. She was beautiful."

David Cassidy arrived in London on Sunday, February 6. After a vacation in France, he stopped in England on this way back to America to promote the release of the first Partridge Family record album in the United Kingdom. He was already a recording sensation in the United States. His pop-idol status, a result of his starring role in the hit television series *The Partridge Family*, drew tens of thousands of youngsters to Heathrow.

David had remained friends with Sal, who understood the overwhelming weight of celebrity, and David could commiserate with him about the problems of teen idol–dom. They had always been supportive of each other.

A couple of days later, with screaming fans and photographers in pursuit, David Cassidy made his way to Westbourne Terrace to visit and dine with Sal and Courtney. It was a startling reversal of roles. Just four years earlier Sal had befriended David, who was still in high school and flirting with the idea of a show business career. And fifteen years before, thousands of screaming fans had chased Sal through the streets, throwing themselves at him at premieres and personal appearances. "When Sal and I walked down the street in London," Courtney said, "nobody looked twice. Nobody knew him. It was bliss."

PAUL DEHN, the screenwriter responsible for *Escape from the Planet of the Apes*, expressed an interest in writing a treatment for *The Wrong People*. Dehn told Sal he required a five-thousand-pound payment in order to proceed. Though Dehn was a favorite of the group, they didn't have the money he requested and had to walk away.

"Things had reached a standstill. There was little money. Neither one of us could work in England, outside of our own company. The film wasn't going anywhere, and it was getting a little tense," Courtney recalled, "so I decided to go back to New York to find some work." Courtney flew to New York on February 24. The night before, he and Sal went to the ballet and had dinner with Sal's friend Rudolf Nureyev at April and Desmond's.

After a couple of weeks in New York, Courtney was cast in *Murder Without Trace*. The play was scheduled for a one-month engagement at Brown's Suburban Dinner Theatre in Louisville, Kentucky. The play opened on March 28, 1972. Sal sent Courtney two telegrams. One read, "Break a leg tonight love from Dov Landau Lord Robin

Maugham Noel Coward Lionel Bart Hermione Baddley Paul Dehn Ewing Arnold Glover Glyn and Chris Martin Potter Nureyev and Sal Mineo." The other read, "If I had the wings of an angel over to Kentucky I would fly with me I would bring steak and kidney pie but you will have to supply the dessert love me too."

When it came to matters of the heart, Sal's devotion to Courtney was undeniable. "I think Courtney was the love of his life," Jill said. "Sal told me he loved him. He told me Courtney kept him calm." Nevertheless, matters of the flesh were another story.

Shortly after Courtney had returned to New York, Sal invited his ex-lover interior decorator Paul Gill to come to London. Sal offered him a job at the Serpentine production office. "Actually," Eric Williams recalled, "he brought him in to have sex with."

"I was never threatened by the presence of these young men in Sal's life," Courtney said. "Perhaps it was arrogance or acute awareness, but we held a unique place in each other's heart that was unshakable. The others were just visitors."

While Courtney was in Kentucky, Sal granted an interview to journalist Bart Mills and talked about his plans to film *The Wrong People*.

"I'm not an old man," Sal told Mills. "I'm only thirty-three. It's been a very heavy ten years, though. None of the films after *Exodus* was really very rewarding at all. I desperately wanted to do *In Cold Blood*, but Richard Brooks felt that it should be done by an unknown. *America, America* with Kazan, I was very close to doing—a plum role, but it was the same story. Wait a minute, I told them. I'm a good actor. What's the difference if they know me? So we went through this 'new-face' phase—still going through it."

Still, Sal assured Mills that he had no regrets. "So what if they're not banging on the doors like they used to with acting offers?" Sal explained. "I'm not disappointed that they're not coming in. More time to work on *The Wrong People*. I can't imagine that this project wouldn't work out. I never even think of it in those terms. It's going to work. It's going to happen. I won't think negatively now under any circumstances."

After his engagement in *Murder Without Trace* ended, Courtney flew back to London on April 26. The following day, Sal and Eric interviewed another writer, London-born Lionel Chetwynd, who worked with the London office of Columbia Pictures. He was about to begin work on the motion picture screenplay adaptation of *The Apprenticeship of Duddy Kravitz*. Ultimately, Chetwynd was not interested in the project.

Sal and Courtney spent the next few days planning their trip to the Cannes Film Festival and to Tangier to scout locations. They met with Ken and Julie Slaven, who had been recommended by Stanley Baker as Moroccan travel guides. Several years earlier, Baker had hired the Slavens to help him scout locations for his picture *Zulu*, which had been filmed in South Africa. They drove to Tangier ahead of Sal and Courtney, and planned their itinerary and booked hotels.

Before leaving, though, Sal and Courtney had a meeting with Eric and their accountant. After funding the trip to Tangier to scout locations for the film, Serpentine Productions had very little pre-production capital left and was in danger of financial collapse. Originally, Eric considered accompanying Sal on the trip. Instead, he stayed behind in London to try to raise funds.

"I raised additional money from American Express," Eric said, "though they really didn't want Sal to direct the picture. Rather, he would have to star in it. We all thought he was too old, actually, and he didn't want to act in it anyway. But I said what I needed to get the money."

A short time earlier, Sal had met an independent film producer named Peter Walker. Using his own production company, Walker had produced and directed a series of cheap sexploitation films beginning with *Cool It Carol!* and followed by *Die Screaming, Marianne*, and *Four Dimensions of Greta*, Britain's first 3D film. All of these low-budget, soft-core sex films were financially successful, and all had been written by Murray Smith.

Walker offered Sal a part in his next sexploitation potboiler, called *Tiffany Jones*. Sal turned down the role of Prince Salvator. The role was given to Damien Thomas, a handsome young actor of Sal's acquaintance who lived in a room above Eric Williams's pub. Eric and Sal thought Walker, who was fast earning a fortune in the B-movie business, might be convinced to invest money in, or even produce, *The Wrong People*. In order to encourage his interest, Eric and Sal hired

Walker's screenwriter, Murray Smith, to write a screenplay of the Maugham novel.

ON MAY 11, 1972, Sal and Courtney flew to Nice, rented a car, and drove to Roquebrune-Cap-Martin. The tiny French village is located on a rocky outcrop high above the Mediterranean Sea east of Nice, between Monaco and Menton and within walking distance of Monte Carlo. They settled into a comfortable villa belonging to Courtney's aunt. "It was so relaxing, and Sal and I were alone at last," Courtney said. "It was like a honeymoon."

In between relaxing on the beach and dining in some of the finest restaurants in the area, Sal and Courtney saw several screenings at the Cannes Film Festival, including Alfred Hitchcock's film *Frenzy*. They attended the awards ceremony following the screening but had trouble getting in, Courtney recalled. "It was overcrowded and there was some sort of mix-up at the door. It was a little embarrassing and humbling for Sal. They didn't seem to know who he was."

There was little opportunity to approach potential investors or even promote *The Wrong People*. The press had no interest in Sal, especially since he was not involved with any current film presented at the festival. In fact, Sal was not engaged in any press interviews whatsoever.

On Sunday afternoon, May 21, Sal and Courtney left the glamorous privileges of Cannes and Monte Carlo and flew from Nice to Madrid. Before boarding an Iberia Airlines flight for Tangier, in order to be allowed entre to Morocco, they had to change on the runway from their short pants to trousers. When they landed in Morocco a short time later, their guide, Ken Slaven, and their new screenwriter, Murray Smith, were waiting to receive them.

For propriety's sake, Sal and Courtney booked separate rooms at the Hotel el Djenina, a small, three-story hotel overlooking the Bay of Tangier. The next day was Courtney's twenty-fourth birthday. That morning, he and Sal visited Potty Peters, an old gay bar that Robin Maugham had written about in *The Wrong People*. After lunch at the hotel, they went shopping in the bazaar and spent some time at the beach. With Sal's encouragement, Courtney stripped to his white jockey shorts and danced in the sand at the water's edge. Sal took pictures of him until the police arrived and told them it was illegal to appear in public dressed only in underwear. "I tried to tell them it wasn't my underwear," Courtney said, "but my bathing suit. But they wouldn't go for it. We finally talked our way out of that somehow."

A friend of Ken Slaven's, a professional Moroccan wrestler, arranged for Courtney's birthday celebration in a Tangier brothel. "We even had dancing girls," Courtney said. Sal gave him an old silver slave bracelet he purchased in the bazaar. After dinner, they went to a bar called Ibsala for drinks. In spite of living his dream, Courtney struggled with his feelings during the trip. "We had a blowup over something in the bar," Courtney recalled. "I was in love, and traveling. I started to have terrible anxiety attacks. And terrible mood swings. It scared me. Sal would ask me, 'What's wrong?' and I'd just snap at him. I had everything I ever wanted and I was afraid I was going to lose it all."

As a birthday gift, Sal hired a Moroccan boy to go to bed with Courtney. "His name was Abdul," Courtney said. "The boys there were very sexy. He was probably twenty. But he didn't want to do anything I wanted. 'I don't do that,' he said, and 'I don't do that.' So I sent him home. I went across the hall to Sal's room, where he was involved with his own Moroccan boy. They looked up at me in the middle of it all and smiled invitingly. I joined them in bed."

The next morning, armed with his camera to photograph potential film locations, Sal joined Courtney, Ken, and Murray on a trip to Grottes d'Hercules (the Caves of Hercules) in Cap Spartel, a thirty-minute car ride from Tangier. Sal, afraid of heights, watched from a safe distance while Courtney and Murray climbed over the rocks.

During the next week, they traveled through Morocco, driving to Asilah on the coast, Casablanca, and then Marrakesh at the edge of the Sahara Desert. Sal took photographs of the exotic landscape, colorful marketplaces, and stunning architecture. They eventually arrived in Rabat, the capital of the Kingdom of Morocco, to visit the British embassy and discuss film permit requirements in the country.

"We planned to return to Tangier and go home after our meeting," Courtney said, "but we were invited to meet the king's brother, Prince Moulay Abdallah. Apparently, he was a huge movie fan." The next day they were driven to the palace to meet the prince's family and treated to an extravagant luncheon by the sea at King Hassan II's palace in Skhivat.

On Wednesday, May 30, Sal and Courtney arranged for their airline tickets to London and sunned for a time on the hotel roof. That afternoon, they attended a birthday party for the prince. "We were driven to an exact replica of a movie Western town in the middle of nowhere," Courtney recalled. "All the buildings were complete, not false fronts. The party was in the saloon. There were John Wayne and Clint Eastwood movie posters framed on the walls, and the royal guards were dressed in drag and performed, some reluctantly, at gunpoint!" As a birthday gift, Sal gave the prince the viewfinder, he had been using to scout locations for *The Wrong People*.

On June 1, they returned to the Hotel el Djenina to spend their last night in Morocco, and the following day, Sal and Courtney flew back to England. As soon as Courtney returned to London, he left the Westbourne flat he shared with Sal and moved into a room at Eric's Bull and Gate pub. "I was so frustrated," Courtney said. "After the trip and then returning to our problems in London, nothing seemed real to me. Our life was about image. It wasn't a real life."

For Courtney, the trip was nothing less than surreal. "Here we were at Cannes and Monte Carlo, then Morocco and all the opulence, and when we get back to London, we had nothing. No money, nothing. It was too much, too stressful for me. I didn't know what to do with myself."

Sal seemed unfazed by their lack of money. It was something he had become accustomed to, and it didn't seem to interfere with his living style.

Courtney quickly began sexual affairs with two young women. And Sal began an affair with a married man. "That's what we did," Courtney said. "Whenever we were feeling things were out of control, we'd start screwing around. That was the one thing we could take control of."

Sal and Courtney had dinner at April and Desmond's and spent the night together the evening before Sal left for Los Angeles on June 18 to make a television movie, *The Family Rico*. It would be the first time in eighteen months Sal worked in front of the camera.

*The Family Rico* was written by Emmy Award–winning writer David

Karp and directed by Paul Wendkos. The dramatic story concerned the pressures experienced by a Mafia chief (Ben Gazzara) who is torn between his love for his younger brother (Sal), who has defected from his underworld family, and his loyalty to the criminal organization. The supporting cast included Michael Anderson Jr., who shared the screen with his friend for the fourth time.

When *The Family Rico* was broadcast in September, *Variety* favorably reviewed the television movie, writing, "The cast was mostly good, especially Ben Gazzara and Sal Mineo."

While Sal was working on the film, he ran into his old friend Perry Lopez. "We were all scrambling around for jobs then," Perry said. "Television paid well and there seemed to be more opportunities there." Perry played the part of a lawman on Richard Boone's show *Hec Ramsey*. He tried to get Sal on the show. "But Boone said no," Perry recalled. "Sal had sort of a reputation in Hollywood. People talked about him being homosexual behind his back. Boone said Sal was too 'soft,' if you know what I mean. Boone wouldn't have it. Sal was such a great guy, but people in the industry seemed to back away from him then. It was a real shame."

Sal returned to England on July 4. Shortly before leaving Los Angeles, he attended Yul Brynner's birthday party on the *Queen Mary* ocean liner dry-docked in Long Beach Harbor. Sal had seen little of Brynner for several years, embarrassed by his inability to repay a $20,000 loan Brynner had made to him years before. Sal was glad to reconnect with "the old man" and told reporters that he regarded Brynner as his second father.

FOR THE next month, Courtney lived and worked at Eric Williams's pub. He liked being around people his own age. "There was a lot going on there," Courtney said. "Sal was working on *The Wrong People*, which didn't seem to be going anywhere, and I needed to be around other artists I could identify with."

Courtney saw Sal frequently for dinner, walks in the park, and sexual intimacy. Still, Sal conducted a casual relationship with Paul Gill, who had moved to London earlier that year. They, too, were sexually compatible. "Paul was highly sexed," Courtney said.

"Sal and Courtney got into a terrible row over Paul once," Eric

Williams recalled. "Sal and I went out for something at the store and when we came back, Courtney was fucking Paul. Sal flew into a rage and tore up my flat, throwing lamps about and screaming. But he got over it quickly and later regretted the outburst."

Sal was angered by Courtney's transgression, but not for the obvious reason. "Sal was jealous, all right," Courtney said. "He wanted to have a three-way with me and Paul. Sal was mad because we were doing it *without* him. He felt left out."

During the month, Sal and Courtney had countless story conferences with Murray Smith. It didn't take long, though, before Courtney became uneasy with the direction the writer was headed with the script.

On August 22, Sal and Courtney attended a screening of Peter Walker's latest film, *The Flesh and Blood Show*. The horror film was about some young actors, rehearsing for a show, who are mysteriously and gruesomely killed off one by one by an unknown maniac. The film had everything: decapitations, psychotic tramps, naked women, deranged killings, drownings, and sex. "It was awful," Courtney said. "And this was the guy we were trying to get to produce our film." His doubts about the project increased.

After mending their differences, Courtney moved back to Sal's flat on August 25. Courtney recalled, "It became a routine. During the day we met with people, always trying to raise money and getting a workable script. We'd send out promotional film packages and wait weeks for replies. It was a whole lot of 'hurry up and wait.' "

In early September, feeling time was running out, Sal and Murray worked diligently to complete the script. But Sal was not happy with the story arc and tone of the rewrite, and Courtney wasn't pleased with his work or his notes. Sal worked late into the night rewriting what he and Murray had written earlier each day. "I know Sal was anxious about the project," Courtney recalled, "and we could almost feel it slipping away." Sal was under enormous stress. One evening, unwilling to put the script work aside but overcome by fatigue, Sal took too much Mandrex and passed out. "I thought he was dying," Courtney recalled.

On September 9, Sal met with Murray Smith and made his feelings known about the direction his script had taken, and gave him a list of proposed changes. Later that evening, David Cassidy, who had returned to London to appear in concert, sent a car to pick up Sal and Courtney. David was Sal's only American friend to ever visit him while he lived in London.

After David's fans had torn apart the Dorchester Hotel during his previous visit, it was impossible to find accommodations in London. He rented the yacht that Liz Taylor and Richard Burton had earlier rented when, famously, no hotel would take their dogs. The yacht, the largest privately owned boat in England at 110 feet, was docked in the Thames River between the Tower Bridge and the London Bridge. Courtney and Sal were driven to a dock, where they were taken to the yacht by a Metropolitan Water Police boat.

"The night before," Courtney mused, "Sal and I had baked beans on toast, we were so poor."

Later in the month, Courtney received a call from a writer and aspiring movie producer named Craig Zadan who was visiting London from New York. He reminded Courtney they had earlier met at an *After Dark* magazine party in Manhattan. Kenn Duncan's sexy photographs of Courtney were earlier printed in the magazine. "We met up," Courtney said. "We talked about work and all the exciting things going on in New York. I immediately felt this strong urge to go back to New York City. He may have had his own agenda but encouraged me and said I could stay with him.

"I was frustrated that the film was going nowhere," Courtney said. "The script wasn't good. I was just sitting around again, watching my life pass by, pursuing another of Sal's dreams. I was afraid the same thing would happen again that happened before with *Fallen Dove*. And that was an even better script. It didn't take much encouragement; I was ready to leave."

Zadan was staying in London with two young men who worked for Robert Stigwood's production company. Stigwood employed many handsome young men whose careers quickly moved forward because of the producer's numerous successful projects. Zadan introduced Courtney to his hosts, Peter Buckley and his roommate Kevin McCormick. McCormick would later produce the hit film *Saturday Night Fever* for the Robert Stigwood Organization.

"Kevin was incredible," Courtney said. "I was taken with him. He was handsome, sexy, and very smart. One night, I was at their apartment drinking and tumbled into bed with each of them."

In late October, Courtney caught Sal off guard when he told him he planned to return to New York to pursue other work. Sal was outraged that Courtney had decided to leave London again. He felt betrayed.

"I spent my own money to furnish our flat there," Courtney said. "I wanted to be reimbursed before I left. Sal and Eric got mad at me and told me to move out, which I did on Halloween." Courtney stayed at David Shaw's house until he flew back to New York City on November 4.

IN AN effort to generate more interest in his project, Sal's agent, Tom Korman, provided a news item that ran in the *Hollywood Reporter* on November 20, 1972. "Sal Mineo, who has been living in London for some time, was set this week to direct *The Wrong People,* from the novel by Robin Maugham. Serpentine Productions will make the picture in Morocco from a screenplay by Murray Smith. Sal, known mainly as an actor and a stage director, is making his debut as a director on this story of the sleazy Tangier set."

Sal sent Courtney his revised screenplay of *The Wrong People* to read over the Thanksgiving holiday. "The script just wasn't any good," Courtney said. "It was disappointing, especially after we had interviewed some of the greatest writers in London. We end up with Murray Smith. I had lost interest."

In early December, Courtney found out he had landed the lead in a production of *Norman, Is That You?* When he called Sal in London to tell him the good news, Eric Williams informed him that Sal was actually in America directing a production of Gian Carlo Menotti's opera *The Medium* in Detroit. Eric also told Courtney that Sal had taken Kevin McCormick with him as an assistant.

Sal was hurt that Courtney had left London. He wasn't used to being left behind by anyone. Sal found out about Courtney's dalliance with McCormick. With resources in London tapped out, Sal needed to return to the States in search of work. The offer to direct the opera came unexpectedly. Sal thought there was no better way to get back at Courtney than to accept the directing assignment and take McCormick along in Courtney's place.

"I was indignant," Courtney said. "I had taken Sal to his first opera in London and he hadn't even called me to tell me about the job. He took Kevin. I was sure Sal was sleeping with him, and I was worried. This was the first time I was jealous. I knew Kevin was a sexual turn-on for Sal, and he was ambitious." Courtney called Sal immediately and confronted him. After numerous, and at times contentious, telephone conversations, they eventually came to an understanding of each other's issues.

Gian Carlo Menotti was an Italian-born American composer and librettist best known for his classic Christmas opera *Amahl and the Night Visitors*. Menotti first produced *The Medium* in 1946, and in 1951 directed a film version starring Anna Maria Alberghetti. *The Medium* was a one-hour-long, two-act dramatic opera. Muriel Costa-Greenspon, a mezzo-soprano from the New York City Opera, portrayed the medium in Sal's opera-directing debut. Sal played the role of Toby, the mute.

When *The Medium* closed after its scheduled performance, Sal returned to Los Angeles to pursue television work.

# 34.

"The idea of settling down goes against my makeup."

Sal found a one-bedroom, first-floor apartment at 8569 Holloway Drive, west of La Cienega Boulevard and south of the Sunset Strip. The two-story building belonged to attorney Marvin Mitchelson. The alley behind the building provided access to the tenants' carports and led to a courtyard crowded with overgrown potted plants and plastic patio furniture. The building was next door to the apartment he had rented years before when he was filming *Escape from Zahrain*. The sparsely furnished apartment rented for $175 a month.

Sal's bad credit prevented him from qualifying for the apartment. "I had good credit. I told him to put it in my name," Courtney explained. "Tom Korman helped him and I actually rented the apartment myself."

Sal was cast in a new pilot for the ABC-TV series *Harry O* in January 1973. "Such Dust as Dreams Are Made On" was written by well-respected television writer Howard Rodman and starred David Janssen playing the part of Harry Orwell, a retired Los Angeles policeman. The ninety-minute film was edited down from two hours for television broadcast. The pilot, which aired on March 11, did not originally sell.

While Sal was working on the pilot, he received the disheartening news that Morocco had rejected his application to obtain film permits to shoot *The Wrong People* in their country. In an article for the *Hollywood Reporter* printed on February 8, Will Tusher wrote, "Moroccan censors turned thumbs down on his script because they felt it kept alive the mystique of Morocco as a center of international intrigue teeming with bars, lice, drugs, prostitutes and skulking natives up to no good." Sal told the reporter that he hoped to find a deal with a co-producer to film in Israel.

In truth, Sal was devastated. He had moved to England hoping he could realize his dream of directing and producing a film of his choosing. He had interrupted what was left of his career in America and dug

324 / *Michael Gregg Michaud*

himself deeper into debt. And, in the process, Serpentine Productions had run out of capital.

When Sal finished working in Los Angeles, he had little choice but to return to London and try to salvage *The Wrong People*. The flat in Westbourne Terrace had been reclaimed by the original tenant, so Eric arranged for a flat on Ennismore Gardens, a tony area on the south side of Hyde Park.

"Sal moved to larger quarters," Eric explained. "He was living next door to Ava Gardner and her little corgi dogs. Sal went out with her one night for a late dinner and she got plastered. He told me he kept looking at her trying to see the beautiful 'Barefoot Contessa,' and all he could see was a puffy old fat blubber of a drunk. She made a pass at him and he did his best to get rid of her, and avoided her whenever he could later on. He said she was so drunk he picked her face out of the soup."

Courtney prepared for his role in *Norman, Is That You?* which was set to open in Miami Beach on February 26, but he was more interested in the other play he had read for, *The Children's Mass*, written by Frederick Combs. Combs had starred in Mart Crowley's smash hit, the groundbreaking *The Boys in the Band*.

Robin Moles, a wealthy Manhattan socialite, originally had the rights to the play and intended to make this her first foray into theater production. One of the original producers she was working with couldn't raise enough money, so the production languished.

With Moles's approval, Courtney sent a copy of *The Children's Mass* to Sal in London. "I really wanted to do the play," Courtney said. "I thought it was edgy and provocative and would be something that Sal would like, too. *The Wrong People* was not happening, and I knew Sal needed the money and this could be something that would help him and keep his name out there. And he would be paid a five-thousand-dollar producer fee."

*The Children's Mass* was not for the faint of heart, but it was the type of shocking material that appealed to Sal. It worked for *Fortune and Men's Eyes*, Sal reasoned, and it could work again. The play explored the life and death of Dutchie, a New York drag queen who is deeply into marijuana, heroin, and other illegal drugs. She eventually brings home a strange young man and taunts him into grotesquely murdering her.

The subject matter of the play, as well as his diminished status in the entertainment world, made it nearly impossible for Sal to interest investors in *The Children's Mass*. He flew to New York and accepted a proposal from his friends, Jack Deveau and Bobby Alvarez, to produce a documentary about the making of the play as a fund-raising tool. Working out of the Ansonia Hotel, the two men owned Hand in Hand Films, an independent film company famous for gay, hardcore pornographic movies. Despite their best efforts, Sal failed to find investors. He wined and dined Robin Moles, introduced her to some celebrity friends, and ultimately convinced her to put up all the money for the production herself. Moles knew Sal could handle the publicity, casting, and crew, and the prospect of producing a play became exciting to her.

On April 5, the *Hollywood Reporter* announced their producing partnership. Courtney was cast as Dutchie. The other three leads were Calvin Culver, Kipp Osborne, and Donald Warfield. Richard Altman would direct. Altman had been Jerome Robbins's directorial assistant on the original Broadway production of *Fiddler on the Roof,* and he directed Tennessee Williams's *Small Craft Warnings* in New York.

In 1971, using the name Casey Donovan, and looking like a "golden-haired, blue-eyed preppie," Cal Culver starred in *Boys in the Sand.* The X-rated, gay film became an instant classic and earned Cal the title "the Golden Boy of Gay Porn." His handsome face, photographed by Kenn Duncan, was featured on the December 1972 cover of *After Dark* magazine.

Duncan and Bill Como, the editor of *After Dark,* suggested Cal Culver as a box office draw to Sal when he was casting *The Children's Mass.* Sal was intrigued by the idea of using a well-known porn star and believed the publicity would be very helpful. New York City newspapers and tabloids ran with the casting news, and *After Dark* heavily promoted Cal's engagement in the play in several consecutive issues. The only problem was that Cal Culver could not act. He was eventually replaced by a young actor named Gary Sandy.

*NORMAN, IS THAT YOU?* was extended at the Carillon Dinner Theatre for a few weeks. When the show finally closed, Courtney jumped on a plane for New York. He was coiffed and photographed with the cast of *The Children's Mass* by Kenn Duncan that same day so the ad could begin running in the *New York Times*.

Courtney found a small one-bedroom apartment on Sixteenth Street. His relationship with his *Norman, Is That You?* costar, singer Eddie Rambeau, proved to be more than just a diversion or a flirtation. They had roomed together during the run of the play in Miami Beach. Courtney characterized it as "a showbiz romance." When Eddie returned to New York City, he was immediately cast in the off-Broadway production of *Tubstrip,* a gay comedy written by Jerry Douglas.

"Sal and I had no secrets," Courtney explained. "He knew about me and Eddie, and he was concerned because it went on for a while." Sal stayed at his agent Tom Korman's apartment.

Sal and Courtney remained cool toward each other. "We were both busy," Courtney recalled. "I didn't see him that often. I was rehearsing. He dropped in once in a while for rehearsals, to go over notes with the director, make suggestions, but he wasn't there very much." Courtney finally told Sal he didn't know how serious his relationship with Eddie was becoming, but they were considering living together. Sal was consumed by an incendiary combination of feelings. He was hurt. And he was jealous.

After several preview performances, *The Children's Mass* opened at the Theatre de Lys on Christopher Street on the evening of Wednesday, May 16, 1973. Sal sent a telegram to Courtney that read, "CB my love tonight my heart bursts with pride as large fragments of our fantasy are realized. I love you, Gibone."

The opening-night performance was sold out. Clive Barnes's review appeared the next day in the *New York Times*. "*The Children's Mass,* which opened last night, is a mixture of good and bad, but as a first play it can be regarded as at least promising. The figure of 'Dutchie'—a little girl lost in a man's body—it has its moment of insight."

Douglas Watts of the *Daily News* wrote, "A lurid story of a drag queen, a curious sense of truth and pity that compels attention." "Courtney Burr," wrote Emory Lewis in the *Record,* "is brilliant, dazzling, one of the best performances of the season!"

Sal found himself in a curious position. *The Wrong People* had fallen apart. Acting jobs were few, and he was producing a play starring his boyfriend, who was heaped with critical praise and carrying on with a handsome new young lover.

On Monday afternoon, May 21, Courtney went to Robin Moles's tenth-floor penthouse for a birthday party the cast and crew had planned for him. It had been a rough day. Eddie Rambeau had called him earlier in the day to tell him he didn't want to move in with him.

As Courtney made his way through the twenty-odd guests to get a drink at the bar, someone said to him, "It's a shame about the show."

"I didn't know what they were talking about," Courtney said. "I said, 'What?' "

"It closed yesterday."

Courtney was stunned. Robin saw that someone had intercepted him and she hurried to his side. "We closed the show yesterday," she quickly told him.

"I couldn't believe it," Courtney remembered. "And I was the only one who didn't know!"

Immediately, Courtney suspected Sal had closed the show out of spite. Courtney's acting career seemed on track; his reviews in Florida, and more importantly in New York, were excellent. Sal's name was barely mentioned in the press in regard to *The Children's Mass*.

A short time later Sal arrived by cab. Courtney saw him walk in the door. "I rushed him and grabbed him," Courtney recalled. "I said, 'How dare you?' I was in such disbelief. Sal was shocked. I said, 'After all I've done. I stood by you for three years on projects you wanted that went nowhere and the one time I ask you to help me, you fucking shut me down!' People rushed over to us thinking I was going to throw him over Robin's balcony."

Sal tried to explain his actions. He said, "We didn't have enough money to keep it open."

"It was a two-hundred-and-ninety-nine-seat theater," Courtney recalled. "The audiences were good. It just opened. They had to keep it open to *earn* the money. I sent him the play so *he* could earn some money. And this is what he did to me. It was unbelievable. I felt it was a terrible betrayal after all I had done. Why hadn't he called me to tell me what was going on?"

Courtney didn't speak to Sal again at the party and soon left.

———

A COUPLE of weeks later, a friend who was one of the producers of the San Francisco production of *Fortune and Men's Eyes* invited Courtney to a party at his home in Manhattan. He was informed Sal was also invited. Courtney hadn't seen or spoken with Sal since their unpleasant encounter in Robin Moles's penthouse.

"Sal walked in the door with Eddie Rambeau," Courtney said, "and I was stunned. I thought, 'Haven't you done enough to me?' "

Within minutes, Sal and Courtney were standing at a buffet table. Surrounded by people, Courtney stared at Sal and said, "You really are a little man and this is why you're going to be known as a lesser talent. You have no class. You have no style. And not just because of your lack of education."

Sal was speechless. "The color drained from his face right in front of me," Courtney said. "I turned and walked away. Eddie said to me, 'What is it with you two? All Sal did was talk about you when I was with him. What you did in bed with me, and did you wear jockey shorts.' Sal wanted to know everything Eddie and *I* did together!"

Before leaving New York for a television job on the West Coast in July, Sal spoke with the press about *The Children's Mass.* "We got marvelous reviews," he said, "but no business, so I had to close the play. However, rather than falling into a cocoon and saying, 'Oh, my God, I produced a failure and blah, blah, blah,' I faced reality and looked at the positive side. At least it opened; it got on the board. It's done. Next? The day that I closed the play I was already working on my next project."

Sal told Frank Torrez that he was currently involved in producing a film he had written called *Sacred Bubblegum* and acquiring the rights to the stage play *Warp*. Advertised as "the world's first science fiction epic-adventure play in serial form," the peculiar play had opened on Broadway on February 14, 1973, and closed after four performances.

*Sacred Bubblegum* was a project that Sal had toyed with for several years. Sal's friend Michael Mason remembered, "The script for *Sacred Bubblegum* was written by Sal. It was the story of a young Hollywood director who tours high schools looking for young men to star in his upcoming film. The voyeuristic plot included several seduction scenes. It bordered on pornography and included many of Sal's own fantasies involving fit, young blond boys wearing jockey shorts. The film was never completed."

With more personal issues, Sal still played a well-practiced game of cat and mouse. He said, "I love Jill. I always will, but I've chosen my lifestyle over marriage." A week earlier, Sal and Jill had attended the opening of Le Jardin, a nightclub located near Times Square in the Diplomat Hotel. Though surrounded by muscled young men in metallic hot pants, Sal playfully told the press that he and Jill were again an item and they planned to marry soon. Bill Como, editor of *After Dark* magazine, said, "Sal was always playing Sal Mineo. He had that star aura. He had a 'Little Caesar' complex. He was always trying to be outrageous, larger than life, to make up for his physical stature."

For several months, Courtney had been having a fling with his female dresser from *The Children's Mass*. One day in July she taunted him and told him he had really blown it with Sal. "And I told her," Courtney said, " 'You don't get it. This is what we do.' " He then called Sal in Los Angeles and told him he missed him and wanted to see him. Sal told him to come, and a couple of days later, Courtney flew to California.

"When I got there," Courtney added, "there were someone else's clothes in the closet!" He and Sal fought and Sal agreed to get rid of the stuff. "I went out for something," Courtney recalled, "and when I got back, all the stuff was gone." Sal and Courtney picked up as if nothing had ever happened.

In September, Sal was cast as Gamal Zaki, the peace-crusading president of a Middle Eastern country, in an episode of a new detective series called *Griff,* starring Lorne Greene. The episode, titled "Marked for Murder," aired a few months later on ABC. Very few people saw Sal deliver one of his worst performances when he played an Arab who looked like an Italian gangster who spoke with a thick Bronx accent on this ill-fated show.

Sal lost the only other acting job of the summer almost as fast as he got it. Telly Savalas, with whom Sal had worked on *The Greatest Story Ever Told,* began filming a television series in Los Angeles called *Kojak.* "We had run into Telly at the London airport one day," Courtney recalled. "He and Sal were both in search of work at the time. They commiserated and Telly said, 'We gotta work together.' The implication was, whoever gets a job first could help the other one out."

Sal was cast as "a big-time drug dealer" in an episode of *Kojak* called "Secret Snow, Deadly Snow." "He went to Universal Studios for the wardrobe tests," Courtney explained, "and when he got home, Tom Korman called and said the producers changed their minds and didn't want him. Tom made up some excuse, but Sal was humiliated."

Although discouraged by his failure to film *The Wrong People,* Sal still had hopes the project could be salvaged. He applied for filming permits in Israel, but his request was quickly rejected. Instead of directing his first film, he found himself back in Hollywood, reading for nondescript roles for the sake of much-needed money.

Elliot Mintz, Sal's old buddy, encouraged him to give radio a shot. In 1966, Elliot began a radio career in Los Angeles. By 1973, he was a successful late-night talk jock on KABC Talk Radio.

Sal began his entertainment-chat radio program on August 20 when he replaced top-rated conservative commentator Marv Gray. The day before, the *Los Angeles Times* cryptically wrote, "This is going to sound like a joke, but beginning [tomorrow], Gray will be replaced by (deep breath) . . . Sal Mineo! SAL MINEO?"

From the beginning, the program struggled with low ratings in the 7–10 P.M. segment. Two weeks later, the programming director at KABC moved Sal's program to another time slot. Frank Torrez wrote in the *Los Angeles Herald Examiner* on September 10, "Mineo believes the key to talk radio is 'being honest with your listeners.' And that belief is now directed into KABC radio's 9–12 P.M. talk slot—a three-hour session devoted entirely to the arts on 790am Monday through Friday."

The format of Sal's program included "call-in time" with listeners; reviews of motion pictures, theater, rock concerts, books, and ballet; and in-studio guests from the entertainment world. "Night after night," Sal said, "you get a pulse on what people are into. What kinds of films, or plays, or music they're digging. And because that's my business, it's more interesting getting it directly from the people whose views often differ from what business people are talking about."

Meanwhile, Sal occupied his days with two television assignments. In an episode of *Tenafly* for the NBC Wednesday Mystery Movie titled

"Man Running," Sal played the part of a parking attendant who holds the key to a rash of high-end burglaries. He then played the part of Stippy, a criminal gang member, in a special ninety-minute episode of *Police Story* called "The Hunters."

Los Angeles became preoccupied with the triumphant return of Josephine Baker in October. The legendary performer appeared at the Ahmanson Theatre. Courtney saw her exhilarating show and reviewed it for Sal's radio program. After he signed off the radio for the evening, Sal joined Courtney at a party in Baker's honor at fashion maven Mr. Blackwell's ornate twenty-eight-room mansion in Los Angeles.

"The guest list," Mr. Blackwell, creator of the annual "Worst-Dressed List," recalled, "was an eclectic mix of high society, old and new Hollywood and personal friends of Miss Baker. Gloria Swanson represented old Hollywood and Sal Mineo represented new Hollywood. Sal looked like a Borsalino Bandit selling fake watches and jewelry from inside his leather jacket as he mingled in the crowd. He was sort of an enfant terrible, and had a bit of a dangerous reputation, but the elite loved him. He had an edge, and he could work a room. He was very appealing."

Courtney returned to New York City in October to begin rehearsals for a play. At Sal's request, Courtney wrote reviews of several Broadway shows for Sal to read during his radio program.

But Sal's days on the radio were numbered. The *Los Angeles Times* had called his radio show "lame." With listenership fast dwindling, Sal was fired on October 27, 1973, after little more than two months on the air.

Courtney had been cast in *Lovers and Other Strangers,* which opened at the Coachlight Dinner Theatre in Connecticut on November 23. Sal sent him a congratulatory telegram. "Another opening another show, with Courtney Burr it's got to glow, and when you bow to a roar of applause, remember I love you mause and mause, a Sondheim I'm not but 8 inches he has not. Love, Sal."

After one week, Courtney fell ill with hepatitis and had to leave the production. He flew to Florida and joined Sal in Jacksonville to recuperate. Sal was appearing at the Alhambra Dinner Theatre with Marjorie Lord in Alan Ayckbourn's comedy, *How the Other Half Loves.*

Courtney had worked frequently in dinner theater. He was working more steadily than Sal and often covered Sal's living expenses as well as his own. Begrudgingly, and at his agent's urging, Sal had accepted a limited dinner-theater engagement of his own in Florida.

"Sal hated it," Courtney said. "It was his first time doing dinner theater. He complained, 'The cast is so amateur.' I told him, 'Sal, you're the worst person on the stage. You're not listening to any of them. You're not present. At least they're trying.' "

WHEN *HOW THE OTHER HALF LOVES* closed, Sal and Courtney flew to New York for a couple of days. With no immediate work, they decided to fly to London and spend a couple of weeks at Ennismore Gardens.

For the next ten days, Sal and Courtney enjoyed the peace and quiet London offered. "We were both in our element there," Courtney said, "and it was a good neutral ground. We spent all of our time re-connecting. We just relaxed."

Sal was a different person in England. Jill thought his time in England was transitional. So far from home, Sal felt at ease and didn't feel the need to live up to anyone else's standard or expectation. "I know he was happy there," Jill said. "I would say he became more comfortable in his own skin. Courtney helped him with that."

On their last night in England, Sal and Courtney attended the opening-night performance of *Aida* at Covent Garden and had a late-night dinner at April and Desmond's. Later, they had a serious conversation back in their flat where they talked about the crushing disappointment surrounding the production of *The Children's Mass*. Courtney explained how hurt he had been by Sal's careless treatment, and Sal finally admitted that he was angry and jealous of Courtney's relationship with Eddie Rambeau. He admitted his spiteful involvement with him, too.

"A lot had changed between us," Courtney added. "We had grown. We had wounded each other deeply, and yet our bond remained strong. It was a very mature conversation."

Sal and Courtney flew back to New York City on January 10, 1974. Courtney returned to the Sixteenth Street apartment to resume the busy pursuit of his career. Sal flew to St. Petersburg, Florida, to star in *Sunday in New York*, another dinner-theater production.

# 35.

"I guess you could say that today I live out of a suitcase."

Sunday in New York was written by Norman Krasna and originally produced by David Merrick on Broadway in 1961. Krasna had written several successful Broadway comedies, including *Dear Ruth* and *Time for Elizabeth*. The thin plot concerns a young woman suffering the breakup of a relationship. She goes to New York City to visit her brother and meets a handsome stranger on a bus.

The Country Dinner Playhouse was located at the Gateway Mall in St. Petersburg, Florida. Admission included a buffet dinner and alcoholic beverage service—just the type of theatrical experience Sal despised. Sal took up residence in the Red Carpet Inn nearby.

*Sunday in New York* opened on January 22, 1974. Local newspapers reviewed the play favorably, and the theater did a brisk business. Ticket sales encouraged the management to extend the show.

Late in January, Tom Korman presented Sal with a job offer. Ernest Criezis, a businessman in Houston, Texas, wanted Sal to stage *Fortune and Men's Eyes* at a basement jazz club he owned called La Bastille, located in the Old Market Square district peppered with other nightclubs, pawnshops, strip clubs, and porn stores. Beginning in the 1960s, La Bastille was a well-known local jazz showcase. Criezis wanted to launch a new theater venture in the club.

On February 7, Sal contacted Ken Waissman and Maxine Fox for a copy of the script, a property and wardrobe list, the soundtrack tape, and a budget breakdown. The next day, Courtney flew to Florida with the package from the New York producers. "Sal was interested in doing *Fortune* again," Courtney recalled. "We talked about it a lot. Sal would direct and play Rocky. I would play Smitty, and our friend Ted Harris would play Queenie."

It was a leisurely time for both men while Sal explored the idea of restaging *Fortune*. They spent a romantic weekend at the Sarasota Hotel on the Gulf Coast of Florida before Courtney flew back to New

York on February 19 and Sal flew to Los Angeles three weeks later to begin work on another provocative project.

SAL MINEO WILL PLAY BOB KENNEDY KILLER was the headline in *Variety* on February 2. The article reported, "Ananke Productions has signed Sal Mineo to portray the role of the convicted assassin of Sen. Robert F. Kennedy, Sirhan Bishara Sirhan. According to Donald Freed, author of the still untitled screenplay, the film will demonstrate the tragic psychological manipulation of Sirhan at the hands of a conspiracy. Mineo will join Freed and researcher Jack Kimbrough in screenplay preparation."

Sal's friend Elliot Mintz was a conspiracy buff. Often impressed by other people's real or imagined knowledge, Sal became very influenced by Elliot's interesting preoccupations and theories about all things—from who killed President Kennedy to chasing flying saucers in the California desert. Sal parroted many of Elliot's ideas about the assassination of John Kennedy to the press. "The Warren Commission is totally bullshit. We know it wasn't Oswald who shot the president," Sal said. "I mean, obviously there can't be one man shooting the president from three different angles."

The assassination of Senator Robert Kennedy in 1968 ended a type of youthful liberalism in America and allowed a wave of conservatism to sweep the political landscape of the day. The killing was monumentally shocking and disenfranchised young voters for generations to come. Sal had political opinions based on youthful energy and snap judgment, but he rarely voted. He rarely endorsed candidates, and they didn't seek his counsel. Nevertheless, he happily shared his thoughts with the press when asked. His sense of the dramatic, though, sometimes made him sound disingenuous.

"I campaigned for Robert Kennedy because I loved him," Sal said. He had actually served as honorary Los Angeles chairman of the Young Democrats for Kennedy in 1968 and appeared at several rallies and fund-raisers. "It was just horrible when I learned of the assassination. At first, I didn't see how I could ever portray Kennedy's killer. I had always been convinced that Sirhan was the lone gunman who killed Kennedy but now I believe there are grounds for doubt. If the film can influence the courts to reopen the case or force out new facts and answer questions, then it will serve its purpose."

Sal began working with writer Donald Freed on the film project, entitled *Sirhan Sirhan*. Freed was a liberal-minded political activist with numerous writing credits as a playwright, screenwriter, and novelist. As work progressed on the screenplay, Sal became excited about the prospect of starring in a feature film again.

But it was not to be. The subject matter of *Sirhan Sirhan* and the assassination of Robert Kennedy, a horrific incident that happened in Hollywood's backyard, proved to be a treacherous political football. Producers wouldn't touch it, and the proposed film died. A year later, Donald Freed published a book based on his research called *The Killing of RFK*.

Sal was disheartened by the failure of the project. He was also having trouble dealing with Ernest Criezis in Houston, Texas. The club owner frequently called Sal at home in Los Angeles. His calls became desperate and pleading as it became more and more apparent that his proposal was not acceptable to Sal. And Sal's required budget was not acceptable to Criezis. Sal canceled a March 5 trip with Courtney to Houston to discuss the production and informed Criezis he would pass on his offer to restage *Fortune and Men's Eyes*. After that, the phone calls took on a threatening tone. Criezis said he had actually advanced money to pay for publicity to promote the upcoming production even though they had no written agreement. He said he had allotted a block of time at the club for this venture and stood to lose money as a result of the cancellation.

"Sal didn't want to deal with the guy," Courtney said. "He told me it was too much trouble. There were no contracts, just talk." Sal turned over communication with Criezis to Tom Korman and accepted an extended engagement directing and acting in *Sunday in New York* for the Windmill Dinner Theatre chain in Texas and Arizona instead.

Requests for interviews had become infrequent. At the age of thirty-five, Sal was considered a part of movie history, not a viable player on the scene. He told a Hollywood reporter, "I guess you could say that today I live out of a suitcase. I have to go where my work takes me, where I can be creative and happy and productive."

For weeks Courtney had been preparing the Sixteenth Street apartment in Manhattan for his and Sal's expected use. With few acting possibilities in Hollywood, Sal intended to spend more time in New York. He had shipped his books and some small household items from storage in Los Angeles. Courtney had driven to Mrs. Mineo's apartment to pick up a stereo and some furniture that had been stored since Sal sold the Mamaroneck house.

On March 27, Sal called Courtney and offered him a costarring role in *Sunday in New York*. The three-city, fifteen-week tour provided Courtney with $250 a week, plus travel and accommodations. Courtney accepted the offer and flew to Dallas on April 1. He took a small apartment near Sal and the company began rehearsals on April 2 under Sal's direction.

The Windmill Dinner Theatre chain owned several theaters in Texas and one in Scottsdale, Arizona. Sal's first stop with *Sunday in New York* was Addison, Texas, a northern suburb of Dallas. The cast began one week of rehearsals. The going was tough. The sets were not finished for the first preview performance. The sound system did not work, and the theater was overwhelmed by traffic sounds from the street. Nevertheless, the show opened on April 10, 1974, to a full house.

John Neville of the *Dallas News* wrote, "*Sunday in New York* is a light-weight show, but amusing. And Sal Mineo's direction (he also stars in the vehicle) keeps things moving apace." The *Dallas Times Herald* reported, "Mineo plays it nicely, displaying a comic flair away from his common work on screen."

Working together and essentially living together proved to be a challenge once again for Sal and Courtney. They tended to get on each other's nerves. After the show, they often went to Bayou Landing, a gay bar in Dallas that presented drag shows. Sometimes they saw a movie in the afternoon before showtime. Both men quickly became bored by the mediocrity of the material and the audiences. After the last performance in Addison, Courtney gave notice to leave the show. He was feeling trapped and professionally stymied again.

*Sunday in New York* opened in Houston on May 8. With a nod of recognition to their tempestuous relationship, Sal sent Courtney an opening-night telegram: "From the ripple through the rapids atop the title [*sic*] wave there is love. Break a leg. S."

The critics were not impressed. "It was a blistering enema from the critics," Courtney said.

With the rules of their open relationship clearly defined, Sal always had an eye for a casual hookup. One night he and Courtney went dancing at a local gay bar, and a young man deliberately spilled his Coke in Sal's lap. He was invited to the next evening's performance and joined Sal and Courtney bar hopping later after the show. "It was all so predictable," Courtney recalled.

During the curtain call after a Sunday matinee, Sal became agitated by a loud drunk in the audience. From the stage, Sal flashed with anger and kicked part of the set, breaking a chair. Courtney stepped in before it could escalate into a confrontation. "I took his arm and pulled him back," Courtney remembered. "I said, 'Sal, that's enough.' And we left the stage."

Later that day, they drove to the gulf and took a motel room on the beach for a rest. Sal was exhausted. He told Courtney he didn't want to do the show either, but with creditors on his back, he had no choice. He could not afford to turn down a steady paycheck.

As a birthday surprise for Courtney, Sal flew in their friend Ted Harris on May 22. Sal and Courtney had known Ted since he worked backstage during the San Francisco production of *Fortune and Men's Eyes*. Ted stayed for several days, and they talked about a new project that interested Sal.

One day, walking through an airport terminal, Sal had stopped at the newsstand to pick up some magazines. He noticed a paperback book that interested him. He bought it and read it on the plane. "It was about hustlers," Courtney said, "and that got his attention."

*McCaffery* was a pulp novel written by Charles Gorham and originally published by Dial Press in 1961. The plot of the book centers around a teenage boy who suffers mental, physical, and sexual abuse. Following his mother's death, seventeen-year-old Vincent McCaffery becomes involved with a street gang that robs homosexual men cruising Central Park at night. One of his victims turns him over to a notorious pimp in Greenwich Village, who "sells" him to a millionaire. McCaffery is kept by the older man in his luxury apartment in Gramercy Park, but he falls in love with a young female prostitute he meets in the Greenwich Village brothel. In a rage, the boy murders his millionaire "protector" and tracks down and attempts to kill his own hated father.

This was a story too good to pass up. Sal wanted Ted Harris to write a screenplay from the book and convinced his friend Billy Belasco to pursue the film rights to *McCaffery*. Sal wanted to produce and direct a film adaptation of the novel.

Courtney's last performance in *Sunday in New York* was on June 2. The next morning he returned to New York City. He resumed an affair he was having with Robin Moles, the producer of the ill-fated *The Children's Mass,* and finished decorating his apartment, picking up some paintings and more furnishings from Mrs. Mineo. After Mr. Mineo's death, Sal's brother Mike had moved into his parents' apartment to help their mother. She and Mike had rented a small storefront on Mamaroneck's main street and opened a health food and vitamin shop called Mamaroneck Nutrition Center.

Sal sent several hundred dollars to Courtney to assist with the makeover of their New York apartment, to purchase a sofa and some dining room chairs, and to pay Josephine for a box of vitamins she had sent him in Texas.

The *Sunday in New York* production moved to Arizona and opened at the Windmill Dinner Theatre in the Phoenix suburb of Scottsdale on June 20 for a successful one-month engagement.

Before Sal left Texas, he was served with a subpoena regarding a legal suit filed against him by Ernest Criezis. On June 4, the owner of La Bastille filed an $800,000 slander suit against Sal. Criezis contended in state district court that Sal made "malicious statements which resulted in a loss of business." The plaintiff asked for $400,000 in actual damages and another $400,000 in exemplary damages. Criezis claimed that Sal had agreed on February 5, 1974, to direct and act in the play *Fortune and Men's Eyes* at La Bastille. The play was scheduled to open in May, he alleged, "launching an avant garde theatre venture for the jazz cabaret." Criezis claimed the "deal" fell through and Sal began appearing in *Sunday in New York* at the rival Windmill Dinner Theatre. Upon initial filing, the suit did not specify what slanderous things Sal was alleged to have said.

Sal handed the suit off to Tom Korman, who hired a Texas attorney. Legal suits and small-claims actions were nothing new to Sal.

Through the years he had been sued many times by utility companies, leasing agencies, and numerous landlords. Still, this particular action was disturbing and potentially costly, and it validated his negative feelings about doing business with Ernest Criezis from the start.

IN LATE July, Sal returned to Los Angeles from Scottsdale. Though Sal may not have felt compelled to settle down with one partner, he didn't like being alone. During the summer, he and Michael Mason dined together, often at the Old World restaurant, a block from Sal's Holloway apartment, and cruised local gay bars and bathhouses in the neighborhood. Sal saw a little less of Elliot since he had become professionally involved as a publicist with John Lennon and Yoko Ono. Sal befriended an actor named David Joliffe, one of the teenage stars of the hit television series *Room 222*, who lived in the building next door. Joliffe recalled, "Sal was a wild man with a sense of purpose and stability. He was a good, straight-ahead guy who didn't live in the past. He was always happy and loving and approachable."

Sal's lifestyle in 1974 seemed a million miles away from his wide-eyed arrival in Hollywood twenty years before. Many things had changed in twenty years, but the public's interest in Sal's most famous costar, James Dean, had never wavered. Dean had become iconic with the passage of time.

In September, Sal was interviewed for a ninety-minute special about James Dean for ABC-TV's *Wide World of Entertainment*. Hosted by Peter Lawford, the special, called "James Dean: Memories of a Gentle Giant," included archival footage of Dean at home and at work, and interviews with his friends and coworkers. Each recounted their personal impressions and recollections of the young actor.

"It's weird," Sal said, "really weird. Jimmy's been dead for nineteen years. Can you believe it? A whole generation of kids have grown up who weren't even born when Jimmy was alive. Yet, the Dean legend persists and grows. The fact that we played such close buddies in *Rebel* has created a situation where I sometimes feel as though I'm frozen in a time capsule. I'm perpetually sixteen, playing Jimmy's buddy, and the legend of Dean continues not only to thrive, but actually to grow stronger and stronger."

# 36.

"They've always tagged me as the delinquent Peter
Pan, the switchblade gang punk, the original Joe
Doper."

S al had starred in Michael McAloney's production of *What Makes
Sammy Run?* at the Royal Alexandra Theatre in 1965. At the time,
Sal had to talk his way into the production. In exchange, he promised McAloney that he would return the favor and appear in a show
at a later date. A new play written by Arthur Marx was scheduled to
premiere at the Royal Alexandra in November as the second offering
in their subscription series. Marx, perhaps best known as the son of
Groucho, had written a couple of books about his famous father and
the Broadway hits *The Impossible Years* and *Minnie's Boys*. McAloney
and theater owner Ed Mirvish, experiencing casting problems, called
in their marker and asked Sal to star in the new thriller *Sugar and Spice*.
Sal arrived in Toronto in mid-October to find the production in a
shambles.

In describing the play, the press release prepared by the theater's
publicist, Gino Empry, read, "the genuine murder-thriller stresses the
changing sexual values of our times, the disorientation of the young,
their demands for total honesty and their rejection of what they see as
hypocritical middle-class morality."

*Sugar and Spice* concerns the impact on a well-to-do Texas couple
of the return of the wife's daughter, Amanda, after the girl's involvement with a group of young people who committed one of the bloodi-
est mass murders in modern times. Given immunity for her testimony,
Amanda is remanded to the custody of her mother.

Gradually the parents realize that their daughter is inherently evil.
As the girl unsuccessfully attempts to seduce her stepfather and gain
his sympathy, her lover (played by Sal) arrives. Shortly, his true nature
as a satanic killer emerges. As they make plans to rob and kill the parents and flee to Mexico, the young killers gain control of the ranch and
begin the brutal and systematic terrorization of the parents. The play

ends when the parents are hacked to death by their daughter and her boyfriend.

Originally cast as the parents in *Sugar and Spice* were film veterans Janet Leigh and John Ireland. Janet Leigh never made it to Toronto. "I knew Arthur [Marx] very well," Janet recalled. "I hadn't done any theater, and I toyed with the idea. I was sent the script. They told me it was a thriller like Hitchcock. It was beyond awful. It was inspired by the Sharon Tate–Charles Manson murders. I don't think I'd ever read anything like it before. I called Arthur and told him I couldn't do the play. I didn't tell him I couldn't even finish reading it."

Virginia Grey, a veteran actress with dozens of television credits and film roles, replaced Leigh. Canadian-born Academy Award nominee John Ireland was a well-known movie "he-man." After several days of rehearsals, McAloney fired Ireland and hired Jack Kelly to replace him. Kelly had starred in the popular television series *Maverick* and hosted the television game show *Sale of the Century*. He arrived in Toronto on October 28 to begin rehearsals.

On November 1, Sal was interviewed in his suite at the Waldorf Astoria Hotel in Toronto by Frank Rasky for the *Toronto Star* newspaper. "I'm just beginning to outgrow those labels people hang on me," Sal explained. "They've always tagged me as the delinquent Peter Pan, the switchblade gang punk, the original Joe Doper. I don't blame them really because I used to play up to those images.

"They call me the handsome baby-faced kid and I smile to myself. I look into the mirror and what do I see? Gray hairs beginning to show at the temple. A broken nose that I once busted in a street fight. Brown eyes that are sad, lonely, and wiser beyond my years. They hang on to this image of me being an actor who specializes in neurotics and psychotics and this role in *Sugar and Spice* is proof positive of the way casting directors think of me.

"I can smile at that image now," Sal said, "because I know I'm a former rebel who has found his cause. I'm going to be a great movie director someday. Just you wait and see."

Plagued by infighting, script rewrites, and artistic differences, the production continued to falter after the dismissal of Jed Horner, the original director. Sal could sense the play was going to be a debacle.

Publicist Gino Empry recalled, "Sal saw it coming, and we all did. He agreed on only one television interview—on CITY-TV Brian Lineham's talk show providing no mention be made of the play. After it opened, Sal wasn't available for any press interviews, and normally he was so cooperative. Sal was so upset over it all that he got terribly sick."

After two dismally received preview performances, for the first time in his life, Sal protested that he was too sick to appear onstage on opening night. He told the producer he had contracted hepatitis. A local actor was asked to step in. After reading the script, he declined. Sal saw a doctor and his blood tests revealed only a case of influenza, so he opened the play as scheduled on November 12, 1974.

Sal immediately called Courtney in New York. "He told me what was going on," Courtney recalled. "He said he was sick and he needed help. I dropped everything and flew up there that day."

Never in Sal's professional life had the critics attacked him with such vigor. And never in his life had an audience booed him off the stage. "The reviews were blisteringly bad," Empry said. "Just horrible. Sal was so worried. I said, 'Are you kidding? When you tell people to stay away, they'll come in droves.' And they did. The play was shocking at that time. Sensational with sex and nudity and violence. Of course, one of the problems was it had a different ending every night [the playwright and director rewrote daily]."

Theatre critic Urjo Kareda wrote in the *Toronto Star*, "A kind of history has been made; a play was last night booed off the stage of the Royal Alexandra Theatre. A steady line of fleeing patrons filled the aisles during the final quarter hour of the piece, there were hisses and catcalls, and in the final curtain call, there was a wall of boos for all the actors. Had the author and director appeared onstage as well, there might have been bloodshed."

Reviewers in the *Toronto Sun* and the *Toronto Globe and Mail* echoed the sentiment, dismissing the production as "a dim-witted, foul-mouthed piece of work" and calling for Ed Mirvish to close the show. The *Toronto Sun* reported, "Veteran theatre-goers said it was the first time any show had been booed in Toronto in living memory."

Some of the worst criticism was directed at Sal. Stephen Weir wrote in the *Toronto Eye*, "What really disappointed the black-tie opening-night audience was the 'star' of the show, Sal Mineo." Writing for the *Ryerson Review*, Ted Kerr was equally dismissive: "Anybody who stayed around for the second act saw Sal Mineo, in his gold-rimmed lifts and basic black, flit around the stage playing Mr. Ordinary Guy, bemoaning that society just isn't 'a groovy scene' anymore."

Arthur Marx and Ed Mirvish were interviewed by Sid Adilman for the *Toronto Star* on November 13. Marx said he wanted the play withdrawn immediately from the theater. "But I can't withdraw it," Marx complained. "It's got to run its three weeks of subscription here. I can only hope that it won't go anywhere else in this form. The trouble is that no one is happy with this production. It's all such a bad effort."

As a normal practice, the Royal Alexandra Theatre refused to make refunds to unhappy patrons. "But if anyone wants to cancel out the rest of their subscription season, I'll give them their money back," Mirvish said. "I certainly won't cancel the play. I wouldn't just cancel because someone doesn't like it. If you don't want to gamble, you don't go into theater."

"Sal was a wreck," Courtney said. "He was so sick. I'd never seen him like that before. He had had some big disappointments with his projects. His debt was like quicksand. And he was doing this horrible show. It was just too much for him. It had all caught up to him and overwhelmed him at that time. It was more emotional than physical. He had terrible night sweats and I stripped the bed and put dry sheets down every night. He was shaking with the chills and I held him and tried to get him warm. It was awful. But he kept going to the theater. He didn't talk about it at all. Not one word. He just did his job. I saw the show. It was terrible. I'd never seen an audience yell at the stage."

As the publicist for the show, Gino Empry was besieged by the press. "There just wasn't much I could do. The play had to run its course. And in spite of it all, audiences *did* come, and the theater did business. And Sal had nice accommodations and twenty-five hundred dollars a week for the six weeks he was here. But I knew he wasn't happy about it."

Not all of the reviews were bad, though one wonders if they saw the same show. McKenzie Porter described Sal's character as "a satanic young satyr" in the *Toronto Sun*. "Mineo is excellent in this evil role," Porter added.

"If you thought Brando was terrific in *Streetcar Named Desire*," wrote the *Varsity* on November 15, "you won't believe Sal Mineo in this. He is like a finely cut diamond. When Mineo was on stage, you could hear a pin drop. You have to admire the talent, the effortless control, the amazing product that has so clearly resulted from months of concentrated work."

*Sugar and Spice* ran its full three-week engagement and closed on November 30.

SAL FLEW to New York City to spend the holidays with Courtney after working five days in Hawaii playing a mobster on another episode of *Hawaii Five-O*. While in Manhattan, he auditioned for the role of Vito in a new Broadway production called *P.S. Your Cat Is Dead*. He was especially intrigued by the provocative elements of the story, which had been written to appeal to a mainstream audience. It was the first role in a long time that truly excited him, and he was desirous to play it on Broadway.

Originally published as a novel, *P.S. Your Cat Is Dead* was written by James Kirkwood Jr., who also wrote the book for the musical *A Chorus Line*, which opened off-Broadway in May 1975. Kirkwood's other novels included *There Must Be a Pony* and *Good Times, Bad Times*. A few years earlier, Sal had tried unsuccessfully to obtain the film rights to *Good Times, Bad Times*. The novel told the story of two young men at a New England prep school who develop a dangerously deep friendship. They are threatened when the disturbed headmaster develops a homoerotic fixation on one of the boys. The novel was suffused with homoeroticism, but like many similar books at the time, homosexuality was disingenuously disavowed.

*P.S. Your Cat Is Dead* told the story of Jimmy Zoole, a hapless, down-on-his-luck actor who is dumped by his girlfriend on New Year's Eve. To make matters worse, he finds out that his beloved cat also died earlier that day at the animal clinic. Jimmy surprises a burglar, Vito, in his apartment when he arrives home. It's the same burglar who has broken in several times before and stolen Jimmy's things. Jimmy overtakes Vito during a brief struggle, strips off his pants and shorts, and ties him to the kitchen counter with his genitals dangling in the sink. He begins to torture his captive, but soon their relationship takes on homosexual undertones when Vito confesses that he is gay. In a short time, Jimmy begins to question his own sexuality. When his ex-girlfriend arrives at his apartment with her new date, Jimmy gets his revenge. She catches him chatting with the handsome young man bare-assed and bound to the kitchen counter.

Unfortunately, Sal lost the role in *P.S. Your Cat Is Dead*. After spending an uneventful holiday with Courtney at their apartment, Sal returned to Los Angeles to resume work.

On January 23, Courtney won a lead role in the premiere of Tennessee Williams's newly reworked play *Kingdom of Earth*, to be staged at the McCarter Theatre in Princeton, New Jersey. Sal had equally good news. He excitedly called Courtney to tell him he had finally secured an option for the film rights to Charles Gorham's novel *McCaffery*.

AFTER PLAYING the part of the crazed leader of a cult of killers in an episode of *S.W.A.T.* called "A Coven of Killers," Sal traveled to New Mexico for a theatrical engagement in February. Energized by the prospects of producing and directing *McCaffery*, Sal aggressively pursued any available work.

His scramble for money brought him to Albuquerque to make his debut in a guest-starring role in a community-theater production of *LUV* at the Little Theatre. Written by Murray Schisgal, the absurdist comedy concerned two old college buddies who meet on a bridge. As they share their hard-luck stories, each discovers the other is equally miserable.

Sal arrived in Albuquerque in a blinding snowstorm to begin two weeks of rehearsal on February 21. In the last few years, he had developed a chronic case of gastritis. At times severe and aggravated by stress, he experienced discomfort during his time in New Mexico, and bouts of insomnia. The professional step backward from dinner theater to community theater vexed him, and he had an especially hard time sleeping in Albuquerque. The first night in town, he didn't sleep at all. Bernie Thomas, an executive at the theater, was dispatched to get a refill for Sal's sleeping pill prescription.

*Kingdom of Earth* opened on March 6. Sal sent Courtney a congratulatory telegram: "CB is champagne bubbles cherished brandy centaur bronzed celebrated bordeaux coltish bohemian colossal brawn and commands bravos love Sal." *LUV* opened the same night to an audience of local students, many of whom were bused to the theater in the snow.

Though Sal cut a fascinating figure in the city of Albuquerque in his blue seersucker shirt with pink and orange flowers, navy blue cords, and wide snakeskin belt, the play was not especially popular with the local critics. The material was painfully dated and the amateur actors were mannered and self-conscious. Carole Gorney reported in the *Albuquerque Journal,* "The script is talky, inconsistent and silly. In short, it is a nonsensical bore."

Nevertheless, she was taken by Sal's Hollywood pedigree: "And herein lies the tragedy. An exceptional performance by Sal Mineo could not rescue the script from the doldrums. Mineo, by the way, is well worth seeing if you are interested in observing a truly polished performer in action. Television and movies do not do justice to Mineo, who is both a vigorous and sensitive actor and a comic with a natural sense of timing."

Urith Lucas wrote in the *Albuquerque Tribune,* "Sal Mineo is a delight." Despite the mediocre notices, *LUV* was extended one day and two shows to accommodate audience demand, eventually closing on March 22.

COURTNEY JOINED Sal in California in mid-April. They had a few meetings with Billy Belasco, who had partnered with Sal in acquiring the option on *McCaffery.* Ted Harris had begun work on an early draft of a script based on the novel. Sal was enthused by the film project, but Courtney was again disheartened by Sal's choice of subject matter. "He picked things that interested him and usually were almost impossible to ever get made," he said. "That's the way I felt about *McCaffery.* I couldn't even finish the book."

Sal shot a guest spot on *Columbo* on Tuesday, April 22. In the episode called "A Case of Immunity," Sal played the part of Rachman Habib, an Arab terrorist who was blown up in the first ten minutes of the program.

At five o'clock the next morning, he flew to Austin, Texas, to begin rehearsals for a school production of *Marathon '33* at St. Edward's University as a guest artist through the theater department's Equity program. A private, Catholic liberal arts university, St. Edward's had a preprofessional undergraduate theater arts program. Written by June Havoc, the younger sister of Gypsy Rose Lee, the play was based on her autobiographical book *Early Havoc*, and recounted her experiences of the sadistic dance marathons of the 1930s.

The large cast of *Marathon '33* was comprised of students from the theater arts department. Ralph Kerns, an artist-in-residence at St. Edward's, was set to direct. Kerns was a teacher, actor, and director, and had worked in regional theater. Sal was cast as Patsy, the "top-banana" of the dance floor. About his character, Sal said, "He's very driven. And maybe a little perverse."

As soon as rehearsals began, Sal was unhappy with the play and with Kern's vision and direction. The director wanted to intersperse the drama with comedy routines, songs, and dances. Sal felt the drama was lessened by the director's approach, and the production risked becoming little more than a minstrel show. He wanted an "edgier approach," and he wanted to explore "the dark angles." Kerns balked at Sal's suggestions. When Kerns refused to accommodate Sal's requests, Sal took his complaints to Edward Mangum, the department chairman. Mangum overruled Kerns. Sal began rewrites and again asked for Courtney's help.

"Sal called me and said the production was a disaster," Courtney recalled. "He asked me to come to Austin and direct it." Courtney flew to Texas on April 25. With only three days left before opening night, the cast began exhaustive, around-the-clock rehearsals. Some of the students skipped classes in order to prepare. After working with Sal and the cast for several days, Courtney returned to Los Angeles after the opening-night performance.

The creative differences that Sal encountered with Ralph Kerns were more than just minor disagreements. Courtney's arrival had only made matters worse. Kerns removed himself from the production and resigned his position after only one year at the school. In a letter to the editor of the *Austin American-Statesman* newspaper, Kerns bitterly complained about "Mr. Mineo's outrageous demands." He wrote, "Mineo disliked the play, calling it pointless and amateurish. He demanded that he be allowed to change it to his own liking. He wanted to turn it into some sort of sadistic, on-stage ritual. It was inappropriate for the students and for the audience."

Students' reaction to Kerns's resignation was mixed. One student cast member said that Sal's changes were basically good for the play, which was "dated," and that the script had needed all the help it could have gotten. Other students believed both sides acted immaturely. The real victim of the unpleasant episode, though, was the theater arts program. Many students expressed apprehension about the future of the program. They said that morale was very low.

*Marathon '33* opened at the Mary Moody Northen Theatre at St. Edward's University on April 29 to tepid reviews and poor sales. After sixteen tedious performances, the play closed as scheduled on May 11. Sal returned to Los Angeles the following day and resumed work on the *McCaffery* script with Ted Harris.

Problems quickly arose when Ted bristled at Sal's notes. Ted had envisioned the film as a love story. Sal had a very different take on the material. "Sal wanted it to be salacious," Courtney recalled. "He wanted some ominous, sexual tone in relation to the boy and his older john. I said, 'Sal, why do you always have to go there?' Ted eventually threw up his hands and walked away from it."

Before Sal returned from Austin, Courtney had moved some small pieces of furniture once belonging to his grandmother to the Holloway apartment. Their relationship had evolved into a comfortable coexistence. "The intensity of our relationship had passed," Courtney explained. "We were more comfortable together. Less volatile. We had both grown. We were trying to survive together and support each other. But we knew each other so well. There weren't any surprises left, and that was a good thing. He did what he wanted, and so did I, but we always came back together, which was what really counted."

At the time, Sal told a reporter that he divided his time between Los Angeles and New York City, and that he contentedly lived alone. "For a while I tried living with someone," Sal said, "but it doesn't work for me. I guess I've spent too many years of being by myself. But I don't mind it. I cherish that kind of privacy. If at four o'clock in the morning I want to get up, have a joint, listen to some music . . . it's not that anybody ever complains, it's just that I know there's a body there, so I don't do it."

After dealing with the press for twenty-five years, it was not unusual that the public face Sal presented was unlike the private Sal. Reporters rarely asked Sal about his private sexual life. He lived his life freely, and his closest friends knew about his sexual orientation. Sal knew that outing himself, declaring his sexuality, would destroy what little was left of his career. Though Sal never publicly came out in a conventional manner, there was a subliminal coming-out that began years before. He wanted his lifestyle and his choices to be accepted. He wanted a normalcy and legitimacy in his life. He believed the fact that he preferred men sexually made him no less of a man.

Sal's agent, Tom Korman, felt differently about any effect Sal's personal life had upon his career. Although Korman was not privy to all of his client's private comings and goings, he felt the downturn in Sal's career was natural. "The business changes, times change," he said. "He grew up and he wasn't a little boy anymore."

COURTNEY RECALLED, "We had such a small circle of friends in Los Angeles, our attempts to socialize with other gay celebrities failed. We kept mostly to ourselves." Unlike London, and New York City to a degree, Hollywood's attitude about sex was oddly guarded, suspicious, and at times homophobic. Gay men and women in the entertainment business lived their private lives under the radar for fear of professional recriminations.

Sal's socializing with his longtime friend Roddy McDowall came to a dramatic end one evening after they got together for dinner. "Roddy had learned we had been frequenting some gay clubs," Courtney explained. "He looked down on that practice. He said Sal shouldn't go to gay bars. He felt it was a bad move. He made it clear that he thought I was the initiator of these outings, which was far from the truth. Roddy said he had *never* danced with a man, and I said, 'Oh, please! Why not, you fuck them.' The next day, Roddy called Sal and told him never to bring me to his house again."

On May 30, Sal again auditioned for the role of Vito for a San Francisco production of *P.S. Your Cat Is Dead.* (The play, starring Tony Musante and Keir Dullea, had opened at the John Golden Theatre in Manhattan on April 7 but closed after only sixteen performances.) Although accustomed to professional rejection, Sal was disappointed when he again lost the role to another actor.

AS HAPPENED often in the past, Sal passed on to Courtney a young man, one he had met while working in Scottsdale, Arizona. Richard Rubadue was a handsome, sinewy young man who became sexually involved with Sal during his dinner-theater run in *Sunday in New York* in 1974. They had stayed in touch, and Richard arrived in Los Angeles to visit Sal. "Sal sort of handed Richard off to me," Courtney said. "Sal was busy and once he had *had* someone, he was sort of over them. He told me to entertain Richard. And I did."

Courtney showed Richard around the city. That evening, Richard accompanied Sal and Courtney when they visited Sal's friend Geoffrey Holder, who was staying at the Chateau Marmont. Holder was preparing for his upcoming show in Las Vegas and invited his guests to the opening. Rubadue returned to Phoenix the next morning.

Sal began work on another episode of *Police Story*. He played the part of Fobbes in an episode of the one-hour drama titled "The Test of Brotherhood." He then shot the two-part season-premiere episode of *S.W.A.T.*, playing the part of a jewel thief in an episode called "Deadly Tide."

With Sal working, Courtney rendezvoused with Richard Rubadue in Las Vegas. They checked into a room at Caesars Palace and attended Geoffrey Holder's show at the hotel that evening. Their "sexy fling" continued briefly when, a week later, Courtney flew to Phoenix to spend a weekend with Rubadue at his home.

Courtney had interviewed and auditioned for numerous acting jobs in Los Angeles with no success. He decided to return to New York City on July 8. Courtney recalled, "Sal and I were very happy and settled. We just needed a steady source of income. I just needed to find some work and I always had more luck in New York."

With Courtney unable to find immediate work in New York, Sal had to send him some money to pay the rent and cover a few bills. On July 25, Sal called Courtney and asked him to act with him in *The Tender Trap* at the Country Dinner Playhouse in St. Petersburg, Florida. The four-week engagement provided Courtney with accommodations and a $350 weekly salary. It was a lucrative offer and supplied both men with an income. Courtney accepted the offer and flew to Florida on August 2 to begin rehearsals. *The Tender Trap*, written by Max Shulman and Robert Paul Smith, opened on Tuesday, August 12.

The play takes place in the New York apartment of a young playboy (Sal) who is visited by a chemist friend (Courtney). The chemist thinks he has formulated a sure cure for the common cold and has come to the big city to prove it. Soon, though, he reappraises his own life when he experiences his friend's carefree ways.

Reviews were mostly good. The *Tampa Tribune* reported, "What Mineo brings to this production is a veteran's self-assuredness and a strong style all his own . . . he makes his character come alive with enthusiasm. Playing opposite Mineo, and practically a costar because of his performance, Courtney Burr does a strong and effective job as, perhaps, the only distinguished other player in the play."

The *St. Petersburg Times* review said, *"The Tender Trap* is one of the funniest, best executed productions, and one of the tightest to hit the Suncoast in many moons; and much of the credit goes to Sal Mineo, who, even in a comedy, exudes a dark, haunting quality that engages the playgoer's attention with a sense of compressed energy. Where Mineo is excitable, nervous and keyed, Burr is relaxed and cool. The actors are as well-balanced off one another as the female leads."

Sal and Courtney had separate rooms at the nearby Colonnades, though they stayed together most nights. "We had a really good time there," Courtney recalled. "It was a very pleasant work experience and we enjoyed ourselves so much."

Before leaving for New York the day after the show closed, Sal gave Courtney a puppy he named CB.

SAL RETURNED to Los Angeles on September 15 and jumped into several jobs arranged by his agent. Sal's first acting role was in a twenty-minute student film called *Sonic Boom* produced by his friend singer Ricky Nelson's wife, Kristin. Later in the month, Sal filmed an episode of *Ellery Queen*. He played the part of Jimmy Danello in "The Adventure of the Wary Witness," directed by Walter Doniger, who had directed him in *Griff*. In early October, Sal filmed an episode of the police drama *Joe Forrester*.

Sal was also interviewed on camera for a documentary film called *James Dean: The First American Teenager*. The film was directed by Ray

Connolly for Ziv International, an independent British production company. Narrated by Stacy Keach, the documentary used archival footage as well as current interviews with those who knew and worked with Dean. Sal was interviewed in his Holloway apartment. He said about James Dean, "He was the first to give teenagers an identification of any kind. Before Jimmy Dean you were either a baby or a man . . . in between was just sort of one of those terrible stages that you had to get out of rather quickly. And he didn't."

Meanwhile, Sal also grappled with the *McCaffery* script, which he now worked on alone, and he and Billy Belasco solicited investors in the project. Sal met with several producers, including Arthur Whitelaw, who had produced *You're a Good Man, Charlie Brown, Butterflies Are Free,* and *Minnie's Boys,* among other shows, for the theater. He expressed a mild interest in Sal's proposed film project but unexpectedly offered Sal a job in a play he had earlier read for and twice lost.

*P.S. Your Cat Is Dead* had opened in early summer in San Francisco at the Montgomery Playhouse. The two-act play enjoyed critical and popular success. Robert Foxworth played the role of Jimmy Zoole, and a young actor named Jeff Druce played the burglar Vito, the part Sal had read for months before. After several months, Foxworth left the show for another commitment and was replaced by Warren Burton. Jeff Druce gave notice to leave the production at the beginning of November. Sal was reconsidered for the role. The producers thought he might generate renewed interest in the play, which had been running for five months, and Whitelaw wanted to give him a shot.

"It's very bizarre how so much of what's happened
in my life I've fantasized way ahead of time as
a kid. . . . I'm just so terrified that one day I'll
become realistic, and when I do, it'll be all over."

Sal arrived in San Francisco on October 25 to begin rehearsals for
*P.S. Your Cat Is Dead.* He took an apartment in the Hamilton at
631 O'Farrell Street in the city's Tenderloin District, less than a
mile from the Montgomery Playhouse on Broadway and Grant.

Under the direction of Milton Katselas, Sal assumed the role of
Vito on November 4, 1975. Katselas had directed the Broadway production of *Butterflies Are Free,* a Broadway revival of *The Rose Tattoo,*
and *The Lion in Winter.* Considered an "actor's director," Katselas was
enthusiastic and his love of actors manifested itself in the considerate
and encouraging nature of his style of direction. Sal loved working
with him, and his performance was well received by the critics. San
Francisco theater critic Bob Kiggins wrote, "Sexy Sal Mineo! Mineo
is wonderful as the wisecracking intruder, only to find himself the
victim of sweet revenge and rather bizarre fantasies. In fact, Mineo
all but steals the show with his outlandish, marvelously antic gestures, his facile facial contortions and his robust delivery. Mineo's
nimble, engaging performance calls for a visit to the Montgomery
Playhouse."

Despite the good notices, the mainstream press had all but written
Sal off. A number of national gay periodicals and magazines courted
his attention, though. James Armstrong interviewed Sal for *After Dark*
magazine. "Sal Mineo's in town," Armstrong wrote, "with his tushy up
eight times a week as Vito, in *P.S. Your Cat Is Dead,* taking over for Jeff
Druce. I raved about Jeff Druce when the play opened, so to say that
Mineo's every bit as good is to pay him a very high compliment. His
Vito is gentler, though; more of a pussycat."

"I read the script a couple of years ago and liked it even then,"
Sal explained. "It's much changed, with a completely different ending.

And Jimmy gets his balls, if you know what I mean." The original play was in three acts. Kirkwood had extensively rewritten the material, shifting the focus from Vito to Jimmy and further exploring the dynamic of their unexpected relationship.

Douglas Dean interviewed Sal for *Mandate* magazine. Sal told the reporter that the author did not approve of him for the part of Vito when he was considered for the role in the New York production. "He said I wasn't vulnerable enough for the part. I was believable enough as the kid from the streets, he thought, but I wasn't soft enough underneath.

"And now," Sal continued, "he told me he is now seeing his play for the first time, the way he conceived it in his mind . . . yes, it's true, Vito can pretend to be a tough guy, but he's really a pussycat underneath."

Kirkwood had watched Sal's career decline as his roles became fewer, smaller, more clichéd, and confined to television during the past decade. The playwright said, "Until I saw Sal in my play, I had dismissed him as an actor. But my admiration for him is inexpressible. He is a professional whose talent grew over the years—a dedicated actor. And there aren't many of those left."

Not surprisingly, Sal had some ideas of his own when it came to creating the character of Vito. At his request, Katselas permitted Sal a flash of full-frontal nudity, which was not in any previous production. "It's natural, isn't it?" Sal said. "Why should Vito turn his back to the audience when he gets down off the sink? The thing is, it has to be done very unself-consciously—I don't make a big production of it." Sal was not an exhibitionist in private, and he had stated many times that gratuitous nudity onstage and in film was boring. Nonetheless, he understood and even courted the shock value of a naked body on public view. "The publicity," he said, "will only help our business!"

Dean asked Sal what his plans were in the near future. "Well," Sal explained, "I'd like to complete the run here in San Francisco. It's wonderful to play a show like this to full houses. We may go to Los Angeles, and there's some talk of doing the show again in New York, off-Broadway."

His days of working the dinner-theater circuit were over, he said. "I've paid my dues in this business," Sal said. "I know every Holiday

Inn in the country, I think! I've earned the right to settle in one place for a while.

"I'm working on a film script of *McCaffery*. It's about a boy hustler and a girl hustler who fall in love. It deals with the essential purity of love. The story's essentials remind me of *Crime and Punishment*, and the boy especially reminds me of Roskolnikov."

Courtney flew to San Francisco on November 26. "That's where it had all started for us years before," he recalled. "We had come full circle and we were in a different but very loving place. He had found peace. He was content, in a sense, he was settling down."

The nature of their relationship was not Sal's invention or Courtney's unwilling cross to bear. Neither was it especially unique for the time. Sexual liberation and exploration, swinging singles, and "open" relationships were endemic to the 1970s. Sal had a keen sense of the changing times and a knack for exploring and experiencing fully "the moment." Just as he was a participant in the fifties era of teenage identity and empowerment, so was he a player in the sexually liberated sixties and seventies.

They still had outside, freewheeling sexual adventures. Their sexual wanderings ran the gamut from casual one-night stands to brief flings. An occasional three-way spiced up their life together, as well. Rather than angering them, though, the affairs and adventures became a topic of conversation. Sal especially enjoyed sharing with Courtney stories of his sexual encounters, including his liaison with Peter Berlin, one of the most famous gay icons in San Francisco. "He told me he brought him to his room," Courtney said, "but rather than being turned on, he was amused by Berlin's narcissism and let him do his show."

Courtney saw the play on November 28. "Sal was really great in it," he recalled. "He inhabited the role with warmth, strength, and humor, and what I believe was his greatest acting asset—vulnerability. I was very moved and very proud, and it gave me great joy to tell him so." After they shared a happy and loving week together, Courtney returned to New York City on December 5.

Jeremy Hughes interviewed Sal for another gay magazine called *In Touch*. Sal admitted that his young life had been a balance of the reality of growing up on the streets of the Bronx and youthful fantasies. "I'm thirty-six now, and I still fantasize. And it's very bizarre how so much of what's happened in my life I've fantasized way ahead of time as a kid. It jolts me sometimes, how it manifests itself, when it was a seed that I planted as a little kid, y'know? I'm just so terrified that one day I'll become realistic, and when I do, it'll be all over. I just won't be stopped if I want something. It may take years, but it will happen."

As Sal prepared to leave for the theater, Hughes referred to the "many hair-raising rumors" regarding his Hollywood activities. He asked Sal if there were any misunderstandings or misconceptions about himself that he would like to clear up once and for all.

"Nope," Sal said, " 'cause I like 'em, if there are any. It's funny. I don't have to lie, in an interview or in a relationship with someone. But sometimes I wonder if not denying a certain fact is the same as lying. Is silence assent?"

*P.S. Your Cat Is Dead* ran successfully through January 4, 1976. It was a satisfying personal and professional experience for Sal. And to a degree, it restored in him a certain confidence level and interest in acting. The eight-week engagement was problem free, except one evening in December when he collapsed on the stage from exhaustion. He spoke frequently on the phone with Courtney, who was in New York. The audiences were responsive, and the material was respected. Sal felt his career had taken a turn in the right direction and he was eager to move on to his next project.

SAL RETURNED to the Holloway apartment in Los Angeles on January 6. The producers, buoyed by the successful six-month run in San Francisco, decided to move the production to Los Angeles. The play was scheduled to open at the Westwood Playhouse on February 25, with rehearsals to begin later in January.

Warren Burton was unable to reprise his role of Jimmy Zoole in Los Angeles. Keir Dullea, who had originally created the role on Broadway, was cast in Burton's place. As he did in San Francisco, Milton Katselas directed the play.

Two other productions in Los Angeles were attracting attention. *Let My People Come* began a long-term, wildly successful run at the Whisky a Go Go on the Sunset Strip in November 1975. The "sexual musical," written by Earl Wilson Jr., featured an all-nude cast and songs including "I'm Gay," "Come in My Mouth," "Give It to Me," and "The Cunnilingus Champion of Company C." The Las Palmas Theatre (a former porno movie theater) presented *Boy Meets Boy,* a gay musical send-up of 1930s musicals. Though local critics were not impressed with *Let My People Come,* their rave reviews of *Boy Meets Boy* drove audiences to the small Hollywood theater.

The time was perfect, Sal felt, to challenge the public with *P.S. Your Cat Is Dead* and his provocative film project *McCaffery.*

As soon as Sal arrived back in Los Angeles, however, he was met with disturbing news from his agent, Tom Korman. The $800,000 slander suit filed against him by Ernest Criezis in Dallas, Texas, had finally gone to trial in late 1975. Unbelievably, the court found in favor of the plaintiff and awarded Criezis $30,000 in damages against Sal. To avoid creditors' claims and collection agents, all of Sal's income had been paid directly to Korman for years. Sal didn't even have a bank account in his name. Korman spoke with Criezis and told him that Sal had no money and no assets. Nevertheless, Criezis filed his court-awarded judgment with the county recorder's office in Los Angeles County on January 21, 1976, in preparation for a collection action.

In spite of working almost nonstop throughout 1975, Sal found himself still in debt. Michael Anderson Jr. said, "I had lunch with Sal after he got back from San Francisco, and we went to his little apartment on Holloway. Sal made a joke, like always: 'How do you like what I've done with the place?' And he hadn't done *anything.* A little bit of rental furniture. Nothing seemed to faze him. He had a great attitude in that way. We had both been on top, and we both hit bottom. We smoked a joint and laughed at how far we had both fallen."

*Playgirl* magazine photographer Bob Seidermann visited Sal at the apartment to discuss the actor being photographed nude for a centerfold in the women's magazine. When describing Sal's apartment, Seidermann recalled, "It was funky, warm, loads of candles, the kind of place where you could put your feet on the coffee table and rap until three in the morning."

Mabel, Sal's loyal housekeeper, still dropped by to clean and wash his clothes even though he had no money to pay her. Sal did not cook, and when he was alone, he didn't eat balanced meals. Mabel brought him sandwiches and other prepared food, which she left in his refrigerator.

During the next few weeks, Sal prepared for his Los Angeles debut in *P.S. Your Cat Is Dead.* He spoke often with Courtney who was in Manhattan, and he frequented gay bars with Michael Mason. One evening he met a handsome young man also named Michael at a bar. The tall twenty-two-year-old, newly arrived in Hollywood from Philadelphia, was an aspiring motion-picture costume designer. Sal brought him home, and they began a heated sexual affair. He was enthusiastic about his new sexual partner and called Courtney. "Sal and Michael were in bed together when we spoke one evening," Courtney said. "Sal told me he wanted me to meet him when I came back to L.A. 'You'll really like him,' he said."

Sal drove his rented, beat-up, blue two-tone Chevelle to the Westwood Playhouse every day for rehearsals. Milton Katselas remembered, "Sal was always a gentleman, always with a joke, and never balked at direction." Sal's costar, Keir Dullea, said, "I had never known Sal before, but I got so I really loved him. He thought this play would be the start of a new career. He was so enthusiastic about it."

Sal felt that Dullea was an affable man and an easy conversationalist but hardly a dynamic actor. He could not find that certain spark he had shared with Warren Burton onstage in San Francisco. And Sal, who was a fast study, quickly became impatient with Dullea's inability to learn his lines. About his costar's problem with remembering lines, Sal joked with Courtney, "Keir today, gone tomorrow . . ." Rehearsals became laborious, but still, Sal was optimistic about his return to a Los Angeles stage.

On Tuesday, February 10, Sal and Michael Mason went for a sauna at the Beverly Hills Health Club. After lunch, they went to Sal's doctor Lee Siegel's office for their weekly testosterone and vitamin-B shots, which they hoped would shore up their lagging sex drives. Mason said, "Sal was depressed because he didn't have [the drive] to screw around anymore. He realized it was partly because he loved Courtney. One reason that he liked Courtney was that he was freer. He was into wilder sex, spontaneous sex." Also, Courtney was coming to attend the opening of *P.S. Your Cat Is Dead.* He planned to stay in Los Angeles with Sal during the run of the play. Sal sent money to Courtney for his plane ticket before going to Westwood for rehearsals that night.

The next evening, Sal met Billy Belasco at the Palm restaurant on Santa Monica Boulevard in West Hollywood for dinner. Sal and Belasco discussed their *McCaffery* film project. Belasco had lined up enough initial independent financing to make a deal with MGM Studios and to begin work on the film. He told Sal he had a commitment from MGM to produce and distribute the finished motion picture. The young producer had worked successfully with MGM in the past, producing *The Carey Treatment, They Only Kill Their Masters,* and *Super Cops.* After years of frustration, Sal was finally set to direct his first feature film.

Thursday morning, February 12, Courtney called Sal and told him he had decided to change his travel plans. Instead of flying from New York to Los Angeles on Friday morning, the thirteenth, he would fly in on Monday, February 16. "Sal said it was okay," Courtney recalled, "he was busy rehearsing, and he said, 'I'm afraid I won't be able to pay enough attention to you.' The last thing we said to each other was, 'I love you.' "

Sal spent a lot of time on the telephone during the day, inviting friends to the February 25 opening of *P.S. Your Cat Is Dead.* "He sounded great," Jack Haley Jr. said, "and was inviting Liza [Minelli, Haley's wife] and me to the opening of his play and to the party afterward. We hosted him at our party for Chita Rivera's show at the Back Lot Theatre at Studio One and had a great evening. Liza loved Sal."

Later in the afternoon, Sal called Jill Haworth in Manhattan. "We talked about birth control," Jill said. "He was concerned about me and wanted me to get an IUD. He always wanted to know who I was dating and what I was doing. I had the abortion before, and he was worried about me. I made an appointment to see a gynecologist the next day."

Michael Mason called Sal and canceled the dinner plans they had previously made for that evening. Instead, Sal drove to the Westwood Playhouse to begin rehearsals a little earlier.

After several hours, Sal left the playhouse shortly before nine o'clock that night. "We were rehearsing at the theater till around nine or so," Dullea said. "Sal was in tremendous spirits. He always said that this play was a major one for him, one which would launch his second career."

Sal stopped at a convenience store on the way home and bought a pack of cigarettes and a package of Hostess Cupcakes for his dinner.

He arrived home shortly before 9:30. He parked his Chevelle in the carport and walked toward the pathway leading into the courtyard separating his apartment building from the one to the east. Suddenly, someone lunged out of the darkness and plunged a knife into his chest. Sal cried out, staggered a few steps, and collapsed, hitting his head on the pavement. His assailant ran east along the wide, dark alleyway behind the apartment complex and onto Alta Loma Road, where he jumped into a yellow car and sped off.

Nancy Barr, Sal's neighbor, was at home. "I was going to walk my dog right around the time Sal got home, but I didn't," Barr recalled. "I stayed in for some reason. I heard him come home. I heard his car in the carport. I'll never forget that night. His screams were so loud. So startling. I heard him yell, 'No . . . no . . . Oh, my God . . . no . . . help! Somebody help me please!'

"I froze. I couldn't move," Barr continued. "I knew it was Sal. In a second, I heard voices and a commotion in the alley, people yelling. And in a minute, I heard sirens."

> "I'm a hero type. Of course, I don't win the girl.
> I get killed as usual."

Though located a couple of short blocks south of Sunset Boulevard, Sal's apartment complex was normally very quiet. His
screams for help were especially startling to his neighbors.

Sal's neighbor Ray Evans heard the screams and ran from his apartment into the alleyway. He found Sal lying on the ground, the left side
of his chest covered with blood. By then, other neighbors ran into the
driveway.

Evans noticed that Sal's keys were lying on the ground beside the
actor's body. He lifted Sal's head to speak to him, but he was semiconscious and his eyes seemed fixed. "I saw he was going into an ashen
color, and I immediately started to give him mouth-to-mouth resusci-
tation. Everyone was yelling, 'Get the police! Get an ambulance!' I was
getting a response, then all of a sudden he gave it [a last breath] back
and that was it. The police arrived at that point."

Responding to the emergency call, Los Angeles County sheriffs
arrived at the scene. Rather than the City of Los Angeles police, the
sheriff's department had jurisdiction because the attack occurred
in the small West Hollywood pocket of unincorporated county territory. Sheriffs found Sal in the driveway behind 8569 Holloway
Drive. He was lying in an east-west position in an incline of the
driveway, with his head toward the east. His body's position and the
blood flow into the incline gave the initial incorrect impression that
he was profusely bleeding from the head. Paramedics from Fire Rescue Unit 7 turned him on his back, cut his jacket and shirt away, and
tried unsuccessfully to resuscitate him. Sal was pronounced dead at
2155 hrs (9:55 P.M. PST).

Authorities prepared case report number 76-1953, noting that the
"homicide" had been committed in an alley between carports R7 and
R6 at the rear of Sal's apartment, number 1, at 2130 hours (9:30 P.M.)
on 2-12-76 by "unknown person(s)."

Sal's body was covered with a sheet while numerous detectives arrived to begin questioning the neighbors. Stephen Gustafson, a security guard who lived nearby, told detectives he saw "a white man with dirty blond or brown hair" who ran away like "a bat out of hell." Another witness, Scott Hughes, said he saw a man fleeing the scene who appeared to him to be "Italian or Mexican." Hughes said the figure got into "a yellow Toyota" and drove away with the headlights off.

The coroner arrived at 1:25 A.M. to photograph and search the body. Sal's wallet, containing $21, was in his left jacket pocket. His pocket watch and chain were in his right jacket pocket. There were a few coins in his pants pocket and eighty-five cents in change scattered on the ground beneath his body. The package of cupcakes and Sal's clipboard with rehearsal notes were also on the ground near his body. His eyeglasses were on the pavement near his feet. A white metal ring was on his left index finger. There were a few restaurant receipts and two cards with men's names and phone numbers in his shirt and pants pockets.

Attorney Marvin Mitchelson preliminarily identified the body. Tom Korman was called to the scene to make a formal ID. In the early morning hours of Friday, February 13, Sal's body was removed to the Los Angeles morgue for autopsy. Investigating detective Sergeant Pia called Josephine Mineo at her apartment in Harrison to tell her the tragic news. He then called Sal's older brother Victor. "I received a phone call from a police officer who told me Sal was killed," Victor said. "I just couldn't believe it."

Courtney had gone to Jack Doroshow's apartment at seven o'clock Thursday evening to finalize paperwork relating to the option he had been offered on a script he wrote called *Possessed*. Doroshow was a cross-dressing actor/artist who starred in a documentary about New York drag queen competitions in 1968 called *The Queen*. Courtney worked at Doroshow's apartment until nearly 1:30 in the morning.

"As I came up the steps to my apartment," Courtney recalled, "the phone was ringing. I got in and answered and it was Richard Rubadue calling from Phoenix. He said, 'Have you heard about Sal?' I said, 'What are you talking about?' He said Sal was killed in Los Angeles. He'd just heard it on the news. I couldn't believe it. I called our answering service in Los Angeles and our operator answered, and I asked her what was going on. She starting crying and said, 'Oh, honey, I'm so sorry . . . I'm so sorry . . .'

"I left New York on the twelve noon flight, the one I had originally booked, and arrived in Los Angeles at 2:45 in the afternoon on Friday the thirteenth," Courtney continued. "I stayed at my friend Peter Brown's house because the police wouldn't let me into the apartment. They said it was a crime scene. The police came to Peter's house to speak with me. They were going through Sal's phone book and didn't know who *anybody* was. They asked me, 'So, who is Cher?' And I said, 'You know, Cher, the singer . . .'

"The police told me it was a good thing I was in New York, because they got some calls about me. At that time, the suspect was described as a man with blond hair. I had blond hair. I asked, 'Who did you get calls from, Roddy McDowall?' And they laughed and nodded yes. Roddy had actually called the police and named me as a suspect!"

Still numb with shock, Courtney joined Michael Mason, Tom Korman, and David Cassidy for a get-together at Billy Belasco's house later that evening. Plans were made for Courtney, Michael, and Elliot to accompany Sal's body back to New York the next day. David Cassidy paid for the casket.

On Saturday, Valentine's Day, Courtney returned to New York with Sal's body on American flight number 10.

ASSISTANT CORONER Donald Drynan said his autopsy revealed that Sal had died of a massive hemorrhage from a single stab wound in the chest that penetrated his heart. Other apparent injuries included a fresh abrasion to his left gluteal (backside) region and a small hemorrhage on the subcutaneous tissue of his scalp, both a result of his collapse to the pavement upon being stabbed. The coroner also noted three intramuscular injection sites, one to the right and two to the left gluteal regions. These injections were a result of Sal's visit to his doctor a few days earlier. The autopsy report noted that the body weighed 144 pounds and measured 68 inches. The body was well developed and normally built and, with the exception of "fairly extensive diverticulosis of the sigmoid colon," appeared to be in good condition and good health. There were no signs of alcohol or any drugs present in the body.

"A heavy type knife," such as a hunting knife, was the murder weapon, the coroner concluded. The coroner's office certified the death as a homicide. In legal terms, "homicide" means the taking of a human life by another human. In terms of legal definition, the word "murder" means the "unlawful" taking of a human life. Such an act is determined and charged by a prosecutor and if taken to trial must be proven beyond a reasonable doubt.

In the course of the autopsy, the coroner excised the stab wound to the skin and heart to preserve it for later investigation purposes. Chief Medical Examiner Thomas Noguchi explained in his book *Coroner at Large,* "In effect we create what I call a 'negative cast' which is the wound itself and which is preserved in its surrounding tissues in formalin. Our goal is to provide a precise means of identifying the murder weapon, if it is recovered, by matching the wound with the knife."

A forensic laboratory analysis was conducted in the coroner's office by a Dr. Breton and completed on February 13. This report provided vital information to investigators and determined the weapon used in the fatal assault.

RESULTS:
1. Wound is triangular with blunt end to decedent's left, appears to have been caused by a single-edged blade measuring approximately 1¼" (3cm) by ⅛" (3mm) in cross section.
2. From the center of the blunt end of the wound extending upward approximately 7mm (⁵⁄₁₆"). There is some bruising to the skin surface, possibly caused by the knife handle.
3. The edges of the wound are straight except for a small defect on lower edge near the blunt end. (This may reflect a defect in the knife.)
4. The angle of entry is clearly from above downward and towards the midline of the body.
5. Some fibers, probably of clothing, are present in the wound.
6. The larger hairs on the chest give the appearance of having been shaved at some time in the past.

OPINION (derived from these observations on the wound as well as observations made during the course of autopsy):
Assailant was right-handed and standing to the decedent's right when the fatal blow was struck. The knife penetrated to the

handle in one powerful stroke. The knife blade was single-edged and measured approximately 1¼″ deep by 6″–7″ long and ⅛″ wide at the back edge. This description better fits a hunting knife than a switchblade.

THE FOLLOWING day, the *Los Angeles Times* reported that homicide detectives had a partial description of a single suspect but no apparent motive to go on. Witnesses told police they saw a young man, possibly Caucasian, with blond hair and dark clothing run from the carport area. Investigators said that Sal had just pulled his car into his carport when he was confronted by a "blond man" without warning.

"The motive—we just don't know," said Lieutenant Phil Bullington of the Los Angeles sheriff's office. "It's a mystery. We know it was not robbery. Mineo still had his watch and ring on and there was money in his pocketbook. It looks like whoever did it knew precisely what they were doing."

Detectives speculated that Sal could have been killed resisting a robbery attempt. When he cried out for help, his assailant may have fled without completing the robbery in fear of capture. The *Los Angeles Times* added, "Detectives were looking into the possibility that the assailant may have been a drug addict lurking in the carport area to rob a returning resident. The area, a middle-class to affluent apartment house district, has a large population of types who might have a drug habit. Sheriff's investigators conducted a house-to-house search for anyone who might have seen the stabbing or the man who fled."

When Detectives Tankersley and Pia entered Sal's apartment on the night of the murder, they discovered evidence that fueled rumors about Sal's sex life. They found gay pornographic magazines, a gay sex manual next to Sal's bed, and a leather vest and pants in his closet. The detectives then speculated about another murder angle. "During the investigation that night," Tankersley said, "we found out that he was homosexual. That opened a whole new field. Is this a disgruntled lover? A prostitute he picked up off the street? Was Sal into bringing home strangers?" This sensational angle, though without any real merit, quickly made its way into the press.

"The papers went berserk," Courtney recalled.

In a February 23 *Newsweek* magazine feature article about the murder titled "The Outcast," the writer speculated, "Partly because of Mineo's recent homosexual roles and partly because the knifing occurred near the notoriously kinky Sunset Strip, long-whispered reports of the actor's alleged bisexuality and fondness for sado-masochistic ritual quickly surrounded his murder. The actor's friends puzzled over the sudden tragedy. 'Sal had some strange tastes,' reflected film director Peter Bogdanovich, 'but he was totally unaffected by it. The murder was so shocking because as a person he was so innocent.' "

Michael Mason said any theories about such a scenario were ridiculous and insulting. "The rumors about S and M started years ago," he said. "He wasn't into it at all, but he loved to put people on. It was all just a joke, and anyone who knew him knew that was the case. The police had no idea where to go with the investigation and the sex angle was just a diversion."

David Cassidy defended his friend in the press. "Sex, dope, and cheap thrills are discussed more than anything else at gay bars," he said. "I've heard about women I've slept with, sheep I've slept with. It's a lot of jive. There's a lot of shit-talking about everybody.

"If you knew Sal, you loved him for what he was as a man, as a human being. It's like Dustin Hoffman said, man, the first time he knew he was a star was when he walked into a party and he heard someone say, 'There's that faggot.' "

David Joliffe, Sal's neighbor, was home the night of the killing. "It was really shocking. It was like just a really bad encounter. If he was being robbed, it would have been in his nature to run, not to fight it."

When Elliot was questioned about Sal's private life, he snapped, "He spent a lot of time at home in bed reading books, mostly to find promising ideas for movies or plays."

SAL'S BODY arrived at Kennedy Airport in New York early Sunday morning, February 15. In a daze of shock and disbelief, Courtney went to his Sixteenth Street apartment and collapsed from exhaustion.

At the Mineo family's directive, an open-casket viewing was prepared, and the wake was conducted at O'Neil Funeral Home in Mamaroneck. Sal had wanted his father's casket closed several years before but lost out to the family's wishes. He had said, "I don't want anybody to see me dead. Just bury me. Then have a big party."

"There were two wakes," Jill recalled. "I couldn't believe any of this was happening. It was an open casket and he wouldn't have liked that at all. They made me kiss him, and I said, 'Oh, my God, Sal, what have they done to you!' It didn't look anything like him, it was a terrible makeup job. It was like a nightmare. I kept thinking he was going to spring up and tell us it was a joke. It all made me sick and I actually threw up all over Elliot."

On Monday evening, Michael Mason had a disturbing encounter with Victor Mineo. Sal's murder marked the beginning of a curious struggle orchestrated by his family about how he would be remembered. Though Sal had proudly lived his adult life the way he chose, his freewheeling sexuality was not a subject he shared with his family. In fact, his family vehemently denied that Sal was homosexual.

At the wake, Victor approached Michael Mason, who was taken aback. "Money was the first thing they asked me about! I finally told his brother, 'It's too bad you didn't know him well enough to find these answers yourself,'" Mason said. "'But I see why he didn't like you or have anything to do with you in recent years. He had no money. He had nothing. Some clothes, a table, some books, and that's it.'"

Michael Mineo actually told the press he had been his brother's manager. "All his life, no matter what Sal did, people drummed up stories about him," he sniped. "He was an innocent, *straight* person. All he was doing was fighting to be an artist!"

On February 17, at ten o'clock in the morning, Sal's funeral mass was said by Reverend Gerard Di Senso, the assistant pastor of the Roman Catholic Church of the Most Holy Trinity. Courtney, Elliot Mintz, and Michael Mason were honorary pallbearers. Once inside the church, they joined Josephine and Michael Mineo, who were sitting in the front pew. Jill Haworth, Desi Arnaz Jr., Michael Greer, and Nicholas Ray sat nearby.

When Greer arrived, he took one look at the crowd of people in the street and said, "Well, my God, it looks like Garland or Presley died. A star is being buried today. It's a standing-room-only smash funeral!"

The *New York Times* reported, "When 'Plato,' the alienated teenager played by Sal Mineo, died at the end of the 1955 film *Rebel Without a Cause,* he was mourned only by the family housekeeper and two high school friends. At Sal Mineo's funeral today, about 250 people crowded into the church, and dozens more stood outside in a cold rain. His mother, Josephine, a tiny, fragile-looking woman, was accompanied by her sons, Michael, 38; Victor, 40 and her daughter, Sarina, 33."

Victor could hardly speak to the congregation. "Sal was sincere," he stammered, "honest, and very dedicated to his family." Josephine was too distraught to say anything. So too was Courtney, although Josephine had invited him to say a few words. Sarina's husband, Charles Meyers, provided the eulogy.

"Sal was a rare and very special person, a gentle man, whose sensitivity and understanding affected everyone he met. Those who love him knew he loved life and that he lived with courage, abandon, humor, style, and grace," he said. "His art, what he created, will always stand. Nothing, not a person nor the passage of time, can take it away from him." Meyers noted that he was sadly standing in the same place Sal had stood three years before to eulogize his own father's passing. He added, "It was such a happy irony of his life that he was so different as a person from the roles he created."

In a misty rain, Sal was buried beside his father in the Gate of Heaven Cemetery in Hawthorne, New York. Buried nearby were Babe Ruth, Fred Allen, Anna Held, Dorothy Kilgallen, New York mayor Jimmy Walker, and legendary 1930s gangster Dutch Schultz.

No contemporary celebrity friends or professional acquaintances spoke out to the press about Sal's murder, with the exception of his most recent director, Milton Katselas, and costar, Keir Dullea. "I've never been so shocked by this kind of senseless tragedy in my life," Dullea said.

Nicholas Ray was stunned and deeply saddened by Sal's death. A lifetime of alcohol and drug abuse had taken a toll on the peripatetic director. His emotions were close to the surface when he spoke to the press a few days after Sal's funeral. "I think to have success so young made the rest of his life unfulfilling," Ray said. "A star needs to have the steel of a Joan Crawford, a restlessness, a selfishness in a creative sense. Actors also have to betray. They are all things to all people. Sal had the will but he didn't have the steel. I doubt if Sal knew when he was being ripped off."

Sal would have been delighted, though, when the *Los Angeles Times* interviewed Mickey Cohen, a former underworld figure. He told the newspaper that Sal had frequented the Brentwood, California, ice cream shop Cohen's sister had owned. "He was my friend," Cohen said. "I just spoke to him seven or eight days ago. He was such a fine young man. It's unbelievable. I guess a bunch of people are running around full of something. I doubt Sal was having trouble with anyone. I think he'd have called me if there was any trouble. It was a terrible, sad thing."

Numerous national magazines and newspapers printed tributes to the actor. *Newsweek* wrote, "On screen, Sal Mineo never outgrew his role as an outcast, a man-child who projected a compelling mixture of violence and vulnerability."

Peter Bogdanovich wrote in *Esquire*, "That Sal was stabbed to death in an alley was so horribly in keeping with so many of the movie deaths he died that its bitter irony might have amused him. After all, he had a black sense of humor and firm grasp of the absurd—a teenage symbol in his late thirties who never had a childhood. To know that newspapers plastered his murder in a banner headline across the country would probably have made him drop his head to his side and snore: 'A lot of good that does me.' "

RICK ARMITAGE, a friend, invited Courtney to come to Miami for a few days to get away from the turmoil and to rest. Courtney flew to Florida late in the afternoon on February 17, immediately after Sal's interment.

The next night, Courtney was awakened by an unnerving telephone call. The friend he had asked to stay in his Sixteenth Street apartment had been attacked in bed by an intruder. In the dark, the assailant broke a vase over the man's head and warned him, "Don't write a book." Shaken, Courtney immediately returned to New York. He feared the Mineos, protective of Sal's reputation, had staged the attack.

Billy Belasco planned a memorial for Sal's Hollywood friends and professional associates who were unable to attend his New York funeral. In his *Variety* column, Army Archerd reported the gathering would take place at Belasco's house on the afternoon of Sunday, February 22.

On February 20, Courtney flew to Los Angeles to attend the memorial and "close up" the Holloway apartment. Before leaving for the

West Coast, though, and acting on a hunch, Courtney collected all the intimate letters and telegrams Sal had sent to him through the years, packed them in a valise, and took them with him to California.

Even though he was the legal lessee, Courtney had been told by the police that he could not go into the Holloway apartment until Sal's family first gained entry. In the meantime, he accepted Michael Mason's invitation to stay at the Cherokee Lane home in Beverly Hills Mason shared with his lover, Beverly Hills clothier "Mr. Guy" Greengard.

After a night on the town and a late-night dinner at the Palm, Billy Belasco invited one of the waiters to return home with him. Too drunk to drive, he asked the waiter to take the wheel. On the way back, the waiter lost control of the car and struck a tree in the early morning hours of February 22. The waiter was unhurt, but Belasco was gravely injured.

"I assumed the task of calling Roddy McDowall to tell him the memorial had been canceled," Courtney recalled. "Roddy said to me, 'I wouldn't be there even if I could. It's because of people like *you* that Sal is dead.' "

On Monday morning, Victor Mineo called Courtney and asked to meet with him at the Continental Hyatt Hotel on the Sunset Strip, less than a mile from the Holloway apartment. "I went there," Courtney said, "and Victor was there and Michael Mineo and an old friend of the family named Joe Cavallero. Victor told me they went through our apartment and found my letters to Sal. He told me they burned them. And they wanted any letters that Sal sent to me. They said they were very concerned about Sal's reputation and anyone doing anything that would hurt his public image.

"I actually had all the letters in the briefcase I took with me to the meeting and it was on the seat next to me, but they didn't know it."

Victor said, "We want the letters."

"I said, 'I'm not giving you the letters,' " Courtney told him.

"Where are they?" Victor asked.

"I told them they were in a safety deposit box," Courtney recalled. "The three of them sat there staring at me like they were trying to strong-arm me. It was so strange. I just sat there and listened. I said I would never do anything to hurt Sal."

The next day, Courtney reluctantly entered apartment number 1 at 8569 Holloway Drive. "Michael and Victor Mineo had gotten in before me," Courtney said. "The place looked like it was ransacked and picked over by vultures. There was a residue of burned paper in the bathtub. They burned my letters to Sal, and his gay magazines, and pictures, whatever they could find. I looked around; there was not much there. I stared at Sal's little sneakers on the floor by the bed. I took Sal's leather jacket from the closet with me when I left. I never went back there."

Billy Belasco never regained consciousness and died five days after the automobile accident. On February 27, Courtney visited Sal's doctor, Lee Siegel. "He told me he saw Sal's body and it didn't look like any accident," Courtney said. "He said it was so precise, so forceful, it looked like a hit. Sal's murder, Billy's death, the Mineos, it was one thing after another, and there was so much going on, it was surreal."

IN THE grandest show business tradition of "the show must go on," *P.S. Your Cat Is Dead* opened on February 25 at the Westwood Playhouse. Actor Jeff Druce, who had played the part of Vito for five months in San Francisco and whom Sal had replaced several months before, stepped into the role following Sal's murder.

"It wasn't easy," director Milton Katselas said just before the play opened. "And it's not a matter of overcoming. There are so many obstacles placed in our paths in this world that it becomes important just to go on. It's been difficult because we loved Sal. He would have wanted it to go well and Keir makes it a vindication."

Keir Dullea recalled, "My initial reaction was that I didn't want to do the play. But that lasted only minutes. Then I went to the opposite extreme. I decided the only way to restore sense to all the senselessness was to pay tribute to this guy. So I want the performance to be so good that it's a lasting tribute to him."

The Playbill for the Los Angeles engagement of *P.S. Your Cat Is Dead* featured a tribute to Sal written by Margy Newman, one of the producers. "As you are probably aware," it read, "this production was originally to co-star Sal Mineo. His tragic and senseless death has robbed the theatre and film world of one of its more talented and well-liked actors. Those of us involved, feel that every performance we present is our tribute to Sal, an actor whose dedication to his craft and to this play would have demanded that we continue. This we do, in his memory."

Roger Rosenblatt wrote an essay called "Plato Dies" that appeared in the *New Republic* on March 6, 1976. "The joke was a kid from the Bronx whose father manufactured caskets, and whose mother sent him to dancing school to keep him off the streets so that he could eventually become an actor and play a kid from the Bronx. He made B movies such as *Crime in the Streets* and *Rock, Pretty Baby,* and never captured an earth angel's heart. Once, though, in *Rebel Without a Cause,* he died very well. 'Do you think the end of the world will come at night?' Plato asked, his last cliché.

"Weeks ago Sal Mineo died again, stabbed outside his West Hollywood apartment house. This time there were no searchlights hailing the American teenager gone berserk—only one man cutting another in a grown-up world that deals with such realities calmly."

On March 3, the investigation took a turn. At first, deputies had reported that they were looking for a Caucasian man with blond hair wearing dark clothing. After talking to new witnesses and further questioning original witnesses, however, the Los Angeles sheriff's department revised the description to that of a young man between twenty and thirty years of age, of "indeterminate race" with "curly or wavy dark brown or black hair" and about five-feet-seven to five-feet-ten inches tall. He fled on foot through the dark alley, jumped into a small yellow car on Alta Loma Road, and escaped. They additionally reported that there was still no obvious motive in the attack.

# AFTERWORD

L.A. MAN CHARGED IN MURDER OF SAL MINEO. The *Los Angeles Times* headline on January 5, 1978, was the answer to a prayer for Sal's friends and family. Reporter Bill Farr wrote for the newspaper, "A young Los Angeles man who has been in a Michigan jail for the last eight months was charged here Wednesday with the murder of actor Sal Mineo in Hollywood nearly two years ago. Lionel R. Williams, 21, was accused of the Feb. 12, 1976, stabbing in a complaint filed by Dep. Dist. Atty. Burton Katz a few hours after Sheriff Peter Pitchess told a news conference that Williams was being held as a suspect.

" 'The sheriff's bulldogs have done it again,' Pitchess told a large gathering of reporters in his office, but he declined to fully disclose how the case against Williams was put together. Pitchess did say that investigators have decided the motive for the slaying was robbery and that the murder weapon was a hunting knife."

Pitchess continued, "Our belief is that it was a premeditated murder because as you will recall Mineo was returning from the rehearsal of a play and came directly there to his place of residence and had just left his car when he was attacked."

The sheriff conceded that Sal was not actually robbed. He said it was most likely that the attacker had been scared off by Sal's screams. Witnesses who responded to Sal's cries for help saw a man run away, jump into a yellow car, and drive off, the sheriff added.

"That man," Farr reported in the newspaper, "was described by those witnesses as a Caucasian. Williams is black, but Pitchess said the witnesses had 'only a fleeting glimpse' and added the discrepancy could be because Williams is 'light-complexioned for a Negro.' "

With Williams safely in jail in Michigan for the preceding eight months, detectives had carefully and diligently worked on building the case. Pitchess concluded, "We will now take steps to extradite him and take the case before the grand jury."

IT HAD been a long, circuitous, and at times discouraging road to an arrest in the case. Some people had given up hope the killer would ever be found. On February 12, 1977, the first anniversary of Sal's murder, Elliot Mintz held a press conference at the Los Angeles Press Club to seek the public's help in finding the killer. "Sal Mineo was my best friend for almost thirteen years," he said. "Tomorrow will be the first anniversary of his death." Elliot said he felt the answer to the case, "riddled with rumors, gossip, and theories," could be reached if anyone with even the smallest bit of information would simply come forward.

Elliot said that he had spent much of the last year trying to help the investigation. He had tried to raise $10,000 from Sal's friends to offer as a reward but was unable to collect more than a few hundred dollars. Elliot added that he would continue his efforts to find the killer "as long as there's any hope."

In an article for *Esquire* magazine, Peter Bogdanovich wrote, "In this racket when you're not hot anymore, or when you're cold, you're dead anyway, so a lot of folks had turned the page on Sal's murder and shrugged. He wasn't up for any picture."

Tom Korman preferred to let the matter rest. "I'd rather not comment," he said. "It just sort of passed over and we've avoided all kinds of publicity for the obvious reasons. It's just passed and we'd all like to forget about it."

In spite of dead-end leads and seemingly little progress, Detective Tankersley speculated about a break in the case. "I'm very optimistic," he said. "It's been my experience that somebody has to talk. It's only a matter of time before somebody tells somebody else and they tell us. It's human nature."

———

ON FEBRUARY 26, 1976, two weeks after Sal's murder, Lionel Williams, a nineteen-year-old, five-foot-five-inch stocky black man and his high school friend, James Green, had been arrested by Los Angeles police. The young men were accused of attacking a motorist with a hammer and tire iron and robbing the driver of small change. Both Williams and his companion spent a short time in jail.

When he was released from the L.A. county jail, Williams told a deputy that he wanted to talk to somebody about the Mineo case. He said he had overheard some "blood dudes" talking about killing Sal Mineo over a drug deal gone bad. Investigators had no evidence that such a scenario existed. Williams's bold statement led detectives to suspect he himself might have been involved in the murder and was trying to concoct a story that would point in another direction should he ever be accused of the crime. Detectives visited Williams's home to determine his whereabouts the night of the murder.

Mattie Snell, Williams's mother, told the press that investigators had questioned her and her son a short time after Sal was killed. She said the officers told them that one of Williams's friends said her son killed Sal. Mrs. Snell provided her son with an alibi, telling the investigators that Williams had been at home with her that evening watching television and said, "The authorities definitely know where he was."

For a short time, Williams was kept under police surveillance. When no other incriminating evidence surfaced, the surveillance ended.

IN APRIL 1977, Williams was again arrested in Inglewood, California, for outstanding traffic warrants. In the course of processing him, police discovered he was wanted in Michigan on a forgery charge. He was subsequently returned to Michigan, where he was convicted of passing a bad check and sentenced to eight months in the Calhoun County jail.

At that time, investigators working on the Mineo case in Los Angeles obtained a statement from La Sonya Armstrong stating that she had been at Williams's home shortly after the murder and he told her he had killed a famous person in Hollywood. According to her statement, Williams showed her some bloodstained clothing and a knife that he kept on his wall. She quoted him as saying he had used the knife in the murder.

More damning information was obtained in May 1977 from

Williams's wife, Theresa, after she was arrested on a solicitation charge. In exchange for the charge against her being dropped, she told police that her husband had come home on the night of Sal's killing covered in blood. She said he told her that he'd stabbed someone. While they watched the television news, they heard a report about the murder of an actor, Sal Mineo. Theresa said Williams pointed at the picture of Sal on the television screen and said, "That's the dude I killed."

She said her husband killed Sal with a hunting knife he had purchased for $5.28. She knew the price, she said, because she had given him the money to make the purchase. She said he carried the knife during a string of robberies on the west side of Los Angeles. Investigators were skeptical of her story but consulted with Los Angeles County Chief Medical Examiner Dr. Noguchi. The coroner inserted "an exactly similar knife" into the section of Sal's chest that had been preserved by pathologists as evidence. It matched the wound perfectly.

Theresa Williams also told investigators she had washed the blood from her husband's clothes, and a couple of weeks after the slaying, he had driven her to the alley where he stabbed Sal to prove he'd committed the crime. She said Lionel told her he had hidden behind some trash cans and attacked Sal after he parked his car in the dimly lit alley. Sal screamed, she said, and frightened her husband off before he could rob him.

In a January 6, 1978, article in the *Los Angeles Times* titled "Mineo Suspect's Boasts Disclosed: Twice Bragged About Killing Actor, Court Records Show," reporter Bill Farr wrote that declarations had been filed to support an arrest warrant for twenty-one-year-old Lionel R. Williams.

Ronald Peek, a deputy sheriff in Calhoun County, Michigan, told Los Angeles County sheriff's deputy Robert Harris that he had overheard a conversation between Williams and another inmate named Philbert Gallard.

The declaration stated, "Dep. Peek overheard suspect Williams state to inmate Gallard, 'I killed a honky awhile back.' To which inmate Gallard stated, 'Who was it?' Suspect Williams said, 'Sal Mineo.' 'You're conning me,' Gallard responded. 'No, I'm serious,' Williams said. 'I have no reason to bull about nothing like that.' "

Investigators also reported they had a transcript of a recorded conversation between Sgt. John Repec of the Calhoun County sheriff's office and a former county jail inmate there. Williams was quoted as telling his fellow prisoner that he had stabbed Mineo.

Farr's report continued, "Michigan authorities disclosed today that Williams' cell in the county jail had been bugged with court permission in a 30-day period last June and five days in September. Calhoun County Sheriff Roger Dean said investigators had used the recordings of Williams' conversations with fellow inmates to develop leads." Sheriff Dean said "certain implications" contained in the recordings had formed the basis of a warrant charging Williams with first-degree murder.

Detectives also tried to connect Williams to the murder through a car that witnesses had seen driving from the crime scene with the headlights off. One witness said he saw a small yellow car, possibly a Toyota, drive away. According to investigators, they discovered that on February 12, 1976 (the day of the murder), Williams borrowed a yellow 1971 Dodge Colt from a Lincoln-Mercury dealer on Crenshaw Boulevard in Los Angeles. They obtained a loan agreement signed by Williams to prove it. Detectives said that the appearance of a Dodge Colt was very similar to that of a Toyota.

At a hearing on January 5, 1978, in Marshall, Michigan, Lionel Williams waived extradition proceedings and agreed to return to Los Angeles to face first-degree murder charges. Williams, who was handcuffed and dressed in jailhouse fatigues and slippers, spoke briefly to reporters and joked with deputies. He claimed to newsmen that he had nothing to do with Sal's death and knew nothing about it. When asked if he was confident he would be found innocent, Williams said, "Oh yeah, I'm cool." As he was led from the Michigan courtroom, he said to a sheriff's deputy, "This is a big deal, ain't it?"

Lionel Williams was returned to California on January 12 to face charges. The convicted forger was booked into county jail in lieu of $200,000 bail. When Williams was interviewed by detectives upon his arrival in Los Angeles, one of the investigators noticed what appeared to be a fresh tattoo on the defendant's arm. It was a knife. Williams said, "I had it done while I was back in Michigan." Detectives believed it looked like the knife they suspected Williams had used to kill Sal.

On Monday, January 16, Lionel Williams stood silent as he was arraigned on a charge that he fatally stabbed Sal two years earlier. Beverly Hills Municipal Court Judge Andrew J. Weisz scheduled a February 9 preliminary hearing on the homicide charge. Williams and his court-appointed attorney, Robert Harris, waived the reading of the murder charge and did not enter a plea.

Deputy District Attorney Burton Katz decided to present his case against Williams to a secret grand jury rather than wait for the preliminary hearing scheduled for February 9. "We took the case to the grand jury for two purposes," Katz explained, "and one of them was to keep the forum from turning into a circus, which it would have been at a preliminary hearing in open court."

Katz said the other reason for going to a secret grand jury was for the protection of witnesses, "some of who fear for their life." The deputy DA was apparently referring to certain inmate informants and acquaintances of the defendant who had cooperated with authorities.

"We've already lost one of our witnesses," Katz said. He was referring to Lionel's wife, Theresa Williams, who refused to testify at the grand jury hearing citing the marital privilege that excuses a partner from testifying against his or her spouse. Once attention had been focused on her husband, Theresa Williams had moved away from California to an undisclosed location.

Williams's attorney, Robert Harris, complained that the prosecution had not given the grand jury all evidence favorable to his client. "Had the case gone to a February 9 preliminary hearing as scheduled," Harris said, "witnesses would have been exposed to vigorous cross-examination and evidence helpful to the defense would have been presented."

Katz called Harris's charges "preposterous." He said he could not specifically reveal to the media what evidence had been presented to the grand jury because of the secrecy of the proceedings. He added that investigators working on the case "had been working around the clock" and still had not completed transcripts of all eighty-two hours of the tape recordings but would soon provide those to the defense.

Williams pleaded innocent to the homicide charge in a brief appearance at the downtown Los Angeles criminal courts building on February 6. He was formally indicted, and Judge Paul Breckinridge then ordered Williams to appear on February 21 for further pretrial proceedings in the courtroom of Superior Court Judge William Ritzi. In the meantime, Williams was held on $500,000 bail. At the same time, Breckinridge denied Burton Katz's request to transfer the case to Santa Monica Court "for convenience of witnesses."

With the formal indictment of Williams accomplished, Katz handed over the prosecution of the case to Deputy DA Michael Genelin. The young prosecutor was determined and very confident. He referred to the knife tattoo on Williams's arm as "the mark of Cain." He described the defendant as "a strange breed of cat, totally unconcerned with any human being. He doesn't give a damn who he hurts. He told his girlfriend that when he felt bad he had to go out and hurt someone."

INVESTIGATORS HAD earlier interviewed a friend of Lionel Williams's named Allwyn Williams. Known as "Rock" by his friends, Allwyn Williams had participated with Lionel Williams in the armed robbery of four people in Beverly Hills on March 7, 1976. Allwyn Williams was currently in jail on an unrelated kidnapping/robbery charge. He stepped forward with information about his acquaintance Lionel Williams and was cut a deal.

Allwyn Williams said that Lionel told him about Sal's murder one night after their robbery in Beverly Hills. According to Allwyn, Lionel said he had been driving around Hollywood below Sunset Boulevard looking for someone to rob. He accosted Sal, and during the failed robbery, he said, he killed him.

Lionel Williams was incensed when word reached him in the Michigan jail that Allwyn was talking to prosecutors in Los Angeles. Lionel gave one of his visitors a note that he had written to pass on to someone named "Big Perry." The note read, "Rock is trying to kill me. I want to do something to Rock right away. He can kill me. So do something about him. He is against me all the way. Important. He is in high power."

The note was intercepted by authorities. A member of Michael Genelin's prosecution team said, "Lionel Williams knew that Allwyn had finked on him and could send him to the gas chamber so he apparently was soliciting his murder—or at least bodily harm—in the county jail."

Defense motions and complaints temporarily bogged down the case's progress. Finally, on March 21, Lionel Williams was ordered to stand trial on May 25 before Superior Court Judge Edward A. Heinz Jr. for Sal's murder. He was held on $500,000 bail.

AFTER ADDITIONAL delays, on May 3, 1978, Williams was finally formally charged with Sal's murder and arraigned on a Los Angeles County grand jury indictment accusing him of committing a series of robberies in the months following the actor's 1976 slaying.

Williams pleaded not guilty to ten counts of robbery and one count of armed robbery when he appeared before Superior Court Judge Paul G. Breckinridge Jr. The twelve-count indictment superseded one filed in January against the convicted forger. Prosecutor Michael Genelin said Williams was reindicted on the homicide count so that all the charges could be consolidated for a single trial.

Los Angeles County sheriff Sergeant John Allender said all the robberies occurred on the street in West Hollywood, Beverly Hills, and the Wilshire area. Williams approached the victims and demanded money, Allender said. He was allegedly armed with a gun or a knife in all the robberies but one. The evidence supporting the robbery charges was developed during the course of follow-up investigations into Sal's murder.

After three postponements, legal maneuvering by both sides, and a transfer to another judge's court, Los Angeles Superior Court Judge Bonnie Lee Martin scheduled Williams's trial for January 3, 1979.

FOLLOWING ANOTHER delay, Williams's trial finally began on Tuesday, January 9. In his opening statement, the prosecutor, Michael Genelin, described Williams as a "night marauder" who had committed a series of violent, strong-arm robberies, during one of which Sal was stabbed to death. Genelin assured the jurors that they would conclude that the defendant "did commit the acts outlined."

Stephen Gustafson was one of the first witnesses to testify before the six-man, six-woman jury. Not only had Gustafson seen the assailant flee the scene of the crime, but he had actually witnessed the attack against Sal. Gustafson said, at the time, he thought the attacker was white, of average height and build, and had "dirty blond or light brown hair with brown highlights." He said the assailant's hair was "somewhere between an Afro and naturally curly." When pressed by the defense, Gustafson said that in the dim light of the alleyway, he thought the man was white only "from the hair" and did not clearly see his face.

The witness testified that he was walking his dog at about 9:30 P.M. on Thursday, February 12, 1976. He said he heard a car enter the apartment parking area and then saw the driver—Sal—get out. Sal walked from his car to the pathway leading into the apartment complex, Gustafson explained. When Sal reached the entranceway, he stopped short and started backing away, shouting, "No! No!"

A figure darted from the dark walkway area toward Sal and "plowed into him," the witness continued. He said Sal fell immediately to the ground, clutching his chest and crying out, "Oh, God! Help me please! Somebody help me!" He did not hear the assailant say anything but did get a glimpse of the shadowy figure as he quickly ran away.

Scott P. Hughes, a security guard like Gustafson, testified he heard Sal screaming for help and seconds later saw a fleeing man jump into what looked like a yellow Toyota and speed away without turning on the car's lights. He said the man had dark hair and, in the dim light, had a yellowish complexion. "I thought he could be Mexican or Italian," Hughes said.

Prosecutor Genelin substantiated the testimony with a police photo of Lionel Williams taken February 26, 1976, two weeks after Sal's murder, when he was booked for the robbery of a man whose windshield he smashed with a hammer in Inglewood. The mug shot was of a black man with a light complexion and long, bleached hair.

The next witness, a man named Richard Roy, identified Williams as one of two men who accosted and robbed him on the street outside his apartment on the night of February 12, 1976. Thirty minutes after Sal's murder, and less than a mile from the murder scene, Roy said two black men knocked him down, beat him, robbed him, and fled on foot. When asked if either of his assailants was in the courtroom, Roy said yes and pointed at Lionel Williams.

Allwyn Williams, a newly enlisted marine at the time of the trial, spent two days on the witness stand. He admitted to participating in an armed robbery in Beverly Hills with Lionel Williams on March 7,

1976. He also testified that Lionel told him about killing Sal. One day in January 1977, he and Lionel were "just talking in general" and "reminiscing" about their gang-fighting days.

"We came to the discussion," Allwyn explained, "that he had killed someone famous. 'Who?' I asked him. He said, 'Sal Mineo.' And he started talking about it. He said he was in Hollywood, driving around below Sunset, somewhere in there, and he was going to rob someone for some money and he stabbed somebody. And he told me how he done it. He demonstrated." When asked by Deputy District Attorney Michael Genelin to show the jury what he meant, using his hand to re-create the stabbing movement, Allywn said, "the right-hand downward thrust kind of motion, a standard stabbing motion."

The witness said the defendant told him Sal then "went back" (demonstrating a backward movement) "and grabbed his chest . . . Ray [the defendant's middle name] kind of demonstrated the man yelling, 'Ah' or 'Oh,' something like that, and whatever actions."

The witness said although the purpose of the assault was robbery, no money was taken by Lionel Williams, who "ran away from the scene and went back to the car." Allwyn, on leave from his duty station in Hawaii to testify under immunity from prosecution, told the court someone else was with the defendant, driving around Hollywood the night of the slaying, but "not at the stabbing, but riding together in the car."

As the trial dragged on, Williams's numerous recorded boasts of the killing were played for the jury. The inmates to whom he'd confessed and the prison guards who overheard his confessions all testified before the court. Various victims of robbery and assault identified Williams as their assailant from the witness stand.

What little character the defendant may have had was effectively sullied by the prosecutor. Williams's past criminal record—beginning with a juvenile conviction at age fourteen—was introduced in court to establish a pattern of criminal behavior.

On Thursday, January 25, Monica Merrem was called to the stand by the defense to testify in the murder case. The twelve-year-old seventh-grader was living with her mother in the apartment complex where Sal was stabbed. She told the court she was sitting at her desk in her room when she overheard Sal's screams. She went to the window, pushed aside the shades, and looked out. "I saw somebody running by," she said, "and I thought that person must have hurt the person who was screaming. I noticed that he was very white because I could see the side of his face."

The young girl said the man's hair was "dark . . . in long, big curls, and as he ran, it bounced." She added that after the figure ran out of her sight, she heard the screech of tires.

To contradict Monica Merrem's testimony and the similar testimony of her mother, Marcia Di Sessa, the prosecution called Elliot Mintz to the stand on January 29. A secretly recorded telephone conversation was played for the jury to discredit Merrem's account. Elliot had recorded the conversation and played the tape in court. Elliot identified the other voice on the tape as that of Marcia Di Sessa. She had earlier testified that both she and her daughter, Monica, saw a suspect fleeing from the murder scene. The key point of their testimony had been that the man they saw running was white.

On the tape, the voice of Di Sessa was heard to say that her daughter did not really see the man's face at all. She saw only the side of his head and "actually did not see any skin." The tape was played shortly after Di Sessa was recalled to the witness stand by Genelin. When pressed by the prosecutor, Di Sessa testified that her daughter saw the side of the man's face—his cheek or the side of his chin. She said she did not remember telling Elliot Mintz that her daughter did not actually see skin.

At the time she testified, Di Sessa seemingly did not know her February 16, 1977, telephone conversation with Elliot was being recorded. Elliot explained that the conversation resulted from a public appeal he had made on the first anniversary of Sal's death for information about the unsolved murder.

FINAL TESTIMONY PRESENTED IN MINEO TRIAL was a *Los Angeles Times* headline on Wednesday, January 31, 1979. "Both the prosecution and defense presented final testimony Tuesday in the murder trial of Lionel R. Williams, the twenty-two-year-old ex-convict accused of slaying actor Sal Mineo. Williams, a former pizza deliveryman, also is on trial in connection with ten other strong-arm robberies committed during the first three months of 1976 in Beverly Hills, West Hollywood and the Wilshire district."

The prosecutor again described defendant Lionel Williams as a "night marauder," as well as a "despoiler," in his closing argument to the Los Angeles Superior Court. "He is a sadist, a man who wants the world to know how tough he is," Genelin said as he pointed to Lionel Williams. "He is a night marauder who would kill you if he had to— even if he didn't have to. He is a person who likes to inflict pain." The prosecutor's closing argument was based heavily on compelling, but nevertheless circumstantial evidence, including testimony from two witnesses who said they heard Williams boast about the killing. Genelin reminded the jury of the testimony of several victims who said they had been assaulted and robbed by the defendant within a few weeks of Sal's death. The prosecutor further asserted that seven of the people in the robberies with which Williams was charged indentified him as their attacker and argued that Sal's killing fit a similar pattern to the other hit-and-run holdups. He accused Williams of striking one victim in the head, causing a permanent deafness in one ear, "for no apparent reason except this man is a sadist."

On the seventh day of deliberations, February 13 (a day after the third anniversary of Sal's slaying), the jury returned their verdicts. Lionel Williams was found guilty of second-degree murder and ten other counts of robbery. The prosecution had contended that Sal was the third victim in a string of eleven holdups stretching from January 24 to March 7, 1976. "My God," Williams said upon hearing the verdicts, "they're going to convict me on every one of these things!"

Williams's attorney, Mort Herbert, said he was "stunned" by the verdict. He told reporters he had wanted Williams tried separately on the murder and robbery charges and admitted the weight of the "cumulative evidence" came down hard on Williams.

Many in the press speculated that the murder case was probably won when Genelin was allowed to try Williams on ten other robberies at the same time as well. "It was one course of continuous conduct, a series of muggings," Genelin said. "That's his modus operandi."

Defense attorney Herbert said evidence that his client had committed the robberies "was extremely strong—and they were bad robberies. Basically, this was a case of ten brutal robberies with Mineo tacked on. It was ironic that Mineo became a very minor part of the trial."

No murder weapon was ever found. The prosecution made their case against the defendant primarily on circumstantial evidence, part of which was Williams's conviction for another armed robbery committed less than thirty minutes after Sal's murder and less than a mile away. The only eyewitnesses to any crimes attributed to Williams were the people he had actually robbed and assaulted, who identified him in court. "Though we were working with circumstantial evidence," Genelin admitted, "it was a mountain of circumstantial evidence, and we buried him."

Both the prosecutor and defense attorney said they felt the second-degree murder conviction was a "compromise verdict." Premeditation is usually a requirement for a first-degree murder conviction.

Williams remained in custody in lieu of $200,000 bail until his sentencing on March 15. After denying a defense motion for a new trial, Judge Bonnie Lee Martin gave Williams the maximum sentence of fifty-one years to life in prison (five years to life for the second-degree murder conviction and identical sentences for each of the nine first-degree robberies, and one year to life for a second-degree robbery that he was convicted of in the single trial). Judge Martin ordered the eleven sentences to run consecutively. After imposing the sentence, the judge credited Williams with 353 days already spent in jail on the case and 60 days spent on another case. She ordered him taken to the men's prison in Chino, California.

"The defendant should be committed to state prison for as long as the law allows," Judge Martin said. "I don't think he's susceptible to rehabilitation, considering his escalating conduct of committing more and more violence." The judge said she ordered the maximum sentence after reading the defendant's probation report that showed his criminal career began at age fourteen and had grown progressively more violent. His weapons, the judge explained, "included guns, knives, and hammers."

Deputy District Attorney Genelin said, "Lionel Williams is a predator. This was a progressive process with him. He enjoyed brutalizing people. These were not just street robberies but one incident after another where he inflicted pain . . . and enjoyed it. He has no socially redeeming characteristics at all. If ever released, he will unquestionably kill again. There is no doubt in my mind."

Although he did not testify at his trial, Williams addressed the court before his sentencing. "I fault you for my going to the penitentiary," he told the judge. "Twice I tried to fire my attorney but you wouldn't let me. I don't feel I was represented. He wasn't in my corner. I didn't want him, but you put him on me."

Referring to Genelin's argument that he had tattooed a replica of the murder knife on his arm, Williams yanked his coat off and displayed the tattoo for all to see. He shouted at Genelin, "That knife don't look nothing like the knife that killed him!"

Referring to Williams's outburst in the court, Genelin later commented, "The defendant made an interesting claim. How did he know his tattoo didn't look like the knife that killed Mr. Mineo unless he had intimate knowledge of the actual murder weapon?"

Judge Martin told Williams she felt his defense attorney, Mort Herbert, had done a fine job on his behalf. "There is no question in the court's mind that you gave Mr. Williams the best defense possible," the judge told Herbert. "I think the defendant got a fair trial."

UNDER CALIFORNIA'S fixed-sentencing law, Williams's sentence was recomputed by the state community release board and a specific term was set. Attorneys estimated that the term of fifty-one years to life would be recomputed to approximately fourteen years in prison, with Williams eligible for parole in about nine years.

Some people speculated that the investigation was actually stymied by the authorities. The belief was that detectives had dismissed a robbery motive in the slaying in favor of an unspoken theory that Sal was the victim of a sexually motivated crime because of his assumed sexuality. When attention was finally focused on Lionel Williams and Sal being the unsuspecting victim of a botched robbery attempt, some investigators quietly admitted that their attention may have been subconsciously pointed in the wrong direction all along. Detective Tankersley said, "In retrospect, I think, 'Why didn't I pursue the robbery angle more?' We might have solved it a lot sooner."

In 1981, the California Supreme Court denied Williams's appeal based on his claim that he had been wrongly convicted. In the early 1990s, Lionel Williams made parole but was soon back in prison, convicted of more violent assaults.

IN 1976, shortly after the murder, Sal's longtime agent, Tom Korman, was named administrator of his estate. A small life insurance policy Sal had with his union, Actors' Equity, named Courtney his beneficiary. Since no will was in effect at the time of his death, a petition for probate was filed with the Los Angeles County recorder on August 18, 1976.

Only three heirs were listed: Josephine, Michael, and Victor Mineo. At the time of his death, Sal's estate was valued at $14,152.98. Creditors' claims totaled $49,707.03. The claims included judgments against Sal from former landlords Bonnie Morse in the amount of $2,333 dating back to August 13, 1965, and Robert Thorgusen in the amount of $4,133 dating from September 25, 1969; the New York Telephone Company for $725 dating from August 5, 1971; and the recent $30,000 judgment in favor of Ernest Criezis of Texas dated January 21, 1976.

Sal owed several personal loans for which no claims had been filed, including a loan made to him years before by his friend Yul Brynner. There were also numerous outstanding bills to settle at Beverly Stationers in Beverly Hills; (Crazy Nate) Turner's TV Rentals for the television set and miscellaneous furnishings at the Holloway apartment; Pacific Telephone San Francisco; Pacific Telephone Sherman Oaks; Theta Cable Television; Effie Sharabie Limousine Service; Sal's Los Angeles attorney Leslie and Rubin; his tax accountant S. Sanford Ezralow; and his medical doctor, Lee Siegel.

The most interesting creditor's claim against Sal's estate was filed on February 17, 1977, in the amount of $6,887.68 in favor of his mother, Josephine. Her claim covered the costs of her son's funeral, including $2,767.68 for the funeral service; $590 for the grave opening; $400 for the grave marker; $200 for flowers; $80 for printed death certificates; $850 for security guards at the funeral and burial, including the Mineos' childhood friend Joe Cavallero; $500 for the airline transportation of Sal's casket and body from Los Angeles to New York; and $1,500 for Sal's gravestone.

The court eventually found Josephine's claim for funeral expenses to be "excessive even for a solvent estate." When the estate was finally settled on July 3, 1978, Josephine was granted a single payment in the amount of $1,549.21.

# NOTES

The author gratefully acknowledges those who shared their recollections for this book. Unless otherwise noted, all quotations from these people are drawn from my personal interviews and our recorded conversations. Subsequent quotations from the same source derive from the identical interviews with that source unless stated to the contrary. Special heartfelt thanks to Jill Haworth, Courtney Burr III, Michael Anderson Jr., Eric Williams, and Perry Lopez, who accommodated my every request.

Nancy Barr, Chris Beeching, Peter Beiger, Mr. Blackwell, Johnny Crawford, Eugene Daniels, Mark Fleishman, Don Grady, Earl Holliman, Dennis Hopper, David Joliffe, Glyn Jones, Zalman King, Tom Korman, Janet Leigh, Diane McBain, Richard Ouzounian, Marvin Paige, Doug Peters, Eddie Rambeau, Tom Reese, George Reinholt, Eva Marie Saint, Kathy Schiano, Clair Sedore, Gene Shuey, Harold Stevenson, Ray Stricklyn, James Whitmore, Walter Willison, Shelley Winters, Lana Wood, and Jack Wrangler, thank you for your invaluable help.

**CHAPTER 1**

3 **"The original pronunciation"** "I'm No Teenager Lover," *Liberty,* December 1957.

3 **"The move"** Art Ryon, "Mineo Proves Youngsters from Tough Districts Can Win Out," *Los Angeles Times,* April 26, 1957.

3 **"My father was born"** Ed Meyerson, "Man, That Mineo's the Most," *Photoplay,* August 1956.

4 **"My mother was born"** Ibid.

4 **"My father was so good"** Ibid.

4 **"We always had plenty"** Ibid.

4 **"Pop and Mama"** Ed DeBlasio, "Sal Mineo's Thanksgiving Miracle," *Modern Screen,* November 1957.

5 **"Some days"** Ibid.

5 **"Sal was just so little"** Author interview with Kathy Schiano, August 5, 2005.

5 **"The first five years"** Meyerson, "Man, That Mineo's the Most."

5 **"I guess that's why"** Ibid.

6 **"Even if they"** Ibid.

6 **"A guy would come up"** "Sal Mineo's Wildest Interview," *Movie World,* September 1959.

6 **"The sisters"** Hedda Hopper, "Have You Met Sal?" *Modern Screen,* July 1956.

7 **"Sal's our baby brother"** Victor Mineo, "My Brother's Tough," *Motion Picture,* September 1956.

8 **"No," Sal said. "I knew"** Aljean Meltsir, "The Gentle Road to Stardom," *Motion Picture,* June 1956.

8 **"If anybody won"** Ryon, "Mineo Proves Youngsters."

8 **"I could have gone"** "No Fake Thrills," *Screen Album,* May/July 1957.

8 **"most soft-hearted person"** Sarina Mineo, "My Brother Is Not Tough," *Motion Picture,* September 1956.

8 **"It was Sal"** Ibid.

9 **"How would you kids"** Sal Mineo, "Call Me Junior," *Seventeen,* January 1957.

9 **"Ma, send me"** Hopper, "Have You Met Sal?"

9 **"Since I was too small"** Sal Mineo, "The King and Me," *Photoplay,* October 1957.

10 **"We didn't have very much"** Lloyd Shearer, "Sal Mineo, He's Got the Magic," *Parade,* July 29, 1956.

10 **"I sold papers"** Hopper, "Have You Met Sal?"

10 **"Salvatore," she said** "A Prince from the Bronx: The Double Life of Sal Mineo," *Hollywood Life Story,* 1957.

10 **"Should I spend all of my time"** Ibid.

10 **"I really want to go"** Ibid.

11 **"It was almost frightening"** Ibid.

11 **"I'd walk in the dirt"** Ryon, "Mineo Proves Youngsters."

11 **"The dancing school"** Victor Mineo, "My Brother's Tough."

11 **"The day after"** Hopper, "Have You Met Sal?"

11 **"Sal is a bright boy"** "I'll Do Anything Once," *Man's Magazine,* January 1970.

12 **"We were just kids"** Ibid.

12 **"This boy will be"** Ibid.

12 **"They told my mother"** Ibid.


**CHAPTER 2**

13 **"I thought it was"** "I'll Do Anything Once."

13 **"Who's your agent?"** Sal Mineo, "Call Me Junior."

14 **"After taking"** "The Year That Mineo Got Hot," *British Photoplay,* May 1957.

14 **"Daniel Mann"** Sal Mineo, "Call Me Junior."

14 **"I cried"** Ibid.

14 **"It was Eli"** Hopper, "Have You Met Sal?"

15 **"I knew what I wanted"** May Mann, "Sal Mineo's Hidden Life," *Movie Mirror,* August 1960.

16 **"I came home one day"** "The Day the Sun Disappeared," *Motion Picture,* September 1959.

16 **"We tried"** Sal Mineo, "Why I'm Sure There Is a God," *Photoplay,* December 1959.

16 **"Before I found"** DeBlasio, "Sal Mineo's Thanksgiving Miracle."

16 **"Because you're home"** Meltsir, "The Gentle Road to Stardom."

16 **"You can always"** Sarina Mineo, "My Brother Is Not Tough."

17 **"Call it ambition"** "Editorial: The Sal Mineo Story," *Modern Screen,* June 1960.

17 **"If Sal was with"** Helen Bolstad, "Mineo's Really Moving," *TV Radio Mirror,* September 1957.

17 **"I want to be"** "No Fake Thrills."

17 **"Even if I am"** Ibid.

18 **"But I didn't mind"** "The Incredible Cost of Stardom," *Motion Picture,* July 1957.

19 **"Rehearsals passed"** Sal Mineo, "Call Me Junior."


**CHAPTER 3**

20 **"Again I began"** Sal Mineo, "Call Me Junior."

20 **"My other children"** Shearer, "Sal Mineo, He's Got the Magic."

20 **"After Sal"** Author interview with Schiano.

21 **"I had to summon"** Sal Mineo, "Call Me Junior."

21 **"This was a brand-new"** Martin Abramson, "Bronx Boy with Box Office," *Coronet,* February 1958.

21 **"I never got tired"** Ibid.

22 **"You gotta"** Sal Mineo, "Call Me Junior."

22 **"I'd rather"** Sal Mineo, "Every Guy Needs a Father," *Screen, TV and Record Stars,* December 1958.

22 **"Look, Jo"** Ibid.

23 **"One night"** Hopper, "Have You Met Sal?"

23 **"I was scared"** Sal Mineo, "The King and Me."

23 **"My knees"** Jhan Robbins, *Yul Brynner: The Inscrutable King* (New York: Dodd, Mead & Company, 1988), 85, 86, 87.

24 **"He whispered"** Sal Mineo, "The King and Me."

24 **"We were more"** Ibid.

24 **"Every night"** Ibid.

25 **"One night"** Ibid.

25 **"There's a scene"** Ibid.

25 **"I was pretty bad"** "18 Is a Crucial Age," *TV Guide,* May 18, 1957.

25 **"fierce earnestness"** "Sal Mineo," *Private Lives,* June 1957.

26 **"It happened backstage"** Natalie Wood, "Spotlight on Sal," *Motion Picture,* May 1957.

26 **"After a while"** Ibid.

27 **"By the time"** "Avanti Interview: Sal Mineo," *Avanti,* January/February 1969.

27 **"Jesus, the sound"** Peter Bogdanovich, *Who the Hell's in It* (New York: Knopf, 2004), 234.

28 **"When I was"** Jack Holland, "I Fall in Love Too Easily," *Silver Screen,* December 1959.

28 **"Whenever I walked"** "Editorial: The Sal Mineo Story."

28 **"I was on Broadway"** Ibid.

29 **"You've got the skis"** "Please Use One of My Coffins," *Photoplay,* October 1956.

29 **"Though he loves"** Ibid.

30 **"Here he was"** Meyerson, "Man, That Mineo's the Most."

30 **"He's the best"** "A Piece of Chocolate Cake," *Movie Teen Illustrated,* March 1958.

30 **"But," Sal told her** Paul Denis, "Sal's Bitter Awakening," *Screen, TV and Record Stars,* October 1958.

30 **"Sal's the finest"** Abramson, "Bronx Boy with Box Office."

31 **"Young Sal"** Howard Taubman, "NBC Televises Superb Salome," *New York Times,* May 9, 1954.

31 **"though, of course"** Sal Mineo, "Call Me Junior."

31 **"When Tony Curtis"** Ibid.

31 **"We knew"** Victor Mineo, "My Brother's Tough."

32 **"a gifted actor"** Tony Curtis and Peter Golenbock, *American Prince* (New York: Harmony Books, 2008), 162.

32 **"He showed me"** Sal Mineo, "Call Me Junior."

33 **"If you don't"** Meyerson, "Man, That Mineo's the Most."

**CHAPTER 4**

34 **"I used to look"** "I Thought It Would Be One Big Disneyland," *Young Movie Lovers,* January 1957.

34 **"Hollywood's calling"** Abramson, "Bronx Boy with Box Office."

34 **"good-time"** Ibid.

34 **"The first time"** Claire Susans, "Prayer Saved My Life," *Movie World,* November 1958.

35 **"My first morning"** *Young Movie Lovers.*

35 **"I didn't know"** Ibid.

35 **"The idea struck"** Helen Gould, "Teacher's Pet," *Movie Stars Parade,* April 1957.

36 **"He was part"** Ibid.

36 **"When Sal took"** Sarina Mineo, "My Brother Is Not Tough."

37 **"On TV"** Alice Styles, "Sal Mineo: 120 Lbs of TNT," *TV Headliner,* November 1956.

37 **"While he was making"** Gould, "Teacher's Pet."

**CHAPTER 5**

40 **"The purpose"** Lawrence Frascella and Al Weisel, *Live Fast, Die Young* (New York: Touchstone, 2005), 56–57.

41 **"I saw this kid"** Ibid., 83.

41 **"He was so excited"** Gould, "Teacher's Pet."

41 **"I was almost sick"** Frascella and Weisel, *Live Fast, Die Young,* 84.

42 **"Definitely you want"** Ibid.

42 **"I had no idea"** Ibid.

42 **"Sal," he said, "stop trying"** Ibid.

42 **"I liked being near him"** *New York* magazine interview, November 8, 1976.

43 **"One afternoon"** "Sal Mineo Tells How Natalie Fascinates Men," *Movie Life,* April 1957.

44 **"I couldn't understand"** *New York* magazine interview, November 8, 1976.

45 **"Sal is rich"** Meltsir, "The Gentle Road to Stardom."

46 **"We all tended"** Frascella and Weisel, *Live Fast, Die Young,* 109.

46 **"He was all she"** Ibid.

47 **"Do you ever get"** Ibid., 125.

47 **"He tried to hang out"** Ibid.

48 **"Sal was withdrawn"** Ibid.

48 **"If anyone"** Ibid.

48 **"Sal was under"** Author interview with Dennis Hopper, July 20, 2007.

49 **"Mineo folded on me"** Frascella and Weisel, *Live Fast, Die Young,* 157.

49 **"Honey, it's his"** Ibid., 161.

49 **"Sal and I"** "Sal Mineo Tells."

51 **"The whole movement"** Frascella and Weisel, *Live Fast, Die Young,* 164.

51 **"After an 'involuntary performance'"** Ibid., 169.

52 **"Warners didn't know"** Ibid., 172.

52 **"It is of course vital"** Ibid.

52 **"This was an important scene"** Ibid., 174.

53 **"I think that under"** Ibid., 175.
53 **"The thing I feared most"** Ibid.
53 **"I heard Jimmy"** Ibid., 174.
54 **"Plato was the one"** Ibid., 173.
54 **"The gay community"** Ibid.
54 **"Jimmy sneaked up"** John Gilmore, *Live Fast, Die Young* (New York: Thunder's Mouth Press, 1997), 190.
55 **"But that round cherub"** Carroll Baker, *Baby Doll* (New York: Arbor House, 1983), 116, 117, 118.
56 **"The day I got killed"** Gilmore, *Live Fast, Die Young*, 185.
56 **"And I wanted"** Ibid.
56 **"Immediately after"** Ibid.
56 **"In Plato's death scene"** Ibid.
56 **"Jim had the hots"** "I'll Do Anything Once."
57 **"Working on *Rebel*"** Gilmore, *Live Fast, Die Young*, 183, 184.

**CHAPTER 6**
62 **" 'Please use one of' "** "Please Use One of My Coffins."
62 **"Stevens was a good director"** "Sal Mineo Answers Your Questions," *Movie Stars Parade,* October 1956.
62 **"He practically rebuilt"** Gould, "Teacher's Pet."
62 **"Story, performances"** Frascella and Weisel, *Live Fast, Die Young,* 228.
63 **"Everyone asks me"** "Sal Mineo," *TV and Movie Screen,* November 1959.

**CHAPTER 7**
65 **"Sal, who was still"** Rock Brynner, *Yul: The Man Who Would Be King* (New York: Simon & Schuster, 1989), 102.
68 **"Sal is a perfectionist"** "Sal Mineo," *Private Lives.*
68 **"It's mainly the family"** Ruth Jackson, "Success Hasn't Spoiled Sal Mineo," *TV and Movie Screen,* November 1956.
69 **"If they want"** Ibid.
69 **"They never developed"** Ibid.
69 **"My Sal"** Ibid.
71 **"We all saw this kid"** A&E, *Biography,* "Sal Mineo: Hollywood's Forgotten Rebel" (1999).

72 **"Paul was not only"** "Sal Mineo Answers Your Questions."
73 **"I think my greatest"** Sal Mineo, "Call Me Junior."
73 **"You know"** "Sal Mineo Answers Your Questions."
74 **"We had a lot of lunches together"** Author interview with Perry Lopez, 2004–2006, numerous phone calls and in person.
74 **"Sal wants"** Jackson, "Success Hasn't Spoiled Sal Mineo."
74 **"Sal Mineo is the only boy I know"** Wood, "Spotlight on Sal."

**CHAPTER 8**
79 **"I want to win the Academy Award"** "Tough and Talented."
79 **"I'm here"** Bob Thomas, "Mineo Sallies Forth," *AP/Mirror News,* March 2, 1956.
80 **"Any time you're with Sal"** Wood, "Spotlight on Sal."
80 **"One of my biggest"** Sal Mineo, "The Girls I Date," *Movie Stars Life,* August 1956.
81 **"No, he told me"** "Has Success Spoiled Sal Mineo?"
81 **"I took my mother"** Meyerson, "Man, That Mineo's the Most."
82 **"When they announced"** Styles, "Sal Mineo: 120 Lbs of TNT."
82 **"It was the first"** Wood, "Spotlight on Sal."
82 **"I thought that"** "Has Success Spoiled Sal Mineo?"
83 **"Each of us"** Meyerson, "Man, That Mineo's the Most."
84 **"When I first got there"** "18 Is a Crucial Age."
84 **"The crowds broke"** "Sal's Big Night," *Movie Stars Parade,* September 1956.
85 **"I just couldn't stand"** Ibid.
87 **"I just usually"** "18 Is a Crucial Age."

**CHAPTER 9**
88 **"The girls"** Sarina Mineo, "My Brother Is Not Tough."
90 **"No villains"** John L. Scott, "Sal Mineo, Star at 17," *Los Angeles Times,* August 19, 1956.
90 **"There's nothing"** Sal Mineo, "Call Me Junior."

91 **"Because I've played"** Fred Brown, "Everything but a Girl," *Movieland*, December 1956.

91 **"I get all those letters"** "The Year That Mineo Got Hot."

91 **"At home"** Sarina Mineo, "My Life with Sal," *Filmland*, October 1957.

91 **"My money that I earn"** Sal Mineo, "The Girls I Date."

91 **"I'd be lost without"** "Please Use One of My Coffins."

92 **"I used to be"** "Boy, What a Man!" *Screen Stars*, November 1956.

94 **"Sal was self-assured"** Author interview with James Whitmore, May 12, 2005.

95 **"His quiet urging"** Sal Mineo, "Call Me Junior."

95 **"It was a rough shoot"** Author interview with Whitmore.

96 **"*Giant* was filmed"** "Don't Quote Me, but . . . ," *Motion Picture*, October 1957.

96 **"When I have troubles"** "The Most Exciting Bachelor of the Year," *Movie Stars Parade*, November 1956.

97 **"Besides," he added** Brown, "Everything but a Girl."

97 **"I like doing juvenile"** Ibid.

97 **"Because our rooms"** Ibid.

97 **"Though not quite eighteen"** "Tender, Tough and Teenage," *TV Star Parade*, April 1957.

**CHAPTER 10**

99 **"When I knew"** "The Incredible Cost of Stardom."

99 **"I need a bodyguard"** Ibid.

100 **"We got pretty"** "*Dino:* Behind the Scenes," *Screen Stories*, July 1957.

100 **"It's like being home"** Ibid.

100 **"I dig brass"** "I Dig Bachelorhood and Brass Buttons," *Movieland*, June 1957.

100 **"I don't have ten"** Ibid.

100 **"I have a lot of"** Ibid.

100 **"I think they idolize"** "Sal Mineo Reveals Some of His Problems," *TV Guide*, May 18, 1957.

101 **"An actor"** Ibid.

101 **"Listen, do me a favor"** Ibid.

101 **"First," Sal explained** "The Incredible Cost of Stardom."

102 **"I spend it"** Ibid.

103 **"Sudden money"** Ibid.

103 **"We have a formula"** Ibid.

103 **"I felt like"** Ibid.

104 **"When he didn't"** "The Truth Behind Sal's Stardom," *Star*, November 1957.

104 **"I wasn't really a good loser"** "Don't Quote Me, but . . ."

**CHAPTER 11**

105 **"Teenagers sense"** Abramson, "Bronx Boy with Box Office."

105 **"I had seen"** Bolstad, "Mineo's Really Moving."

105 **"I'd like to"** Ibid.

106 **"You'd have thought"** Ibid.

107 **"I don't know"** "Adults Are Attacking Sal," *TV Star Parade*, August 1957.

108 **"We parked the car"** Bolstad, "Mineo's Really Moving."

110 **"He gave me"** "Sal Mineo's Fight to Save His Eyesight," *Movieland*, September 1957.

111 **"I want to thank you"** Ibid.

112 **"My father has no interest"** Sal Mineo, "Every Guy Needs a Father."

113 **"I have changed"** Ibid.

114 **"The back part"** Abramson, "Bronx Boy with Box Office."

114 **"There's no question"** Dick Clark and Richard Robinson, *Rock, Roll and Remember* (New York: Thomas Y. Crowell Company, 1976), 10–13.

117 **"We started hoping"** Sidney Homer, "I'm Not a Mixed Up Kid," *Movie Mirror*, April 1958.

117 **"I lost about two months"** Denis, "Sal's Bitter Awakening."

117 **"I want the best"** Henry Mitchell, "Is Sal Mineo Burning Himself Out?" *Motion Picture*, December 1957.

118 **"Who needs"** Ibid.

119 **"Someday I'd like"** ". . . But I Had Aladdin's Lamp," *Movie Life*, March 1958.

119 **"There's *Tubie's Monument*"** Ibid.

**CHAPTER 12**

121 **"In case I'm ever"** "Sal Is Girl Crazy," *Movie Fan*, June 1958.

121 **"For me"** "Date Sal If You Dare," *Motion Picture*, August 1958.

122 **"This is a sure way"** "Television Magic Conjures Up Another Memorable Week," *TV Guide*, February 15–21, 1958.

123 **"They wanted three hundred thousand dollars"** Fred Dickerson, "Mansion via Lamp," *American T-Vue Time*, February 16, 1958.

123 **"We're moving in"** Ibid.

124 **"My home is in New York"** "Mineo's on the War Path," *Teen*, March 1959.

126 **"How is anyone"** Author interview with Lopez.

126 **"This is the first time"** "A Young Man's Fancy," *TV Star Parade*, September 1958.

126 **"The folks moved in"** Ibid.

**CHAPTER 13**

127 **"We put our heads"** "The Jinx That Haunts Sal Mineo," *Screen Album*, February 1959.

128 **"At the bottom"** Ibid.

129 **"It gets bad"** Claire Susans, "Sal Mineo's Restless Search for Happiness," *Movie World*, March 1959.

129 **"It's a love story"** Charles Stinson, "Sal Mineo: Young Man on the Go," *Los Angeles Times*, September 28, 1958.

129 **"The girls I met"** Holland, "I Fall in Love Too Easily."

129 **"was too young"** Stinson, "Sal Mineo: Young Man on the Go."

131 **"This house"** "Mineo's on the War Path."

**CHAPTER 14**

133 **"We tried so hard"** May Mann interview for *Movie Mirror*, April 27, 1959, original transcript.

134 **"There was a time"** Mann, "Sal Mineo's Hidden Life."

135 **"It was bad enough"** Studio press release for *A Private's Affair*.

136 **"If there's one thing I like"** William Tusher interview for *Movieland*, May 21, 1959, original transcript.

136 **"Victor's marriage"** "Marriage Looks Different to Me Now," *Movie Stars Parade*, December 1958.

136 **"We didn't"** Tusher interview for *Movieland*.

137 **"He acts like"** Robert Peer, "How Sal Mineo Behaves on Dates," *Movie Mirror*, January 1960.

137 **"He's so interested in himself"** Dena Reed, "Susan Digs Sal," *Movie World*, April 1958.

137 **"Sal was a real pleasure"** Mann interview for *Movie Mirror*.

137 **"His reputation"** "Sal Thinks of Marriage," *Movie TV Secrets*, January 1960.

137 **"He told me"** Bill Tusher, "They Warned Me Sal Was a Playboy," *Motion Picture*, September 1959.

139 **"Went to a party"** "I Stole Ricky's Girl," *Movie TV Secrets*, January 1960.

139 **"He finally cut me off"** "What Sal Mineo's Secret Diary Says About . . . ," *Motion Picture*, December 1959.

139 **"As usual"** "Just a Little Bit Square," *Screen Album*, February–April 1960.

140 **"I've never been more happy"** "My Neighbor Sal Mineo," *Movieland and TV Times*, May 1959.

141 **"You'd think"** "Sal Mineo and the Love Witch of Fiji," *Modern Screen*, April 1961.

141 **"It was like"** Ibid.

141 **"The shows were"** Ibid.

141 **"I was fifty dollars"** Ibid.

142 **"But the beach"** Ibid.

143 **"She told me"** "The Gene Krupa Story," *Screen Stories*, February 1960.

**CHAPTER 15**

144 **"We're not losing any sleep"** Dean Jennings, "The Boy Called Sal," *Saturday Evening Post*, October 31, 1959.

145 **"I think it's because"** "Just a Little Bit Square."

146 **"Seems like old times"** Ibid.

146 **"I'm no Pat Boone"** Charles Denton, "Sal Mineo Tells How He Battles to Stay Popular," *Los Angeles Examiner*, July 30, 1959.

147 **"I'm consumed"** Kathy Johnson, "Please Try and Understand Me," *Movie Teen Illustrated*, March 1960.

149 **"I don't think"** Mann interview for *Movie Mirror*.

150 **"It's just nervous"** Mann, "Sal Mineo's Hidden Life."

CHAPTER 16

152 **"The next morning I read"** "Exodus Casting," United Artists press release, February 1960.
152 **"Stop!"** "Sal Mineo's Choices," *Dallas Morning News*, February 19–25, 1961.
153 **"Back then"** Author interview with Eva Marie Saint, November 1, 2004.
153 **"I think she is beautiful"** "Sal Mineo's Israel Diary," *Silver Screen,* October 1960.
153 **"They said I was a big fan"** Author interview with Jill Haworth.
154 **"Mr. Preminger knew"** Ibid.
154 **"Whenever we step out"** "Sal Mineo's Israel Diary."
154 **"When I got the role of Dov"** "Bible Comes to Life for Actor Sal Mineo," *Citizen News,* July 20, 1960.
154 **"Mr. Preminger can be so harsh"** "Sal Mineo's Israel Diary."
155 **"Sal was a wonderful actor"** Author interview with Saint.
156 **"SOL!"** "Sal Mineo's Israel Diary."
156 **"The funny thing was"** Ibid.
156 **"But where"** "The Saga of Exodus," *Cosmopolitan,* November 1960.

CHAPTER 17

159 **"It just didn't work"** Erskine Johnson, "The 'It' Factor and Sal Mineo," *Los Angeles Mirror,* March 2, 1961.
159 **"It seems"** "I Had to Date Older Women," *Motion Picture,* January 1961.

CHAPTER 18

167 **"They saw me"** Johnson, "The 'It' Factor."
167 **"I'm not a good"** "Sal Mineo's Choices."
167 **"I made one mistake"** Ibid.
167 **"I'm determined"** Don Alpert, "Sal: I Want a Fight in Life," *Los Angeles Times,* February 26, 1961.
168 **"Andrea is a role"** "Sal Mineo's Choices."

169 **"I was a kid"** Author interview with Haworth.
170 **"First I was"** Johnson, "The 'It' Factor."
172 **"I've never done"** Ibid.
172 **"For about a week"** Author interview with Gene Shuey, September 28, 2007.
172 **"That was *my* fucking Oscar"** Frascella and Weisel, *Live Fast, Die Young,* 259.

CHAPTER 19

174 **"Sal was cast"** Brynner, *Yul: The Man Who Would Be King,* 143.
176 **"How do you plead?"** "Is Sal Mineo Too Fast for His Own Good?" *Photoplay,* February 1962.

CHAPTER 20

179 **"Jesus"** Author interview with Haworth.
180 **"I have one, he didn't"** Author interview with Eric Williams.
180 **"How about me giving"** Ibid.
181 **"I had a large studio"** Author interview with Harold Stevenson, May 21, 2005.
182 **"The part of the Israeli"** Jack Garver, "Sal Mineo Is Still Trying to Shake His Rock 'n Roll Reputation," United Press International, May 26.

CHAPTER 21

186 **"Finally, Sal drove up"** Author interview with Michael Anderson Jr.

CHAPTER 22

194 **"As I walked"** Susan Braudy, "The Slow Fade," *Crawdaddy,* March 1978.
195 **"It's got three bedrooms"** "Two Loves Against the World," *Modern Screen,* March 1964.
197 **"Must know"** John L. Scott, "Hollywood Calendar," *Los Angeles Times,* August 26, 1963.
200 **"It's frankly nobody's business"** "Two Loves Against the World."

CHAPTER 23

202 **"Every time"** Ronald L. Davis, *John Ford: Hollywood's Old Master* (Oklahoma City, OK: University of Oklahoma Press, 1995), 321.

203 "It's typical" Ibid., 322.
204 "Whoever had an accent" Author interview with Williams.
204 "My father" Dan Ford, *Pappy: The Life of John Ford* (New York: Da Capo Press, 1998), 297.
204 "Well, you see" Davis, *John Ford*, 324.
204 "He's no longer" Ibid.
205 "Do you wanna do it" Scott Eyman, *Print the Legend: The Life and Times of John Ford* (New York: Simon & Schuster, 1999), 504.
205 "The prevailing winds" Bogdanovich, *Who the Hell's in It?* 235–36.
205 "I have never" Ibid.
205 "I never saw" Ibid.
206 "You know what day" Ibid., 232.
207 "Do not let" Author interview with Haworth.
208 "Sal attended" Author interview with Stevenson.

CHAPTER 24

211 "After several postponements" Bogdanovich, *Who the Hell's in It?* 237.
215 "Sal was wonderful" Author interview with Alex Gildzen, July 10, 2009.
215 "The play was a little tough" Author interview with George Reinholt, July 20, 2009.
215 "But I'm by no means" Dorothy Manners, "He Works for the Money," *Los Angeles Herald Examiner*, September 6, 1964.

CHAPTER 25

220 "I was a lesbian" George Hatch, "Who Killed Teddy Bear," *Scarlet Street*, Winter 1995.
221 "*Who Killed Teddy Bear?* bolstered" Ibid.
222 "I played a telephone freak" Jeremy Hughes, "Sal Mineo, the Eternal Original," *In Touch*, May/June 1976.
222 "a real actor" Hatch, "Who Killed Teddy Bear."
224 "cute, a little weird" Jon Provost and Laurie Jacobson, *Timmy's in the Well: The Jon Provost Story* (Nashville, TN: Cumberland House Publishing, 2007), 229.
224 "He had a motto" Ibid., 230.
224 "Sal took" David Cassidy and Chip

Deffaa, *C'mon, Get Happy* (New York: Warner Books, 1994), 33.
225 "His career was not" Ibid.
227 "Long before" "I'll Do Anything Once."
228 "When I started" Boze Hadleigh, *Conversations with My Elders* (New York: St. Martin's Press, 1972), 8.
228 "I went through a time" "I'll Do Anything Once."

CHAPTER 26

231 "Sal hit" Interview with Gino Empry, February 23, 2006.
231 "I really dig" Sid Adilman, "Sal Mineo 'Digs' Village," *Toronto Telegram*, December 20, 1965.
232 "I don't dig" Frank Morriss, "Sal Mineo and His Philosophy of Life," *Globe and Mail*, December 21, 1965.
233 "I won't be a loser" Michael Sherman, "Sal Is a Young Man in a Hurry," *Movie Life*, December 1965.
234 "He even signed" Braudy, "The Slow Fade."
235 "The actors had already" Author interview with Peter Beiger, February 8, 2008.

CHAPTER 27

238 "I felt terrible" "I'll Do Anything Once."
239 "*The Flower Children* is a" "In Love Only Once," *Cineavance*, March 1967.
239 "He was so charismatic" Provost and Jacobson, *Timmy's in the Well*, 226.
240 "Sal was one" Cassidy and Deffaa, *C'mon, Get Happy*, 32.
240 "I'll show you" Provost and Jacobson, *Timmy's in the Well*, 231.
241 "I knew he was trying to shock" Ibid., 232.
241 "There were many" Eugène Lourié, *My Work in Films* (New York: Harcourt Brace Jovanovich, 1985), 281.
242 "But each" Ibid., 301–2.
244 "I took LSD" "I'll Do Anything Once."

### CHAPTER 28

247 **"All of a sudden"** "Catching Up with Sal Mineo," *Modern Screen,* December 1973.
248 **"My agents were frank"** Ibid.
249 **"You're wrong"** Provost and Jacobson, *Timmy's in the Well,* 243.
249 **"Sal had to be in control"** Ibid.
249 **"It's okay"** Ibid., 246.
249 **"What's wrong with *you*"** Ibid.
250 **"I found the play"** "Avanti Interview: Sal Mineo."

### CHAPTER 29

255 **"I didn't have"** "Catching Up with Sal Mineo."
255 **"I have literally"** Ibid.
256 **"Don arrived"** Author interview with Walter Willison, March 30, 2005.
257 **"I'd heard of Sal's reputation"** John Marvin, "Interview with Don Johnson," *In Touch,* May 1974.
258 **"While he didn't"** "Avanti Interview: Sal Mineo."
259 **"None of us"** Margaret Hartford, "Mineo's Star on the Rise Again," *Los Angeles Times,* January 2, 1969.
259 **"I never really thought about it"** Marvin, "Interview with Don Johnson."
260 **"This is the worst piece of shit"** Author interview with Williams.
261 **"was able to live"** Provost and Jacobson, *Timmy's in the Well,* 247.
261 **"My intention"** "Rape on Stage," *In,* July 1969.
262 **"I don't consider"** "Avanti Interview: Sal Mineo."
266 **"Some directors"** Stephen Lewis, "Sal Mineo: Rebel with a New Cause," *After Dark,* May 1969.
267 **"The film"** A. H. Weiler, "Mick Jagger Rolling Cowboy," *New York Times,* July 13, 1969.
267 **"It's about"** Ibid.

### CHAPTER 30

269 **"It would be easy"** Lewis, "Sal Mineo: Rebel."
270 **"But Sal was too proud"** Quoted in Braudy, "The Slow Fade."
270 **"I was living"** Author interview with Marvin Paige, June 5, 2005.
271 **"Sal would lease"** Quoted in Braudy, "The Slow Fade."
272 **"What difference"** Bart Mills, "Sal Mineo Rolls the Dice with 'The Wrong People' in London," *New York Times,* May 13, 1972.
274 **"The thing I worried"** Interview with John Bustin, *Austin Citizen,* April 29, 1975.
275 **"I was fourteen"** Braudy, "The Slow Fade."

### CHAPTER 31

278 **"To this day"** Author interview with Courtney Burr III.

### CHAPTER 32

301 **"I remember"** Quoted in Frascella and Weisel, *Live Fast, Die Young,* 262–63.
307 **"We got on well"** Author interview with Glyn Jones, May 28, 2008.
310 **"I spent the last five days"** "Catching Up with Sal Mineo."

### CHAPTER 33

313 **"I'm not an old man"** Mills, "Sal Mineo Rolls the Dice."
318 **"We were all"** Author interview with Lopez.

### CHAPTER 34

323 **"The idea of settling down"** "Catching Up with Sal Mineo."
328 **"We got marvelous reviews"** Ibid.
329 **"Sal was always playing Sal"** Braudy, "The Slow Fade."

### CHAPTER 35

334 **"The Warren Commission"** "Avanti Interview: Sal Mineo."
334 **"I campaigned for"** Ibid.
335 **"I guess you could say"** "We Find the Guys You Wanted the Most," *Photoplay,* April 1974.
339 **"Sal was a wild man"** Author interview with David Joliffe, October 29, 2004.
339 **"It's weird"** "We Find the Guys."

CHAPTER 36

341 **"I knew Arthur"** Author interview with Janet Leigh, January 15, 2004.
341 **"I'm just beginning"** Frank Rasky, "Sal Mineo No Longer Delinquent Peter Pan," *Toronto Star,* November 2, 1974.
342 **"Sal saw it coming"** Author interview with Empry.
343 **"There just wasn't much"** Ibid.
347 **"He's very driven"** "Mineo to Star in Marathon '33," *Citizen Marquee,* April 26, 1975.
347 **"edgier approach"** A. Peter Thaddeus, "Resignation Causes Turmoil," *Hilltopper* (Austin, TX), May 15, 1975.
348 **"For a while I tried"** Hughes, "Sal Mineo, the Eternal Original."
349 **"The business changes"** "Murders: The Outcast," *Newsweek,* February 23, 1976.

CHAPTER 37

353 **"Sexy Sal Mineo"** Bob Kiggins, "San Francisco," *The Advocate,* December 3, 1975.
353 **"Sal Mineo's in town"** James Armstrong, "P.S. Your Buns Are Showing," *After Dark,* January 1976.
354 **"He said I wasn't vulnerable"** Douglas Dean, "P.S. Your Play's a Hit," *Mandate,* January 1976.
354 **"Until I saw Sal"** George Carpozi Jr., "Sal Mineo, Behind the Baby Face, A Lonely Man," *Motion Picture,* June 1976.
354 **"It's natural, isn't it"** Dean, "P.S. Your Play's a Hit."
355 **"I'm thirty-six now"** Hughes, "Sal Mineo, the Eternal Original."
357 **"It was funky"** Braudy, "The Slow Fade."
358 **"Sal was always"** Sylvie Drake, "It's a Matter of Overcoming," *Los Angeles Times,* February 19, 1976.
358 **"Sal was depressed"** Braudy, "The Slow Fade."
359 **"He sounded great"** *Variety,* February 17, 1976.
359 **"We were rehearsing at the theater"** John Kendall, "Detectives Unable to Discover Motive for Fatal Stabbing of Actor Sal Mineo," *Los Angeles Times,* February 14, 1976.
360 **"I was going to walk"** Author interview with Nancy Barr, October 4, 2004.

CHAPTER 38

361 **"I'm a hero type"** "Mineo, the Hero Type Who's Usually Killed," *Los Angeles Herald Examiner,* February 14, 1976.
361 **"I saw he was going"** Kendall, "Detectives Unable to Discover Motive."
364 **"In effect"** Thomas T. Noguchi, *Coroner at Large* (New York: Simon & Schuster, 1985), 179.
364 **A forensic laboratory analysis** County of Los Angeles, Office of the Coroner, Ronald L. Taylor, Ph.D., Director, Case Report no. 76-1953 (Mineo, Sal), February 12, 1976, Homicide.
365 **"The motive"** John Kendall, "Motive in Sal Mineo Slaying Baffles Police," *Los Angeles Times,* February 13, 1976.
365 **"Detectives were looking"** United Press International, *New York Times,* February 14, 1976.
366 **"The rumors about"** Braudy, "The Slow Fade."
366 **"Sex, dope, and cheap"** Ibid.
366 **"It was really shocking"** Author interview with Joliffe.
366 **"He spent a lot of time"** "Sal Mineo Liked Things Candlelit," *People,* November 8, 1976.
366 **"I don't want anybody"** Author interview with Haworth.
367 **"Money was the first thing"** Braudy, "The Slow Fade."
367 **"All his life"** "Sal Mineo Liked Things Candlelit."
367 **"Well, my God"** Braudy, "The Slow Fade."
368 **"Sal was sincere"** "Hundreds of Mourners Jam N.Y. Funeral for Sal Mineo," *Los Angeles Times,* February 17, 1976.
368 **"Sal was a rare"** Ibid.
368 **"I've never been"** Associated Press interview with Diane Dalbey, March 1976.
368 **"I think to have success"** Braudy, "The Slow Fade."

369 **"He was my friend"** Kendall, "Detectives Unable to Discover Motive."

369 **"On screen"** "Murders: The Outcast."

369 **"That Sal was stabbed"** Peter Bogdanovich, "The Murder of Sal Mineo," *Esquire*, March 1, 1978.

371 **"It wasn't easy"** Drake, "It's a Matter of Overcoming."

371 **"My initial reaction"** Ibid.

**AFTERWORD**

374 **"Sal Mineo was my best friend"** "Sal Mineo: New Hunt for Clues," *Los Angeles Herald Examiner*, February 11, 1977.

374 **"In this racket"** Bogdanovich, "The Murder of Sal Mineo."

374 **"I'd rather not comment"** "Sal Mineo's Murderer Still at Large," *Los Angeles Free Press*, July 29, 1977.

374 **"I'm very optimistic"** Ibid.

375 **"The authorities"** John Kendall and Bill Faar, "Suspect Bragged of Killing Sal Mineo," *Los Angeles Times*, January 6, 1978.

376 **"That's the dude I killed"** "Murderer's Wife Tipped Police in Mineo Case," *Variety*, February 15, 1979.

377 **"Oh, yeah, I'm cool"** John Kendall and Bill Farr, "Mineo Suspect's Boasts Disclosed," *Los Angeles Times*, January 6, 1978.

377 **"I had it done"** Ibid.

378 **"We took the case"** Bill Farr, "Mineo Suspect's Lawyer Hits DA's Handling of Case," *Los Angeles Times*, January 28, 1978.

380 **"dirty blond"** Dorothy Townsend, "Witness Recalls Slaying of Mineo," *Los Angeles Times*, January 11, 1979.

381 **"I thought"** "Mineo Suspect Robbed Man 30 Minutes Later Witness Says," *Los Angeles Times*, January 12, 1979.

382 **"We came to the discussion"** Dorothy Townsend, "Accused's Tale of Mineo Slaying Related in Court," *Los Angeles Times*, January 18, 1979.

382 **"I saw somebody"** "Man at Sal Mineo Death Site was White, Girl Testifies," *Los Angeles Times*, January 26, 1979.

383 **"actually did not see"** Gene Blake, "Tape Contradicts Witness in Sal Mineo's Slaying Trial," *Los Angeles Times*, January 30, 1979.

384 **"He is a sadist"** Bill Hazlett, "Accused Slayer of Mineo Denounced," *Los Angeles Times*, February 2, 1979.

384 **"My God"** "The Sal Mineo Case," *Newsweek*, February 26, 1979.

384 **"stunned"** "Lionel Williams Found Guilty of Mineo Slaying," *Variety*, February 14, 1979.

384 **"It was one"** "The Sal Mineo Case."

385 **"The defendant"** Bill Farr, "Sal Mineo's Slayer Gets Term of 51 Years to Life," *Los Angeles Times*, March 15, 1979.

385 **"Lionel Williams is a predator"** Ibid.

385 **"I fault you"** Ibid.

386 **"That knife don't look"** "Sal Mineo's Killer Gets Maximum," *Los Angeles Herald Examiner*, March 16, 1979.

386 **"In retrospect"** *Los Angeles Herald Examiner*, March 24, 1979.

387 **"Only three heirs"** Los Angeles Superior Court, Petition for Probate, Case Number WEP 12850/9-10-1976.

# SOURCES

**RESEARCH INSTITUTIONS**

Albuquerque Public Library, Albuquerque, New Mexico

The Little Theatre (archives), Albuquerque, New Mexico

Los Angeles County Court, public records, Los Angeles, California

Los Angeles Public Library, Los Angeles, California

Margaret Herrick Library of the Academy of Motion Picture Arts and Sciences, Beverly Hills, California

New York Public Library, New York, New York

New York Public Library for the Performing Arts, New York, New York

San Francisco Public Library, San Francisco, California

**SELECTED BIBLIOGRAPHY**

Alexander, Paul. *Boulevard of Broken Dreams: The Life, Times and Legend of James Dean.* New York: Viking, 1994.

Baker, Carroll. *Baby Doll.* New York: Arbor House, 1983.

Blackwell, Mr., and Vernon Patterson. *From Rags to Bitches.* California: General Publishing Group, Inc., 1995.

Bogdanovich, Peter. *Who the Hell's in It.* New York: Knopf, 2004.

Brynner, Rock. *Yul: The Man Who Would Be King.* New York: Simon & Schuster, 1989.

Carey, McDonald. *The Days of My Life.* New York: St. Martin's Press, 1991.

Cassidy, David. *Could It Be Forever?* London: Headline Publishing, 2007.

——, and Chip Deffaa. *C'mon, Get Happy.* New York: Warner Books, 1994.

Clark, Dick, and Richard Robinson. *Rock, Roll and Remember.* New York: Thomas Y. Crowell Company, 1976.

Colacello, Bob. *Holy Terror.* New York: HarperCollins, 1990.

Curtis, Tony, and Peter Golenbock. *American Prince.* New York: Harmony Books, 2008.

Darin, Dodd. *Dream Lovers.* New York: Time Warner, 1994.

Davis, Ronald L. *John Ford: Hollywood's Old Master.* Norman, OK: University of Oklahoma Press, 1995.

Edmonson, Roger. *Boy in the Sand: Casey Donovan, All-American Sex Star.* Los Angeles: Alyson Publications, 1998.

Eyman, Scott. *Print the Legend: The Life and Times of John Ford.* New York: Simon & Schuster, 1999.

Ford, Dan. *Pappy: The Life of John Ford.* New York: Da Capo Press, 1998.

Frascella, Lawrence, and Al Weisel. *Live Fast, Die Young.* New York: Touchstone, 2005.

Gilmore, John. *Laid Bare.* Los Angeles: Amok Books, 1997.

——. *Live Fast, Die Young.* New York: Thunder's Mouth Press, 1997.

Gorham, Charles Orson. *McCaffery.* London: Secker & Warburg, 1961.

Granger, Farley, and Robert Calhoun. *Include Me Out.* New York: St. Martin's Press, 2007.

Hershkovits, David. *Don Johnson.* New York: St. Martin's Press, 1986.

Hudson, Rock, and Sara Davidson. *Rock Hudson: His Story.* New York: William Morrow, 1986.

Hunter, Tab, and Eddie Muller. *Tab Hunter Confidential.* Chapel Hill, NC: Algonquin Books, 2005.

Lambert, Gavin. *Natalie Wood: A Life.* New York: Knopf, 2004.

Lourié, Eugène. *My Work in Films.* New York: Harcourt Brace Jovanovich, 1985.

Malden, Karl, and Carla Malden. *When Do I Start?* New York: Simon & Schuster, 1997.

Maugham, Robin. *Escape from the Shadows*. London: Hodder and Stoughton, 1972.

———. *The Wrong People*. New York: McGraw-Hill, 1972.

Noguchi, Thomas T. *Coroner at Large*. New York: Simon & Schuster, 1985.

Provost, Jon, and Laurie Jacobson. *Timmy's in the Well: The Jon Provost Story*. Nashville, TN: Cumberland House Publishing, 2007.

Quirk, Lawrence J. *Paul Newman*. New York: Taylor Publishing, 1996.

Robbins, Jhan. *Yul Brynner: The Inscrutable King*. New York: Dodd, Mead & Company, 1988.

Russo, Joe, Larry Landsman, and Edward Gross. *Planet of the Apes Revisited*. New York: Thomas Dunne Books, 2001.

Sherman, Bobby, and Dena Hill. *Still Remembering You*. New York: Contemporary Books, 1996.

Spoto, Donald. *Rebel: The Life and Legend of James Dean*. New York: HarperCollins, 1996.

Stack, Robert, and Mark Evans. *Straight Shooting*. New York: Macmillan Publishing Co., 1980.

Stapleton, Maureen, and Jane Scovell. *A Hell of a Life*. New York: Simon & Schuster, 1995.

Stevens, George Jr. *Conversations with the Great Moviemakers of Hollywood's Golden Age*. New York: Knopf, 2006.

Stricklyn, Ray. *Angels and Demons: One Actor's Hollywood Journey*. New York: Belle Publishing, 1999.

Tropiano, Stephen. *Rebels and Chicks*. New York: Back Stage Books, 2006.

Wallach, Eli. *The Good, the Bad, and Me*. New York: Harcourt, Inc., 2005.

Walsh, Raoul. *Each Man in His Time*. New York: Farrar, Straus and Giroux, 1974.

Winters, Shelley. *Shelley II: The Middle of My Century*. New York: Simon & Schuster, 1989.

Courtney Burr III and Sal, Niagara Falls, Canada, July 1974.
*Collection of Courtney Burr III*

# SAL MINEO FILMOGRAPHY,
# TELEVISION AND THEATER CREDITS,
# AND AUDIO RECORDINGS

All features are given with release dates, all TV shows with date of first showing.

Also included are Sal's discography and a list of his theatrical credits.

## FILM

*Six Bridges to Cross* 1955. Universal International Pictures. Producer: Sydney Boehm. Director: Joseph Pevney. Screenplay: Sydney Boehm, from a story by Joseph F. Dinneen. With Tony Curtis, George Nader, Julie Adams, and Sal Mineo as Jerry as a boy.

*The Private War of Major Benson* 1955. Universal International Pictures. Producer: Howard Pine. Director: Jerry Hopper. Screenplay: William Roberts and Richard Alan Simmons, from a story by Joe Connelly and Bob Mosher. With Charlton Heston, Julie Simmons, William Demarest, Tim Hovey, Tim Considine, and Sal Mineo as Cadet Colonel Sylvester Dusik.

*Rebel Without a Cause* 1955. Warner Bros. Producer: David Weisbart. Director: Nicholas Ray. Screenplay: Stewart Stern, from a story by Nicholas Ray. With James Dean, Natalie Wood, Jim Backus, Ann Doran, Dennis Hopper, Nick Adams, and Sal Mineo as John "Plato" Crawford.

*Academy Award Nomination, Best Actor in a Supporting Role.

*Crime in the Streets* 1956. Allied Artists Pictures. Producer: Vincent M. Fennelly. Director: Don Siegel. Screenplay: Reginald Rose, from a teleplay by Reginald Rose. With John Cassavetes, James Whitmore, Mark Rydell, and Sal Mineo as Angelo "Baby" Gioia.

*Somebody Up There Likes Me* 1956. Metro-Goldwyn-Mayer. Producer: Charles Schnee. Director: Robert Wise. Screenplay: Ernest Lehman, based on the book by Rocky Graziano and Rowland Barber.

With Paul Newman, Pier Angeli, Everett Sloane, Eileen Heckart, and Sal Mineo as Romolo.

*Giant* 1956. Warner Bros. Producer: George Stevens. Director: George Stevens. Screenplay: Fred Guiol and Ivan Moffat, from a story by Edna Ferber. With Elizabeth Taylor, Rock Hudson, James Dean, Carroll Baker, Jane Withers, Chill Wills, Mercedes McCambridge, Dennis Hopper, Rod Taylor, Earl Holliman, and Sal Mineo as Angel Obregón II.

*Rock, Pretty Baby* 1956. Universal International Pictures. Producer: Edmond Chevie. Director: Richard Bartlett. Screenplay: Herbert H. Margolis and William Raynor. With John Saxon, Luana Patten, Edward Platt, Fay Wray, Shelley Fabares, Rod McKuen, and Sal Mineo as Angelo Barrato.

*Dino* 1957. Allied Artists Pictures. Producer: Bernice Block. Director: Thomas Carr. ·Screenplay: Reginald Rose, from a teleplay by Reginald Rose. With Brian Keith, Susan Kohner, Frank Faylen, Joe De Santis, Pat DeSimone, and Sal Mineo as Dino Minetta.

*The Young Don't Cry* 1957. Columbia Pictures. Producer: Philip A. Waxman. Director: Alfred L. Werker. Screenplay: Richard Jessup, based on the book by Richard Jessup. With James Whitmore, J. Carrol Naish, and Sal Mineo as Leslie "Les" Henderson.

*Tonka* 1958. Walt Disney Productions. Producer: James Pratt. Director: Lewis R. Foster. Screenplay: Lewis R. Foster and Lillie Hayward, based on the book *Comanche* by David Appel. With Philip Carey, Jerome Courtland, H. M. Wynant, Joy Page, Slim Pickens, Rafael Campos, and Sal Mineo as White Bull.

*A Private's Affair* 1959. 20th Century

Fox. Producer: David Weisbart. Director: Raoul Walsh. Screenplay: Winston Miller, from a story by Ray Livingston Murphy. With Christine Carère, Barry Coe, Barbara Eden, Gary Crosby, Terry Moore, Jim Backus, Jessie Royce Landis, Bob Denver, Tige Andrews, and Sal Mineo as Luigi Maresi.

*The Gene Krupa Story* 1959. Columbia Pictures. Producer: Philip A. Waxman. Director: Don Weis. Screenplay: Orin Jannings. With Susan Kohner, James Darren, Susan Oliver, Yvonne Craig, Red Nichols, Bobby Troup, Anita O'Day, Shelly Manne, Buddy Lester, and Sal Mineo as Gene Krupa.

*Exodus* 1960. United Artists. Producer: Otto Preminger. Director: Otto Preminger. Screenplay: Dalton Trumbo, from the book *Exodus* by Leon Uris. With Paul Newman, Eva Marie Saint, Ralph Richardson, David Opatoshu, Peter Lawford, Lee J. Cobb, Jill Haworth, John Derek, Hugh Griffith, Gregory Ratoff, and Sal Mineo as Dov Landau.

*Academy Award Nomination, Best Actor in a Supporting Role.

*Golden Globe Award Winner, Best Supporting Actor.

*Laurel Award, Top Male Supporting Performance.

*Escape from Zahrain* 1962. Paramount Pictures. Producer: Ronald Neame. Director: Ronald Neame. Screenplay: Robin Estridge, based on the book by Michael Barrett. With Yul Brynner, Madlyn Rhue, Jack Warden, James Mason, Anthony Caruso, Jay Novello, and Sal Mineo as Ahmed.

*The Longest Day* 1962. 20th Century Fox. Producer: Darryl F. Zanuck. Director: British exterior episodes by Ken Annakin, American exterior episodes by Andrew Marton, German exterior episodes by Bernhard Wicki. Screenplay: Cornelius Ryan, based on the book by Cornelius Ryan. With John Wayne, Robert Mitchum, Henry Fonda, Robert Ryan, Rod Steiger, Robert Wagner, Richard Beymer,

Mel Ferrer, Jeffrey Hunter, Roddy McDowall, and Sal Mineo as Pvt. Martini.

*Cheyenne Autumn* 1964. Warner Bros. Producer: Bernard Smith. Director: John Ford. Screenplay: James R. Webb, suggested by the book by Mari Sandoz. With Richard Widmark, Carroll Baker, Karl Malden, Dolores del Rio, Ricardo Montalban, Gilbert Roland, Arthur Kennedy, John Carradine, Victor Jory, James Stewart, Edward G. Robinson, George O'Brien, and Sal Mineo as Red Shirt.

*The Greatest Story Ever Told* 1965. United Artists. Producer: George Stevens. Director: George Stevens. Screenplay: James Lee Barrett, Henry Denker, George Stevens, from the book by Fulton Oursler. With Max von Sydow, Michael Anderson Jr., Carroll Baker, Ina Balin, Victor Buono, Richard Conte, José Ferrer, Van Heflin, Charlton Heston, Martin Landau, Angela Lansbury, Roddy McDowall, Dorothy McGuire, Shelly Winters, Sidney Poitier, Claude Rains, Telly Savalas, John Wayne, Ed Wynn, and Sal Mineo as Uriah.

*Who Killed Teddy Bear?* 1965. Phillips Productions. Producer: Everett Rosenthal. Director: Joseph Cates. Screenplay: Leon Tokatyan and Arnold Drake, based on a story by Arnold Drake. With Juliet Prowse, Jan Murray, Elaine Stritch, Daniel J. Travanti, and Sal Mineo as Lawrence Sherman.

*Krakatoa, East of Java* 1969. American Broadcasting Company and Cinerama. Producer: Philip Yordan. Director: Bernard L. Kowalski. Screenplay: Cliff Gould and Bernard Gordon. With Maximilian Schell, Diane Baker, Brian Keith, Barbara Werle, Rossano Brazzi, John Leyton, and Sal Mineo as Leoncavallo Borghese.

*80 Steps to Jonah* 1969. Warner Bros. Producer: Steve Broidy. Director: Gerd Oswald. Screenplay: Frederick Louis Fox, based on the story by Frederick Louis Fox. With Wayne Newton, Jo Van Fleet, Keenan Wynn, Mickey Rooney, and Sal Mineo as Jerry Taggart.

*Escape from the Planet of the Apes* 1971. 20th

Century Fox. Producer: Arthur P. Jacobs. Director: Don Taylor. Screenplay: Paul Dehn, based on characters created by Pierre Boulle. With Kim Hunter, Roddy McDowall, Bradford Dillman, Natalie Trundy, Eric Braeden, William Windom, and Sal Mineo as Milo.

## TELEVISION

*Hallmark Hall of Fame* "The Vision of Father Flanagan." March 30, 1952, NBC-TV. Sal played Les.

*Hallmark Hall of Fame* "A Woman for the Ages." May 11, 1952, NBC-TV. Sal played Charles.

*Omnibus* "The Capital of the World." December 6, 1953, CBS-TV. Sal played Paco.

*Janet Dean, Registered Nurse* "The Garcia Case." March 1954, syndicated. Sal played Jose Garcia.

*NBC Television Opera Theatre* "Salome." May 8, 1954, NBC-TV. Sal played the Page.

*Omnibus* "A Few Scenes out of the California Boyhood of William Saroyan: The Bad Men." October 16, 1955, CBS-TV. Sal played Señor Cortez.

*Big Town* "Juvenile Gangs." November 1, 1955, NBC-TV.

*The Philco Television Playhouse (aka The Philco-Goodyear Television Playhouse)* "The Trees." December 4, 1955, NBC-TV.

*Frontiers of Faith* "The Man on the 6:02." December 25, 1955, NBC-TV.

*Studio One* "Dino." January 2, 1956, CBS-TV. Sal played Dino.
    *Emmy Award Nomination, Best Single Performance by an Actor.

*Look Up and Live* "Nothing to Do." January 15, 1956, CBS-TV.

*The Twenty-eighth Annual Academy Awards* March 21, 1956. NBC-TV. Sal presented the Oscar for Best Sound.

*Lux Video Theatre* April 5, 1956, NBC-TV. Sal appeared as himself to promote his motion picture *Crime in the Streets*.

*Screen Director's Playhouse.* "The Dream." May 16, 1956, NBC-TV. Sal played Charles Monet.

*The Alcoa Hour* "The Magic Horn." June 10, 1956, NBC-TV. Sal played Tommy Angelo.

*Juke Box Jury* August 3, 1956, NBC-TV. Sal appeared as a guest star on the music-themed game show.

*Perry Como Show* September 15, 1956, NBC-TV. Sal appeared as a musical guest star on an episode of the music/variety program.

*Climax!* "Island in the City." October 4, 1956, CBS-TV. Sal played Miguel.

*Can Do* November 26, 1956, NBC-TV. Sal appeared as a guest star on an episode of the game show.

*Person to Person* December 14, 1956, CBS-TV. Sal appeared as a guest on an episode of the interview program.

*The Steve Allen Show* January 4, 1957, NBC-TV. Sal appeared as a guest star on the late-night talk show.

*Kraft Television Theatre* "Drummer Man." May 1, 1957, NBC-TV. Sal played Tony Russo.

*Alan Freed's Rock 'n' Roll Revue* May 4, 1957, ABC-TV. Sal appeared as a musical guest star on the music/variety program.

*What's My Line?* June 30, 1957, CBS-TV. Sal appeared as the mystery guest on the game show.

*The Arthur Murray Party* July 1957, NBC-TV. Sal appeared as a musical guest star on the summer music/variety program.

*The Ed Sullivan Show* July 14, 1957, CBS-TV. Sal appeared as a musical guest star on the music/variety program.

*American Bandstand* August 13, 1957, ABC-TV. Sal appeared as a musical guest star on the music program.

*The Ed Sullivan Show* August 25, 1957, CBS-TV. Sal appeared as a musical guest star on the music/variety program.

*The Big Record* September 18, 1957, CBS-TV. Sal appeared as a musical guest star on the variety program.

*Kraft Television Theatre* "Barefoot Soldier." October 2, 1957, NBC-TV.

*Perry Como Show* November 2, 1957, NBC-TV. Sal appeared as a musical guest star on the music/variety program.

*The Steve Allen Show* December 8, 1957, NBC-TV. Sal appeared as a musical guest star on the music/variety program.

*The Patrice Munsel Show* January 3, 1958, ABC-TV. Sal appeared as a musical guest star on the music/variety program.

*American Bandstand* January 10, 1958, ABC-TV. Sal appeared as a musical guest star on the music program.

*The Big Record* February 19, 1958, CBS-TV. Sal appeared as a musical guest star on the variety program.

*The DuPont Show of the Month* "Aladdin." February 21, 1958, CBS-TV. Sal appeared as Aladdin on the television special.

*The Ed Sullivan Show* April 27, 1958, CBS-TV. Sal appeared as a musical guest star on the music/variety program.

*Hollywood Diary* October 2, 1958, syndicated. Sal appeared as a guest on the interview program.

*Pursuit* "The Vengeance." October 22, 1958, CBS-TV. Sal played Richie Rogart.

*The Dick Clark Saturday Night Beechnut Show* "Dick Clark Birthday Show." November 29, 1958, ABC-TV. Sal appeared as a guest on the music/variety program.

*I've Got a Secret* January 7, 1959, CBS-TV. Sal appeared as a guest star on the game show.

*May Mann—What's Your Problem?* May 4, 1959, syndicated. Sal appeared as a guest on the talk show.

*Juke Box Jury* May 9, 1959, syndicated. Sal appeared as a guest star on the music-themed game show.

*An Evening with Jimmy Durante* September 25, 1959, NBC-TV. Sal appeared as a musical guest star on the television special.

*The Big Party by Revlon* October 28, 1959, CBS-TV. Sal appeared as a musical guest star on the music/variety program.

*The Ann Sothern Show* "The Sal Mineo Story." November 2, 1959, CBS-TV. Sal played Nicky Silvero on the comedy series.

*The Ed Sullivan Show* January 3, 1960, CBS-TV. Sal appeared as a guest to promote *The Gene Krupa Story* on the music/variety program.

*The Mike Wallace Interview* July 6, 1960, syndicated. Sal was interviewed by Wallace.

*The Jack Paar Show* January 3, 1961, NBC-TV. Sal appeared as a guest on the talk show.

*The Ed Sullivan Show* January 8, 1961, CBS-TV. Sal appeared as a guest to promote *Exodus* on the music/variety program.

*Cry Vengeance!* February 21, 1961, NBC-TV special. Sal played Andrea.

*Disneyland* "Comanche: Part I." February 18, 1962, NBC-TV. Part 1 of the serialization of the Walt Disney feature film *Tonka*.

*Disneyland* "Comanche: Part II." February 25, 1962, NBC-TV. Part 2 of the serialization of the Walt Disney feature film *Tonka*.

*The DuPont Show of the Week* "A Sound of Hunting." May 20, 1962, NBC-TV. Sal played PFC Charles Coke.

*The Tonight Show Starring Johnny Carson* October 9, 1962, NBC-TV. Sal appeared as a guest to promote the film *The Longest Day*.

*The Greatest Show on Earth* "The Loser." October 22, 1963, ABC-TV. Sal played Billy Archer.

*Dr. Kildare* "Tomorrow Is a Fickle Girl." March 19, 1964, NBC-TV. Sal played Carlos Mendoza.

*The Match Game* June 22–26, 1964, NBC-TV. Sal appeared as a guest star on the daytime game show.

*Kraft Suspense Theatre* "The World I Want." October 1, 1964, NBC-TV. Sal played Ernie.

*Combat!* "The Hard Way Back." October 20, 1964, ABC-TV. Sal played Larry Kogan.

*What's This Song* November 16, 1964, NBC-TV. Sal appeared as a guest star on the game show.

*Shindig!* January 3, 1965, ABC-TV. Sal appeared as a musical guest on the music/variety program.

*The Patty Duke Show* "Patty Meets a Celebrity." January 20, 1965, ABC-TV. Sal played himself on an episode of the comedy series.

*ABC's Nightlife (aka The Les Crane Show)* February 17, 1965, ABC-TV. Sal appeared as a guest star on the late-night show.

*Burke's Law* "Who Killed the Rabbit's Husband?" April 14, 1965, ABC-TV. Sal played Lew Dixon.

*The Match Game* May 24–28, 1965, NBC-TV. Sal appeared as guest star on the game show.

*The Celebrity Game* August 19, 1965, CBS-TV. Sal appeared as a guest star on the game show.

*Mona McCluskey* "The General Swings at Dawn." January 27, 1966, NBC-TV.

*Live at T.J.'s* "The Dave Clark Five." July 15, 1965, ABC-TV. Sal hosted an episode of the music program.

*Combat!* "Nothing to Lose." February 1, 1966, ABC-TV. Sal played Vinnick.

*Run for Your Life* "Sequestro!: Part I." March 14, 1966, NBC-TV. Sal played Yanio.

*Run for Your Life* "Sequestro!: Part II." March 21, 1966, NBC-TV. Sal played Yanio.

*Court Martial* "The House Where He Lived." April 29, 1966, ABC-TV.

*The Match Game* October 17–21, 1966. Sal appeared as a guest star on the game show.

*Combat!* "The Brothers." October 4, 1966, ABC-TV. Sal played Marcel Paulon.

*The Dangerous Days of Kiowa Jones (made-for-television film)* December 25, 1966, ABC-TV. Sal played Bobby Jack Wilkes.

*Bob Hope Presents the Chrysler Theatre* "A Song Called Revenge." March 1, 1967, NBC-TV. Sal played Doctoroff.

*Stranger on the Run (made-for-television film)* October 31, 1967, NBC-TV. Sal played George Blaylock.

*Happening '68* April 6, 13, 20, 27, 1968, ABC-TV. Sal appeared as a guest star on the music/variety program.

*The Donald O'Connor Show* October 15, 1968, syndicated. Sal appeared as a guest star on the talk/variety program.

*Hawaii Five-O* "Tiger by the Tail." October 10, 1968, CBS-TV. Sal played Bobby George.

*Funny Valentines: The Buddy Greco Special* February 14, 1969, syndicated. Sal appeared as a musical guest and played the drums with Greco.

*The Challengers (made-for-television film)* March 28, 1969, CBS-TV. Sal played Angel de Angelo.

*The Joe Pyne Show* May 24, 1969, syndicated. Sal appeared as a guest on the talk show.

*The Name of the Game* "A Hard Case of the Blues." September 26, 1969, NBC-TV. Sal played Sheldon.

*The Square World of Ed Butler* November 23, 1969, syndicated. Sal appeared as a guest on the talk show.

*The Mike Douglas Show* February 26, 1970, syndicated. Sal appeared as a guest on the talk show.

*The Name of the Game* "So Long Baby, and Amen." September 18, 1970, NBC-TV. Sal played Hillary.

*Mission: Impossible* "Flip Side." September 29, 1970, CBS-TV. Sal played Mel Bracken.

*My Three Sons* "The Liberty Bell." January 2, 1971, CBS-TV. Sal played Jim Bell.

*The Immortal* "Sanctuary." January 7, 1971, ABC-TV. Sal played Tsinnajinni.

*Dan August* "The Worst Crime." February 11, 1971, ABC-TV. Sal played Mort Downes.

*In Search of America (made-for-television film)* March 23, 1971, ABC-TV. Sal played Nick.

*How to Steal an Airplane (aka* Only One Day Left Before Tomorrow *and* The Scavengers *made-for-television film)* December 10, 1971, NBC-TV. Sal played Luis Ortega.

*The Family Rico (made-for-television film)* September 9, 1972, CBS-TV. Sal played Nick Rico.

*Harry O* "Such Dust as Dreams Are Made On." March 11, 1973, ABC-TV. Sal played Walter Scheerer.

*Griff* "Marked for Murder" (aka "Prey"). October 27, 1973, ABC-TV. Sal played Gamal Zaki.

*Tenafly* "Man Running." January 26, 1974, NBC-TV. Sal played Jerry Farmer.

*Police Story* "The Hunters" (aka "Big John Morrison"). February 26, 1974, NBC-TV. Sal played Stippy.

*Dr. Simon Locke (aka Police Surgeon)* October 19, 1974, syndicated.

*ABC's Wide World of Entertainment* "James Dean: Memories of a Gentle Giant." November 13, 1974, ABC-TV. Sal appeared as himself.

*Hawaii Five-O* "Hit Gun for Sale." February 25, 1975, CBS-TV. Sal played Eddie.

*Harry O* "Elegy for a Cop." February 27, 1975, ABC-TV. Sal played Broker. This episode is edited from the original pilot, including Sal's previously recorded scenes.

*S.W.A.T.* "A Coven of Killers." March 3, 1975, ABC-TV. Sal played Joey Hopper.

*S.W.A.T.* "Deadly Tide: Part I." September 13, 1975, ABC-TV. Sal played Roy.

*S.W.A.T.* "Deadly Tide: Part II." September 20, 1975, ABC-TV. Sal played Roy.

*Columbo* "A Case of Immunity." October 12, 1975, NBC-TV. Sal played Rachman Habib.

*Police Story* "The Test of Brotherhood" (aka "Jurisdiction"). November 14, 1975, NBC-TV. Sal played Fobbes.

*James Dean: The First Teenager* Documentary broadcast in the UK on January 9, 1976. Sal appeared as himself.

*Ellery Queen* "The Adventure of the Wary Witness." January 25, 1976, NBC-TV. Sal played James Danello.

*Joe Forrester* "The Answer." February 2, 1976, NBC-TV.

**THEATER**

*The Rose Tattoo*
Salvatore
December 29, 1950–January 25, 1951
Erlanger Theatre, Chicago, IL

*The Rose Tattoo*
Salvatore
February 3–July 15, 1951
Martin Beck Theatre, New York City

*The Little Screwball*
Candido
July–August 1951
Westport Country Playhouse, Westport, CT

*Dinosaur Wharf*
Shoeshine Boy
November 8–10, 1951
The National Theatre, New York City

*The King and I*
Understudy
November 1951–October 1952
Prince Chulalongkorn
October 20, 1952–March 20, 1954
St. James Theatre, New York City

*Operation Madball*
Pvc. Petrelli
April 26–29, 1961
Casa Manana Theatre, Fort Worth, TX

*Something About a Soldier*
Jacob
December 1–7, 1961
Wilmington, DE
December 8–16, 1961
Forest Theatre, Philadelphia, PA
December 18–30, 1961
Colonial Theatre, Boston, MA
January 4–13, 1962
Ambassador Theatre, New York City

*Awake and Sing!*
Ralph Berger
July 7–19, 1964
Theatre by the Sea, Venice, CA

*End as a Man*
Director; Jocko
August 11–16, 1964
Canal Fulton Summer Theatre, Canal Fulton, OH

*What Makes Sammy Run?*
Sammy Glick
December 27, 1965–January 8, 1966
Royal Alexandra Theatre, Toronto, Ontario, Canada

*Fortune and Men's Eyes*
Director; Rocky
January 9–July 29, 1969
Coronet Theatre, Los Angeles, CA

*Sal Mineo's Fortune and Men's Eyes*
Director

October 22, 1969–May 10, 1970
Stage 73, New York City

*Sal Mineo's Fortune and Men's Eyes*
Director
November 1969–January 1970
Nontheatrical venue (a gay bar),
Honolulu, HI

*Sal Mineo's Fortune and Men's Eyes*
Director
April 22–May 24, 1970
Committee Theatre, San Francisco, CA

*The Children's Mass*
Producer
May 5–16, 1973
Theatre de Lys, New York City

*How the Other Half Loves*
William
November 1973
Alhambra Dinner Theatre,
Jacksonville, FL

*Sunday in New York*
Mike Mitchell
January 22–March 15, 1974
Country Dinner Playhouse,
St. Petersburg, FL

*Sunday in New York*
Director; Mike Mitchell
April 10–May 1, 1974
Windmill Dinner Theatre, Dallas, TX
May 8–June 1974
Windmill Dinner Theatre, Houston, TX
July 15–August 10, 1974
Windmill Dinner Theatre,
Scottsdale, AZ

*Sugar and Spice*
the Stranger
November 12–30, 1974
Royal Alexandra Theatre, Toronto,
Ontario, Canada

*LUV*
Harry Berlin
March 7–22, 1975
The Little Theatre, Albuquerque, NM

*Marathon '33*
Director; Patsy

April 29–May 11, 1975
Mary Moody Northen Theatre,
St. Edward's University, Austin, TX

*The Tender Trap*
Charlie Reader
August 2–September 14, 1975
Country Dinner Playhouse,
St. Petersburg, FL

*P.S. Your Cat Is Dead*
Vito
November 4, 1975–January 4, 1976
Montgomery Playhouse,
San Francisco, CA

## AUDIO RECORDINGS

### 1957

Epic (5-9216) 45 rpm
Side 1: "Love Affair"
Side 2: "Start Movin' (In My Direction)"

Epic (9227) 45 rpm
Side 1: "Lasting Love"
Side 2: "You Shouldn't Do That"

Epic (5-9246) 45 rpm
Side 1: "The Words That I Whisper" ·
Side 2: "Party Time"

Epic (9260) 45 rpm
Side 1: "Little Pigeon"
Side 2: "Cuttin' In"

Epic Promotional Record (EG-7187)
45 rpm
Side 1: "Dino," "Death in a Warehouse"
Side 2: "First Love," "Saturday Night"

### 1958

Columbia Label (CL-1117) LP *Aladdin*,
television movie soundtrack

Epic (5-9271) 45 rpm
Side 1: "Seven Steps to Love"
Side 2: "A Couple of Crazy Kids"

Epic (5-9287) 45 rpm
Side 1: "Souvenirs of Summertime"
Side 2: "Baby Face"

Epic (LN-3405) LP *Sal*
Side 1: "Too Young," "My Bride,"
"Not Tomorrow but Tonight,"
"The Words That I Whisper,"
"Blue-Eyed Baby," "Tattoo"
Side 2: "Now and for Always,"
"Down by the Riverside,"
"Secret Doorway," "Oh Marie,"
"Deep Devotion," "Baby Face"

Epic (ZTEP-27283) 45 rpm *Sal Sings*
(Scotch cellophane tape promotional)
Side 1: "Too Young," "Baby Face"
Side 2: "Little Pigeon," "Start Movin'
(In My Direction)"

**1959**

Epic (9327) 45 rpm
Side 1: "Make Believe Baby"
Side 2: "Young as We Are"

Epic (9345) 45 rpm
Side 1: "I'll Never Be Myself Again"
Side 2: "The Words That I Whisper"

**1962**

Decca Custom Records (Style H)
Christmas Seal Campaign 1962 celebrity
spot announcements

Side 1 (MG 79238): Jimmy Durante,
Richard Widmark, William Bendix,
Jack Webb, Jack Lemmon, Lee Remick,
Tony Curtis, Edgar Bergen, James
Stewart, Robert Stack

Side 2 (MG 79239): Bing Crosby, Frank
Sinatra, Jack Benny, Bob Hope,
Robert Young, Walter Brennan,
Sal Mineo, Susan Hayward, Charlton
Heston, George Burns, Robert
Horton, Gene Berry, Jose Jimenez
(Bill Dana)

**1964**

Fontana Records (F-1540) 45 rpm
Side 1: "Take Me Back"
Side 2: "Save the Last Dance for Me"

Courtney Burr III and Sal, Marrakesh, Morocco, May 1972.
*Collection of Courtney Burr III*

# ACKNOWLEDGMENTS

Sal, Florida, August 1975.
*Collection of Courtney Burr III*

Thank you, Jill Haworth and Courtney Burr III, for your patience, constant encouragement, and, most important, trust in me. Thank you, Michael Anderson Jr. and Eric Williams, for your stories, humor, and friendship. Thank you to Perry Lopez, who was gracious till the end. Thank you, Larry Robins, for your enthusiasm from the start, and Jeri Coates, for countless hours of grammatical corrections. Thanks, Mel Berger (see you in the movies). Thank you, Julia Pastore, for seeing a book in the rubble, and Domenica Alioto, for long-distance technical assistance. Thank you to the wonderful libraries and thoughtful librarians who assisted me. And thanks to the many wonderful people who graciously spoke with me about Sal Mineo.

# INDEX

# ABOUT THE AUTHOR

MICHAEL GREGG MICHAUD's work has appeared in numerous magazines and publications, including the *Los Angeles Times*. He is also a playwright, editor, artist, and award-winning photographer. An animal-rights defender, he is a founding director of the Linda Blair WorldHeart Foundation. He lives in Los Angeles.

www.MichaelGreggMichaud.com